"Dr. Carver is the best-known and most highly regarded scholar and practitioner in the field of not-for-profit corporate governance and the leading exponent, throughout the world, of the value and necessity of improving the governance of these organizations. Indeed, he is the father of contemporary governance practices in the extremely large not-for-profit sector."

>—**Dr. James M. Gillies,** professor emeritus, York University Schulich School of Business, Toronto; former Member of Parliament and senior policy adviser to the Prime Minister; coauthor, *Inside the Boardroom*; author of *Boardroom Renaissance, Facing Reality,* and *Where Business Fails*

"John Carver has given board effectiveness a unifying vision, a logical and coherent base—an integrated theory of governance. This collection of his writings brings home the intellectual rigor of his thinking and the coherence of his Policy Governance model. We have waited long for a book which analyzes the roles of boards from first principles. The Policy Governance model fills that bill and thereby makes a fundamental contribution. For the first time, we are offered a fully integrated and coherent system of governance, a significant advance in management thinking, as near a universal theory of governance as we at present have."

>—**Sir Adrian Cadbury,** former director, Bank of England; former chairman, Cadbury Schweppes; former chancellor, Aston University; chairman, UK Committee on Financial Aspects of Corporate Governance (source of the "Cadbury Report"); recipient of the 2001 International Corporate Governance Network award; author of *The Company Chairman* and *Corporate Governance and Chairmanship*

"Dr. John Carver is internationally recognized as the leader in improving the governance of nonprofit organizations. His Policy Governance model has been adopted by numerous organizations on five continents. Widely considered the leading pioneer in reconceptualization of the board-executive partnership, Dr. Carver offers a visionary yet practical approach to governance design that is truly transforming, powerful, and attainable."

>—**Drs. Jeffrey L. Brudney and Thomas P. Holland,** codirectors, The University of Georgia Institute for Nonprofit Organizations, Athens

"John Carver is the new guru of nonprofits."

>—**Books for Business,** Toronto

"The conceptual clarity of Dr. Carver's approach provided us an excellent basis for development of new governance arrangements in defence, helping us to sharpen our focus on results and the associated accountability framework."

>—**Dr. Allan Hawke,** former Secretary of Defence, Australian Department of Defence, Canberra

"In the Company Secretary's Office of BP, we owe a great deal of debt to Dr. Carver, and, in our opinion, his ideas on how boards should work are without equal."
> —**Rodney L. Insall,** former vice president, corporate governance,
> British Petroleum, London

"John is not only refreshingly revolutionary in his thinking but he matches his bold thinking with the ability to communicate with both passion and precision. Add to these qualities his thorough professionalism and you have an individual who towers over others in the field."
> —**Jerry Cianciolo,** editor, *Contributions*

"John Carver's *Boards That Make a Difference* was required reading for board members of the Calgary Philharmonic Society. It provided a clear and concise road map with which we carried out significant governance restructuring of the society."
> —**James M. Stanford,** past chairman, Calgary Philharmonic Society;
> former president and CEO, Petro-Canada, Alberta, Canada

"John Carver, like Robert K. Greenleaf before him, is a revolutionary of the very best kind. Carver's Policy Governance model has provided the means for trustees to live out Greenleaf's challenge to boards to act as both servant and leader. In so doing, John has proven himself to be one of our greatest servant-leaders."
> —**Larry C. Spears,** CEO, The Greenleaf Center for Servant-Leadership;
> editor, *Reflections on Leadership, Insights on Leadership, Servant Leadership,*
> *The Power of Servant Leadership;* coeditor, *Practicing Servant Leadership* and
> *Focus on Leadership*

"*Boards That Make a Difference* is a unique contribution to the field of governance. Its insights into the use of policy and the need to separate governance from management are carried throughout the analysis to produce a governance model that is conceptually complete and internally consistent. Dr. Carver's ideas—his Policy Governance model—on how boards should work makes an unparalleled contribution to this essential subject."
> —**Judith C. Hanratty,** former company secretary, British Petroleum, London

"Carver's Policy Governance model focuses our directors on developing the ends for which our organization exists, while holding the CEO accountable through written policies for their accomplishment."
> —**T. Wayne Whipple,** CFA, former executive director,
> New York Society of Security Analysts, New York

"John Carver's Policy Governance model has taught me the board is not supposed to be the better alternative to management, but has to set ends and limit means for management. Many boards do not understand their own role and try to duplicate management."
> —**Folkert Schukken,** chairman, Council on Corporate Governance and
> Board Effectiveness of the Conference Board Europe, The Netherlands

Boards
That Make
a Difference

Other Carver Resources

Reinventing Your Board: A Step-by-Step Guide to Implementing Policy Governance, Revised Edition, by John Carver and Miriam Carver

John Carver on Board Leadership: Selected Writings from the Creator of the World's Most Provocative and Systematic Governance Model, by John Carver

Board Leadership: Policy Governance in Action, co-executive editors John Carver and Miriam Carver

The Board Member's Playbook: Using Policy Governance to Solve Problems, Make Decisions, and Build a Stronger Board, by Miriam Carver and Bill Charney

Corporate Boards That Create Value: Governing Company Performance from the Boardroom, by John Carver and Caroline Oliver

The CarverGuide Series on Effective Board Governance (12 guides), by John Carver and Miriam Carver

John Carver on Board Governance (video)

Empowering Boards for Leadership: Redefining Excellence in Governance, by John Carver (audio)

The Policy Governance Fieldbook: Practical Lessons, Tips, and Tools from the Experiences of Real-World Boards, editor Caroline Oliver

Boards That Make a Difference

A New Design for Leadership in Nonprofit and Public Organizations

THIRD EDITION

John Carver

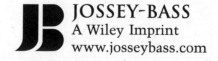

JOSSEY-BASS
A Wiley Imprint
www.josseybass.com

Published by Jossey-Bass
A Wiley Imprint
989 Market Street, San Francisco, CA 94103-1741   www.josseybass.com

Jossey-Bass books and products are available through most bookstores. To contact Jossey-Bass directly call our Customer Care Department within the U.S. at 800-956-7739, outside the U.S. at 317-572-3986, or fax 317-572-4002.

Jossey-Bass also publishes its books in a variety of electronic formats. Some content that appears in print may not be available in electronic books.

Library of Congress Cataloging-in-Publication Data

Carver, John.
    Boards that make a difference: a new design for leadership in nonprofit and public organizations/John Carver.—3rd ed.
        p. cm.
    Includes bibliographical references and index.
    ISBN-13: 978-0-7879-7616-3 (cloth)
    ISBN-10: 0-7879-7616-4 (cloth)
    1. Directors of corporations. 2. Associations, institutions, etc.—Management.
3. Nonprofit organizations—Management. I. Title.
    HD2745.C37 2006
    658.4'22—dc22

                                                            2005033970

Printed in the United States of America   THIRD EDITION
HB Printing   10 9 8 7 6 5

Contents

Preface to the Third Edition   vii

Preface   xiii

The Author   xxiii

Prologue: Beginning and Ending with Purpose   xxvii

Introduction   1

1. Leadership by Governing Boards:
   A Vision of Group Accountability   5

2. Policy as a Leadership Tool:
   The Force of Explicit Values   37

3. Designing Policies That Make a Difference:
   Governing by Values   55

4. Focusing on Results: The Power of Purpose   79

5. Controlling Ethics and Prudence:
   What's Not OK, Even if It Works   115

6. Strong Boards Need Strong Executives:
   The Board-Executive Relationship   153

7. The Board's Responsibility for Itself:
   Governing Oneself Precedes Governing Others   185

8. Officers and Committees: The Chief Governance
    Officer and Other Divisions of Board Labor   215

9. Policy Development by Levels:
    Adding Details Judiciously   239

10. Making Meetings Meaningful: Creating the
    Future More Than Reviewing the Past   257

11. Maintaining Board Leadership: Staying on
    Track and Institutionalizing Excellence   287

12. But Does It Work? Criticisms, Effectiveness
    Research, and Model Consistency   319

Resource A: Varieties of Policy Governance
            Applications   345

Resource B: Bylaws   365

Resource C: Glossary   371

References   379

Index   405

Preface to the Third Edition

The Policy Governance conceptual model that I created in the mid-1970s has now spread internationally, arguably becoming the approach to board leadership that is most frequently identified by name worldwide. Indeed, becoming "Carverized" is a frequently used eponym. My wife, Miriam Carver—who has joined me as the authoritative source on model theory due to her extensive knowledge of Policy Governance—and I have trained over 250 consultants and board leaders from eight countries, providing them with intensive advanced instruction in the model's theory and practice. Some of those persons have gone on to establish the International Policy Governance Association.

Since the first edition of this book was published in 1990, at least eight other books consistent with the Policy Governance model have **WANT MORE?** been published, as well as over two hundred articles. The bimonthly newsletter *Board Leadership*, which I co-edit with Miriam Carver and which is entirely devoted to Policy Governance theory and implementation, passed its eightieth issue in mid-2005. Policy Governance materials have been published in Spanish, Portuguese, French, Russian, and Dutch. Direct personal consulting and presentations have taken Miriam and me to nineteen countries.

My interest in governance began in the mid-1970s, a story I retold in detail in the Foreword to *The Policy Governance Fieldbook* (Oliver and others, 1999). That interest, and my frustration at the patchwork of practices that governance had become (and largely still is), impelled me toward as conceptually coherent a set of universal governance principles as I could devise. My scientific and research background undoubtedly had much to do with my pushing as far as I could toward an integrated system of thought. I was suspicious of what Thomas Kuhn (1996) called "development by accumulation" (p. 2) and was by nature in agreement with E. R. Dodds's sentiment: "Where men can build their systems only out of used pieces the notion of progress can have no meaning—the future is devalued in advance" (Dodds, 1973, iii, 633).

Unfortunately, however, it was that same scientific mentality that led me to describe the Policy Governance system as a "model," meaning the scientific sense of conceptual coherence rather than the more mechanical sense of organizational structure. I could as easily have spoken of a governance "technology," "theory," "operating system," or "philosophy." Inasmuch as the word *model* has led to some unnecessary resistance to my concepts it is not clear to me that I made the best choice. My search, however, was intended to uncover principles of governance that were not only universal in their application but integrated into a seamless and practical whole that would deserve to be designated a model.

Over the years, the model has been received with interest and even enthusiasm in a number of countries. Endorsements have been received from, among numerous others, Peter Dey and James Gillies

WANT MORE?

2

in Canada, Robert Monks and Earnest Deavenport in the United States, John Hall in Australia, and former British Petroleum company secretary Judith Hanratty. Perhaps the most pleasing endorsement was that from Sir Adrian Cadbury, who in 1990 unleashed the modern international flood of corporate governance reform. Sir Adrian (Cadbury, 2002b) said of Policy Governance, "For the first time, we are being offered a fully integrated and coherent system of governance" (p. xiii).

I published the earliest form of my theory in the late 1970s, then expanded on it with increasing frequency in the ensuing years. It was not until 1990 that the Policy Governance model found expression in book form in *Boards That Make a Difference*. Unexcelled sales for this kind of book led to a second edition in 1997. I am delighted now to present the third edition.

This edition differs more from the second edition than the second did from the first. I have added explanatory diagrams that tens of thousands of seminar participants have found useful. Policies created by real organizations that are used to illustrate my points have been updated, and more explanation on monitoring performance is given. An additional chapter on the problems and challenges of governance research has been added. Due to the mountain of Policy Governance publications since 1990, I have changed my approach to references. References clutter the text, even though they give readers further sources of information. So except for citations for quotations or other specifics, references are found in the "Further Reading" lists at the end of each chapter but are keyed to the text with "Want More?" icons inserted near the topics they augment.

I am grateful to the organizations that have allowed me to use their board policies to illustrate various points in the text, as well as to the individuals who have allowed their words to be quoted. To all the individuals and organizations who made statements and policies available that space constraints kept me from using, I am as grateful as if they had been published.

As always, I thank the countless boards, board members, executives, consultants, and other governance enthusiasts who have given my work so satisfying a reception for three decades.

Atlanta, Georgia   John Carver
December 2005   www.carvergovernance.com

WANT MORE?

Further Reading

1. Carver, J. "Leadership du conseil: 'The Policy Governance Model'" [Board leadership: The Policy Governance model]. *Gouvernance Revue Internationale* (Canada), Spring 2000, *1*(1), 100–108.

Reprinted under the title "A Theory of Corporate Governance: Finding a New Balance for Boards and Their CEOs" in J. Carver, *John Carver on Board Leadership*. San Francisco: Jossey-Bass, 2002.

Carver, J. "Model corporativnogo upravleniya: novyi balance mezhdu sovetom directorov i managementom companii" [The model of corporate governance: New balance between the board of directors and company's management]. *Economicheski Vestnic* (Yaroslavl, Russia: Yaroslavl State University), 2003, no. 9, pp. 101–110.

Carver, J. "Teoriya Corporativnogo Upravleniya: Poisk Novogo Balansa Mezhdu Sovetom Directorov i Generalnym Directorom" [Corporate governance theory: New balance between the board of directors and the chief executive officer]. A summary. In E. Sapir (ed.), *Russian Enterprises in the Transitive Economy: Materials of the International Conference*. Vol. 1. Yaroslavl, Russia: Yaroslavl State University, 2002.

Carver, J., and Oliver, C. *Conselhos de Administração que Geram Valor: Dirigindo o Desempenho da Empresa a Partir do Conselho* [Boards that create value: Governing company performance from the boardroom]. (P. Salles, trans.). São Paulo: Editora Cultrix, 2002.

Carver, J. *Una Teoria de Gobierno Corporativo* [A theory of corporate governance]. Mexico City: Oficina de la Presidencia para la Innovación Gubernamental, 2001.

Carver, J. "Un modelo de Gobierno Corporativo para el Mexico moderno" [A corporate governance model for a modern Mexico]. *Ejecutivos de Finanzas* (Instituto Mexicano de Ejecutivos de Finanzas), in press.

Maas, J.C.A.M. "Besturen-op-afstand in de praktijk, Het Policy Governance Model van John Carver" [To bring "non-meddling governance" to life, the Policy Governance model of John Carver]. *VBSchrift*, 1997, 7, 7–10.

Maas, J.C.A.M. "Besturen en schoolleiders doen elkaar te kort" [Boards and principals fail in their duties toward each other]. *Tijdschrift voor het Speciaal Onderwijs*, Nov. 1998, 71(8), 291–293.

Maas, J.C.A.M. "Besturen-op-afstand in praktijk brengen" [To bring "non-meddling governance" to life]. *Gids voor Onderwijsmanagement, Samsom H. D. Tjeenk Willink bv*, Oct. 1998.

Maas, J.C.A.M. "De kwaliteit van besturen, Policy Governance Model geeft antwoord op basisvragen" [The quality of governance: Policy Governance answers fundamental questions]. *Kader Primair*, Jan. 2002, 7(5), 26–29.

Maas, J.C.A.M. "Policy Governance: naar het fundament van goed bestuur" [Policy Governance: To the foundation of good governance]. *TH&MA, Tijdschrift voor Hoger onderwijs & Management*, 2004, 11(3).

2. Cadbury, A. "Foreword." In J. Carver and C. Oliver, *Corporate Boards That Create Value: Governing Company Performance from the Boardroom*. San Francisco: Jossey-Bass, 2002b.

   Cadbury, A. "Foreword." In J. Carver, *John Carver on Board Leadership: Selected Writings from the Creator of the World's Most Provocative and Systematic Governance Model*. San Francisco: Jossey-Bass, 2002c.

Preface

This is a book about boards, particularly boards of nonprofit and public organizations. But rather than describe nonprofit and public boards, councils, and commissions as they are, *Boards That Make a Difference* prescribes how they can be.

This is a hopeful book. Boards can be the forward-thinking, value-oriented, leading bodies we claim them to be. In my consulting work with a multitude of boards and chief executives, I have found a great deal of cynicism and resignation. Knowledgeable skeptics think boards can never get beyond being spoon-fed by their executives and that, because of their nature, boards must remain fundamentally reactive. With good evidence, many people believe that boards will always stumble from rubber-stamping to meddling and back again. They believe the realities of group decision making forever destine boards to be incompetent groups of competent people. My impressions, too, are just as dismal, but I believe the cynicism is justified *only so long as boards continue to be trapped in an inadequate design of their jobs*.

Board members are as conscientious and as giving a group as one could ever hope to find. Members of volunteer boards and underpaid public boards interrupt their personal and occupational lives to support something in which they believe. There is not adequate space to give sufficient credit to the works wrought by board members in any given community in one year. The personal drive of board members has accomplished formidable tasks. The perseverance of board members has surmounted seemingly intractable barriers. The patience of board members has outlasted drudgery. The generosity of board members has made the impossible possible.

Board members arrive at the table with dreams. They have vision and values. In many cases, their fervently held beliefs and sincere desire to make a difference impel them to board membership in the first place. Symphony board members want to improve community culture. City councilpersons want to increase the benefits of citizenship. A trade association board wants to augment business opportunities. School board members want to prepare children for life. Boards of hospitals, port authorities, social agencies, chambers of commerce, credit unions, and other organizations want to offer their constituents a better life.

Yet, by and large, board members do not spend their time exploring, debating, and defining these dreams. Instead, they expend their energy on a host of demonstrably less important, even trivial, items. Rather than having impassioned discussions about the changes they can produce in their world, board members are ordinarily found listening passively to staff reports or dealing with personnel procedures and the budget line for out-of-state travel. Committee agendas are likely to be filled with staff material masquerading as board work. Even when programs and services are on the agenda, discussion almost always focuses on activities rather than intended results. Boards are less incisive, goal directed, and farsighted than their average members.

Much as board members and executives unintentionally conspire to water down the powerful work of genuine governance, they often have a nagging awareness that something is not quite right. Usually, however, their recognition is focused on a specific aspect of board folly. It is rarely the basic design, the system of thought. Concern is often expressed as complaints about time spent on trivial items, time spent reading reams of documents, meetings that run for hours and accomplish little, committees that are window dressing for what staff members want to do, meddling in administration, staff members who are more in control of board agendas than is the board, reactivity rather than proactivity, an executive committee's becoming the de facto board, confusion about what is going on, a rubber-stamping of staff recommendations, and the lack of an incisive way to evaluate the executive.

Some of the preceding complaints apply to all nonprofit and public boards. In my experience, most of what the majority of boards do either does not need to be done or is a waste of time when done by the board. Conversely, most of what boards need to do for strategic leadership is not done. This sweeping indictment is not true of all boards all the time, of course, but I contend that it is startlingly true enough of the time to signal a major dysfunction in what we accept as normal.

In these pages I argue for dissatisfaction with what we now accept as ordinary and outline a path that boards can follow to become extraordinary. The failures of governance are not a problem of people, but of *process*. The problems lie squarely in our widely accepted approach to governance, including its treatment of board job design, board-staff relationships, the chief executive role, performance monitoring, and virtually all aspects of the board-management partnership. This book is a strong indictment of what is, but it is intended to make a compelling case for what can be.

The model presented here originated in the mid-1970s. Like many managers, I had training in a professional discipline rather than in management. As a CEO, or chief executive officer, I worked for years learning how to do what I was already paid to do. Those who worked for this manager-in-training endured that travesty far beyond what I can even now appreciate. As my skills as a manager grew, I became increasingly aware of the shaky foundation upon which management rests—the determination of purpose, which is largely a product of governance. Increasingly schooled as administrators, we worked toward haphazardly established ends as if we were introducing computer guidance into a Conestoga wagon. I was driven to discover what could bring governance into the modern age. Out of that quest, I developed an approach to governance that severely departed from much of conventional wisdom. Boards here and there wanted to hear more about it, so a consulting practice grew that subsequently made regular employment impossible.

I have worked with boards and their executives around the world, particularly in the United States and Canada. I meet with them twice in the average week. These clients have assets ranging from near zero to over $25 billion. In the course of this work, I have written articles on governance and executive management for such organizations as the U.S. Department of Health and Human Services (Carver, 1979b), the Canadian Hospital Association (Carver, 1989a), the Association of Mental Health Administrators (Carver, 1979a, 1981b), the Human Interaction Research Institute (Carver, 1984a), the National Association of Corporate Directors (Carver, 1980a), the University of Wisconsin (Carver, 1981a), the Florida League of Cities (Carver, 1984c), the Nonprofit Management Association (Carver, 1984b), the Indiana Library Association (Carver, 1981c), the National Association of Community Leadership Organizations (Carver, 1983), the Center for Community Futures (Carver, 1986b), and others (Carver, 1988a, 1988b). My work has been featured in audiotapes for the Public Management Institute (Carver, 1985a) and Family Service America (Carver, 1985b) and in videotapes for the Georgia Power Company (Carver, 1986c), the National Recreation and Park Association (Carver, 1987), and the University of Georgia (Carver, 1989b). Quite a few other unpublished writings of mine have been circulated (Carver, 1980b, 1985c, 1986a; Carver and Clemow, 1990).

I have run hundreds of governance and chief executive workshops for communitywide groups, state and national conferences, trade associations, and political bodies. The attraction for these clients was a model or framework that enabled them to see their roles and gifts in a new light. They were not always able to implement the model in full, but they had a new standard to shoot for.

So the past couple of decades have provided me with rich relationships with members and chief executives of literally thousands
of boards located in every American state and in every Canadian
province. The probing and challenging of these insightful clients
contributed to the widespread applicability of my governance
model. The model that emerged is generic, capable of whatever tailoring is necessary to fit any type of organization. And while I do
adapt the model to business board settings, particularly to parent-
subsidiary systems, the exclusive focus of this text is on nonprofit
and public organizations. This extensive dialogue in which I forged
a generic application of the model for nonprofit and public governance included a wide array of organizations.

public schools	city councils
private schools	county commissioners
liquid waste disposal	libraries
Third World development	architects' societies
YWCA	real estate boards
hospitals	sports facilities
mental health centers	industrial associations
poverty agencies	local churches
mental retardation	family services
junior league	family planning
airport authorities	adult learning
parks and recreation	credit unions
women's centers	regional planning
national church bodies	zoos
housing authorities	postrelease programs
art guilds	economic development
pest control districts	women's shelters

chambers of commerce

dental societies

county fairs

community theaters

agriculture cooperatives

wilderness programs

alcoholism treatment

private industry councils

League of Women Voters

child protective services

health departments

Hispanic leadership

holding companies

retirement funds

rehabilitation centers

national associations

state boards of education

state mental health systems

medical specialty societies

planning and zoning commissions

health maintenance organizations

community leadership training

golf course superintendents

employment services

vocational centers

extension services

I cannot begin to describe the personal and professional sustenance that these many boards and their executives continue to give me. Working routinely with organizations whose pursuits exceed my understanding and dedication is humbling even to a consultant's robust ego. Their boards have educated me about topics such as waste disposal, international relief, public housing, and the ravages of racism. Their work and their determination have awed me time and time again. Not infrequently have I been literally moved to tears by their perseverance and commitment to make a difference in the world. Their contribution to me is not only one of the mind, in helping forge an approach to governance, but one of the spirit as well.

Out of that profound appreciation and respect, my counsel to boards minces few words. I am hard on boards simply because *I know how good they can be.* Out of what is, frankly, a love affair with boards, I have written this book for board members who want to make a difference. I have written it for board leaders who wish to guide deliberation toward the big questions. I have written it for executives who want a strong rather than a weak board, one that demands a strong executive as well. I have written it for executives who know that management can be only as good as its governing foundation. I have written it for the long-term benefit of taxpayers and donors, as well as the clients, patients, students, and other beneficiaries whose needs are to be served.

So come with me on an adventure into what strategic board leadership might be. Let us consider how a board can do in the boardroom what it sought to do in the first place: project a vision, infuse an organization with mission, bid a staff to be all it can be, and make itself grow a little in the process.

Organization of the Book

Chapter One recounts the varieties of boards, their predictable difficulties, and the need for more precise principles of governance. I seek to establish not only that individual boards need to function better, but that our idea of what "better" means is sorely in need of revision.

Chapter Two makes a case for a new approach to policymaking and what types of policies boards should make. Even though there is more to the board job than policymaking, I argue that reconceiving the nature of policy allows a new level of leadership to be born. Rather than use the traditional categories of board policies borrowed from administration, I develop four new categories tailored for the governing role.

In Chapter Three, I deal with the depth and breadth of board policy in a way that frees boards from staff details and even from the endless stream of approvals.

Chapter Four deals with policies about organizational results and initiates the next five chapters, which explain the four categories of board policy. These policies engage the board in governing outcomes rather than activities and resolve such issues as mission, priorities, and target recipient groups.

Chapter Five covers those policies that give the board control over administrative and programmatic action. These policies enable the board to fulfill its fiduciary responsibilities and to control the prudence and ethics of organizational practice without resorting to "meddling."

Chapter Six deals with policies that establish an effective relationship between board and staff through a CEO. We explore the meaning of the CEO's role and the board's approach to delegating and to evaluating the performance of this important person.

Chapter Seven addresses the board's relationship to its stockholder equivalents and its primary accountability to that trust. Policies covered in this chapter address the board's governing process and its job description.

Chapter Eight extends the discussion of board roles to subgroups of the board. I explore ways to minimize committees and officers and ensure that they do not interfere with either CEO or whole board roles.

In Chapter Nine, I demonstrate how to make board policies "grow" by adding depth to initially very broad policy statements.

Chapter Ten focuses on keeping the board on track by building structured discipline and agendas into the long view.

Finally, in Chapter Eleven, I discuss the importance of thinking big, keeping the dream in front, and including other ingredients of strategic leadership.

I promise readers that they will never see governance in quite the same way again. In the midst of the great quality revolution in American management, I submit a new standard of what quality means in a board's work. This book redefines excellence in governance. And because we have so far to go, it is an urgent argument for revolution in the boardroom.

Consequently, however gentle my intent, *Boards That Make a Difference* is a presumptuous book. It is presumptuous in broadly lumping together such apparently different organizations as governmental bodies, social agencies, quasi-public entities, private clubs, and foundations. It is presumptuous in claiming that virtually all such boards, councils, and commissions, *even those that are not perceived to be in trouble*, are currently performing at a distressingly low percentage of their leadership potential. It is presumptuous in depreciating finance and personnel committees; in belittling financial reports, budget approvals, and the office of the treasurer; and in exhorting boards to get out of long-range planning. And it is presumptuous in claiming that time-honored, virtually unquestioned beliefs and practices of nonprofit and public boards are the major impediments to their being the strategic leaders they could be. "The whole industry," to borrow from an unidentified observer from Waterman (1988, p. 9), "seems trapped in a disastrous set of habits."

I propose a sweeping revision, a new conceptual framework, so that we can conduct ourselves with purpose and performance. This is not a book of helpful hints, nor is it written to suggest incremental improvements in current board operation. The need I see is not so much to make boards better at the work they are doing, but to reinvent that work and its fundamental precepts, to design from the ground up a general theory—or at least a technology—of governance. My commitment is that boards and managers, impelled by a new comprehension of what governance is all about, will do no less than transform how we conceive and proclaim leadership in the boardroom.

Acknowledgments

For the intellectual spark that led me to question the conventional wisdom and thereby to create a new model, I am indebted to Wolfgang S. (Bill) Price. When I discovered his work in program policy planning in 1975 (it was later published in 1977), I thought it the most refreshing approach to governance I had ever come across. Bill's acceptance of me as co-consultant changed the direction of my career.

In addition, the board members of Quinco Consulting Center in Columbus, Indiana, boldly accepted the challenge to adopt an untested governance method in 1976. In my eight-year association with that board, it remained faithful to its commitment. In doing so, it helped fine-tune a new approach, a contribution for which tens of thousands of nonprofit and public boards are unknowingly in Quinco's debt.

Furthermore, the extensive support I have received from those close to me had much to do with my completing this work. Ronald P. Myers brought my board model to the attention of Jossey-Bass Publishers. Ken and Melanie Campbell, Rob and Kathy Kenner, Tom Lane, and Mary D. Shahan made their homes available for get-away writing. Sandra Meicher, Ronald and Sue Myers, David Mueller, and Sally Jo Vasicko offered commentary on the manuscript. My former secretary, Virginia Haag, chased references and made the painstaking transfers from one word processor to another. Lynn D. W. Luckow and Alan Shrader, my long-suffering editors at Jossey-Bass, offered more support and patience with my intermittent writing schedule than I had any right to expect. I am also grateful to the many former clients who allowed me to use their policies for illustration and to quote their words to make my points.

Carmel, Indiana   John Carver
February 1990

The Author

John Carver is a theorist, consultant, and arguably the world's most published author on the design of governance by boards. With extensive name recognition in the field, he is widely regarded as the world's most provocative authority on the topic. Sir Adrian Cadbury, who was instrumental in starting the current international renewal in corporate governance, recently called his work "as near a unifying theory of governance that we at present have."

A native of Chattanooga, Tennessee, John Carver served four years' active duty with the U.S. Air Force Electronic Security Command (1956–1960). He received his B.S. degree in business and economics (1964) and his M.Ed. degree in educational psychology (1965) from the University of Tennessee at Chattanooga and his Ph.D. in clinical psychology (1968) from Emory University, Atlanta. In 1968, he was inducted into the honorary scientific research society Sigma Xi. His formal education was augmented by frequent continuing education from Tulane University, Wharton School of Business, and the American Management Association.

After several years in the administration of a small manufacturing company, Carver spent the bulk of his time first in managing public mental health and developmental disability services, then in developing and applying governance and executive management concepts. His work in governance has spanned nonprofit, governmental, and corporate boards and consulting assignments on every populated continent. His consulting and public presentations are conducted under the name Carver Governance Design.

Carver incorporated the National Council of Community Mental Health Centers (now the National Council for Community Behavioral Healthcare), America's oldest and largest trade association for providers of mental health, substance abuse, and developmental disability services in 1970 and served as its first chairperson. He presented testimony to U.S. House and joint Senate-House conference committees in 1969, 1970, and 1971. He has served as an adjunct and visiting faculty member at the University of Tennessee Space Institute, Tulane University, the University of Texas, and the University of Minnesota. He is currently adjunct professor at the Schulich School of Business, York University, Toronto, and at the University of Georgia Institute for Nonprofit Organizations, Athens, Georgia.

He is author of *John Carver on Board Leadership* (2002g). He and his wife, Miriam Carver, coauthored *A New Vision of Board Leadership* (Carver and Mayhew, 1994), *Reinventing Your Board: A Step-by-Step Guide to Implementing Policy Governance* (Carver and Carver, 1997c, 2006), and The CarverGuide Series on Effective Board Governance. He and Caroline Oliver coauthored *Corporate Boards That Create Value* (2002b). He is featured in the audiotape program *Empowering Boards for Leadership* (1992b) and the videotape *Reinventing Governance* (1993o). Carver has authored and co-edited the Jossey-Bass periodical *Board Leadership* since 1992 and has written a regular column for *Contributions* since 1997. He has published in Canada, the United States, the United Kingdom, Singapore, India, Australia, Brazil, Mexico, and Russia in publications such as the *Times* of London, *Economic Development Review*, *American School Board Journal*, *Solicitors' Journal*, *Gouvernance Revue Internationale*, *Chronicle of Philanthropy*, *Nonprofit World*, *Hospital Trustee*, *Leader to Leader*, *Public Management*, *Institute of Corporate Directors Newsletter*, *National Association of Corporate Directors' Directors Monthly*, *Corporate Governance Quarterly*, *Corporate Governance: An International Review*, *Nation's Cities Weekly*, and others.

John Carver and Miriam Carver live in Atlanta and operate independent consulting practices from there. Together, they conduct the Policy Governance Academy, a specialized advanced training program for consultants in the theory and practice of the Policy Governance model. Their joint Web site can be accessed at www.carvergovernance.com. John Carver can be reached at 404-728-9444 or johncarver@carvergovernance.com.

To Miriam Carver, my wife and colleague,
for her love, support, and keen intellect
and for her authoritative mastery
of the Policy Governance model

With recognition to Ivan Benson,
our executive assistant,
for over ten years of faithful, competent,
and trustworthy service

Prologue
Beginning and Ending with Purpose

Governing boards do not exist in nature. They are social constructs, which is to say that their purpose is what we say it is. The job design, rules, and processes of governing boards—which taken together I will call *governance*—are dependent on the purpose we assign to such bodies.

Although any group of people is capable of many roles, a serious paradigm of governance must be founded not on what a board *can* do but on what it *must* do—the essential elements rather than the optional ones that peculiar circumstances and inclinations may dictate. If we are to produce a science of governance, it is important to begin with an expression of purpose so fundamental that it applies to any body of persons with primary and topmost accountability for an enterprise. Such a universal underpinning could be called a *theory of governance*, a *technology of governance*, a *governance operating system*, or—the term I shall frequently employ—a *model* of governance. Given conceptual integrity in such a foundation, all further idiosyncratic elements and practices can be considered in light of whether they add to or at least do not impede fidelity to the basic principles.

[handwritten margin note: theology of governance]

The Policy Governance model is founded on just such a statement of essential purpose, one I contend to be true wherever the governing board phenomenon exists. Reduced to its minimum, *the purpose of governance is to ensure, usually on behalf of others, that an organization achieves what it should achieve while avoiding those behaviors and situations that should be avoided.*

That purpose may appear so obvious as to be worth little attention. But the governance practices typical in all types of organizations in all parts of the world neither fulfill that purpose nor are consciously designed to do so. Furthermore, widespread publications on governance and a host of consultants' counsel about governance demonstrate the frequently unstated hodgepodge of purposes of governance. In the following chapters, I will make a case not only for the universality and utility of this simple purpose but for the concepts, principles, and discipline necessary for its fulfillment. If the core purpose is satisfied, all other board contributions and practices are optional. If it is not satisfied, all other board contributions and practices—no matter how intelligent or well conducted in themselves—will fail to yield accountable board leadership. A carefully crafted, conceptually rigorous purpose of governance itself, then, forms the heart of board effectiveness.

Introduction

It is virtually impossible to escape contact with boards. We are on boards, work for them, or are affected by their decisions. Boards sit atop almost all corporate forms of organization—profit and nonprofit—and often over governmental agencies as well. The elected forums of our political jurisdictions are boardlike structures: Congresses, parliaments, state legislatures, city councils, and county commissions. In all kinds of human activity, we find formally constituted, empowered groups deciding courses of action and future conditions toward which some body of people will aspire.

This book calls for a profound transformation in the way we think about and practice the governance of organizations. It is not a book of tips but a description of a governance *system* that departs radically from the norm. Systems require considerable explanation and understanding but promise commensurate benefits. More vexing, they require a great deal of unlearning, because in most cases, they are not simply an overlay of new knowledge on old.

To explain the application of the Policy Governance model in governmental and nonprofit boards, Miriam Carver and I have written (or coauthored with others) a set of four books:

> *Boards That Make a Difference:* This book is the starting point and the primary source. It is written not as a "how to" book

but to establish the concepts and principles that constitute the Policy Governance model.

Reinventing Your Board: A Step-by-Step Guide to Implementing Policy Governance. This book, which I coauthored with Miriam Carver, is recommended as the implementation guide for boards that have read *Boards That Make a Difference.*

The Board Member's Playbook: Using Policy Governance to Solve Problems, Make Decisions, and Build a Stronger Board. This book by Miriam Carver and Bill Charney presents Policy Governance boards a set of structured exercises with which to hone their governance skills and prevent deterioration of those skills.

John Carver on Board Leadership: Selected Writings from the Creator of the World's Most Provocative and Systematic Governance Model. This anthology of over one hundred of my articles is meant to be used for sporadic reading on specific governance topics.

WANT MORE?

1

For those seeking an overview of the entire model in condensed form, there are a few publications available. Most article-length pieces, however, are constrained to one or another aspect of the model rather than its totality.

The explication of the Policy Governance model in the following twelve chapters is intended to change forever the way people see the process, functions, and obligations of governing boards. The model borrows from truths long known but introduces unique concepts and principles as well. The intention of it all is to allow human beings to increasingly fulfill their intentions through servant-leadership, rich diversity of ideas, clear and supportive roles, and sturdy frameworks for their dreams.

WANT MORE?

2

The servant-leadership I refer to is the social accountability concept of Robert Greenleaf, a formula for leadership that is rooted in servanthood. Greenleaf's ideal of servant-as-leader is a necessary component of responsible governance.

WANT MORE?

Further Reading

1. Carver, J., and Carver, M. M. *Basic Principles of Policy Governance.* The CarverGuide Series on Effective Board Governance, no. 1. San Francisco: Jossey-Bass, 1996a.

   Carver, J., and Carver, M. "Le modèle Policy Governance et les organismes sans but lucrative" [The Policy Governance model and nonprofit organizations]. *Gouvernance Revue Internationale* (Canada), Winter 2001, *2*(1), 30–48.

   Carver, J. and Oliver, C. "Crafting a Theory of Governance." *Corporate Governance Review,* Oct.–Nov. 2002d, *14*(6), 10–13.

   Carver, J. *Empowering Boards for Leadership: Redefining Excellence in Governance.* San Francisco: Jossey-Bass, 1992b. Audiotape.

   Carver, J. "Leadership du conseil: 'The Policy Governance Model'" [Board leadership: The Policy Governance model]. *Gouvernance Revue Internationale* (Canada), Spring 2000d, *1*(1), 100–108. Reprinted under the title "A Theory of Corporate Governance: Finding a New Balance for Boards and Their CEOs" in J. Carver, *John Carver on Board Leadership.* San Francisco: Jossey-Bass, 2002g.

2. Greenleaf, R. K. *Servant Leadership: A Journey into the Nature of Legitimate Power and Greatness.* New York: Paulist Press, 1977.

   Spears, L. C. (ed.). *Reflections on Leadership: How Robert K. Greenleaf's Theory of Servant Leadership Influenced Today's Top Management Thinkers.* New York: Wiley, 1995.

   Spears, L. C., and Lawrence, M. (eds.). *Practicing Servant Leadership: Succeeding Through Trust, Bravery, and Forgiveness.* San Francisco: Jossey-Bass, 2004.

Leadership by Governing Boards
A Vision of Group Accountability

The vision I have for boards aims for far higher quality in the boardroom than has been common. My aim in this opening chapter is to broadly describe that vision, setting the stage for more detailed description in the following chapters. To begin, I look at ways of classifying boards in order to then limit the scope of the book to governing boards. Next, I describe the peculiar market circumstances that justify grouping nonprofit and public organizations together. I then step back to view the difficulty all boards—business, nonprofit, and public boards alike—have in fulfilling their opportunities, difficulties so prevalent as to require radical reform in governance thought. I summarize the normal prescriptions for board ills along with the reasons that these existing answers are insufficient, including those associated with the recent international flurry of corporate governance codes. I make the case that governance deserves special attention apart from other elements of organization. The chapter concludes with an argument for a new model of governance and the contributions this model should make to boards' capacity for strategic leadership.

The Vision

This book is not about making incremental improvements in boards. It is written primarily not for boards in trouble but for the best of today's boards. It describes and urges nothing less than a transformation in the practice of governance and, more important, in how people think about governance. My intent is to explain a compelling logical, philosophically founded yet completely practical approach to every governing board's job, one that renders it impossible to ever think of boards the same way again. Undertaking that aim is recognition that—analogous to Kant's compromise between extreme rationalism and extreme empiricism—governance theory without practicality is empty and governance practice without theory is blind.

Although this entire book is devoted to detailing my vision, I can give a broad-brush preview here of the kind of governance I have in mind. Boards will truly be leaders—not by invading territory best left to management but by controlling the big picture, the long term, and the value-laden. Boards will delegate powerfully yet safely to those who carry out the work of the organization, empowering them to the maximum extent that is consistent with maintaining the board's own accountability. Boards will seek diversity and inclusion but will express their decisions with one voice, not with the multiple voices of individuals. Boards will be grounded in an allegiance to a base of legitimacy that I will describe as tantamount to shareholders—that is, owners of the organization. In fact, the importance of the owners-to-board link is so great that the proper board job is best described as ownership one step down rather than management one step up. This concept alone completely changes the nature of governance.

This vision of board leadership applies equally to all governing boards, whether new or old, whether large or small, whether operating charitably or for profit. In the words of Adalberto Palma Gómez, senior partner of Aperture, S.C., a consulting firm in Mexico City, the Policy Governance model "provides a new vision for boards in all kinds of institutions, from governmental to private and nonprofit ones." In a similar vein, Sir Adrian Cadbury, the father of corporate governance codes, opined that the Policy Governance paradigm "is all embracing; it can be applied to any type of board or organization" because it is "a unifying theory of governance that covers both the corporate and voluntary sectors."

The vision I will describe here goes to the heart of why a governing board needs to exist by identifying the irreducible number of principles that apply to the task. Doing so enables the construction of a model or paradigm or theory or operating system—each of these words will work—that applies to any governing board of anything anywhere. I will deal with the deceptively appealing but ill-informed one-size-fits-all objection to this universality as the story unfolds.

WANT MORE?
1

In much the same way as it has been said that management is management is management, I will defend the idea that governance is governance is governance. Prospective board members, executives, and consultants who learn the basics of such a universal governance theory can then apply it to any board situation in which they find themselves. Such a claim, of course, calls for great integrity in the fundamentals—an integrity of design I hope to explain to the reader's satisfaction.

It is important to note that the governance framework presented here is just that, a framework. It could be called a *foundational technology* of governance in that many other techniques can be adopted if kept within this framework. That is, as long as the principles of the paradigm are preserved, others' methods of problem solving, prioritizing, or interacting—for example, various problem-solving approaches, Myers-Briggs interpersonal dynamics, mind mapping, force field analysis, affinity diagramming, and other methods—can be very useful. If rigorously framed by the discipline of Policy Governance, good board work can be assisted by adapting all or parts of the great amount of study that has been devoted to decision makers. (Caroline Oliver's analogy of an operating system that is able to run many programs is fitting.) But since such aids—regardless of how good they are in themselves—were likely not developed with Policy Governance principles in mind, they can

WANT MORE?
2

harm governance if not used judiciously. For example, the most sophisticated problem-solving techniques are useless if they are applied to the wrong level of problems.

I deal with governance as it shows up in nonprofit and governmental organizations in this book, leaving governance in equity corporations to the more specifically targeted *Corporate Boards That Create Value: Governing Company Performance from the Boardroom*, which I wrote with Caroline Oliver in 2002. (The reason for omitting detailed discussion of profit-oriented boards here is not that the same fundamentals do not apply but that the language and owner intentions are so very different. My reason for this exclusion will be explained more fully in this chapter. But a very brief treatment of equity corporations can be found in Resource A.)

Moreover, because it is so critical that boards fully understand the new ideas or, at least, the new way in which old ideas fit together, this book is not a "how to" text but one of principles and concepts. Although practical implementation is not overlooked in these pages, much of the detail on implementation is left to *Reinventing Your Board: A Step-by-Step Guide to Implementing Policy Governance*, which I coauthored with Miriam Carver in 1997, the revised edition of which is scheduled for publication in 2006.

In other words, I present a radically modernized *way to think* about governance, a conceptual coherence on which all real-world specifics and tailoring must be based. But before I can even begin to fulfill my intention to describe my vision for governance integrity and leadership, it is necessary to carve out some distinctions and to demonstrate the need for change in the first place.

Varieties of Boards

At one end of the decision-making scale, decisions are made by individuals and by small groups such as families or associates. At the other end, decisions are made in plebiscites and elections. In between, decisions are made by empowered bodies called boards. Two considerations delineate those bodies to whom my commentary directly applies: (1) the organizational position of the board and (2) the economic nature of the organization.

Boards Considered by Organizational Position

Governing board. The most important kind of board is that of ultimate corporate accountability—the governing board. The governing board is always positioned at the top of the organization. *Corporate board, board of directors, board of trustees, board of regents,* and similar titles denote groups that have authority exceeded only by owners and the state. The governing board is as high in the formal structure as one can go. Its total authority is matched by its total accountability for all corporate activity.

Advisory board. There are also boards whose function is to give counsel, not to govern. Advisory boards may advise the governing board, the CEO, or other staff. They can be positioned anywhere **WANT MORE?** in the organization, as long as they formally attach to some **3** proper organizational element. Advisory boards are optional and have only as much authority as the authorizing point within the organization chooses to grant. In some fields, it is common to find advisory boards that have been given extensive authority and whose advice is virtually certain to have an effect. As long as some position within the organization can retract the group's authority, it is not a governing board. An advisory board's authority can be curtailed only by the advisee, by law, or—in the case of membership organizations—by the membership.

Line board. Considerably more rare is the line board. The word *line* describes a heretofore unlabeled board type. Management lit-**WANT MORE?** erature has paid little attention to this form, except for the **4** modified form discussed by Ackoff. The line board is not advisory, for it wields definite authority over subordinate positions. But it is not at the top of the organization and does not, therefore, qualify as a governing board. It is merely a group inserted where a single manager might have served.

Workgroup board. Sometimes people speak of a "working board" when they simply mean a board that stays busy. Hence, a governing, advisory, or line board might be a working board. My term, *workgroup board*, however, denotes a governing board with little or no staff. It must govern and be the workers as well. Frequently, boards that confine their role solely to governing began as this type of dual-function group.

Very small organizations, such as civic clubs, often have boards in this dual position. The group is incorporated, so a corporate governing board exists. Absent enough funds to pay a staff, board members are the only workforce in sight. This kind of board is not a true type in the way that governing, advisory, and line boards are; it is merely a governing board with another set of responsibilities. The organizational position of a workgroup board is not only at the top but everywhere else as well. It is very important for such boards to remember that they have two different, simultaneous roles and that they can best perform those roles by keeping them clearly separated.

WANT MORE?

5

Boards Considered by Economic Nature of the Organization

The power and responsibilities of advisory and line boards are determined by the specific organization rather than by a commanding generic principle. The foregoing discussion serves only to distinguish governing boards as the sole subject of this text. Throughout this book, I deal only with boards in their governing role.

It has long been common practice to differentiate the vast and disparate array of organizations governed by boards into three groups: *profit* (*equity* or, loosely termed, *business*), *nonprofit*, and *governmental*. Additional characteristics distinguish subgroups of each of these three main groups. For example, equity corporations are grouped as *public* (publicly traded) and *private* (no public trading). Nonprofits are also divided into *public* (directly related to government, sometimes quasi-governmental) and *private* (related minimally or not at all to government). Nonprofits range from purely charitable to trade or professional associations whose aim is to serve the interests of their members. Governmental organizations include not only the jurisdictional governance of cities, townships, counties, provinces, and states but also districts for water supply, schools, pollution control, and a host of other authorities. For the present discussion, I ignore the subgroups and concentrate on the three major types: profit, nonprofit, and governmental.

Profit boards. Equity corporations engage in trade in order to produce a return for shareholders. These companies ordinarily compete in markets that range from free markets to markets that enjoy considerable governmental protection. Governing boards in business range from the obligatory figurehead board of an entrepreneurial business to a highly formalized, paid group representing diverse stockholders.

Nonprofit boards. Corporations chartered for charitable purposes (or, at least, not for return on equity) have no stock ownership, though statutes may require a formal membership as a stockholder-equivalent. Internationally, such organizations are often referred to as *nongovernmental organizations* (NGOs). In the United States, the term *private voluntary organization* (PVO) is frequently used to describe international nonprofits. NGOs and PVOs are included among nonprofit agencies.

Although nonprofit corporations may accumulate surpluses, their accounting systems have no place for profit. They differ from other corporations in that they are exempt from certain taxes and are unable to distribute their surpluses to holders of equity. (In the United States, this exemption includes not only the familiar 501(c)(3) but several other categories of preferred tax status.) Nonprofit corporations frequently receive a large proportion of their revenues from funding from other organizations and donations from individuals rather than from sales of a product. Obligations of nonprofit governing boards under the law, however, are similar to those of boards of other corporations.

Governmental boards. Governmental boards, elected or appointed, are bound by more legal requirements in both their composition and their process than are the foregoing types. Governmental organizations are like nonprofit organizations with respect to profit and distribution of earnings. Governmental boards may be quasi-governmental (for example, boards for water systems or airport authorities) or fully governmental (for example, city councils). They may or may not have taxing authority. Governmental organizations are similar to nonprofit organizations in that they derive their revenues not from sales but from taxation and user fees.

Profit, nonprofit, and governmental governing boards have much in common. They are alike in that they all bear ultimate accountability for organizational activity and accomplishment. They are unlike in how they are situated in the larger context of political and economic life. They differ in how much public scrutiny they receive, a factor that produces differences in the amount of posturing involved in board dynamics. They vary in the degree to which the procedures of governance are prescribed by law. They differ greatly in the strength of the traditions that drive their methods. Many governmental boards have traditions that were established long before twentieth-century management appeared on the scene. Powerful precedents make it difficult for legislatures and county commissioners, for example, to behave as though modern management principles were ever developed.

This book focuses specifically on governmental and nonprofit governing boards. I am concerned not with what those boards are called but solely with their function as governors. Some of the alternate terms for *board* are *council, commission, assembly, house of delegates,* and *elders,* among many others.

From here on, the word *public* will refer to the various types of governmental entities, because in common perception, *public* bridges the gray area between special-purpose governmental groups and quasi-governmental nonprofits. This focus is useful as we explore governance, even though there is nothing inherent in the nonprofit or public organization per se that causes governance to be different from that in profit companies. Then why do I address public and nonprofit governance, particularly in view of the extremely disparate array of organization types included under that rubric? After all, are they not more different than they are alike? The Ford Foundation, a community arts guild, and a credit union may not appreciate membership in this mixed club. The justification for classifying them together is that the boards of most nonprofit and public organizations share a compelling factor: the peculiar nature of their markets and what their owners want the organizations for.

Life in the Muted Market

Companies organized for profit typically receive money through sales. Sales revenues are the result of an exchange between the company and consumers. Consumers judge whether the good or service is worth the price. If it is not, they do not buy; if it is, they do.

WANT MORE?
6

By and large, then, the success of companies competing in such a market is revealed in their financial statements. But for nonprofit and public organizations, income statements not only fail to express success and failure but may even obscure them. In other words, the "bottom line" does not show up in their financial reports.

Nonprofit and public organizations ordinarily receive money from sources other than those who use their products. Direct consumers may pay a discounted price or even nothing. The organization may receive a subsidy from donors and tax sources to make up the deficit. There is no consumer judgment of the product's rightful price, because the consumer is not confronted with that choice. Consequently, although nonprofit and public organizations may be buffeted about by budget pressures and funding squeezes, there is no direct market force bearing on the relationship between product and price.

One relevant variable that separates the governance of most public and nonprofit enterprises from most profit organizations is the automatic market test of product worth. I define a market test as consumers' free decisions about whether a given product, among alternatives, is worth the cost of its production. If alternatives are unavailable because of artificially blocked competition, there is no clean market test. If the consumer does not pay the entire price, there is no clean market test. This definition focuses on the *automatic consumer judgment* aspect of market. The absence of this automatic judgment does not mean that the word *market* cannot be used. For example, public schools and family planning centers each operate in some identifiable market and may fare better if their staff does a good job of marketing. This use of the terms *market* and *marketing*, however, is unrelated to the integrity of the market test I have described.

Without a market to summarize consumer judgment, an organization literally does not know what its product is worth. (Later, I will argue that it may not even know what its product is!) An organization may know what the product costs to make and what the staff thinks about product quality. It may know that consumers are raving with delight. It may even know precisely how effective the product is. But without a market, the organization still does not know what its product is worth.

From a governance perspective, then, the relevant factor that sets most nonprofit and public organizations apart from profit organizations is not how they are managed, for the principles of management are the same in each setting. The difference is not in distribution of earnings, for this is a matter of accounting rather than substance. What is different—with profound effects—is that most nonprofit and public organizations lack a behavioral process to aggregate the many individual evaluations of product and cost. The organization is missing the foundation that would enable it to define success and failure, to know what is worth doing, and, in the largest sense, even to recognize good performance.

Does PCNS even try to measure this?

So the typical public or nonprofit board is faced with a challenge that business boards never have to confront. In the absence of a market test, the board must perform that function. The board must bear this peculiar additional burden if it is to act responsibly. It is not enough to be efficient, nor is it enough even to produce fine products. Any reasonable definition of productive excellence must relate chiefly to whether a good or service is worth the full economic cost of its production.

From this point on, I refer to public and nonprofit organizations as if they all lack a rigorous market test. That will prove sufficiently true to justify the simplification, though exceptions exist. Nonprofit hospitals, for example, operate in a harsh market environment, albeit one of great artificiality imposed by regulation and insurers, depending on the country. For nonprofit and public organizations that are truly subject to an unsubsidized market judgment, the peculiarity discussed here is not true. In these cases, the board's task is easier, though the concepts and principles in the model presented here will still contribute to their governance. Among the vast array of public and nonprofit organizations, however, such truly market-tested instances are in the minority. With this proviso, I consider public and nonprofit boards to be engaged in serving a muted market.

Producing What Owners Want

Consider three intentions persons might have for organizing. First, if persons organize for the purpose of making a monetary return on their investment, they would seek corporate status under for-profit **WANT MORE?** statutes. Second, if persons organize in order to make their **7** own lives better (but not in direct monetary ways), they might incorporate as a professional society or trade association. Such an organization might be a nonprofit, but it would have no access to the most favorable tax treatment. In a special case of this type, if the persons wish to wield coercive police power over

themselves and others, they would seek a state or provincial charter as a municipality. Third, if a group organizes in order to make
life better for others, it would incorporate as a nonprofit and would
be eligible for considerable tax advantages.

In each case, the purpose of the organization flows from what its
owners want it for, but the task of defining what a nonprofit or governmental organization is for is a far more multifaceted task than
defining intended monetary shareholder value for the equity corporation. An equity corporation, to be sure, must manage the market
well, but its board never has to speak for the market (to determine
what products are worth) in the way that nonprofit and governmental boards must.

The Flaws of Governance

Even boards that are free of the "market surrogate" burden have
shown that the challenges of governing are almost too great. Governing boards have not been vessels of exemplary efficiency, even
in the best of situations. Writing of corporate boards, Drucker
(1974) said, "There is one thing all boards have in common, regardless of their legal position. *They do not function.* The decline of the
board is a universal phenomenon of this century" (p. 628, emphasis added). Geneen (1984) of ITT complained that boards are
unable to protect the interests of stockholders whom they represent:
"Among the boards of directors of Fortune 500 companies, I esti-
mate that 95 percent are not fully doing what they are legally,
morally, and ethically supposed to do. And they couldn't, even if
they wanted to" (p. 28).

Smith (1958) found it to be "ironic . . . that we in the United
States have so neglected this most vital area" (p. 52). While every
other management function has been exhaustively studied and ana-
lyzed, "the responsibilities of the board and the distinction between
board and management have been sorely neglected. Management literature on the subject is pitifully brief and strikingly devoid of any real

depth or new ideas." Juran and Louden (1966) pointed to the same root for the problem: "It is an astonishing fact that the job of the board of directors is, in proportion to its intrinsic importance, one of the least studied in the entire spectrum of industrial activities. . . . As a consequence, the job of the board of directors has received neither the benefit of the broad exchange of practical experience nor the intensity of study which has been available to other corporate activities" (p. 7).

Despite years of potential improvement, later observers made equally damning comments. Boards have been "largely irrelevant through most of the twentieth century" (Gillies, 1992). They are "like ants on a log in turbulent water who think they are steering the log" (unknown source quoted by Leighton and Thain, 1997). Leighton and Thain (1997) explain, "The truth is that boards are too often self-perpetuating, more interested in retaining power than in responding to the wishes of shareholders" (p. 39). Arthur Levitt (1998), chairman of the U.S. Securities and Exchange Commission, complains, "There are too many boards that overlook more than they oversee. Too many that are re-active instead of pro-active."

Though possessed of ultimate organizational power, the governing board is understudied and underdeveloped. Here we confront a flagrant irony in management literature: where opportunity for leadership is greatest, job design for leadership is poorest. The worldwide flurry of attention to governance codes in the corporate world that began as the twentieth century ended serves as an indictment of existing governance thinking and practice.

It is against this uninspiring backdrop of governing boards in general that I deal here specifically with boards of public and nonprofit organizations. It is little wonder that such boards have difficulty, for their faults include those of profit boards plus those peculiarly contributed by their artificial market situation and their more complicated delineation of purpose. If the governance of supposedly rational, modern business corporations is not without underlying weaknesses, it should not be surprising that the governance of nonprofit and public enterprises presents an extensive array of blemishes.

What Goes Wrong

It doesn't take a scholar to find the problems in nonprofit and public governance. Random observation of a few nonprofit and public boards will expose many of the normal shortcomings. Nonprofit and public boards stumble regularly and visibly. Individual board members and executives have often felt that one specific act or another is silly or empty. They rarely say so, however, for the charade has a commanding history, eliciting an almost conspiratorial agreement not to notice organizational fatuousness.

It is predictable in almost all organizations that employees know what their respective jobs are with more confidence and accuracy than the board knows its own. Moreover, there is normally more precision about, more studied attention to, and more monitoring of performance in staff tasks than governance. Try to find an arts board as skilled in governance as its artists are in their work. Look for a hospital board as skilled in governance as surgeons, nurses, and even building maintenance personnel are in their arenas. For that matter, seek an automobile manufacturer board as deft in governance as its engineers are in their calling.

The problem is not that a particular board or an individual board member occasionally slips into poor practice but that intelligent, caring individuals regularly exhibit procedures of governance that are deeply flawed. Chait, Holland, and Taylor (1996) provocatively and accurately remark that effective governance is "a rare and unnatural act" (p. 1). Certain common practices are such obvious drains on board effectiveness that one does not need a sophisticated model to recognize them. Although some boards may avoid a few of the following conditions, rarely does any one board avoid them all.

Time spent on the trivial. Items of trivial scope or import receive disproportionate attention compared with matters of greater scope or importance. Richard J. Peckham, on joining a major public board in Kansas, found it so lost in trivia that "I thought I'd been banished to outer darkness." Major program issues go unresolved while boards conscientiously grapple with some small detail. An Illinois school board proudly proclaimed the "active role the members of our board take in purchasing decisions. . . . The administration [in replacing desks in two classrooms] was directed to select three chairs from different companies and have them available for the next board meeting. The board then made the decision on warranty, durability, price and color." A national survey found that almost half of America's school boards made the purchasing decisions for tape recorders, cameras, and television sets (National School Boards Association, n.d.). Little wonder that Chait, Holland, and Taylor (1996) claim, "Trustees are often little more than high-powered, well-intentioned people engaged in low level activities" (p. 1).

Short-term bias. The time horizon for board decisions is more distant than anywhere else in the organization. Yet we find boards dealing mainly with the near term and, even more bizarre, with the past. Last month's financial statement gets more attention than the organization's strategic position.

Reactive stance. Boards consistently find themselves reacting to staff initiatives rather than making decisions proactively. Proposals for staff action and recommendations for board action so often come from staff that some boards would cease to function if they were asked to create their own agenda.

Reviewing, rehashing, redoing. Some boards spend most of their time going over what their staff has already done. "Eighty-five percent of our time was spent monitoring staff work," says Glendora Putnam, Boston, about a prominent national board. "We can't afford that. We have too much wisdom to be put to use." Just keeping up with a large staff can take prodigious hours and even then can never be done fully. But the salient point is that reviewing, rehashing, and redoing staff work—no matter how well—do not constitute leadership.

Leaky accountability. Boards often allow accountability to "leak" around the chief executive. Having established a CEO position, the board members continue to relate in their official capacities with other staff, either giving them directions or judging their performance, rather than allowing the CEO to do his or her job.

Diffuse authority. It is rare to find a board-executive partnership wherein each party's authority has been clarified. Often, a vast gray area exists. When a matter lies in this uncertain area, the safe executive response is to take it to the board. Instead of using this opportunity to clarify to whom the decision belongs, the board simply approves or disapproves. The event has been settled, but the boundaries of authority remain as unclear as they were before.

Complete overload. Unless a board rubber-stamps decisions or just ignores issues, it is likely to be overwhelmed by a seemingly impossible job. The board just cannot get to everything and is likely to miss important red flags.

Moving Toward Solutions

Many board flaws that seem to be cosmetic blemishes are indicative of more fundamental errors. "These are just symptoms of a problem," says Barry Romanko of the Alberta Ministry of Parks and Recreation in St. Paul, Canada. "The problem is that we are giving boards the wrong job." Attacking the superficial flaws might in itself be a worthy undertaking. Similarly, it might be useful to invoke the usual admonitions: "Stick to policy!" "Let your CEO manage!" "Don't rubber-stamp!" But it would be even more instructive to build a healthier infrastructure of governance concepts. Framing the governance challenge more effectively can go far beyond merely eliminating common problems; it can provide a clearing in which boards can be strategic leaders.

Inadequate Prescriptions

At some level, boards and executives are well aware of the historical deficiencies in the ways they operate. An explosion of popular interest in management issues beginning in the 1970s sharpened the perception that governance is not all it can be. (The effects of a further upsurge of interest in the governance of publicly traded companies as the twentieth century came to a close will be dealt with later in this chapter.) Board training has received more attention because of this awareness. Many board members, executives, and observers have offered counsel for ailing board practices all along. But somehow the prescriptions, though quite rational, have fallen short. At best, they have cleaned up some of the clutter and the more striking inefficiencies in board operation. But because few previous efforts have been based in a complete conceptual model, prescriptions have largely been piecemeal, anecdotal wisdom. Most prescriptions have concerned the level of board activity, the board-staff relationship, or the nature of board work. The appeal of each is that it accurately assesses one part of the elephant.

Prescriptions About Activity and Involvement

More involvement. One solution to the problems of governance is that boards should be more involved. They should participate directly in the work of the organization, volunteering time and energy to become physically involved in doing things. A board operating at a distance is a board too detached to understand, much less to make a difference. Board membership means having access to the good works of an organization without having to go through the hiring process to get there. Those who espouse greater board activity greatly need to "know what is going on" in the organization. Reflecting the hyperinvolvement, the board agenda is likely to be drawn out and committee work may be heavy.

Less involvement. Boards should be less involved. By participating directly in the work of the organization, the board tends to become lost in the trees and to lose sight of the forest. While equity corporate boards are criticized for insufficient independence from management, nonprofit boards' involvement in internal affairs hinders their independent judgment just as much. Board members are better as governors around a board table than as a prestigious auxiliary staff. The board's job is "to choose a CEO, then stay out of the way," confided a hospital trustee in Wisconsin. Persons who call for less involvement often propose keeping up with relevant facts through reports, particularly financial ones. Agendas are likely to be crisp and "businesslike." Committee work may be light.

Prescriptions About Board-Staff Relations

Board as watchdog. The board, as the ultimately accountable agent, should keep a sharp eye on staff activities. This close oversight limits the degree of power delegated, requiring many board approvals and close questioning of staff. A utility commissioner in Minnesota claimed that the commission's main function is to "keep a wary eye on the staff." Boards acting as watchdogs become heavily involved in administration, often in busy committees related to staff activities. Tight control is seen as the road to accountability or, at least, to safety. Some boards take the watchdog posture so far that they develop an adversarial relationship with staff; anything brought before the board becomes a trial. In an alternate watchdog role, the board may ally itself with lower-echelon staff members and—as reported by a poverty agency board member in Ohio, for example—may perceive issues in terms of protecting staff from administrators. At their best, such boards are constructive skeptics.

Board as cheerleader. Staff members are basically honest and capable, so the best board role is to be supportive and cheer them on. The hallmark is trust. After all, the key to governing well is choosing a chief executive in whom you can believe and then standing behind him or her. Cheerleader boards stay out of administration because it is none of their business. They may even refrain from asking the hard questions, because to do so would show a lack of faith. Rubber-stamping executive requests is an expression of gratitude that things are going so smoothly. Often, the governing board's role is seen as advisory after a CEO is installed. Loose control is the best approach ("After all, we are just volunteers"). A part-time board should not get in the way; its role is not so much to govern the staff as to be its apologist and champion.

Prescriptions About Board Work and Skills

Board as manager. Boards, though one step removed from daily operation, should become more proficient in management skills so as to act as managers. Board members are chosen in part because of their skills in personnel, finance, program leadership, and so forth. The board is likely to pore over financial statements, staffing patterns, and maintenance reports. It engages staff in the intricacies of management. Committees are structured along the lines of staff departments such as personnel and public relations. The board, more or less autocratic, is seen as the supermanager or at least as sharing management responsibilities with its top staff.

Board as planner. Because planning is an integral part of managing, boards should predominantly plan. Boards plan the elements of personnel, finance, and so forth, rather than engaging in current implementation. Boards develop long-range plans and, with their committees, spend long hours to create a plan document.

Board as adviser. Because boards are composed of experienced persons, they should make those skills and knowledge available to staff. Boards primarily exist to provide useful advice. There may even be several board committees that are devoted to specific advisory areas.

Board as fundraiser. While the staff go about the business of the organization, the board's challenge is to make sure there is enough philanthropic funding to keep the organization afloat. "Give, get, or get off" is the board's mantra.

Board as communicator. The board should communicate better among its members and with staff. If board and staff could only hear each other better, the organization would have a more satisfying process and, hence, a more satisfactory product. Particularly on multiethnic community boards, the existence of barriers to communication lends credence to this approach. The path to better governance lies in better human relations.

Why the Prescriptions Disappoint

These are not the only prescriptions, nor are they really distinct types. They illustrate the range and divergence of proposed solutions to board ineffectiveness. And from the standpoint of slight improvements, they do not all fail. What is confusing is that each prescription contains just enough truth to be considered plausible. At one time or another, they can all be good approaches.

The problem with anecdotal wisdom, however, is its spotty applicability. A former rubber-stamp-type board that has been duped by its CEO will surely improve by being more involved, exerting tighter control, or acting as supermanager. A board fatigued by interminably long meetings may be wise to move toward shorter meetings with more businesslike agendas. In slightly different circumstances, however, these solutions would themselves be the problems.

Problem-based prescriptions sow the seeds of the next difficulty, because the solution often outlives the problem that justified it. Soon the board that shifted to shorter meetings finds it cannot keep up with issues as well as it desires. Or a good CEO is lost because he or she will not tolerate the tight control and suspicion left over from the previous pendulum swing.

Prescriptions for board improvement are often based on current problems or problems that board members have experienced elsewhere. Problem-based improvements may be absolutely sensible and still miss the mark. They may cure present difficulties yet not prevent a wide range of potential future problems. Correcting insufficiencies by looking backward at what they have been simply invites the next, perhaps opposite error. It is like trying to drive down the highway with a firm grip on the rearview mirror.

Governance as Unique Management

A paradigm tailored to the special circumstances of governance would enable us to apply wisdom more coherently. When a function has been assembled from bits of historical practice, it cannot as gracefully incorporate wisdom but must patch it on here and there. Tailoring management principles for governance, however, assumes that boards call for special treatment. This section argues that governance certainly is special, though not for the reason most frequently cited.

The Red Herring of Voluntarism

Boards of nonprofit and some public organizations think of themselves primarily as volunteers. This identity adds little and potentially costs a great deal. Responsibility, authority, job design, and demands of a board are not affected by being paid or unpaid. Beyond strengthening the sense of public service, being a voluntary board is irrelevant to governance and its attendant burden of accountability. On the other hand, some connotations of voluntarism can detract from the board's job, severely reducing its ability to lead.

Volunteers are a tradition of North American life, offering many skills, insights, and hours in a commendable expression of helpfulness. Volunteers help get a job done without compensation. For an existing organization, that usually means helping the staff, inasmuch as staff is engaged in the actual work. Governing boards, however,

WANT MORE?
8

exist not to help staff but to own the business—usually in trust for some larger ownership. If anyone is helping, it is the staff. Volunteers on governing boards are expressing an ownership interest rather than a helpfulness interest. Owning the business conveys a power that cannot be responsibly grasped as long as board members think they are there to help. Power not used is power defaulted on and, ultimately, power irresponsibly used. It is destructive to confuse helpfulness with ownership. By emphasizing their volunteer status, boards risk weakening their effectiveness.

Because the same person can wear two different hats, board members may also be volunteers at a staff level. It is important that

WANT MORE?
9

the hats be kept distinct in everyone's mind. The board as an official body (as opposed to individual members) is well advised to limit its role to owner representative only. It is not necessary for the board to be a source of advice to staff; in fact, that can be problematic. But it is *crucial* that the board be in charge; the chain of command—or chain of moral authority, if you will—will tolerate no less. Consequently, the board's pivotal role is not adviser or helper, but commander.

Boards as Trustees

Unlike other managers who work for a well-defined superior, boards ordinarily work for either a vaguely defined group or a well-defined but difficult-to-communicate-with group. The former is illustrated by a public radio station board, the latter by a city council. There is someone out there for whom the board acts in trust, but it is difficult to tell who that someone is. Consequently, boards have more difficulty than other managers in getting their marching orders and their evaluations.

This book promotes the concept of moral ownership in order to isolate the various stakeholders to whom the board owes its primary allegiance. The concept results in a more carefully defined group than what is normally meant by *stakeholders*. For community boards, this ownership is the community at large; for membership associations, the membership is the ownership. I will deal later with how the ownership concept is of critical importance in designing governance, even in organizations where the concept of owners seems foreign. For now, however, it suffices to say that a board cannot optimally fulfill its responsibilities without determining who is included in its ownership and how those owners can be heard.

Boards as Unique Decision Makers

Although management principles are relevant to governing, it is better for boards to think of their task as an extension downward of ownership rather than an extension upward of management. Governance is ownership one step down, not management one step up. The management skills that might be helpful are similar to the overview management skills a CEO needs rather than specialized management skills, such as purchasing, marketing, and personnel administration. But the board's job is not just to act as a part-time über-CEO, for there are peculiarities that render governance unique. Several decision-making features are inherent only in the governing body:

- Boards are at the extreme end of the accountability chain. Other managers must deal with persons both above and below their station. The buck stops with the board. It has no supervisor to carve out what portion of a given topic it is to oversee.

- The board acts, in a moral sense and sometimes a legal one, as the agent of a largely unseen and often unde-cided principal, an entity that may express itself in curious and spotty ways, if at all.

- The board is a set of individuals operating as a single entity. Melding multiple peer viewpoints and values into a single resolution is peculiar to a group acting col-lectively as an authority.

- Individuals' discipline tends to suffer when they belong to groups. A board is likely to have less discipline than any one of its members operating alone.

- Boards are ordinarily more than the usual managerial arm's length from the next lower organizational level. They are not only part-time but also physically removed. *not true of pens.*

- Boards are groups that oversee one person, whereas managers are single persons who oversee groups; gover-nance structure is like management upside down. Mueller (1981) argues that governance in its essence differs from management. It is, he claims, an unfolding, always incomplete phenomenon driven by "soft realms of thought and deportment. They are value-laden, sub-jective, intuitive and characteristic of the art forms dealing with social interaction" (p. xii).

Effects of Recent Corporate Governance Reforms

The most recent wave of reform in corporate governance began in 1990 with publication of the Cadbury Committee report in the United Kingdom. The corporate world owes a debt to Sir Adrian Cadbury for this breakthrough, though it had little direct effect on **WANT MORE?** nonprofit or public boards. In successive steps, the movement in the United Kingdom challenged the combined **10** CEO/chair, the proportions of executive (inside) to non-executive (outside) directors, and other widespread practices. As the 1990s wore on, however, a series of governance debacles caused a flurry of governance codes to be developed or enhanced over much of the world. Because of its position in the world of capital markets, the United States joined the fray with a vengeance with passage of the Sarbanes-Oxley legislation in 2002. Although the legislation was similar to codes arising elsewhere and is only binding on publicly traded companies, many nonprofit and public boards began treating its provisions as the gold standard in governance, worth emulating even without a mandate to do so.

Corporate governance codes in general and Sarbanes-Oxley in particular do little to improve the nature of governance but much to protect investors from governance. They represent "development-by-accumulation" (Kuhn, 1996, p. 2) rather than being grounded in a conceptually coherent theory. Their focus on transparency and independence is hard to fault, but these are hardly prescriptions for how to govern. Moreover, codes' prescriptions regarding committees and the roles of CEOs and chairs are, frankly, dysfunctional. Corporate boards in the United States, suddenly getting religion about governance, spent huge amounts in legal costs to conform to the new law. It can easily be argued that they are no more interested in good governance than they were before but are very, very interested in lawful compliance.

Consequently, existing codes, to their credit, prohibit a number of bad practices, requiring more stringent controls on conflict of interest and management dominance. They are much like traffic laws that impose rules for stops, turns, speed, and licensing. But everyone knows that meticulous observance of traffic laws, while clearly a desirable thing, does not in itself make one a good driver. Policy Governance boards already exceed the substantive requirements of corporate governance codes. They can easily conform to the nonsubstantive elements by using the consent (automatic approval) agenda described in Chapter Ten.

Being without a theoretical base, corporate governance reforms take on a fad-like quality, driven by the political heat of the moment and adding one piecemeal solution on top of others. The greater involvement of directors, for example, easily becomes greater meddling instead of greater policy control. The understandable backlash discredits even the useful part of the involvement message. Writing to American corporate directors, Rehfeld (2005, p. 1) wishfully reported, "The thought of requiring directors to put their noses into everything the company does but maintain a traditional hands-off posture seems to have run its course." Indeed, Canadian corporate magnate Conrad Black called ongoing corporate governance reforms a fad. Interestingly, his own corporate empire was subsequently plagued by a host of widely publicized governance problems.

WANT MORE?
11

Toward a New Governance

In light of all these factors, I have translated principles of modern management to address the peculiar circumstance of governing boards. The adaptation goes beyond a collection of helpful suggestions; it is a fundamentally reordered paradigm for governance. Governance as widely practiced is a farrago of historical accidents and disjointed elements no doubt contrived by intelligent people. But having not arisen from a coherent sense of the whole, it is gravely flawed.

A model of governance is a framework within which to organize the thoughts, activities, structure, and relationships of governing boards. A designed model yields a new nature of governance, quite unlike a collection of even wise responses to specific governance problems. What should we expect from a model? What conditions would be better if there were a better framework within which to build governance actions? Keeping in mind that *model* in this context means a set of principles rather than a one-size-fits-all structure, I think we have a right to expect a good model of governance to do the following:

1. *"Cradle" vision.* A useful framework for governance must hold and support vision in the primary position. Administrative systems cause us to devote great attention to the specifics. Such rigor, while commendable, can overshadow the broader matter of purpose. There must be systematic encouragement to think the unthinkable and to dream.

2. *Explicitly address fundamental values.* The governing board is a guardian of organizational values. The framework must ensure that the board focuses on values. Endless decisions about events cannot substitute for deliberations and explicit pronouncements on values.

3. *Force an external focus.* Because organizations tend to focus inward, a governance model must intervene to guarantee a marketlike, external responsiveness. A board would thus be more concerned with needs and markets than with the internal issues of organizational mechanics.

4. *Enable an outcome-driven organizing system.* All functions and decisions need to be rigorously weighed against the standard of purpose. A powerful model would have the board not only establish a mission in terms of an outcome but procedurally enforce such a mission as the central organizing focus.

5. *Separate large issues from small ones.* Board members usually agree that large issues deserve first claim on their time, but

they have no common way to discern a big item. A model should help differentiate sizes of issues.

6. *Force forward thinking.* A governance scheme should help a board thrust the majority of its thinking into the future. Strategic leadership demands the long-term viewpoint.

7. *Enable proactivity.* So that boards do not merely preside over momentum, a model of governance should press boards toward leading and away from reacting. Such a model would engage boards more in creating than in approving.

8. *Facilitate diversity and unity.* It is important to optimize the richness of diversity in board composition and opinion yet assimilate that variety into one voice. A model must address the need to speak with one voice without squelching dissent or feigning unanimity.

9. *Describe relationships to relevant constituencies.* In either a legal or a moral sense, boards are usually trustees. They are also, to some extent, accountable to consumers, neighbors, and staff. A model of governance should define where these various constituencies fit into the scheme.

10. *Define a common basis for discipline.* Boards have a tough time sticking to a job description, being decisive without being impulsive, and keeping discussion to the point. A model of governance should provide a rational basis for a board's self-discipline.

11. *Delineate the board's role in common topics.* A model of governance should enable a board to articulate its own roles with respect to the roles of others, so that the board's specific contribution on any topic is clear.

12. *Determine what information is needed.* A model of governance would introduce more precise distinctions about the nature of information needed to govern, avoiding too much, too little, too late, and simply wrong information.

13. *Balance overcontrol and undercontrol.* It is easy to control too much or too little or even, ironically, to do both at the same time. The same board can simultaneously be a rubber-stamper and a meddler. A model of governance would clarify aspects of management that need tight versus loose control.

14. *Use board time efficiently.* Members of nonprofit and public boards receive token or no pay in exchange for their time. Though they willingly make this contribution, few have time to waste. By sorting out what really needs to be done, a model should enable boards to use the precious gift of time more productively.

15. *Enable simultaneously muscular and sensitive use of board power.* The board has the difficult task of being powerful, yet not stultifying. A model should provide a way to fulfill such a balancing act.

A conceptually coherent way to approach governance would be strong medicine for nonprofit and public organizations. Ian R. Horen, CEO of Painting and Decorating Contractors of America in St. Louis, agrees, noting that while "forces within the organization will suggest that the uniqueness of not-for-profits is anchored in shared decision making," this "point of view simply dismisses the dramatic change that has occurred in not-for-profit management." The most significant management breakthrough that could occur would be in the highest-leverage element of the organization—the governing board. Both the leverage and the room for improvement scream urgently for attention.

But boards have been around so long that it is hard to see that the emperor has no clothes. We have grown accustomed to mediocrity in nonprofit and public board process, in the empty rituals and often meaningless words of conventional practice. We have watched intelligent people tied up in trivia for so long that neither we nor they notice the discrepancy. We have observed the ostensible strategic leaders consumed by the exigencies of next month. Mindful people regularly carry out mindless activity and appear to be, as Phillip T. Jenkins of Bryn Mawr Associates in Birmingham, Michigan, put it, "the well intentioned in full pursuit of the irrelevant." Inexplicably, effective people have a different standard of excellence for public and nonprofit boards than for other pursuits, "often [tossing] aside the principles of good management, and sometimes even common sense, when they put on trustee hats" (Chait and Taylor, 1989, p. 44). The forum in which vision should be the chief order of business is mired so chronically in details that, growing weary, we come to see nothing amiss. Boards, after all, will be boards!

We need strong boards, and we need strong executives as well. "One of the key problems," observes Robert Gale, "is that many boards are either too weak to accomplish anything or so strong they wind up managing the organization." When increased strength is dysfunctional, the solution is not, of course, to weaken the strong. It is better that the blessing of a strong engine be augmented by an improved chassis, not "solved" by shorting out a few spark plugs. When their strength causes boards not to do their job better but to intrude on the jobs of others, something is awry in the design. We must take a fresh look at governance concepts and the board-management partnership. The stark truth of Gale's comment is reason enough for a new model of governance.

It need not bespeak paranoia to observe along with Louden (1975) that "if we do not concern ourselves with how we can rule organizations, the organizations will rule us" (p. 117). But the paradigm according to which we traditionally rule is worthy neither of the people who give their time and talent nor of the missions they serve. Governance is overdue for a rebirth. Though much has been written over the past several decades about governing boards, with rare exceptions the efforts offer incremental improvement to an inadequate vehicle via new paint and tires. The purpose of this book is not to indict previous efforts or current performance so much as to prescribe a better way. My message is that strategic leadership is both exciting and accessible.

Next Chapter

The chapters that follow lay out a new vehicle for governing, a model whose premise is not incremental improvement in the capacity to govern but *transformation*. Seeing policies in a more exacting light is the first step toward creating the new model, one now widely known as the *Policy Governance model*. Therefore, I begin in Chapter Two by arguing that the opportunity for greater strategic leadership lies first in the redefinition of policy and policymaking.

WANT MORE?

Further Reading

1. Carver, J. "Is Policy Governance an All-or-Nothing Choice?" *Board Leadership*, 1997k, no. 34.

   Carver, J. "Is Policy Governance the One Best Way?" *Board Leadership*, 1998j, no. 37. Reprinted in J. Carver, *John Carver on Board Leadership*. San Francisco: Jossey-Bass, 2002.

   Carver, J. "So How About Half a Loaf?" *Board Leadership*, 2004h, no. 73.

   Carver. J. "FAQ: You Claim That Policy Governance Is a Universal Model for Governance. Why Is a Universal Model Even Needed?" *Board Leadership*, 2004b, no 73.

2. Chrislip, D., and Larson, C. *Collaborative Leadership: How Citizens and Civic Leaders Can Make a Difference*. San Francisco: Jossey-Bass, 1994.

   RE-THINK Group. *Benefits Indicators: Measuring Progress Towards Effective Delivery of the Benefits of Parks and Recreation*. Calgary, Canada: RE-THINK Group, 1997.

   Buzan, T., and Buzan, B. *The Mind Map Book: How to Use Radiant Thinking to Maximize Your Brain's Untapped Potential*. New York: NAL/Dutton, 1994.

Oliver, C. (gen. ed.), with Conduff, M., Edsall, S., Gabanna, C., Loucks, R., Paszkiewicz, D., Raso, C., and Stier, L. *The Policy Governance Fieldbook: Practical Lessons, Tips, and Tools from the Experiences of Real-World Boards*. San Francisco: Jossey-Bass, 1999.

3. Carver, J. "Tips for Creating Advisory Boards and Committees." *Board Leadership*, 1994k, no. 11. Reprinted in J. Carver, *John Carver on Board Leadership*. San Francisco: Jossey-Bass, 2002.

4. Ackoff, R. *Creating the Corporate Future*. New York: Wiley, 1981.

5. Carver, J. "When Board Members Are the Only Staff in Sight." *Board Leadership*, 1993r, no. 9, pp. 6–7. Reprinted in J. Carver, *John Carver on Board Leadership*. San Francisco: Jossey-Bass, 2002.

6. Carver, J. "What Use Is Business Experience on a Nonprofit or Governmental Board?" *Board Leadership*, 2001p, no. 58. Reprinted in J. Carver, *John Carver on Board Leadership*. San Francisco: Jossey-Bass, 2002.

7. Carver, J. "Organizational Ends Are Always Meant to Create Shareholder Value." *Board Leadership*, 2002h, no. 63.

8. Carver, M. "The Board's Very Own Peter Principle." *Nonprofit World*, Jan.–Feb. 1998a, *16*(1), 20–21.

   Carver, J. "All Volunteers Can Be Good Board Members—Not!" *Board Leadership*, 1997a, no. 32.

9. Carver, J. "Who Is in Charge? Is Your Organization Too Staff-Driven? Too Volunteer-Driven?" *Board Leadership*, 1995p, no. 22. Reprinted in J. Carver, *John Carver on Board Leadership*. San Francisco: Jossey-Bass, 2002.

   Carver, J. "The Founding Parent Syndrome: Governing in the CEO's Shadow." *Nonprofit World*, 1992e, *10*(5), 14–16.

   Carver, M. "FAQ: In Policy Governance, the Board Is Supposed to Speak with One Voice to the CEO. Yet Our Board Relies to Some Extent on CEO Advice When We Make Our Decisions. Is This OK?" *Board Leadership*, 2004a, no. 75.

   Carver, J. "Boards Should Be Not the Final Authority but the Initial Authority." *Board Leadership*, 1996c, no. 23. Reprinted in J. Carver, *John Carver on Board Leadership*. San Francisco: Jossey-Bass, 2002.

Carver, J. "Governing in the Shadow of a Founder-CEO." *Board Leadership*, 1995g, no. 22. Reprinted in J. Carver, *John Carver on Board Leadership*. San Francisco: Jossey-Bass, 2002.

10. Carver, J. "Now Let's *Really* Reform Governance." *Directors Monthly* (National Association of Corporate Directors), Nov. 2004f, pp. 16–17.

Carver, J. "Rules Versus Principles: Comments on the Canadian Debate." *Institute of Corporate Directors Newsletter*, Nov. 2002i, no. 105, pp. 14–15.

Carver, J. "Compliance Versus Excellence." *Board Leadership*, 2003d, no. 67.

Carver, J. "What Do the New Federal Governance Requirements for Corporate Audit Committees Mean for the Policy Governance Board?" *Board Leadership*, 2003u, no. 67.

11. Carver, J. "Is Governance a Fad?" *Board Leadership*, 2003h, no. 70.

Carver, J. "If Corporate Governance Is a Fad, We Need More Fads." *Board Leadership*, 2004d, no. 71.

Financial Post (Canada), May 23, 2003.

Rehfeld, J. "Nose In, Hands In, Too: Optimizing the Board's Talent." *Directors Monthly*, 2005, 29(5), p. 1.

Globe and Mail (Toronto), Nov. 22, 2003.

2

Policy as a Leadership Tool
The Force of Explicit Values

Public and nonprofit managers have incorporated much of modern management into their operations. Boards that would provide strategic leadership for increasingly sophisticated management require an equally modern governance. Modern governance is not simply modern management practiced by a governing board. To be sure, the principles of management and governance are closely related. But governance is more than management writ large. And it is more than a quality control board of expert managers and technicians running inspections and approvals to maintain order.

The pressure toward better management has created an awkward gap between the sophistication of management and the sophistication of the board. Although public and nonprofit management is not known for its rigor, it has advanced considerably in the past few decades. Governance, on the other hand, has scarcely moved at all. When chief executives are becoming more skilled as managers while their boards are not becoming more skilled as governors, leadership becomes a brittle commodity or, at worst, a mockery. Executives may end up patronizing the board in order to manage well. Boards can be led to busy pursuits that interfere as little as possible with management. The resulting scenario is not unlike that of a very mature child dealing skillfully with an immature parent. Most public and nonprofit CEOs expect, as part of their job obligations, to stage-manage board meetings so their boards will not wander aimlessly or go out of control. Such a game of seemingly necessary manipulation jeopardizes the fragile balance of leadership. For this reason alone, governing boards must modernize the process of governance.

A modern approach to governing will enable a part-time, possibly inexpert group of persons to lead. They have neither the time nor the ability to control every action, circumstance, goal, and decision. Even if perchance they did have both the time and the ability, the organization would slow to a halt as they carried out their task. The most expensive resource of public and nonprofit organizations, the staff, would be significantly wasted as the official second-guessing process ground on. Boards caught in the trap of being better staff than staff, and boards bewildered by unending details or confused by technical complexities cannot lead. A modern approach to governance must enable a board to cut quickly to the heart of an organization, being neither seduced into action nor paralyzed into inaction by trappings along the way.

This chapter argues that the secret to the new governance lies in policymaking, but policymaking of a freshly designed and finely crafted sort. I begin by defining the term *policy* as it is used throughout this text. After making a case that policy clarification is the central feature of board leadership, I consider how a board might get a handle on policy in real board life. I end the chapter by describing the four categories of board policy that will be used throughout the text.

Policies as Values and Perspectives

The essence of any organization lies in what it believes, what it stands for, and what and how it values. An organization's works, rather than its words, are the telling assessment of its beliefs. Studies of corporate culture look at the way people deal with problems, differences, customers, decision making, and one another as a way to penetrate to the essence of an organization. These values and perspectives form the bedrock on which the more mechanical and visible aspects of an organization are based.

By *value,* I mean the common connotation of "belief" or "relative importance," as when we speak of right and wrong, prudent and imprudent, ethical and unethical, proper and improper, worthy and worthless, acceptable and unacceptable, tolerable and intolerable, and so forth. An example of a board value might be "Cost-of-living raises should be consistent with those in other organizations in our county." By *perspective,* I mean the common connotation of "way of looking at," "guiding principle," "approach," or "conceptual point of view." An example of a board perspective might be "CEO evaluation will be based on total organization performance."

Consider an organization's goals, compensation, inventory procedures, cash management, plant maintenance, paint scheme, promotion practices, market penetration plans, and innumerable other factors. With enough patience and inference, we could construct from these concrete realities a picture of the organization's values and perspectives. It is probable, however, that decisions about such things were made explicitly but the values or perspectives that underlie them were not. Consequently, not only are values and perspectives unspoken, but, having gone unstated, they are likely to be inconsistent across the organization and across time as well.

As with individuals, organizations' frameworks of values and perspectives determine specific decisions and behaviors in the face of specific facts. And the same frameworks determine what they regard as relevant facts about the environment. So subtle is this effect that boards often do not regard their selection of facts as a choice; after all, facts are facts. They are caught in a self-perpetuating, circular phenomenon that does untold damage to vision and to thinking about possibilities. Being thus captured is the chief impediment to what is popularly called "thinking outside the box." The unlocking of thought enabled by getting beyond single events to the underlying policy "has taken us so far outside the box that the box no longer exists," according to Gerald L. Anderson, president of the Alberta Institute of Agrologists, Sherwood Park. He continues, "It encourages the mind to explore options that have no bounds, allowing one to consider all possibilities." Values and perspectives are

thus powerful, often invisible forces that determine not only organizational circumstances, activities, and goals, but even the data
that organizations admit into their assessment of reality.

Excellence in governance begins when boards recognize this
central, determining feature of organizations. Setting goals, deploy-
ing staff, writing procedures, formulating plans, developing strategy,
establishing budgets, and all other board and staff activity depend
on values and perspectives, whether those values result from debate
or default. Unrecognized values can result in pernicious disparities,
difficulties, and unfulfilled potential. Leaders may develop goals and
plans without being mindful of their underlying meaning, the binding glue that transforms disjointed parts into a whole. But when recognized and properly used, an organization's foundational values and
perspectives offer leaders the key to effectiveness.

It has been my experience with boards that a simple shift away
from detailed and event-specific decision making and toward values and valuing produces a powerful change in board leadership. In
focusing directly on perspectives and values, a board moves closer
to the underpinnings of organizational behavior and, as I will argue,
becomes far more capable of delegating the actual event-by-event
decision making safely and profitably to staff.

In the language of this text, values and perspectives are blended
into a fresh version of the concept of policy, so in most contexts
henceforth, I refer to them in undifferentiated fashion simply as policies. It is only important to remember that policy as used here can
refer to values, perspectives, or both. When I refer to *values*, the
reader may safely conclude that I mean both values and perspectives.

Policy is a familiar and useful word, but the strength of familiar-
ity is also a weakness. There is nothing new about the word in board
life; it has long been a mantra that boards should make policy—or
even confine themselves to policymaking. While that is true, the
case I make here is that governing well requires policies that are far
more carefully derived from rigorous concepts than before and
crafted accordingly. If we are to build a more exacting framework

for policy-based governance, we must avoid the looser definitions currently attached to the word *policy*.

Governing boards must learn to govern by creating and adjusting policies as I define them here. Because sophisticated management processes will then use board policies as their point of departure, these documents must be conceived with care.

Leadership Through Policies

Because policies permeate and dominate all aspects of organizational life, they present the most powerful lever for the exercise of leadership. Peters and Waterman (1982, p. 291) write, "Clarifying the value system and breathing life into it are the greatest contributions a leader can make." Leadership through explicit policies offers the opportunity to think big and to lead others to think big. Leaders, acutely aware of the value aspect of life's events, continually link day-to-day exigencies with the underlying important elements of life. They tap into something deeper, perhaps more uniquely human, than the accountant, supervisor, or technician in all of us. Work becomes not so much a series of structured mechanical activities as a process of creating and becoming. Policy leadership clarifies, inspires, and sets a tone of discourse that stimulates leadership in followers.

There are four reasons that policy-focused leadership is a hallmark of good governance:

1. *Leverage and efficiency.* By grasping the most fundamental elements of an organization, the board can affect many issues with less effort. However high-flown their intentions, boards have only so much time available, often measurable in hours per year.

2. *Expertise.* Board members rarely have all the skills required to operate their organization. To compensate, some boards focus their recruiting on skills that match those of staff more than

those of governance. Governing by policies requires none of the specialties and can often be done better without them.

3. *Fundamentals*. When a board sifts through and sorts all the material it might deal with, the real heart of the matter is the body of policy those materials represent. Boards that govern by attending directly to policies are more certain to address that which has enduring importance. Dealing so directly with the fundamentals has a compelling legitimacy.

4. *Vision and inspiration*. Dreaming is not only permissible for leaders, it is obligatory. Dealing meticulously with the trees rather than the forest can be satisfying, but it neither fuels vision nor inspires.

Directing an organization can be like rearing a child. Controlling every behavior is a fatiguing and ultimately impossible charge. Inculcating the policies of life is far more effective, and even if some slippage occurs on individual behaviors, it is the only serviceable approach in the long run. So whether a board wishes to control narrowly or to lead more expansively, governing through policies is the efficient way to operate.

To the extent that a board wishes to provide strategic leadership, it must clarify policies and expect organizational activities to give them life. Making policies explicit and consistent, consciously choosing policies from among alternatives, and obsessively keeping the spotlight on the chosen policies prevents the governing focus from wavering from policies and the organization's fidelity to them.

Reinventing the Meaning of Board Policy

Boards have not been well enough equipped with language or useful conceptual categories to discuss policies. Even though we are all accustomed to speaking of policies, and even though boards claim to be "policy boards," the promising idea of Policy Governance is handicapped by our inexperience with managing policies. Which policies must be addressed? What should a board policy look like? Are there inherent differences among types of policies? If a board addresses policies, what are the nonpolicy issues that it stops addressing? In preparation for proposing a classification system for board policies, let's look at the relationship between policy and the unending stream of organizational decisions.

Let us consider how boards ordinarily see their reality. Organizations present themselves to boards as a collection or sequence of concrete decisions, documents, arrangements (for example, staffing patterns or plans), and persons. Boards are accustomed to dealing with specific decisions and with resolving specific problems about this unending list. In fact, they pride themselves on being decision makers and problem solvers. They gauge their performance by such decisions and solutions, not by the clarity of the policies that led to them.

A board approval to increase a specific staff member's salary by $500 might really represent a board policy that would allow any salary to be adjusted up to 15 percent, as long as budget balance is maintained. A board decision to reimburse staff for use of private vehicles at some specific rate might flow from the board's belief that the rate should be consistent with that of local governments. A board presented with a staff plan for clinic hours might approve the extension of operating time to 8 P.M. if its own value is that service hours not penalize patients who hold daytime jobs. A board's only policy concern, when asked to approve purchase of certain insurance coverage, may be that equipment is insured to 80 percent of replacement cost.

A board would do well to examine the policy implications of any initiative it is asked to approve. It can rise above the technical complexities by being a guardian of values rather than a superstaff. "What policies are represented here?" should be a constant board query. "How do these actions relate to previous policies adopted by the board?" "What resolution of competing policies does this program, budget, or plan embody?"

For example, in many service agencies, a "sliding fee" schedule
(also called a "sliding scale") adjusts the price of services or products on the basis of recipients' ability to pay. Such schedules are
ordinarily developed by staff, then inspected and approved by the
board with great attention to form and content. Not uncommonly,
the policies that the fee schedule represents receive no systematic—
much less rigorous—airing at all. Above all, fee markdowns in a
public agency are implicitly based on how the organization's economic nature is conceived. If, to put it simply, the organization is
to plug holes in the market mechanism (meaning, provide for those
whom the market price system would leave behind), there are many
value choices to be made about which holes are plugged and which
are not. In other words, if we are to subsidize some persons or some
needs more than others, on what basis will we establish differential
subsidy? These values will, at some level, be decided within the
bounds drawn by an organization's fundamental purpose. In fact, the
policies relevant to this issue could be seen as subsidiary to the
broader intent. If these policies have been clearly stated, administrative writing of the specifics of a fee adjustment schedule could
proceed without board involvement.

To use another example, budgets are adopted with exhaustive
attention to detail but with only cursory review of the important
policies inherent in the array of numbers. Zero-based budgeting
arose primarily in response to the unstated value in conventional
budgeting that ongoing activity has the benefit of the doubt over
marginal additions. That undeliberated, unstated policy had gone
largely unnoticed in millions of annual budget approvals. Budgets
make powerful, albeit nonverbal, commentary on policies regarding financial risk, conservatism in projection of revenues, and apportionment of resources among competing intentions. Budgets are
often cited as the most important policy statement. And so they
may be, but they are usually poorly conceived policies. The policies
represented are buried so well in numbers that few boards get past
the numbers to any rigorous debate about the underlying policies.

If anything, the numbers seduce board members into a myriad of interesting but peripheral details.

We pore over the many pages of personnel "policies" (a misnomer), even though there are a mere handful of important policies underlying—and usually hidden in—the ample specifics. Similarly, boards often overinvolve themselves in the many aspects of a long-range plan rather than isolate and resolutely deal with the very small number of large value issues on which a staff planning process can be based.

In other words, because of the allure and handy concreteness of specifics, boards are no more accustomed to dealing directly with policies than are their staffs. Individual board members do hold values, of course, and sometimes state them clearly. The problem is that the board job design and process do not focus on the policy aspect of organization, nor do they provide a systematic way of collecting, deliberating, and enunciating those policies. Indeed, boards occasionally make a clear value pronouncement about an encompassing issue, only to "lose" the statement by burying it in a far longer document or in the minutes. Wisdom expressed but uncodified slips away.

By attending to policy content, a board can gain far more control over what matters in the organization and be at less risk of getting lost in the details. Even then, the board will be trapped into reactivity if its policy deliberation is limited to what it receives from the staff. James P. Weeks, member of the elected park commission in Naperville, Illinois, captured this thought when he said, "My philosophy will affect a process rather than react to a function already under way." There is no proactivity in inspecting what is already developed. Moreover, by that time, the organization already has a sizable investment in the document or the staff recommendation. Beyond being reactive, this after-the-fact value inspection is shaped by the interests, initiative, pace, and categories of staff work. Further, there is a great deal of executive prerogative about what to bring to the board and what not to bring. Inasmuch as boards often

answer only what they have been asked, the resulting board response is hardly leadership.

To lead instead of follow, boards must get to the other end of the
parade. Rather than following agendas driven by what the staff
wants approved, boards should initiate the agendas. Of course, no
board knows what is going on in the staff domain well enough to
do this. I am not suggesting that boards try to connect in a real-time
sense to staff activity. I am saying that boards can know what is
going on—and what should go on next—in the board's own job.
The board is not responsible for managing, but it can surely be
responsible for governing.

The objective is not to bring the board more knowledgeably into
an ongoing administrative process, as if staff operations is the train
to be caught. The point is to establish the board's policymaking
process as both preliminary and predominant. If boards are truly
governing, then board members are not obliged to tag along behind
management. And they need not become superstaff in a conscientious attempt to tag along more professionally. They need only tend
to their job of proactively establishing organizational policies.

Categories of Board Policy

Boards can scarcely lead the parade if their categories of work are
derived from staff work. Normally, when a board addresses matters
of policy, it is likely to do so within categories that mimic the
administrative realm. Administrators are accustomed to breaking
their domains down into certain areas: financial, personnel, program, data processing, and so on. Our tradition of board work
encourages boards to derive their agendas from staff-based divisions
of work. That these are sensible divisions of labor within a paid staff
does not make them optimal divisions of thought at the board level.

This common board practice is tantamount to classifying a manager's functions on the basis of his or her secretary's job areas. Con-

sider a new manager who asks his or her secretary just what categories of work have been successful in the clerical position. The manager finds that the secretary divides the job into typing, filing, telephone answering, and scheduling. So informed, the manager proceeds to divide the managerial job into managing about typing, managing about filing, managing about telephone answering, and managing about scheduling. Such a course of action would be ludicrous. We would think that such a manager had given little thought to the design of his or her own job, preferring thoughtlessly to mimic the concrete, handily available arrangement of a subordinate's duties. In fact, it is hard to conceive of any manager behaving in this way, unless the manager is a board! This error is so routine that we fail to see there can be another way to operate. Thus, conventional governance is subtly managed by management, a far cry from management governed by governance.

In constructing a new wisdom of governance, I found it necessary to create categories to guide a board's debate and pronouncements, groupings not derived from administration but from the nature of governance. These categories also serve as vessels to contain board policies as they accumulate, and thereby become divisions of the board policy manual. The categories embrace board policies about (1) ends to be achieved, (2) means (defined simply as non-ends) to be avoided, (3) the interface of board and management, and (4) the practice of governance itself.

Policymaking does not constitute all of a board's job. Linkage with the external environment, assessment of executive performance, and, in some cases, fundraising must be mastered as well. Policymaking, however, is the central role and one that verbally contains board positions and intentions about the other activities. Well-considered and well-ordered policymaking fashions all other board tasks into a coherent whole. Let us consider each of the four categories, derived from a consideration of the board's distinct role rather than copied from categories present in management.

Ends

What should the results be? How will our being in business affect the world? Our choices range from the broad (effects on whole populations) to the specific (outcomes for a particular client, student, patient, or other beneficiary). They relate to both the long and the short term. This set of values about an intended impact on the world is at the root of an organization's reason for existence.

Both the cost and the benefit to the world must be taken into account when a board considers the organization's transaction with its environment that represents its purpose for existence. Ends, the most critical of all policy areas, are concerned with what human needs are to be satisfied, for whom, and at what cost. The governing board's highest calling is to ensure that the organization produces economically justifiable, properly chosen, well-targeted results. Ends are about what the organization is *for*, not about what it *does*. I cannot overstate the importance of keeping the ends definition pure, for the Policy Governance model depends on this distinction being honored rigorously.

Strategic leadership is proclaimed more through wisely developed organizational ends than through any other aspect of governance. This policy category could be called *results*, *impacts*, *goals*, or *outcomes* as well as *ends*, each title having its own specific connotations. The ends concept unique to Policy Governance is a simple one; but because it had not been used prior to the model, it can cause stumbling due to its pairing of a familiar word with an unfamiliar concept. The board's governance of ends is specifically addressed in Chapter Four.

Means

Having isolated all values about organizational ends, we can legitimately refer to all the remaining values as *means*. When we have dealt with where we want to go, we are left with how we can get there and how we will behave in getting there. Speaking for myself as an individual, keeping ends and means separate is important, particularly because I have a pernicious habit of confusing means with ends. But suppose I supervise a team and delegate portions of the intended results to the members of that team. To maintain clarity in our communications, it is even more important that I differentiate the activities from the results to which the activities lead.

Beyond the need for clear communication, however, there is another important reason to keep ends and means separate. As a delegator, I am dealing not only with my own means but with those of others as well. And what we know about managing people draws a sharp distinction between my means and theirs. I must tell myself how to do my part, but telling my subordinates how to do their jobs (rather than simply what results I expect) has unintended negative effects. Unless they are unable or unwilling to make decisions, people do not work best when told how they must do things. Their creativity is thwarted; they feel more like machines. If left free to choose the methods and to be held accountable only for results, people make the best of their hierarchical burden.

When applied to an organization larger than a simple team, controlling methods at the top becomes a major source of organizational stress and even pathology. Bottlenecks develop because the part-time board cannot keep up with staff activities fast enough to prescribe them. The CEO cannot empower staff by decentralizing decision making because the board has withheld the power to make decisions. Having chosen to control a wide range of methods, boards frequently look like amateurs trying in vain to play a professional game. Moreover, when organizational dialogue is so heavily invested in the "how," the "why" receives less attention. And issues of "why" are those most in need of board involvement.

Because policies concerning one's own means and policies concerning subordinates' means are such different topics, they must be kept separate. Policies about board means are addressed in the two categories yet to be discussed. Policies about staff means represent board values about methods and conduct employed as staff pursues organizational ends. What expression is proper for board values in the domain of staff means? As we examine this question, remember that the most effective governance controls what needs to be controlled, yet sets free what can be free.

At the outset, the board's only interest in staff means is that they be effective, prudent, and ethical. I have never found any other legitimate reason to interfere with a subordinate's means. The main test of means, of course, is not means at all, but ends. The board's concern about effectiveness manifests in the degree to which the staff fulfills the board's policies about ends. That leaves only one direct board interest in staff means: that staff operations be prudent and ethical. This category of board values concerning the "how" of

WANT MORE? achieving results is composed, then, of policy statements

1 defining prudence and ethics. This is truly what it means to govern an organization as opposed to managing it. Folkert Schukken, chairman of the Council on Corporate Governance and Board Effectiveness of the Conference Board Europe, agreed with the unique Policy Governance approach, summarizing it accurately by saying, "The board is not supposed to be the better alternative to management, but has to set ends and limit means for management. Many boards [mistakenly] try to duplicate management." Chapter Five explores the board's governance of staff means.

The distinction between ends and means, though it seems counterintuitive, proves rather easy to negotiate. Using the Policy Governance definitions, they are quite distinct. This is fortunate, because it enables *board-management delegation* to be robust in its accountability yet optimally empowering at the same time. As Jack Gallon, attorney and board chair of Toledo Area Metroparks, expressed it, "Separating the ends from the means allows [all persons] to play their roles to the fullest and creates a system of checks and balances that holds everyone accountable."

Board-Management Delegation

The only remaining area is the board's own means. For mechanical ease rather than conceptual purposes, I divide the board's means into two parts: how the board relates governance to management and how the board goes about the job of governing.

Policies about relating to staff include the board's approach to delegation and its manner of assessing performance. *Executive* in this context means the staff organization that executes rather than governs. If the board has chosen to create a chief executive role, then it refers to that role. I deal directly with the board-executive relationship in Chapter Six.

Process of Governance

It is in policies about the process of governance that the board addresses the nature of its trusteeship and its own job process and products. Nonprofit and public boards ordinarily govern on behalf of someone else, an often undefined group tantamount to stockholders of equity corporations. Board effectiveness can be sensibly assessed only if we know on whose behalf the board acts. For whom is it in trust?

In carrying out the top job in the organization, the board, like any manager, makes specific contributions beyond just a summation of what subordinates do. What are those contributions? To put it another way, what is the board's job description? What principles or ground rules does the board use to discipline the process of leadership? What are and what are not legitimate board topics? What is the board's approach to its own discipline? How can the board structurally organize itself? Which committees will the board have, and what will be their jobs?

The issues are numerous, but the question in this category is simple: How does the board approach the process and products of governance itself? These subjects form the content of Chapters Seven and Eight.

Summary of the New Policy Categories

Values that govern an organization can be profitably divided into the foregoing four categories. I will show that explicit use of these categories will profoundly alter the nature of board dialogue, documents, and accountability and, ultimately, the board's capacity for strategic leadership. These categories of policy, as further explained in subsequent chapters, can replace all other board documents except

WANT MORE?
2

bylaws, minutes, and pronouncements of the state (articles of incorporation, letters patent, or enabling statutes)(They embrace *and necessarily replace* all that boards traditionally call *values, beliefs, philosophy,* and *mission,* as well as other such categories] They are designed to be the centrally available, exhaustive] repository of board wisdom.

Throughout the remainder of this text, I will capitalize the names of board policy categories, but if the same words are used to refer to a concept, they will be in lowercase. For example, *governance process* simply means the process of governance, while *Governance Process* refers to the policy category. Similarly, *ends* stands for the concept, while *Ends* is one of four board policy categories. As construed by the Policy Governance model, then, all board policies fall into these groups:

1. *Ends.* The organizational swap with the world. What human needs are to be met (in results terms), for whom (outside the operating organization), and at what cost or relative worth. It is important that no means be included in this category.

2. *Executive Limitations.* Boundaries that limit the choice of staff means, normally for reasons of prudence and ethics. While *means* includes practices, activities, circumstances, and methods, the most comprehensive definition for *means* is simply "non-ends."

3. *Board-Management Delegation.* The manner in which authority is passed to the executive or staff component of the organization and the way in which performance using that authority is reported and assessed.

4. *Governance Process.* The manner in which the board represents the ownership, disciplines its own activities, and carries out its own work of leadership.

These policy category titles (one for ends and three for means) will be used throughout this text, but the exact titles are not important except to maintain continuity of meaning. Indeed, over the years, Policy Governance boards have used a number of variants. One referred to Ends policies as *Mission-Related policies*. The Executive Limitations category has been referred to as *Management Limitations*, *Administrative Parameters*, or *Staff Means Proscriptions*. The Board-Management Delegation category is often called *Board-Executive Linkage* or *Board-CEO Linkage*, even in my own publications. The title is not important, but the concepts differentiating these policy types are crucial.

Next Chapter

Having established universal and exhaustive policy categories in which to conceive and store the board's values, I will now investigate policymaking in more depth. In Chapter Three, I will look at the traps in policymaking and the characteristics of effective policymaking. I show how the board can gain greater control with shorter documents and demonstrate how the revered practice of approving budgets, plans, and other administrative material—a process that cripples strategic leadership—becomes unnecessary when boards enact policies that make a difference.

WANT MORE?

Further Reading

1. Carver, J. "Boards Lead Best When Services, Programs, and Curricula Are Transparent." *Board Leadership*, 1995b, no. 19. Reprinted in J. Carver, *John Carver on Board Leadership*. San Francisco: Jossey-Bass, 2002.

Carver, J. "The CEO's Objectives Are Not Proper Board Business." *Board Leadership*, 1995c, no. 20. Reprinted in J. Carver, *John Carver on Board Leadership*. San Francisco: Jossey-Bass, 2002.

2. Carver, J. "What to Do with Your Board's Philosophy, Values, and Beliefs." *Board Leadership*, 1997r, no. 34. Reprinted in J. Carver, *John Carver on Board Leadership*. San Francisco: Jossey-Bass, 2002.

Carver, J. "How Can an Organization's Statements of Vision, Beliefs, Values, and Philosophy Be Integrated into Policy Governance Policy?" *Board Leadership*, 2002e, no. 64.

Designing Policies
That Make a Difference
Governing by Values

Most governing boards conceive of themselves as policy boards. We have a general understanding that board leadership is largely a policy task. A policy approach prevents a flurry of events from obscuring what is really important. Yet it is rare to find a board that seriously attends to policy more than to the various details of policy implementation. Except for boards influenced by Policy Governance, very few of the boards I have encountered in over thirty years could furnish me with even a handful of board policies! Either they did not have them or what they had was scattered through years of minutes. Documents that purported to be policies were almost always executive compendiums in which the board had played a reactive part. Even searches of minutes failed to turn up much more than single-event decisions disguised as policies. To be sure, there were "personnel policies" and "administrative policies" or general "policies and procedures manuals." But these were basically staff documents on which the board had stamped its approval. In none of these was it clear what portions or aspects the board itself had created or decreed.

The most frequent exceptions to this state of affairs have been school boards. They have so many policies that they cannot possibly keep up with them. As would be expected, their policies mainly concern staff practices and are usually prescriptive in detail. Few would qualify as legitimate board policies under the definition described here.

In Chapter Two, I divided board policies into four categories that are based on the nature of governance, not borrowed from **WANT MORE?** management. These categories were derived from governance theory and as such are not mere conveniences or preferences. They must be kept cleanly separate. That is, a board policy is in one category or the other, never in two or more at the same time.

Before investigating each category separately, beginning in Chapter Four, I will explore principles that apply to all categories. This chapter begins by describing what is often wrong with board policy and the general characteristics of effective policy. I next consider how a board can use the different "sizes" of policies to govern more efficiently and how those sizes must be reflected concretely in the format of policies. Then I argue that proactive policymaking can replace approvals as the dominant style of board leadership—and why it should.

Getting Serious About Policy

Traditional definitions and formats of policy impede a board's ability to govern by policy. Moreover, in some cases, whatever the board decides is called *policy*, the word being used to denote authorship rather than a characteristic of the decision. The fuzziness of the definition is a loud signal that the whole area of policy has not been taken seriously. Consequently, the claim of being a policymaking board is ordinarily contradicted by having policy that is really staff material with a large component of implementation specifics. Such policies are usually created by staff and only "blessed" by the board. In practice, I have found that a board's professing to be a policy board offers few clues as to what the board actually does.

Board policy can be dead but unburied. I once supervised the collection of all existing (still official) board policies of a large public organization in Indiana. They had been painstakingly assembled at considerable cost, for they were sprinkled through a wide range of documents. The paperwork was inches thick. Many of the policies had been long forgotten but were still on the books. How could these policies really be useful in running the organization? For all the rhetorical glamour afforded the board's policies, they turned out to be an impotent, self-contradictory collection too unimportant to be kept up to date.

Board policy can be alive but invisible. Although it is hard to find true board policy in written form, it is always possible to find it in unwritten form. Actually, it may not be found so much as suspected. Ironically, unwritten policy is sometimes thought to be so clear that no one feels the need to write it down and, at the same time, so variously interpreted as to border on being capricious. In reality, there is never a lack of policy; it always exists in the actions taken. Implicit policy not only fills in for the missing explicit policy but is used to excuse the absence of the latter.

Unfortunately, both unwritten policy and written policy left untended are of questionable utility. We have difficulty both in agreeing on what the unwritten policy actually is (what it would say if it were explicit) and in knowing which old written policies are still in effect. Curiously, the criterion used to judge which written statements should be taken seriously and which should be ignored is itself always an unwritten policy! Why? Because boards are loath to admit that their policies do not make a difference. Making a major investment in board policymaking means first establishing principles and formats to guide policy content. Board policymaking, within the categories set out in Chapter Two, must be correctly classified, explicit, current, literal, centrally available, brief, and encompassing.

Appropriate classification. The importance of keeping policies both conceptually and physically in categories designed for governance has already been stressed. Any given policy must fit within one and only one of the four categories described in Chapter Two.

Explicitness. Policies must exist in written form. This is the only way that all parties (including the policymakers) can know just what the policy is. It is the best way for board members to realize which policies should be questioned or changed. Two forces often make explicitness difficult to achieve. First, because "everyone understands" this or that precept, it seems silly to dwell on actual language. It seems silly, that is, until the writing begins and we discover that our agreement was not as precise as we thought. Second, being explicit carries a danger similar to that of being proactive. It means laying one's values on the table, exposing differences, and confronting them openly.

Currency. Up-to-date policies are the only ones that work. A board can ensure that it keeps policies current by compulsively operating from its policy manual rather than by vowing to review policies annually. When a board lives from its policies, the policies will either work or be changed. They will not collect dust. Policies must never end with a whimper but a bang; they must not be allowed to fade away into oblivion. Staff can help by acting as if the board sincerely means every policy that the board has not yet rescinded.

Literalness. Policies must mean what they say. If they do not, then they should be amended or deleted. We have come to accept organizational language that is meaningless. Learning a job is time-consuming when you must discern bit by bit which words mean what they say and which do not. Governing is a verbal job; if a board's words have little integrity, governance cannot be excellent.

Central availability. When board pronouncements are all kept in one place, the task of determining what the organization represents becomes easier. Policies done properly are virtually the only medium through which the board speaks and thus should not be scattered about, discoverable only by scouring years of minutes and multiple staff documents. Centrally visible board values go far in preventing board intentions from being idiosyncratically interpreted by individual members, officers, or committees. To make a difference, board policies must be in a single repository that has obvious preeminence over other organizational documents.

Brevity. Brevity may be the unheralded secret of excellence. An organization can be tied up in procedure manuals. Similarly, in board policies, "too long" and "too many" are enemies of good leadership. Organizations seem to be impressed with complexity, however, so brevity in policymaking confronts the need to look sophisticated ("It just can't be that simple!"). Boards need to seek compelling simplicity. Michael F. Paskewicz, superintendent of Adams 12 Five Star Schools in Thornton, Colorado, spoke of "a simple elegance to the governance process."

Comprehensiveness. The board policy framework must encompass the entirety of that which is governed. That is, the design must enable all aspects of the organization to fall within the stated values of the board. In this way, the board need not address all value issues, only the larger ones. By sticking to the discipline of resolving larger questions before smaller ones, starting with the broadest in each category, the board ensures that its policies will encompass the entire range of corporate possibilities. It can then be truly said that board policy embraces *everything*. By examining the nature of policy "sizes," the next section explains how policy can be encompassing.

Policies Come in Sizes

Inasmuch as there are fewer policies than decisions based on those policies, the board's task is already easier than if it had tried to address all the single organizational decisions. Dealing with policies moves the predicament from the impossible to the merely improbable, for there are also more policies than a board has time to consider. Because policies merely represent our values or perspectives, written or unwritten, they can be revealed in every event that occurs in an organization. We value one pen over another. We have values about the length of meetings, economy airfare, group insurance, wax for the floor, and the need for a waste treatment plant. How can the board address such an inherently pervasive, large body of policy material, yet have a manageable task and product? This quandary of too many policies to deal with has, happily, a simple key: policies come in all sizes.

Logical Containment of Policies

Larger values or perspectives logically contain—that is, logically limit the content of—smaller ones. Once a board has chosen an encompassing value, a plethora of narrower value issues still remain to be settled. It is this characteristic that leads many board members to see policy as vague or not specific. A board is just as likely to be too broad as to be too detailed, so board members' anxiety is not without foundation. Happily, the phenomenon of logical containment can help boards debate the question of policy breadth in an organized manner.

No matter how broad a policy is, it is always more specific than if it had not been said and less specific than it might have been. Therefore, it delimits the universe of specificity yet to be encountered, though it does not resolve those specificities. In other words, the range of further possible choices is smaller because the large value has been resolved. Say that you personally place more value on owning a new $45,000 car than on having $45,000. This value statement both introduces and delimits further value issues about colors, models, and stereo systems. Similarly, selecting a purpose for the organization involves the broadest level of values about organizational results. Making that choice leaves many questions of priorities unresolved, but it clearly circumscribes the range of remaining choices.

A community may feel that the goal of establishing a healthier local economy is sufficient reason to operate an economic development agency. Whether to establish a broader employment base or to be a regional retail center is a subsequent and slightly smaller value choice that can be confronted within the more broadly stated intention. Similarly, a public school aim to produce competent, employable citizens still leaves large issues to be decided, though at a lower level of abstraction—for example, the balance among academic, job skill, and life-planning competencies.

Policies within each category described in Chapter Two can be arranged by size. Like mixing bowls, they can be nested, largest to smallest (see Figure 3.1). After addressing the largest value choices (the biggest bowl), the board can either address the next level (the second largest bowl) or be content with having clarified the first level. A delegate is granted the right to make choices within the second and subsequently smaller levels (see Figure 3.2).

By attending to the largest issues in each category, the board can responsibly limit the work it must do. As it attends to the specificity in each decreasing level of policy, it reaches a point at which a majority of board members are willing to accept any reasonable interpretation of the policy language. Until the board feels that the full range of choices permissible under this rule are acceptable to it, it has not reached the stopping point. When it does reach that point, the board can safely stop. It is not relevant whether the remaining

Figure 3.1. A Nested Set of Policies

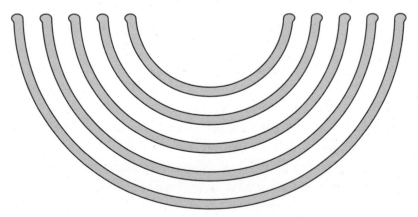

Note: Smaller issues fit within larger issues, as smaller bowls fit within larger ones. The entire set can be controlled by handling only the outermost bowl.

Figure 3.2. Hands-On, Hands-Off Control

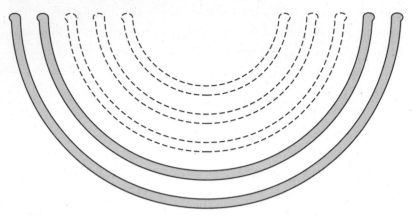

Note: Direct control of the outer bowls in a nested set allows indirect control of the smaller bowls. A board will decide to have hands-on control over the largest issues (depicted here by bowls drawn with a solid line) but indirect, hands-off control of smaller issues (depicted by bowls drawn with a broken line).

range is vague, only whether it is acceptable. In Ends, for example, how much the board trusts its CEO doesn't matter, only whether the range is acceptable. Trusting the CEO to make a certain choice means the board is harboring an unspoken expectation that should be detailed through further policy specificity. When Ends and Executive Limitations policies are created with this integrity, management can safely be authorized to make all further choices.

WANT MORE?

2

Phyllis Field of the Rhode Island Board of Regents referred to this phenomenon as "controlling the inside by staying on the outside." As the board writes its policy, there should be no ambiguity about the size of "bowl" at which the board stopped or what the board has explicitly pronounced. Without such a scheme for creating policy, boards tend to make a policy about this, that, and the other. A patchwork of policies can leave dangerous gaps. Boards are reasonably fearful of having overlooked some important policy feature, so they fall easily into the trap of becoming supermanagers, reviewing and approving everything. Powerful delegation is impossible in these circumstances, as is the freedom of the board to attend unceasingly and vigorously to the big issues. Making use of the logical containment principle in its decision making enables a board to have its hands firmly on, though not in, an organization.

Board Policy Versus Staff Policy

Starting with the big questions first is simply a good problem-solving technique, even for individuals. But when delegation is involved, the utility of this approach goes beyond merely good problem solving. It enables the board to define the boundary between itself and its executive.

Let me emphasize that a clear distinction between "policy and administration" (as it used to be expressed) does not exist, at least not in a universal way. There must be a line between board and staff for role clarity, to be sure, but that line is established by each board and can change over time. Such flexibility, however, does not mean there are no principles for a board to use when establishing or changing that line.

The boundary always lies just below the point that board policy last addressed. There is no set boundary for all boards or even for the same board at different times. As long as the board approaches all policymaking from the largest to the smallest issue, this method will redefine the boundary as circumstances and board values shift.

The board's job differs from staff jobs, then, not by topic but by levels within topics. Exceptions to this rule are the unique elements of the board's job that are discussed in Chapter Seven. This approach recognizes and validates that everybody, not just the board, makes policy. Every clerk and janitor, by her or his actions, is making implicit policy at all times. It is inescapable that everyone does so, though the policies made are of vastly differing sizes. What is important is that all policies that live in the organization be consonant with the broader policies enunciated by the governing leadership. Thus, the board can control without meddling.

In dealing with policy issues of different sizes, then, the board can create policies that make a difference if it observes the following principles:

- *The board should resolve the broadest or largest policy issue in each category before dealing with smaller issues in any category.* This means having the discipline to stick with the highly subjective, tough choices that are found in the broader policy issues. Explication of the general thereby precedes the more particular. Somewhat counterintuitively, stating the largest decisions accurately requires as much precision of thought and language as doing so for the smaller ones.

- *If the board wishes to address smaller levels, it should never skip levels but should move to the next smaller levels in sequence.* This requires having the discipline not to reach into the organizational decision process for instant fixes, even if specific board members are more expert in a subject than staff.

- *The board should grant the CEO authority to make further operational choices, as long as they are in accordance with the board's Ends and Executive Limitations policies.* This requires the discipline to let go, to delegate.

The provisions of Ends and Executive Limitations policies are binding directives. But within the performance ranges they represent, the executive is free to choose and move, free of stultifying, over-the-shoulder involvement by the board. Not only is such

WANT MORE?

3

detailed involvement unnecessary if the board has done its job, but it also destroys staff creativity and efficiency. Only boards that have failed to be proactive policymakers have any need to meander in or retain approval authority over staff activity and plans. Moreover, unless the CEO has such authority, he or she can never delegate parts of it to subordinates without onerous bureaucratic strings. It is no wonder that conventional governance practices often result in an organization that is either unable or afraid to make decisions.

Decision making below the board's in the categories of Governance Process and Board-Management Delegation may be granted to the board chairperson. Inasmuch as they deal with the board's own means, they should not be delegated to the CEO. But within the Ends and Executive Limitations categories, the CEO must be the person authorized to make further decisions. In any event, it is in delegation to the CEO that board fidelity to good principles is most critical. Even when the staff is small, by far the preponderance of further decisions lie in the executive's arena. Consequently, almost all of my further comments on the concept of residual decision latitude relate to the Ends and Executive Limitations categories.

How far a given board delves into the smaller issues is completely up to the board, as long as it starts with the largest issues and progresses in sequence. The likelihood of a board's going too far (even in the judgment of staff!) is small, simply because the further it goes, the more complex the task of balancing all the ramifications of any one choice becomes. Lower-level issues branch out much like a table of organization or family tree does, so the number of factors to coordinate increases at lower levels. Juggling such permutations is one reason that a full-time staff stays busy.

As later chapters explain in more detail, board decision making will go from broad toward narrow based on the board's values and need not be in reaction to current problems. However, in some

WANT MORE?

4

cases, issues do arise that cause a board to rethink the level or content of decisions it has made in the top-down manner. After all, the world does not conveniently present itself to us in neat categories and articulated levels of breadth. Being willing to reconsider previous board decisions based on current realities is commendable, but it is wise only if the board abstracts up from the specific issue to a policy level it consciously chooses.

It is helpful to envision the "size of issue" phenomenon as a matrix (see Figure 3.3). The board's level of involvement is across the top of all subjects. Just beneath the board's level is the CEO's level of involvement; just below that is the first echelon of staff, and so forth throughout the organization. Everything below the board's chosen level is in the CEO's domain; in turn, the CEO delegates issues below his or her chosen level to staff.

Columns cutting through all levels contain any topic with which the organization might deal. Each topic includes issues that are very large (at the top) and those that are very small (at the bottom). A budget, for example, embodies a few sweeping values and

Figure 3.3. Decision Levels Within Organizational Topics

	Budgeting	Personnel	Any other topic
Board level of direct concern			
CEO level of direct concern			
Sub-CEO level of direct concern			
Further levels			

Note: This matrix contrasts traditional board control of staff functions with Policy Governance board control. Typical management documents that traditionally require approval by the board in order to become official are represented by the dashed lines. Such documents include decisions from very high (or broad) to very low (or narrow) levels. The approval process causes the board to be drawn into low-level decision making, impedes agile decision making at the corresponding low levels of the organization, and tends to be reactive. In contrast, board control as exercised in Policy Governance is represented by the dotted lines. The board addresses all topics at their broadest level. The board decisions constitute filling in each of the top cells with an applicable policy. Subsequent decisions by the CEO and his or her subordinates must be within a reasonable interpretation of the board's higher, proactive policy.

a great many small ones. The board fills in the top cells with policy. The CEO and his or her subordinates fill in all other choices, remaining consistent with the board's statement. Board policies are recorded in a board policy manual consisting of all the board's pronouncements but not cluttered by the more voluminous decisions subsequently made by staff.

In other words, instead of a policy and procedures manual, there should be a board policy manual that is separate from staff-written, staff-owned documents. Rather than a board-approved budget, there should be a board budget policy separate from and controlling a staff-written budget. Instead of a board-approved personnel manual, there should be a board policy on the treatment of personnel. Rather than a board-approved wage and salary administration plan with compensation schedules, there should be a board policy on compensation. In practice, it turns out that for most boards, each policy might be approximately one page in length. The board's central document would be a conceptually horizontal collection of these three and other board policies.

Contrast this with the conventional approach, in which operational documents are arranged vertically by topic. Commonly, there is a personnel manual, a budget, and a compensation plan. Each document is a mixture of the trivial and the profound—mostly trivial, simply because the greatest number of issues are at the lower levels. Moreover, the documents are rarely explicit about values at all. Board-level choices cannot be distinguished from staff choices. The content overwhelmingly consists of the specifics of implementation, generated largely by staff, from which the broader controlling values can only be inferred.

Policy Architecture

When a board policy addresses more than one level (or breadth) of a value, it is necessary for the format of the policy to reflect the nesting of the lower levels inside the larger. A simple outline form serves this need handily. The policy preamble would be the highest level, major headings the next highest level, and so on throughout the out-line format. The board will have debated and resolved higher levels prior to lower levels within what will become a single policy. It will not have dealt with the document as a whole, except in its final review. Miriam Carver and I have explained in step-by-step detail a process for creating policies in this way in *Reinventing Your Board* (Carver and Carver, 1997c; revised edition scheduled for 2006).

Consequently, the very format of board policies in nested levels reflects the discipline of the board's determination of governing val-ues. Policies can be rigorous yet succinct. If a policy is going to be a compact document wherein every word counts, it should not repeat what can be found elsewhere.

The Approval Syndrome

This kind of unembellished policymaking may appear stark and sus-piciously terse to boards accustomed to adopting omnibus docu-ments in monolithic rather than articulated policy format. It can be quite difficult to find, much less to extract the broadest, most encompassing policy issues from such conglomerations. It is cus-tomary not only to adopt various levels of policy in an undifferen-tiated mass but also to adopt whole documents such as budgets, personnel "policies," and compensation plans. These include mul-tiple levels of detail or, put more frankly, a preponderance of trivia. This kind of board approval of whole management documents is the long-standing norm in governance.

Only respect for tradition prevents our noticing how ritualistic, trivializing, bottlenecking, and reactive this "approval syndrome" is. The inherent flaws in this time-honored and virtually ubiquitous method are severely detrimental to the quality of both governance and management. Let's examine these flaws.

Reactivity. Document approvals place the board in a reactive position. The board is moving after the fact inasmuch as the document has already been created (using criteria the board did not establish). For practical reasons, the board can often do little but approve the measure. Many times, to avoid feeling like rubber stamps, boards nitpick, particularly in approving budgets. No matter how much intelligence goes into playing this reactive role, it is clearly not leadership.

Sheer volume of material. Board members must read and understand sufficiently to critique. That calls for studious attention to many low-level issues. The resultant tomes of background information are necessarily filled with staff-level material and issues, on which board members conscientiously spend prodigious amounts of time. It is unlikely that boards can be truly complete in this endeavor, and they are likely to overlook important items in the flurry of small ones.

Mental misdirection. A strategic leader must continually struggle against smallness. The larger, important values are vulnerable and easily displaced by concrete, short-term matters. The approval syndrome invites boards to deal primarily with low-level issues and distracts their attention from more subjective high-level issues. One board I worked with spent time going over every nook and cranny of an almost $200 million budget each year. Looking back over several years of such exhausting work, they were hard pressed to find even one half of 1 percent of budget improvement thus produced. Yet during the same time, they had failed to wrestle with and clarify just what this large organization was to produce!

Letting staff off the hook. When the board gives formal approval, it becomes the owner of the document. Whatever is inconsistent with what would have been a board policy (had there been one) can no longer be held against the CEO. Who is to be held accountable when a board-approved staff plan fails to accomplish the desired results? The board has been co-opted in the process. But staff judgment may have been co-opted as well, inasmuch as staff plans are designed not only to accomplish results but also to garner board approval, approval that is normally granted in accord with board members' unstated (not committed to policy) values. It is not uncommon for a staff to give disproportionate attention to this political feature. Under these conditions, CEO accountability to the board loses both legitimacy and rigor.

Unfairly putting staff on the hook. Despite having taken ownership of documents by virtue of approval, boards frequently disavow their decision subsequently by blaming management for some shortcoming that was not noticed at the time when the document was approved. Staff are caught not knowing what they might be judged on and cannot rely on the board's approval to be the final test. Even if this revocation of approval never occurs, the approval process itself is usually a board judgment of staff work against no obvious criteria.

Short-term bias. Low levels of an organization generally have a short time horizon. Because the document is created from the bottom up, rather than on the basis of high-level values pronounced by the board, it may have a short-term bias.

Lack of clarity in the board's contribution. When the document is approved, it is impossible to determine just what the board said! The board either said everything because it officially took ownership of the document in its entirety, or it said nothing because it merely passed what someone else contributed, or it said something between these extremes. But no one can tell. There is no distinct pronouncement expressing the values of the board. Thus, the voice of leadership cannot be heard. Under such obscure conditions, a board may remain busy reviewing and approving but making no substantive contribution at all, and no one notices.

WANT MORE?

5

Hampered staff agility. Since we cannot tell what the board has said, we cannot tell what others in the hierarchy have said. Consequently, we cannot tell who has the right to restate or change some part of what has been decided. Any request for change must be put to the board, regardless of how undeserving it may be of board attention. Thus, the board is involved in trivial matters both in the initial approval and in subsequent amendments. The management either floods the board with staff-level issues in order to preserve flexibility in their activities and plans as circumstances change or accepts the bottleneck caused when plans and procedures cannot be amended in a natural flow by the persons most intimate with implementation.

Fragmentation. The board faces a sequence of disconnected and unmanageably voluminous vertical slices of the whole (budget, personnel, program, and so forth) instead of a holistic, manageable fabric of horizontally connected policies. We all profess that boards should deal with the big picture, but it is difficult to picture the forest by inspecting one tree at a time.

The approval process provides boards with a handily available, easy, tradition-condoned method of imitating leadership. Instead of separating the board's domain from the staff's domain, the approval syndrome confounds both domains, resulting in an undifferentiated mass. The stage is set for the board to do unnecessary work at the staff level and for the staff to wield undue influence at the board level. The former result, depending on one's point of view, is perceived as detailed, trivial, burdensome, or involved. The latter is perceived as rubber-stamping, staff dominance, or comfortable passivity. Of course, both situations may exist at the same time, with the board doing staff work and the staff doing board work. Whichever way talent is wasted, neither strategic leadership by the board nor effective management by the staff occurs. When the approval process is taken too lightly, it reduces board action to a charade. When it is taken too seriously, it reduces the CEO concept to a charade.

WANT MORE?

6

Curiously, there are times when the board goes through the approval process not intending to withhold authority from the CEO but to confirm it. A board might declare its support for the CEO by cloaking some controversial executive decision with the prestige of the boardroom. Board motivation is usually expressed thus: "We want the staff (or others) to know the board is really behind the

CEO on this." As long as the board and CEO understand that the decision is truly the CEO's, this approval not only seems harmless but appears to be a healthy show of solidarity. However, such a gesture of board support is called for only if the board has been sending weak signals about the nature of delegation. This kind of support is rarely warranted if the board has made it clear to all that *all* CEO decisions that are within board-stated bounds are always supported by the board. Official support of a specific action implies that such sporadic backup is necessary or, conversely, that the general philosophy of delegation is weak.

Board approvals are an unnecessary and dysfunctional method of board control, then, regardless of the ubiquity of the practice. Chapters Four, Five, and Six will build a case for a more proactive, fair, and detrivializing approach to fulfilling the board's moral and legal obligation to control the organization.

Policy Development

Good policymaking, then, is proactive on the broadest issues rather than reactive on issues of all sizes. Policies of the board, brief though they may be, become parents to all executive action. Because these policies are central, their currency is critical. Brevity will make it far easier to keep them up to date. Such brief, current policies developed by a state board in Ohio were said to "reduce the Board's Policy Manual to 34 pages from 422 pages and make it a constantly used reference rather than a collector of dust," according to Ohio educator Robert Bowers. Governing by policy means governing out of policy in the sense that no board activity takes place without reference to policies. Most resolutions in board meetings will be motions to amend the policy structure in some way. Consequently, *policy development is not an occasional board chore but its chief occupation*.

Board policies categorized as in Chapter Two and nested as in the mixing bowl example now wrap around every possible result, action, behavior, process, and other characteristic of the organization. Using the policy circle shown in Figure 3.4, Figure 3.5 illus-

Figure 3.4. The Policy Circle

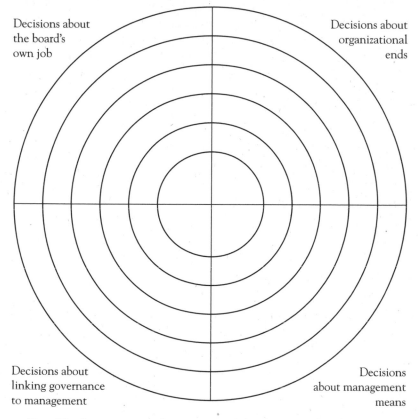

Decisions about the board's own job

Decisions about organizational ends

Decisions about linking governance to management

Decisions about management means

Note: The four categories of organizational decisions are shown as four sets of bowls, brought together to form four quadrants of a circle. Larger and smaller issues within those categories are shown as larger and smaller bowls.

trates the all-embracing nature of the resulting board policies. The board's arms are around the organization without its fingers being in it; control without meddling has been achieved.

From time to time, a board discovers that its values have changed. Perhaps a previous statement was not fully cognizant of the range of options, or the risks and opportunities in the external world have shifted. Even large shifts in board values can usually be accommodated by altering existing language rather than by adding to it, thus changing the volume of policies very little. The body of

Figure 3.5. Board Policymaking

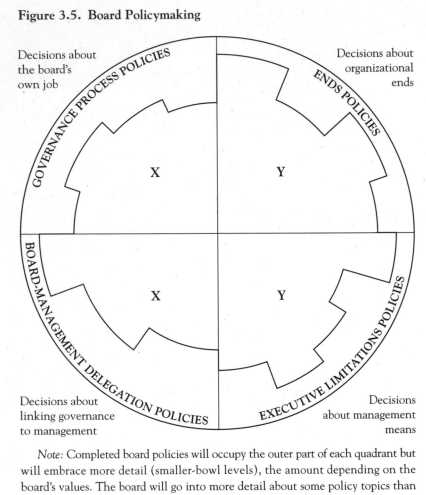

Decisions about the board's own job

GOVERNANCE PROCESS POLICIES

Decisions about organizational ends

ENDS POLICIES

X   Y

BOARD-MANAGEMENT DELEGATION POLICIES

X   Y

EXECUTIVE LIMITATIONS POLICIES

Decisions about linking governance to management

Decisions about management means

Note: Completed board policies will occupy the outer part of each quadrant but will embrace more detail (smaller-bowl levels), the amount depending on the board's values. The board will go into more detail about some policy topics than others, even within a given quadrant. Notice that the quadrant containing all staff means issues will be addressed by the board in a constraining or negative fashion (hence the policy category titled "Executive Limitations"). Empty space in the middle represents smaller decisions that the board is content to leave to delegatees. The CGO will be given authority to make decisions in the spaces marked X. (Foreshadowing later discussion of this role, CGO is used to indicate the chief governance officer, a function normally fulfilled by the board chair.) The CEO will be given authority to make decisions in the space marked Y.

policies can remain a truly living document as long as the number of policies remains small and the categorization among types remains distinct.

Policies or policy changes can be brought to the board's attention from any source. It is not important to restrict the pathways through which the board receives its impetus to establish or change its policies. But it is important to affix the responsibility for continual, informed weighing of policy issues. That responsibility must rest squarely on the board itself, not on the CEO. In practice, the CEO plays a meaningful role in the board's continuing inquiry. But to remove from the board the central responsibility for its own job would be a rash flight from responsibility. The board may charge its officers or committees with parts of its task, but let there be no mistake about whose responsibility is being assigned.

In an optimally functioning board, the nature of its discourse constantly presents it with ways to develop policy. Proper boardroom dialogue spots value inconsistencies, seizes on value issues, and is impelled toward exciting discoveries in verbalizing relative

WANT MORE?

7

worth. Meaningful policies are an expression of the board's soul. While they may not embody everything a board believes, when created in the Policy Governance manner, they embody everything about which one can be certain the board is and stands for. In an environment of value awareness disciplined by principles relating to value size and category, a board can enact policies that make a difference.

Next Chapter

Having better defined the nature of effective policymaking, I will examine each policy category, visualizing the emerging board policies by using the policy circle. In Chapter Four, I examine the Ends category, the policies that direct the most critical feature of any organization. In these policies, the board makes clear what the organization is *for*, as opposed to what it *does*. The Ends policies are a more sophisticated, more rigorous extension of what is typically called *mission*. No feature is more central to the policymaking responsibility than the governing of organizational ends.

WANT MORE?

Further Reading

1. Carver, J. "A Board Learns That Proper Policy Categories Aren't Just a Nicety." *Board Leadership*, 1998c, no. 36.

2. Carver, J. "The 'Any Reasonable Interpretation' Rule: Leap of Faith or Sine Qua Non of Delegation?" *Board Leadership*, 1996a, no. 28. Reprinted in J. Carver, *John Carver on Board Leadership*. San Francisco: Jossey-Bass, 2002.

3. Carver, J. "Hands On or Off?" *Contributions*, May–June 2004c, *18*(3), 22.

   Carver, J. "Controlling Without Meddling—The Role of Boards." *Business Strategies*, Oct. 2003e, pp. 10–11.

   Carver, J. "Good Governance Is Not About Control—It's About Remote Control." *Board Leadership*, 2000b, no. 49.

   Carver, M. "Of Potted Plants and Governance." *Board Leadership*, 2004d, no. 76.

   Carver, J. "If You Want It Done Right, Delegate It!" *Board Leadership*, 1997j, no. 29. Reprinted in J. Carver, *John Carver on Board Leadership*. San Francisco: Jossey-Bass, 2002.

4. Carver, J. "Abstracting Up: Discovering the Big Issues Among the Trivia." *Board Leadership*, 1994a, no. 15. Reprinted in J. Carver, *John Carver on Board Leadership*. San Francisco: Jossey-Bass, 2002.

5. Carver, J. "Boards Should Have Their Own Voice." Board Leadership, 1997d, no. 33. Reprinted in J. Carver, *John Carver on Board Leadership*. San Francisco: Jossey-Bass, 2002.

6. Carver, J. "Board Approval and Monitoring Are Very Different Actions." *Board Leadership*, 1996b, no. 24. Reprinted in J. Carver, *John Carver on Board Leadership*. San Francisco: Jossey-Bass, 2002.

7. Carver, J. "Policies 'R' Us." *Board Leadership*, 1995i, no. 20. Reprinted in J. Carver, *John Carver on Board Leadership*. San Francisco: Jossey-Bass, 2002.

4

Focusing on Results

The Power of Purpose

The most important work of any governing board is to define and redefine the reason for organizational existence. It is ironic that in so many texts, boards are counseled to "support the organization's mission," a weak role indeed. The passivity and reactivity in that advice falls short of the authority and obligation of a board to *decide, enunciate, and enforce* the organizational mission. Moreover, the board's job in doing this is more crucially related to its relationship with owners than with staff. The board is obligated to express owners' prerogatives, not to champion management choices. It is not simply the approval of a purpose statement. Nor is this a task done once, then forgotten. It is a perpetual obligation, deserving of the majority of board time and energy. It is far more important than any other board undertaking, even its choice of chief executive.

The only justifiable reason for organizational existence is the production of worthwhile results. Worthwhile results always relate to the satisfaction of human needs. Whose needs, which needs, and what constitutes satisfaction are the unending, subjective quandaries confronting a board. Resolving the important, even existential value quandaries inherent in these questions is the very heart of leadership in governance.

In this chapter, I begin by arguing for boards to focus more on the world outside the organization than the one inside. I then relate that external focus to the creation of Ends policies. I also look at two powerful distractions that draw boards away from ends: the confusion of ends with means and premature anxiety about evaluating ends. I conclude with the board's largely ends-related role in long-range planning.

Transcending the Organization

Board leadership of an organization is jeopardized more by the organization itself than by any other threat. I am referring not to the reluctance of staff to be governed but to a more insidious phenomenon: the captivating allure of organizational events and issues. Typically, a high percentage of board time is spent on internal matters. Even when the subject matter is related to services or programs, the focus tends to be on personnel, financial, logistical, or other organizational aspects of programming. In other words, the most compelling subject matter deals with structure and method, not results. Leadership for results begins outside, not inside the organization. Because of the seductive intrigue of organizational activity, board discipline must be designed to overcome entanglement in internal matters. Our understanding of what constitutes board involvement must change. The most effective way to help board members rise above organizational myopia is for the board to develop a taste for the grand expanse of the larger context.

The Larger Context

Although organizations are worlds in themselves, each is part of something bigger. We must start from this larger context to grasp the underpinnings of an organization. This outside world existed prior to, is larger than, and likely will go on after the organization. It is this larger context that gives meaning to the organization's purpose and makes the organization's very existence possible. Further, board members' primary identity lies not within the organization but in some part of the external context.

To the extent that a board fails to consider its results from a context external to the organization, it narrows the vision of which it is capable. Sometimes, leadership differs from nonleadership only in that leadership views the world with a slightly wider lens. That wider lens or, if you will, taller perspective, is achieved in governance by viewing not the organization but its environment as the setting for analysis and debate.

Transaction with the Environment

The organization lives within the larger context of the world and, hence, affects it. That the organization exists makes a difference to this larger world, and the difference it makes can be characterized in two ways: (1) the world is richer, happier, and less in pain because of the care, knowledge, cure, beauty, order, peace, or support produced; and (2) the world is poorer, more depleted, and more in pain because of the talent, capital, and space consumed. These two impacts on the world, corresponding to benefit and cost, should be the chief interest, even obsession, of the governing board. The board should ask itself, "What good shall we accomplish, for which people or needs, and at what cost?" It is important that boards view organizational results in terms of cost, benefits, and beneficiaries.

The concept here is exchange, a transaction between the organization and the world. Something of value that is consumed is swapped for something of value that is produced. I use the word *ends* to mean three elements of that exchange: the intended and

WANT MORE?

1

actual results in people's lives for which the organization exists, the intended and actual persons or populations who experience those results, and the cost of those results or of those results for those particular persons. These elements describe the organization's swap with the world. So the ends concept, as used throughout this book, refers to the organization's product (changes in or for people), the organization's beneficiaries (which people), and efficiency (worth of that change in terms of monetary cost or cost in other results or recipients foregone). It is particularly important to note that there are no activities or methods included in the ends concept.

To summarize: in the terminology of Policy Governance, *anything that is not ends is by definition means*. (It is easy to speak of "means to the ends," but that is wording that can mislead. For example, keeping the organization's lawn mowed is a means in the Policy Governance use of the term, but it is hardly a means to the organization's ends.) To reduce wordiness, when I refer to *results*, it will mean the special type of results included in the ends concept, not just any kind of results (avoiding, then, results of getting the roof leak fixed or the staff satisfied). Further, *ends* is not synonymous with *results*, but includes them along with beneficiaries and cost.

The usual organizational vocabulary contains the terms *goal* and *objective*. But, alas, both *goal* and *objective* can be applied to either means or ends. Therefore, it is misleading to equate goals or objectives with ends. Although I myself use these terms according to their common meaning of some desired achievement, I do not employ them in addressing the board's job, for they are management concepts that are misleading in governance because they obscure the difference between ends and means. Instead, I will refer to the *ends-means distinction*.

WANT MORE?

2

Similarly, *strategy* as commonly used includes both ends and means components. A planned shifting of outcome priorities over the next five years is an ends issue. Long-term staff retraining and replacement strategies to make the shifts possible are means issues. As important as strategy is in management, in governance usage, the concept confuses ends and means. So as much as this text is a plea for boards to be strategic leaders, good governance strategy demands the board's focus on the ends-means distinction, not on strategy per se.

Confusing Ends and Means

My point is not that means are unimportant, just that means and ends should not be confused. Means are best decided by the people who must use them.

Kirk (1986, p. 40) charged that boards "become so engrossed in doing an infinite variety of discrete things, pursuing an endless number of routines, that they lose sight of the results, if any, that the activities are supposed to accomplish." The distinction between

WANT MORE?

3

ends and means seems simple. Ends and means appear often in the common language as a way of usefully classifying events around us. But closer inspection reveals difficulty in this apparent simplicity. For a board to take advantage of the Policy Governance ends-means distinction, it must recognize the ways in which ends and means are confounded.

Mission Versus Ends

One of the mantras of modern organization is the importance of writing a mission statement. Indeed, the concept of mission is crucial to any enterprise from military action to business to social service to religion. There is power in focusing our minds and actions toward a pointedly stated, thoughtfully defined outcome.

Traditional mission statements might summarize in a few words the major values to which an organization aspires—for example, "We will be the most respected regional provider of widgets by our customers, our employees, and our suppliers." Similar phrasing can be found at car rental agencies, grocery stores, hotels, plumbing companies, and uncountable other corporations. The nonprofit equivalent might be "quality mental health services for all" or "effective services by friendly people."

Although there is nothing wrong with the word *mission* per se, there are several flaws in its typical meaning that are important to avoid. First, missions as commonly written tend to include means as well as ends, thereby contaminating the careful separation of ends and means. Habits in mission writing were formed before the importance of the ends-means distinction was widely understood. Second, having built means into the mission concept, the empowerment of staff creativity and innovation in finding new and better means is cramped unnecessarily by prescription. Third, mission statements are just that—statements—rather than simply the broadest, most inclusive explication of results, recipients, and costs of results that is tied integrally to further, highly structured refinements of the values represented. In fact, it is common to think of a single mission statement followed immediately by a work plan or methods. Instead of that leap from a broadly defined purpose directly into how to achieve it, the global ends statement in Policy Governance is further defined by the board, then by the CEO and staff in a level-by-level articulation, still in terms of ends. Done properly, ends expressed in increasingly narrower levels never become means simply by virtue of finer description.

So the chief reason for avoiding the word *mission* is to prevent diluting the Policy Governance ends concept with characteristics associated with a less rigorous, less finely crafted, less theory-based practice. If a staff decides to publish a mission of the traditional sort as a matter of public relations or internal inspiration, that is acceptable and is itself a staff means decision. However, the board's concern with organizational purpose is not mission in the usual sense at all but rigor and brevity in the expression of ends.

Consequently, in this book I rarely use the word *mission*, because its usual connotations do not measure up to the importance of the concept. For years, I did use the word in connection with Policy Governance, but I have ceased doing so after finding how misleading the term can be. When I mean the most inclusive, briefly stated form of ends, instead of *mission*, I use the term *global ends*. This is, I admit, a less inspiring term than the word it replaces, but it embodies more rigor in directing organizational achievement and more sophistication in empowering subordinates.

Means Mistaken for Ends

In the absence of clear dictates about intended effects on the world, boards may treat a number of means as if they were ends themselves. In some nonprofit and public endeavors, these counterfeit results have received the blessing of tradition, an unearned legitimacy that is accorded to the familiar more through default than through deliberation.

Commendable Activities

The most insidious counterfeits are activities associated with good intentions or with well-accepted reasoning. For example, because making more handouts available for training sessions shows good intent or sense, the number and quality of handouts might come to be judged as more important than the effect of the training. The areas to which such confusion can extend are endless. In response to public clamor to compensate teachers on the basis of competence, it is not uncommon for the education establishment to propose incentives for teachers who take more graduate courses!

In social service fields, a revered counterfeit is unit cost. Unit cost is the cost in dollars of providing a time unit of service. *Pupil-day expenditure* is a comparable public school term. Unit cost comes to be the measure of whether a service organization is doing as much per dollar as it should. But unit cost is not related to the effectiveness of a service, so it does not measure productivity (efficiency in producing benefits per dollar), as social programs pretend it does. For example, the unit cost mentality leads to the assumption that $80 per hour of professional activity is better than $110 per hour, although there is absolutely no reason to believe so. Perhaps the $110-per-hour service is 150 percent more effective in attaining the results sought! Unit cost would simply be an innocuous measure if institutions had not come to believe it to be a true productivity measure.

An organization can become so permeated by the belief that well-intended or reasonable actions (rather than results) are the reason for existence that no one realizes something is awry. A striking example is the allegiance given to services and programs as if they were results. Services and programs are often treated as if they have value in themselves; however, they are only packages of prescribed activities. In Policy Governance, services and programs are always and only means. The ends concept prevents righteous busyness from becoming just as meaningful as results, or perhaps even more so.

The threat of good activity being perceived as an end is so great that it can hardly be overstated. Without constant vigilance and systems to support that vigilance, says Odiorne (1974), "People tend to become so engrossed in activity that they lose sight of its purpose. . . . They become so enmeshed in activity they lose sight of why they are doing it, and the activity becomes a false goal, an end in itself. . . . Falling into the activity trap is not the result of stupidity. In fact, the most intelligent, highly educated people tend to be those most likely to become entrapped in interesting and complex activities" (pp. 1–7).

It is not that good intentions or sensible actions by staff are unimportant. It is that they in no way constitute the reason for an organization's existence. Commendable activities are only means.

Commendable Conditions

Similarly, commendable conditions can also masquerade as results. Staff credentials may be the foremost of these conditions. Understandably, credentials and training can inspire admiration. It seems reasonable to think that a person with impressive training will do a better job than one without such training. Such reasoning has been called "paying persons for where they've been, not for what they are contributing." On this basis, for example, a professor with an impressive publications list is assumed to be a better teacher than a professor without such credentials.

High staff morale is another commendable condition. Some boards show more interest in staff morale than in results. They think, "If morale is high, then we must be okay; if turnover is high, something is wrong." One does not have to favor low morale or high turnover to see that although these indices may be symptoms, the organization exists neither for high morale nor for low turnover. The point here is not to ignore the signs of possible problems, only to put them in perspective. Boards that monitor morale but not ends have an unfortunately inverted ends-means perspective. Commendable conditions are only a means.

Commendable Structure

The arrangement of jobs, reporting lines, and distribution of decision centers through an organization constitute the structure of an organization. A shorthand representation is the organizational chart. Structural factors have great influence on how an organization functions.

To illustrate, narrow spans of control may reflect undeveloped management potential and superfluous hierarchical levels. The existence of a majority of staff officers (as opposed to line officers) in close proximity to the CEO suggests fragmented delegation and underutilized, underdeveloped line managers. A very wide span of CEO control may demonstrate unusually precise delegation but could also mean that the CEO is too busy and not sufficiently reflective. A deputy CEO to whom everyone else reports when the CEO is unavailable is almost sure to represent wasted managerial power. More than two executives vertically configured, each with supervision over only one person, almost certainly means someone has a position but no job. Structure does make a difference.

Streamlined, efficient structure is to be admired and much sought after. But an organization neither deserves points for it nor loses points for lack of it. Whether an organization is good or bad is revealed in its results and in its prudence and ethics. If performance is measured against the criteria set forth in board policies and shows no problems, then the concern was misplaced.

Organizational structure is important. Yet even the best structure is not the reason an organization exists. Structure is only a means.

Commendable Technology

High-technology electronics has become increasingly important, but the technology of operations has long been an issue for managers. Examples range from the hardware technologies of computers, filing systems, and telephones to the conceptual technologies of queue theory, operations research, and decision-making techniques.

Management has graduated to e-mail, slick presentation programs, and the Internet. But techniques and technologies can be undeservedly promoted from supporting to leading actors.

The U.S. Environmental Protection Agency (EPA) once planned to require use of a certain type of scrubber to rid smokestack discharge of particulates. The EPA intended that particulate emission be no greater than some critical level. Yet its published criterion was that certain technology be used to reach the result. By diverting attention from the desired result, the EPA may have sabotaged its own long-term effectiveness. Government bureaucracies often operate in this manner. Although they sacrifice long-term effectiveness, in the short run they maximize control (even if over the wrong things). In a supervisory situation, this might be viewed as the difference between managing and bossing. Supervisors may also trade long-term effectiveness for short-term control.

Technology-driven operation, very much like commendable activity–driven operation, is susceptible to what has been called the "tool illusion." To a child with a hammer, objects to be pounded become the most important things in the world. An object's "poundability" becomes its most salient characteristic. Technology within an organization is important, but even the best technology is not the reason an organization exists. Technology is only a means to an end.

Ends Mistaken for Means

In failing to focus on the ends-means distinction, we may also confuse ends with means. In some instances, there is such a single-minded focus on means that results are not recognized when they do come along. I observed a public school board spend its usual long, cluttered meeting moving from one executive means issue to another. Most of the means issues were not very large. In the midst of this unnecessary flurry was an agenda item concerning the outcome of extensive tests of reading ability throughout the system. The busy board spent only enough time to notice the item, say something nice, and move quickly back to the flurry of trivia!

The confusion that surfaces most often is between means and the results component of lower-level ends. In normal English usage, parts of the overall result can be viewed as means to the final result. But in Policy Governance, *means* is a shorthand term that simply means non-ends, so any part of a result counts as an ends issue because it meets the ends test. (*Activities* that lead to that subresult, however, are always means.)

Assume that the results and recipients components of the board's broadest ends statement is "normal community living for the developmentally disabled" (the desired megaresult). The board, in dealing with the next lower level of abstraction, determines which "products" make up the mixture that most closely corresponds to its vision of the broad result. Perhaps the board will decide that the desired mixture comprises independent living skills, occupational skills, and receptive employers (the subresults). The megaresult will contain several subresults, which in turn will contain subsubresults, regardless of where the board chooses to stop and allow executives to take over. This procession of ever-smaller subresults continues until it reaches the most specific short-term result concerning an individual consumer. You can see how any subresult could be seen as a means to the next higher result (occupational skills can be viewed as a means to normal community living), but in using Policy Governance, it is important to avoid diluting the ends concept in this way.

"Occupational skills" is quite different from the pure means represented by, say, "skills training." Skills training, an activity, is a means now and forever; it cannot be an outcome. On the other hand, it is easy to conceive of occupational skills as an outcome, a reasonable organizational result in themselves. Occupational skills can easily be imagined as the single product of a smaller or less ambitious organization—that is, as the megaresult itself. Occupational skills can be mistaken for a means only if there exist broader results of which they are a part.

In the ends-means differentiation discussed in this book, the sense in which a subresult like occupational skills can be considered a means will never be used. The powerful utility of the ends-means differentiation in enabling better governance rests on using one definition rather than the other. *Organizational activities, no matter how complex or important, are always means. External outcomes, results, and impacts are ends, whether or not they are subordinate parts of a broader result.*

Expressing the Global Ends

Although ends can be considered at various levels, it is only the broadest expression that should initially concern a board. The briefest, broadest ends statement does not determine everything about an organization's intended results, beneficiaries, and costs of results, but it tells us the range within which all further results, beneficiaries, and costs will occur. This broadest of ends statements, then, defines the arena of achievement, answering these simple questions: What is this organization for? That is, how much of what difference will be made, and for whom?" The board's answer at the broadest possible level will constitute the global Ends policy.

Let me say a word to distinguish this task from that faced by equity corporations, particularly publicly traded ones. To the ownership (shareholders), the purpose of the company is to produce a return on investment. While stating ends is just as important for corporations as it is for nonprofit organizations, the ends are not in terms of what is accomplished for another group but in terms of what is accomplished for the shareholders themselves. Hence, a corporate board may have to do nothing more to express global ends than to state, for example, that the company will achieve "a rolling three quarters average of no less than 10 percent compounded growth in annual earnings per share." For a nonprofit or governmental board, the ends-stating task normally has more elements and requires more study.

Making the global ends statement will be the most powerful single action a board takes. This intense exercise takes much more time than most boards foresee, particularly in the light of the few words yielded. But the purpose of the process should not be to produce a statement that finds a quiet resting place in a grant application, annual report, or brochure. In Policy Governance, the powerful and compelling global ends statement has the following attributes:

1. *Strict results focus.* As already stated, ends are never couched in terms of the activities necessary to achieve some change. The change itself is the point.

2. *Succinctness.* Long statements clutter and smother the core of the matter with excess verbiage. When the global ends message is buried in several paragraphs or even a single one, not only is the originating board hard pressed to identify it, but the CEO is not able to organize around it.

3. *Authoritative generation.* The global ends determination is too close to the heart of governance for the board to act passively and simply approve someone else's statement. If the board is not actively involved in deciding what the organization is for, why should it be involved in anything else?

4. *Horizontal integration.* Ends are developed from the context beyond the organization by a board accountable to an ownership. That same ownership may have other boards doing its business; therefore, it is important for an organization to see how it fits into the larger context of organizations. Disjointedness in public service and weakening of the public fabric result when boards do not speak with other boards. There is no more meaningful topic that community boards can discuss with one another than the various differences they purpose to make in the world.

5. *Properly categorized.* Ends must stand out from other topics in order to be compelling and in order to avoid dilution. When they are mixed with other topics (which, by definition, would

have to be some form of means), their pointed clarity is sacrificed. In Policy Governance, ends are separately addressed in
a distinct Ends category.

6. *Vertical integration.* Ends must be the theme and the backbone
   of the organization. A board decision does little good if it is
   not connected to the goings-on of the organization. A focus
   on ends, beginning with the global level, is comparable to a
   bottom-line mentality. Because of their peculiar market status, nonprofit and public organizations have been able to
   develop disjointed, internal islands of excellence that are
   not forced to aggregate to a bottom-line purpose.

7. *Starkness.* Although it is possible for the board's broadest
   ends statement to be a presentable slogan, being a slogan is
   not its purpose. Its purpose is best fulfilled by being straightforward with bare-bones directness, even if it would never do
   well on a brochure. A slogan can be created that is consistent
   with the global ends statement, but such an effort is one of
   public relations, not of governance.

Here are some examples of statements that fulfill the requirements for a global Ends policy:

"The citizens and visitors of Durham Region have a safe community in which to live and work at a competitive cost, relative to the Ontario communities of Halton, Hamilton, Niagara,
Ottawa, Peel, Toronto, Waterloo, and York." (Durham Regional Police Services Board, Oshawa, Ontario)

"At a reasonable cost, students are equipped with the spiritual
discernment, the moral courage and the academic excellence
to impact society through responsible, effective Christian living." (board of Colorado Springs Christian School)

"People have the knowledge and skill resources they need for
maximising their potential in their work-places; families; and

communities." (governing body of Castlereagh College, Belfast, Northern Ireland)

"The California Park & Recreation Society exists for the success of its members at dues no greater than comparable associations." (California Park & Recreation Society, Sacramento) (Exhibit 4.4 shows an expansion of this global statement.)

You will notice that all but one statement says something, even if very broadly, about the results to be achieved in the world, who is to experience or receive those results, and the efficiency of producing those results. The Castlereagh College governing body chose to omit the cost element. I don't recommend doing that, but as I will explain later, the board prohibition against being imprudent (discussed in Chapter Five) imposes a ceiling on costs in relation to benefits anyway, albeit a less demanding one than what normally would show up in ends language.

Expanding on the Global Ends

The first instance of vertical integration takes place in the clear connection of the global Ends policy to further Ends policies that the board itself creates. The board, not the CEO, is therefore likely to be the first to further define the broad beginning statement, and it does this by creating a second level of Ends policies, just one order of abstraction below the global statement.

As explained earlier, the broadest ends statement should be phrased in a few carefully chosen words that can stand on their own, to which can then be added more detailed statements that further define the organization's results, beneficiaries, and costs of results. Ends expressions espoused here are in an articulated form—that is, they are characterized by a progression of cautiously segmented parts beginning with the broadest and moving toward the more discrete. The process of deciding on headings before subheadings (as in an outline) yields greater integrity in establishing the board's intentions than lumping them into an undifferentiated narrative mass.

One product of articulation into separable, descending parts is a "value map" that both boards and staffs find informative, with respect to not only what has already been resolved but also what is to be addressed next. The board can pinpoint single elements for further debate and possible change. Furthermore, if the various levels of the policy cannot be displayed in a precise outline form, it is probable that the board has not done its work well.

Though it is unlikely to do so, the board may choose not to address more detailed specifications after it has adopted the top statement. If the board agrees that any reasonable interpretation of the global ends language on the part of the CEO would be acceptable, then it need say no more. That is, if all the possible priorities among subresults, subrecipients, and costs are acceptable, there is no reason for the board to narrow the expected results by passing more policies. The board can simply refrain from further pronouncements and allow the CEO to resolve all smaller or narrower choices among ends. Most boards are understandably reluctant to leave such broad issues to the CEO, so they rarely stop at this point.

Throughout the text, I will illustrate various aspects of policy development by reproducing policies that were actually drafted by real boards. In each case, I will cite the organization by name. However, due to the possibility of amendments and other governance changes, I make no claim that the policies shown are currently in effect.

Expanding on Results, Beneficiaries, and Costs

The board's next step after the global ends statement is to discuss which portions of the topic it wishes to define more narrowly, thereby reducing the latitude available to the CEO. The board may choose to create further policy about results, beneficiaries, or cost of results. Exhibits 4.1 through 4.4 show global Ends policies that

Exhibit 4.1. Law Society of Manitoba, Winnipeg Ends Policy

The aim of the Law Society of Manitoba is a public well-served by a competent, honorable and independent legal profession.

1. Lawyers are qualified upon entry to the profession.

2. Lawyers are honorable and ethical in the practice of their profession.

3. The legal profession is independent of government.

4. Legal services are reasonably available to the public at a reasonable cost.

5. The public are protected from financial loss arising from dishonest or negligent lawyers.

6. There is an absence of systematic barriers to entry to and practice within the profession to persons who are members of groups against whom discrimination is prohibited by law.

Note: The board chose not to state cost or priorities.

Exhibit 4.2. Southeast Booksellers Association, Columbia, South Carolina Ends Policy

SEBA exists for conditions conducive to core member success, to the extent that justifies expenditure of available resources. Accordingly, in order of priority

1. Core members will have skills/capabilities.

    A. Management skills to include at least financial for smaller and newer bookstores, personnel, technology, inventory

    B. Marketing skills to include at least publisher relations, advertising, public relations

2. The public values core members, individually and collectively, as an important part of community life.

    A. Members have a forum for exchange of information and collegiality.

**Exhibit 4.3. Lancaster County
Bible Church, Lancaster, Pennsylvania
Ends Policy**

People who come in contact with LCBC will experience life change through Christ at a cost that demonstrates an increased efficiency and effectiveness in the utilization of the human and financial resources provided for by God.

1. As a first priority, unconnected people in the surrounding communities will connect with Jesus Christ and the LCBC body of believers.

2. As a second priority, believers who are connected to LCBC as their church home will find a supportive community of believers and will grow towards becoming fully devoted followers of Jesus Christ.

3. As a third priority (not to exceed X% of resources), unbelievers in select communities on each continent of the world will accept Jesus Christ as their personal savior and grow in their faith through the efforts of the community of believers of LCBC.

4. As a fourth priority (not to exceed X% of resources), other like-minded organizations will effectively reach non-believers and encourage the growth of believers through interacting with and learning LCBC's approach to local church ministry.

Note: This policy is an abridged version. "X%" still in debate.

have been expanded to one or more further levels of detail by real boards using the Policy Governance model. Exhibits 4.5 and 4.6 show policies that begin at the second level and go into further depth. The format is identical, but most boards choose to clerically separate subtopics of ends into separate policies, thereby beginning a topic-specific policy where the one above it left off. I have shortened some for sake of brevity.

Results

The board's broadest ends statement necessarily encompasses a wide range of potential results. These results—changes or effects in ben-

Exhibit 4.4. California Park & Recreation Society, Sacramento Ends Policy

---

The California Park & Recreation Society exists for the success of its members at dues no greater than comparable associations.

1. Members are united around a common vision and a strategic plan that describes and realizes the benefits of parks and recreation for all Californians.

   A. Members are able to demonstrate and articulate the role of parks and recreation in creating community.

   B. Members are able to communicate with decision-makers at both a state and local level.

2. Members' concerns are heard by legislators in the creation of relevant public policies that affect parks and recreation.

   A. Members are informed of proposed public policies of substantial importance to the profession.

   B. Members are able to use the political process.

3. Members recognize common core competencies essential to meet the changing needs of the profession.

   A. Members have skills and knowledge to advance within the parks and recreation profession.

   B. Members benefit from professional interaction.

4. Parks and recreation is recognized by elected officials as an essential community service in agencies that employ CPRS member(s).

---

eficiaries' lives—are the benefits to be produced, such as cure, knowledge, broad employment base, housing, or job skills.

Organizations produce many results. But the results referred to in the ends concept apply only to (1) changes in the lives of intended beneficiaries outside the staff organization and (2) changes that form the purpose of the organization rather than simply unintended effects. In regard to the first criterion, results for staff or for the board qua board are not admissible. In regard to the second criterion, only

**Exhibit 4.5. Project Management Institute,
Newton Square, Pennsylvania
Ends Policy**

1.1 Project management is recognized as a profession for project management practitioners at a reasonable investment.

   1.1.1 A universally accepted body of knowledge of project management exists for the project management profession.

      1.1.1.1 The expansion of the body of knowledge of project management is dynamic and deliberate for the project management profession.

      1.1.1.2 The expansion of the body of knowledge of project management addresses industry, general, national and global considerations for the project management profession.

      1.1.1.3 The content of the body of knowledge of project management is codified and accepted for the project management profession.

   1.1.2 Generally accepted standards exist for the project management profession.

   1.1.3 Accredited formal degree programs in project management exist for the project management profession.

   1.1.4 Project management is practiced ethically by business, government and society-at-large.

      1.1.4.1 Generally accepted project management standards of conduct exist for the members of the project management profession.

   1.1.5 Credentialling and licensing programs exist for project management.

      1.1.5.1 Universally recognized and accepted credentialling programs exist for the project management profession.

      1.1.5.2 Licensing programs exist through government or appropriate government-sponsored agencies for the project management profession.

Note: This policy begins at the second level and expands to the fifth.

Exhibit 4.6. Oxfam Community Aid Abroad, Melbourne, Australia Ends Policy

There will be an increase in the number of people, in particular people who are currently oppressed or marginalised due to their gender, ethnicity, cultural or indigenous identity, who have equal rights and status with the majority groups in their community, within all areas where Oxfams operate. Consequently there will be:

1. Recognition and respect given by governments, companies and the population to the individual and collective rights of indigenous people;

2. A significant reduction in active forms of discrimination based on ethnic, religious, cultural and social differences and a greater respect for diversity;

3. Increased compliance, especially by governments in our regions of operation, with their obligations under international treaties, especially the Universal Declaration of Human Rights;

4. Much more equal social and political participation by women and greater protection of women's rights, including the right to freedom from violence.

Note: This policy begins at the second level and expands into the third.

the results that the board considers part of organizational performance count. And, with apologies for the repetition, the results component in the ends concept is never, ever what staff will be doing in order to accomplish, safeguard, or perpetuate those results (for example, programs, activities, curricula, services, or financial prudence).

Beneficiaries

The word *beneficiaries* refers to those who will benefit, be affected, or otherwise be changed by the organization; it is they in whom or for whom the results that justify the organization's existence will occur. The board's broadest ends statement necessarily encompasses a wide range of potential beneficiaries. Beneficiaries might be differentially targeted by age, type of disorder or deficit, severity of need, party membership, location, income, or other personal or demographic characteristics. Varieties of benefits, all fitting reasonably within the broadest statement of ends, can be given differing priorities as well. In fact, even if no decision is made explicitly, the very act of operating will cause them to be given varying priorities. The issue for board members is whether they themselves will decide the relative worth of various results or recipient groups.

Cost

Although putting a monetary value on changes in the human condition is not an easy task, we do so implicitly all the time. The board may decide how much any given benefit is worth or, at least, the cost not to be exceeded in providing units of that benefit. *Cost* refers to the resources consumed in order to produce the results, not the price (if any) charged to the person affected. This concept is important in many nonprofit and governmental organizations—for example, those that use sliding fee schedules or provide free services—but it is not an ends issue. (Such apportionment of cost—for example, the subsidy of certain consumers by other consumers, by donors, or by the public—is a means issue that the board can address with Executive Limitations policy. The board might, for example, prohibit the organization from charging low-income direct recipients more than some percentage of cost.)

There is interaction among the three components of the ends concept. Consider, for example, a dental health project in a disadvantaged neighborhood. For a given level of expenditures, we can cause 500 children to be cavity-free or 150 to have beautifully straight teeth. Which is the best choice? We must juggle product and worth to resolve the issue. In a public school system, students with behavior problems cost more to educate. The extra costs mean that other children do not get as much as they otherwise would. To what extent should the benefits to some children be sacrificed so that troubled children can be more fully served? The results of a public library cost more per user in rural areas than in urban areas.

What is the right balance between the cost for rural results and the cost for urban results?

The cost component of the ends concept, though seemingly straightforward, has proven a difficult one for boards in actual practice. It should always refer to how valuable the intended results are. Their value can be expressed in terms of money or in terms of other results. At the global ends level, expression in terms of money is the only option, but below that level (when multiple subresults may be considered), results can be compared with one another. It is never legitimate, for example, to express the ends cost concept in terms of "without exceeding available revenues," for that is a matter of prudence, simply meaning "don't spend more than we have," and tells nothing about the swap between resources and results.

It should be noted that the board's setting of priorities in regard to the cost component of its Ends policies is never a matter of priorities among programs or services. Setting priorities is with respect to various results or various beneficiaries of those results.

It is legitimate for the board, at the global ends level, to say that the organization should produce the results at about the cost achieved in other organizations, thereby referring more or less to a market test. It is legitimate for a board to express that cost per result will always be less than the previous year. It is also legitimate for the board to say that results should justify the cost. Any one of these phrasings requires the CEO to produce monitoring data driven by that wording. It is not a good practice for the board to omit all reference to cost, but if it does, the board must be willing to accept a great deal of CEO latitude on the matter. That is because in the absence of a board ends instruction on cost, the only limiting factor is the board's prohibition in Executive Limitations against being imprudent. So the CEO would have to run costs per result high enough to run into that broad barrier in order to be seen as failing to fulfill board policy.

Obviously, these are but a few of the thousands of value choices that organizations regularly face. Usually they are hidden from direct view, buried in the many pages of program descriptions, budgets, and other staff documents. Board leadership, newly aware of this hidden richness, will at first seem to have uncovered an unmanageable number of value questions. These were always present but were previously settled by default; the board had decided on these massive value choices about organizational nature and destiny by not deciding.

These all-important variations on "What are we here for?" should be the board's consuming business. Reducing the clutter of conventional governance enables boards to approach these choices systematically. The first step is determining the global (broadest) expression of ends. The second step is establishing which aspects of results, beneficiaries, and costs the board feels strongly enough about to make more specific by making further pronouncements. The third step is to analyze, gather information, debate, and finally select further policy language.

With these policies in place, the board has the opportunity to venture still further. The policymaking process is fluid. Policymaking stops at whatever point the majority of the board is willing to allow the CEO to make further decisions. The idea is not to extend policymaking to the smallest possible value choice. It is necessary for the board to go only as far as its values compel it to go. The point is not that the board should control all it *can* but that it should control all it *must*.

Staff sometimes worry that a board will address lesser values so extensively that no latitude will be left for staff decisions. Such overextension by the board is improbable. As a board addresses issues at increasingly lower levels, relatedness among issues grows geometrically. It becomes exceedingly difficult to coordinate all the many value choices. Traditional personnel and finance committees get an inkling of this problem when they have to take extra time to deal with the interface of their respective facets of staff compensation. The board finds that time requirements get out of hand. Coordination of these many interdependent variables is part of the reason a staff is needed. As long as the policymaking principles presented here (particularly, descending only one level at a time) are followed, a board's incursion into lower and lower levels of involvement will be self-limiting.

Policy Product

The concrete product of this series of value considerations by the board is a set of Ends policies. Most boards are able to govern well with only a handful of Ends policies, including the global one. Because the number of policy issues and the depth of value levels addressed vary from board to board, the exact number of such policies a board should have cannot be stated. Under usual conditions, it would be surprising for an ordinary community social service board to have much more than a half-dozen Ends policies averaging a page in length. Of course, reams of program descriptions will be developed by staff on the basis of these brief board directives.

The Ends policies illustrated in this chapter are targeted to a single level of achievement in the sense that organizational performance either achieves a reasonable interpretation of their provisions or does not. It is certainly conceivable for a board to create Ends policies in terms of that which minimally passes and, say, that which meritoriously passes. Indeed, a carefully reasoned argument can be made for this two-or-more-tier approach.

WANT MORE?
4

I have chosen not to present Ends policies in this manner, for two reasons. First, the format is a more complicated one for illustration. Second, any board can convert to a two-tier method once its Ends policymaking is in good order. My experience is that the self-discipline required to craft a full set of pass-fail Ends policies such as those shown here is a momentous achievement in itself.

Long-Range Planning

It is important that the board prescribe ends from an appropriately long-term perspective. *Creating Ends policies with a long-range perspective is the greatest board contribution to long-range planning.*

It is mandatory that boards be forward thinking. It is important that organizations have long-range plans. By extension of these two ideas, one might assume that boards should be involved in long-range planning. Boards should, indeed, make long-range decisions and even short-range ones with a long-range perspective, but boards whose organization has a CEO should never be involved in actually constructing the myriad parts of a planning document.

Good governance calls for the board role in long-range planning to consist chiefly in establishing the organization's reason for planning. Planning is done to increase the probability of getting somewhere from here. Enunciation of that "somewhere" is the board's highest contribution. In a manner of speaking, boards participate most effectively in the planning process by standing just outside it. Boards can make an invaluable contribution to planning; however, except for planning the improvement of governance itself, *boards should not do the actual long-range planning.*

By casting its Ends policies out toward the planning horizon, a board lays out the values that form the basis of staff plans. Of course, planning can become mere "blue-skying" if the board has been cavalier in stating its Ends policies. In establishing Ends expectations, stretch must be tempered with sobriety. To deliberate responsibly, a board must interact greatly with staff and outside parties. This interaction does not relate to the staff's day-to-day concerns and job undertakings. Staff-board interaction here is designed to ensure inclusion of staff insights, passions, and environmental scanning in board deliberation. It should not be, as is common in conventional board-staff communication, that the board shifts its focus to staff-level issues. To the contrary, this process should richly stretch staff upward to the board's long-term, deeply value-laden world, so that all participants grow a little.

The board's creation of Ends policies requires penetrating deliberation about big questions. There is simply no time to drift into current staff issues. Difficult as this challenge might be, it is easily the most exciting, creative, responsible task in which a board can engage. Board data, dialogue, and decisions include the probable environmental circumstances of the future, shifting public needs, big-picture strategic swaps, and the intentions of other boards working on their own visions—in other words, highly informed dreaming.

Planning is more effective when kept simple, yet the greatest resistance to board leadership as defined here is that, although it is not easy, it seems so simple. The principle is not "so complicated that it's hard to grasp," as R. James LeFevre of Planned Parenthood of Northern New England in Burlington, Vermont, put it, "but rather, because it is so maddeningly simple it's easy to have it slip away." There is a fair amount of rigor involved in determining even at a broad level what an organization's contribution to the world should be. But when that has been done, the nuts and bolts of planning become merely the executive tool with which to bring it about. Waterman (1988) counsels managers to "think and rethink basic direction, but keep the statement of it simple and general [even though] you will frustrate the people who are looking for 'the strategy.' Our idealized image of strategy as a complete game plan is so strong that general statements . . . seem unsatisfying" (p. 71).

In short, the board's job in long-range planning is not long-range planning itself but explication of vision in ends terminology. The board's job is to maintain and behaviorally demonstrate a long-range mentality. And the board demonstrates that critical mentality by obsessively deciding what good is to be accomplished for which people at what cost. These value issues about ends lie at the core of organizational existence. They are reduced to a few succinct Ends policies. So it is that with the same stroke, boards can do their part in long-range planning and govern organizational results.

Evaluating Ends

Evaluation is an integral part of the management process, and it must be integral to governance as well. Evaluation should ideally be a precise, systematic, nonintrusive, criteria-focused method that constantly answers the question "How are we doing?" Although evaluation or performance monitoring is discussed in Chapter Six, I also include remarks here on the peculiar difficulties commonly encountered in evaluating organizational results.

The word *evaluation* has come to be associated with service or program success more than with other areas of performance, such as financial status or compliance with purchasing guidelines. The model presented here does not differentiate, however, among these various instances of performance monitoring. The board is obligated to check performance against those matters that it found important enough either to prescribe (in the case of ends) or to proscribe (in the case of staff means). As with other policy types, then, evaluation of ends is important to leadership for three reasons: it discloses unacceptable deviation from desired values; enables the board to relax about the present so that it can keep its mind on the future; and keeps board policies constantly in the spotlight, thereby making them more likely to be amended as they grow out of date.

Well-Placed Concern About Evaluation

Nonprofit and public organizations, which are generally free of the harsh, inescapable ends evaluation of the market, often find their results difficult to evaluate. If, through the mechanism of the market, consumers could tell nonprofit and public organizations what their products are worth, the topic of evaluation would never have attained its lofty status. Business organizations do market research and product research but never have to do the type of program evaluation popular in nonprofit and public agencies—at least, not for the same reasons.

Public and nonprofit organizations need to evaluate their impacts precisely because they have no natural, consumer-based behavioral measure of whether their results are effective enough to be worth the cost of producing them. Public and nonprofit organizations claim that evaluation is difficult because they are producing services, not widgets, but the argument is specious. They are not producing services at all; they are producing results in people's lives by *using* services—for services are means, not ends. And there is nothing inherently difficult in evaluating the effects of organizational pursuits when consumers do the evaluating.

Evaluation of ends assesses not simply whether organizational activity is effective but whether it is sufficiently effective to be worth the cost. If a board is to overcome the muted market voice (that is, if evaluation is even possible), the relative worth issue cannot be neglected. The separation of effectiveness from worth is a rampant disease among nonprofit and public organizations, and it is a fundamental flaw of public administration. This is why the model presented here assiduously focuses on the simple idea of the organization's swap with the world: what is consumed compared with what is produced.

In the face of this difficulty, it is understandable that professional evaluators and laypeople alike bemoan our inadequacies in evaluating nonprofit and public services. The field of process evaluation attempts to circumvent the problems by intentionally evaluating the means rather than the ends. Texts on the problems of measurement validity and reliability often suggest well-considered strategies to get around the difficulties. Evaluation of effectiveness is primitive even without the conceptually burdensome question of whether what is achieved is worth the cost. We truly are not very good at it.

This technical inadequacy in how to evaluate is not the largest evaluation problem facing nonprofit and public boards, however. The biggest problem, far and away, is that we do not know what to evaluate! Misplacing our concern about evaluation is part of the cause of this predicament.

Misplaced Concern About Evaluation

Ironically, premature concern about evaluation of ends can be a formidable deterrent to leadership. Although this problem also occurs in evaluation of the prudence and ethics of staff means, it is particularly prevalent in the evaluation of ends.

Driven by anxiety about evaluative shortcomings, board members often stop short their discussions of desired outcomes, saying,

"But we can't evaluate it" or the milder "But how would we evaluate that?" People are loath to answer such an obvious stopper. An enthusiastic "Oh, yes we can!" would surely brand the speaker as naive, perhaps accurately. It seems that well-read people are armed with impressive proofs that evaluation schemes just do not work well enough to even merit discussion. Given the obvious inadequacies, these people make a fine case.

Fearing that they might decree something that cannot be evaluated cleanly, boards retreat from decreeing at all. They let a reasonable worry about evaluating prevent them from saying what the outcomes should be. This process can deteriorate into their deciding where to go based on whether evaluators can determine when they have arrived there. "What do you want to accomplish?" is answered, for practical purposes, with "It depends. Tell us what you can measure."

Imagine that board members are in a taxi surrounded by fog. Though their view of the surroundings, their progress, and even their arrival might be clouded, they would not refrain from telling the driver where they want to go. Yet that is exactly what many boards do in the face of countless admittedly tough questions about evaluating results. The stage is set for them to slip into the trap of evaluating means, because they can see means better and count them more easily than ends. Professional evaluators and boards miss the most relevant point: stating the desired ends is too important for them to wait for defensible evaluation.

An authoritative, clear statement of what is to be accomplished has a powerful effect on organizational behavior, even if the results are never evaluated. This is not an excuse for omitting evaluation. But there is merit in letting people know what you want, even if you cannot be certain that you got it. The single most intimidating aspect of program evaluation is not the technical difficulty but the blockage resulting from premature consideration. We simply place the concern for evaluation too early in the governance process.

Where to Place the Concern About Evaluation

No place. One option is not to be concerned about evaluation at all. Start at the beginning by stating what the organization is to contribute to the world, what condition is worth achieving, and what you would evaluate if you could. That process is best done in the ends-oriented, stepwise fashion I have described, and must be done without regard for evaluative difficulties.

Wrong place. Another strategy is simply to avoid evaluating the wrong things. Measuring the wrong things is damaging in two ways: (1) "You get what you inspect, not what you expect" is a valid principle of behavior. Measuring the wrong things sends a strong message through the organization about what matters. If, in understandable frustration, you throw up your hands and yield to measuring busyness, you are sure to get more busyness. (2) The pressure, even the embarrassment, of having no stated outcomes to evaluate is a powerful motivator toward developing at least a first, faltering approximation of the results to be achieved. Evaluating the wrong things removes much of the healthy pressure, especially if you do it well. When we are able to take pride in how well we do the wrong things, there is little incentive to begin a wobbly start toward the right things.

Right place. Only when the board has created Ends policies should it stop to consider evaluation, because only when the board knows what it wants the organization to accomplish can it intelligently discuss evaluation. Evaluation without these targets is ludicrous; fretting over evaluation prior to setting these targets is dysfunctional. The issue of evaluation is merely this: What is the most convincing evidence that a reasonable interpretation of what the board sought is being produced? Evaluative purity is wonderful, but purity is not mandatory. What is called for in evaluation is reasonable assurance of the cost, not academic accuracy.

We forget that evaluation in the form of performance monitoring is an issue not of research but of management. The topic of evaluation is dominated, even handicapped, one might say, by the academic mentality. We unthinkingly apply standards of pristine, laboratorylike evaluation to the real-world need to determine whether what we do is worthwhile. A managerial mentality, unlike an academic mentality, would counsel us thus: with respect to influencing organizational behavior, *a crude measure of the right thing beats a precise measure of the wrong thing.*

The best approach a board can take in evaluation, then, is to stick rigorously to the ends, not to cop out by prescribing means. If the evaluation is crude, so be it. But never, never forsake specifying the desired results in favor of a more precise evaluation of the wrong things.

The most important real-world evaluation in almost all nonprofit and public organizations—public judgment of an organization's worth—is extremely crude. These evaluations tend to be too global to be managerially useful. They are usually too hard or too soft on management, because authoritatively pronounced criteria on which to base fair judgment are rarely available. In other words, implicit crude evaluation of results occurs anyway. The board's task is to make that judgment explicit, to direct it at preestablished criteria and away from capricious or confounding expectations, and only then to fret, deliberate, and attempt to make the evaluation less crude.

Board leadership in the matter of ends evaluation lies not in being seduced by sophistication but in persevering in a compelling, disarmingly simple quest to answer the questions "What did we want to accomplish? Are we achieving it?"

No Pain, No Gain

The ends concept and developing model-consistent policies about ends are thought by many to be the most difficult aspect of Policy Governance, despite the idea itself being quite simple. But the agony of sticking to the principles in doing ends work holds far more promise than simply setting goals or adopting a long-range plan. Jane H. Adams, CEO of California Park & Recreation Society,

Sacramento, found that by adopting Policy Governance ends principles, the board could "move much faster on issues critical to our members" and be "much more focused on what truly is important: making our members' worlds better." Lois Rockhill, executive director of Second Harvest Food Bank of East Central Indiana in Anderson, found that "Developing Ends policies was the fun part of the process, as the exercise enabled the board to look forward and to see our organization as an important agent of change."

My contention, of course, is that what really matters in the long run is the effect an organization has on its world. Boards betray their trusteeship when the attractions of staff practices prevent boards from having an undeviating obsession with attaining desired ends. To return to the cab ride example, as long as board members know they are not being cheated, it is usually best to let the taxi driver choose the route and the lanes in which to drive.

I may strain the reader's patience in reiterating that *ends* is shorthand for a very specific concept, one not found in any other system of governance even now. If in using the word, boards allow themselves to import other definitions of it (that is, if the word becomes the point rather than the concept), Policy Governance will not work as designed. It would be as if the baseball concept represented by the word *foul* were confounded with the basketball concept represented by the word *foul* just because the word is the same. Consequently, when someone argues that in their organization, financial soundness, fairness in hiring, or a good image is an ends issue, you can be absolutely certain that he or she has made that error.

Perhaps it is that error—if not simply lack of precision—that leads some boards to create Ends policies that do not pass the ends test. For example, in what were meant to be Ends policies, a hospital board said, "The patients are respected"; a community service board said, "Provide single-counter education and training services in all small and remote communities in the state"; and a college board said, "Productive relationship with the community." All were being careless with the ends concept. Hospitals don't exist so that patients can be respected, though respecting patients is important. Community organizations don't exist to provide services but to achieve results, which services may perhaps produce. Colleges don't exist so that they can have a relationship with their community, though having a good relationship is important. Ends are only about what results for whom justify an organization's existence, not how it would be good for the organization to conduct itself or to accomplish those ends. Keeping this distinction rigorously in focus prevents an organization from becoming another example of the sadly common fact that many organizations persist due not to their results but to their methods.

The Policy Governance concept of ends ties cost and benefit together, precluding any need to continue the old efficiency-versus-effectiveness argument. The Policy Governance model eliminates the shortsighted features of the "cult of efficiency" that were criticized by Stein. Accomplishing an acceptable amount of the right effect for the money spent is all wrapped into the single summarizing idea of ends. It is for this reason that treating the ends concept as if it embraces just results or just cost spoils its utility.

WANT MORE?

5

Ends Policies on the Policy Circle

At this point, let me remind you of the policy circle described in Chapter Three (Figure 3.3). Figure 4.1 illustrates how a given board might have filled in the outer levels of the Ends quadrant. Each board, of course, will choose a different level of detail at which to stop, beyond which the CEO is allowed to make any reasonable interpretation. The number of policies and their depth in Figure 4.1 are not intended to portray the right depth or number of policies but are only one example among many possibilities. Moreover, whatever the depth, number, and content of board policies, the board retains the right to change them whenever its wisdom so dictates.

Next Chapter

Strategic leadership lies in the board's Ends policies more than anywhere else. But the board is also accountable for how its staff mem-

Figure 4.1. Ends Policies Completed

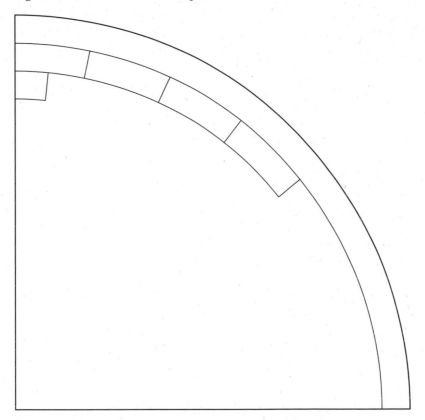

Note: The board has established its Ends policies deeply enough that any decisions or choices made by staff will be acceptable to the board if they are a reasonable interpretation of the broader statements. Thus, the board can safely delegate all further ends decisions.

bers achieve these ends and how they conduct themselves. In Chapter Five, I invite you to consider how the board can safely keep out of staff business yet still be accountable for the conduct of business. We will see how a relatively few Executive Limitations policies can give both the board and its CEO the freedom to be innovative, bold, and attentive to their respective jobs.

WANT MORE?

Further Reading

1. Oliver, C. "The Cult of Efficiency." *Board Leadership*, 2002b, no. 61.

   Carver, J. "FAQ: Why Shouldn't a Board Set Ends Policies One Program at a Time?" *Board Leadership*, 2004a, no. 76.

   Carver, J. "Beware the Quality Fetish." *Board Leadership*, 1998a, no. 37. Reprinted in J. Carver, *John Carver on Board Leadership*. San Francisco: Jossey-Bass, 2002.

   Argenti, J. *Your Organization: What Is It for? Challenging Traditional Organizational Aims*. London: McGraw-Hill Europe, 1993.

   Carver, J. "The Market Surrogate Obligation of Public Sector Boards." *Journal of Mental Health Administration*, 1981b, 8, 42–45.

   Carver, J. "Profitability: Useful Fiction for Nonprofit Enterprise." *Administration in Mental Health*, 1979b, 7(1), 3–20.

   Carver, J. "Your Board's Market Surrogate Obligation." *Board Leadership*, 1997t, no. 30. Reprinted in J. Carver, *John Carver on Board Leadership*. San Francisco: Jossey-Bass, 2002.

   Carver, J. "Evaluating the Mission Statement." *Board Leadership*, 1993e, no. 5. Reprinted in J. Carver, *John Carver on Board Leadership*. San Francisco: Jossey-Bass, 2002.

   Carver, J. *Creating a Mission That Makes a Difference*. The Carver-Guide Series on Effective Board Governance, no. 6. San Francisco: Jossey-Bass, 1996f.

2. Carver, J. "Why in Policy Governance Are Customary Management Words Like *Goal*, *Objective*, *Procedure*, and *Strategy* Discouraged?" *Board Leadership*, 2003w, no. 68.

   Carver, J. "Does the Balanced Scorecard Have Governance Value?" *Board Leadership*, 2001f, no. 58.

3. Odiorne, G. S. *Management and the Activity Trap*. New York: HarperCollins, 1974.

4. Argenti, J. *Your Organization: What Is It for? Challenging Traditional Organizational Aims*. London: McGraw-Hill Europe, 1993.

5. Oliver, C. "The Cult of Efficiency." *Board Leadership*, 2002b, no. 61.

   Stein, J. G. *The Cult of Efficiency*. Toronto: Anansi, 2001.

Controlling Ethics and Prudence
What's Not OK, Even if It Works

It is important that the board have control over the complexity and details of staff operations. Yet it is also important that a board be free from the complexity and details of staff operations. The board needs control because it is accountable for all organizational activity, however obscure or far removed. Yet the board needs to be free from operational matters because it is a part-time body with little time to get its own job done.

It is common to sacrifice one need for the other. Some boards relinquish control to be free from details or to grant the CEO freedom from board intrusion; such boards may be guilty of rubber-stamping. Others forgo freedom in order to control many details; such boards may be guilty of meddling or micromanaging.

The responsible board cannot escape its obligation to prescribe at least the broad sweep of ends (which I have been calling the *global level*) and perhaps a few levels below. In other words, with a broad brush, the board determines the organization's future impacts on the world. In this chapter, however, I am concerned not with the organization in terms of its impact on the world but with what staff members do in getting it there. I deal with the myriad of "how to" questions facing the CEO and his or her staff. More accurately, I deal with how the board might best relate to the staff's "how to" issues. The board's challenge is to be reasonably certain that nothing goes awry and at the same time to grant as much unimpeded latitude as possible to those with the skill and talent to get the work done.

To make the case for freedom through limits, I start with the often dizzying array of organizational means, their seductive appeal, and the board's legitimate interest in them. I then look at how a board can maintain control of internal operations by setting limits instead of becoming directly involved. Next, I deal with developing the documents capable of exercising proactive control (Executive Limitations policies), and I follow this with a demonstration of typical policy topics in this category.

The Enticing Complexity of Operations

For most boards, the greatest source of complexity and, unfortunately, interest is not ends but staff operations. Boards struggle with budgets, personnel procedures and issues, purchasing, staffing patterns, compensation, and staff plans. Self-perpetuating cycles are in effect wherein staff members bring their issues to the board because they think the board wants to hear them. Board members request information and attend to staff-level issues because they believe that the staff will feel abandoned if they do otherwise. Sometimes, staff members bring matters to the board to avoid making choices: "This item is a hot one; we'd better get the board to decide." Often, no prior board guidance has been given; consequently, there are no parameters within which the board protects the staff's right to make such choices.

On the other hand, boards may delve into staff matters because a particular board member has either the relevant expertise or mere curiosity about some aspect of operations. It is not uncommon for an entire board to be drawn into an issue only because it is a concern of one or two persons. The board's job is thus defined not by a carefully constructed design of the task but by a laundry list of individual interests. Perhaps most distressing is that much of the literature for and advice to boards accentuate just this kind of flurry-governance.

Boards study, invest meeting and committee time in, and worry and argue about the complex, never-ending, intriguing body of staff activities. To the detriment both of carefully deliberated results and of effective board process, boards are entangled in and seduced by the means of their subordinates. As if by an irresistible force, board members are drawn into staff issues like the following:

Personnel: job design, hiring, firing, promotion, discipline, training, grievances of staff from the most junior to the CEO, deployment, evaluation

Compensation (except that of the CEO): salary ranges, salary grades, salary adjustments, incentives, benefits, pensions

Supply: purchasing, bidding, authorization, storage, inventories, distribution, salvage

Accounting: budgeting, depositories, controls, investments, retrenchment, growth, cost center designation

Facilities: space allocation and requirements, rentals, purchases, sales, upkeep, refurbishing

Risk management: insurance, exposures, protective maintenance, disclaimers

Consumer record keeping: consumer forms, waivers, consents, service tracking, service design

Reporting: grant reports, tax reporting, law and regulation compliance

Communications: telephone systems, meetings, postings, mail distribution

Management methods: objective setting, staffing patterns, team definitions, feedback loops, planning techniques, control methods, on and on ad nauseam

The foregoing list is not exhaustive. Means issues with which staff members contend are endless. There are always far more issues than any board can keep up with, even if the board totally neglects its own job in order to do so. Keeping up with all these issues—much less providing leadership for them—is utterly impossible. The ideal of reviewing and approving everything is illusory. Yet the board has no choice but to attend to its legitimate interest in these matters, an interest that can be overlooked only with severe damage to the organization's concept of board accountability.

The challenge for the board is to exercise oversight with respect to staff operations without obscuring role differences and without taking the staff off the hook for making decisions. The appropriate expression of the board's legitimate interest is not to redefine a staff issue as a board issue but to curtail or confine the available staff choices to an acceptable range.

The Board's Stake in Staff Practices

The preceding partial list of executive means includes important aspects of corporate life. Such material in board mailings and meetings may be so impressive that it seems to capture the essence of the enterprise. But no matter how important, how technically sophisticated, how impressively carried out, or how great the professional training of experts in the various areas, these items are means, not ends. They are not what organization is all about; they serve what organization is all about. And for the most part, the degree to which they serve board-desired ends well is the source of their value.

For the most part, but not totally. Boards have more than one interest in staff practices. The Policy Governance model provides a unique mechanism for boards to control what needs to be controlled about staff means in a way that is as economical as it is rigorous.

Effectiveness

By far, executive means are of most importance to a board because of their effectiveness. Do they work? That is the primary test. Judging the effectiveness of means is not done by looking at the means but at what they were intended to produce. Means are assessed best by focusing on ends. In fact, the greatest impediment to measuring the effectiveness of means is looking at the means themselves.

In this area, nonprofit and public administrative practice is prone to a monumental flaw. People inspect means through site visits, certifications, and organization evaluations, but there is very little inspection of results. Rewards are handed out on the basis of the means' purported excellence rather than attainment of results. Organizational means come to have a life and momentum of their own, driven by the overpowering tendency to assess them apart from their ability to produce results. Perhaps this source of managerial perversity should not surprise us. Individuals and particularly disciplines or professions are heavily invested in and, in large part, formed around distinctive methods or practices—that is, means.

So if a board is willing to make judgments about means based primarily on attainment of ends, then this largest single concern about executive means can be laid aside. I dealt with it in Chapter Four, and the board deals with it by measuring how well its organization performs with respect to the board's Ends policies.

Approvability

Granting that the board discharges its central legitimate interest in executive means by assessing achievement of ends, we must now deal with the fuzzy concept of approvability. Most boards would be unwilling to rest with mere effectiveness as the only test but would require that, apart from effectiveness, executive means be carried out in an approvable manner.

What is meant by an approvable staff activity or plan? By observing as boards proceed through a traditional approval process, I've noted three phenomena. First, as a body, a board may not be quite sure what *approvability* means. Consequently, a board may tend to go through the motions. Different board members question different items, usually against idiosyncratic criteria. Sometimes they question effectiveness, but they are likely to fall back into the trap of trying to judge effectiveness by closely inspecting the means. A telling test is for a board to ask itself what it would *disapprove*. If a board does not know what it would disapprove, its approval is a process without direction and, at worst, a sham.

Second, board members may equate approvability with the question "Would I do it this way?" When an approval is rendered from this point of view, the real chief executive finds that there are a number of would-be executives to contend with. Board members sometimes see it as their prerogative to play part-time CEO. This phenomenon leads a politically inclined CEO to manipulate documents so as to satisfy the various board member interests. Such maneuvering is not without cost. Ends suffer a loss of primacy, and the staff's selection of means is less true to its own best judgment. CEO accountability for ends achievement is reduced when the board dictates the means.

Third, board members want to ensure that staff means—however effective in reaching prescribed ends—are prudent and ethical. And to the extent that inspection and approval of executive means fulfill this board interest, they are justifiable.

Legitimate Control of Means

Let me summarize the foregoing points: (1) effectiveness requires no inspection of means and, in fact, is best measured by intentionally not looking at means; (2) a simple preference that means be arranged or selected in a certain way is an indulgence that the board may want to allow itself, but it is one that reduces the integrity of management and cheapens the meaning of staff accountability; and (3) boards cannot ensure prudence and ethics by measuring the attainment of ends. But unlike a desire to enforce what are mere preferences, the board has a moral obligation to ensure the prudence and ethics of operations.

Consequently, the only legitimate, direct interest a governing board need have in how the staff conducts its business is that all be prudent and ethical. Stated more pointedly, *apart from being pru-*

dent and ethical, the activities that go on at and below the level of chief executive are completely immaterial. The board need only involve itself in executive means to make sure that acceptable standards of prudence and ethics are being met. This can save much board time, as well as a great deal of executive frustration. And it becomes clear what values in any given document or recommendation the board in its most clearheaded moments was approving or disapproving.

Control Through Proactive Constraint

Most means are justified by the ends because producing results is normally what justifies means. Some means, however, are not justifiable regardless of how effective they are. If this were not so, a board would not need to test anything about executive means except their effectiveness. Focusing on which means are *not* approvable, rather than on those that are simplifies the board's work and makes it less onerous for management as well.

A board that wishes to ensure that its organization's actions are prudent and ethical must delineate *ahead* of time exactly what is imprudent and unethical. Any staff action that does not violate the board's standards, then, is automatically approvable. Note that the board's standards are negative or limiting rather than positive or prescriptive. The board has neither the time nor the expertise to state everything that should be done. It does have the sense of ethics and prudence necessary to recognize what should not be done. Although counterintuitive, this principle is deceptively simple, given the excellence in governing that it enables.

Although the board speaks to ends prescriptively, with regard to executive means, the board should remain silent except to state clearly what it will not put up with. A small number of policies can enunciate the board's values with respect to minimum levels of prudence and ethics. The board can govern the vast array of executive means through policy, not through direct involvement in staff activities. I call the category of policies that limits or constrains executive authority *Executive Limitations*.

The total message the board sends to staff, then, consists of what outputs are to be achieved (ends) and what may not be done in the process of achievement (limits on staff means). Board thought is proactive and general rather than reactive and specific. Thus, the board is saved from making countless separate decisions in the future.

Despite the breakthrough in board effectiveness that this approach makes possible, some board members find it difficult to place limits on staff means. As persons and as governors, they desire to be positive rather than negative. Such a motivation is commendable, but it overlooks an irony of delegation. The most positive approach a board can take toward its subordinates' means is verbally negative. Conversely, the most negative approach is prescriptive and positive. Telling a subordinate how to do a task automatically eliminates all other methods. Telling a subordinate how not to do it leaves open all other possible methods. Good supervision leaves as much freedom as possible.

No one can presume to know ahead of time all the innovative combinations of means. No one can divine all the possible ways to improve tasks, systems, structures, and relationships. Even the people who are carrying out a task stumble across innovation as often as they bring innovative ideas to the task at the outset. Moreover, running an organization involves not only innovation within single tasks but also continual re-creation of interrelationships among tasks and persons. The ability to make and change decisions and to move quickly, particularly on the part of those closest to the action, is of paramount importance. In the best of enterprises, leaders "define the boundaries, and their people figure out the best way to do the job within those boundaries" (Waterman, 1988, p. 7).

Board prescription of means is a stultifying and anti-innovative process of control. This would be true even if a board were available full-time and fully versed in all organizational areas of expertise. But boards are available to render decisions only a few hours per year and do not have knowledge of every part of organizational life. The common, albeit incomplete prescription of means not only produces an untenable amount of work for the board but unduly hampers staff effectiveness. Such board positiveness is a serious cause of lost staff potential. Given the availability of a more effective alternative, it is completely unnecessary as well. In Fram's fictional exploration of what he terms the *corporate model*, a character boasts, "We have a REAL BOARD. . . . A real board tells its executive director exactly what to do." Fram's protagonist politely withholds his thought: "You don't have a real board. What you have is a parent-child relationship" (Fram, 1988, p. 74).

There is a subtler way in which a board can inflict the same kind of damage without directly prescribing executive means: by retaining approval authority over staff plans. When staff must bring specific decisions to the board (for example, approval of annual budgets and compensation changes), the board implies that only the staff actions it approves are legitimate. Although staff members author the board-approved actions, the board authorizes them. For staff, operational choices that have board approval, regardless of their origin, are frozen in place until the board has time and sees fit to approve changes. The effect on management is only a little better than if the board had generated the means prescription itself. Consequently, board approvals, even of staff-submitted documents, constitute unnecessary interference with the CEO's staff delegation system and decision flow.

Consider the effect of the board's being minimal but negative in dealing with staff means. Ignoring staff means except to prohibit them with explicit policies frees both board and staff. Regarding the unusual proscriptive language, Jo Luck, CEO of Heifer Project International, Little Rock, says that the Executive Limitations category can mistakenly be seen "as negative, largely because it is written in negative terms. However, the way it is written actually provides a greater amount of flexibility for management." In addition, the board is free of the endless details of staff work and can attend better to its own job. G. Taft Lyon, Jr., board chairperson of Life Management Center, El Paso, Texas, was happy that he "didn't have to get involved in [the CEO's] business and tell him what he needed to do." Anne Saunier, board chairperson of Planned Parenthood Federation of America, speaks of the ability to "safely withdraw, as a national board, from administrative details, with the emphasis on being 'safe.'" The staff is left free to choose, change, and create within clearly stated boundaries. Norman Barth, CEO of Lutheran World Relief, New York, is happy to be "freed. . . . Not that I can do anything I want to, but rather I know the bounds of my authority. . . . The board does not second-guess me."

WANT MORE?
1

Without this explicitly bounded freedom, the CEO of a large zoo wrote that "[I] continue to feel as though I am walking through traps and land mines. Fortunately, I am guessing where most of them are; I am guessing a lot." J. Gregory Shea, CEO of Tri-County Mental Health Services of Lewiston, Maine, says his board "clearly feels . . . that it knows . . . how far the CEO can and will go . . . that both my day-to-day functioning and the board's policy setting and oversight are done with much greater freedom . . . and [with] flexibility . . . to [adapt to] sometimes very rapidly changing circumstances. Without those policies, there would be a lot of 'Monday-morning quarter-backing.'" Lois Rockhill, executive director of Second Harvest Food Bank of East Central Indiana in Anderson, Indiana, says that even though she "already enjoyed a great deal of freedom from board interference in operations," she is "amazed that Policy Governance has provided even greater liberation." Similarly, Jeanette Andrews, executive director of the Association of Registered Nurses of Newfoundland and Labrador, St. John's, claims, "Policy Governance has empowered our staff and unleashed their creativity and innovation. At the same time, we feel it has increased our accountability to our governing Council . . . ; it is a true innovation in governance."

As long as the board's ends are accomplished and the board-stated Executive Limitations policies are not violated, staff action is by definition supported by the board. Using this approach, the board is proactive. Approval of staff documents, which is discussed more fully in Chapter Three, is reactive. Further, approval is a practice in which the board is always "one down"; it can never know quite as much about the details of staff action and planning as the staff itself. Moreover, by being proactive, the board can be more confident that it has dealt with the issues of prudence and ethics. As painstaking as many approval processes might be, they ordinarily focus on the acceptability of specific actions or documents rather than on the underlying values that form the basis for board decisions on those actions and documents. Consequently, after the board approves specific actions or documents, its policy remains unstated. Another payoff, which is more important than it seems, is reducing the board's burden of paperwork. The board can invest the bulk of its leadership in determining expected results rather than in helping staff be staff.

Policies to Limit Staff Action

The task, then, with respect to board oversight of staff means is to create a workable set of policies that constrain or limit executive latitude. In this section, I first review the necessity of saying what seems unnecessary to say, even at the broadest and most obvious level, in a negative or limiting fashion. Second, I argue that broad policies should grow out of the board's, not the staff's, values. Last, I consider the board's worry areas as a natural origin of these Executive Limitations policies.

Starting with Broad, Proscriptive Language

As with all policy control, proper governance lies an arm's length from the action, which can be uncomfortable for some board members. There may be discomfort, but there will not be difficulty, because it is not hard to write policies that safely allow board withdrawal from the prescriptive details of staff means. Doing so does require close attention to the few simple rules proposed here for policy development. For example, as discussed in Chapter Three, boards must start with the largest, most inclusive level before moving on to lesser levels.

Remember that the intent of the Executive Limitations category of policies is to prohibit staff practices that the board regards as imprudent or unethical. This intent will be further defined; however, it is important to note from the outset that preventing imprudent and unethical behavior is the board's *sole* aim in setting these policies. Note further that the wording here is negative. We could as easily say—using positive language—that the board is trying to ensure that behavior is prudent and ethical, for the meaning would be essentially the same. However, because boards face the almost irresistible temptation to slip back into prescribing staff means, they are wise to maintain a proscriptive demeanor throughout, even when it seems pedantic to do so. Establishing the negative approach right from the beginning at the global level helps a board maintain the necessary discipline in subsequent, more complex issues.

It is important to remember that the reason for Executive Limitations policies is to place off-limits any staff means that are unacceptable *even if they work,* not to give the board a backdoor method of prescribing staff means. By backdoor method, I mean requiring certain methods of operating simply by placing out-of-bounds all methods that are not the ones to be imposed. For example, an executive limitation that says, "Don't use any management method other than total quality management" would be such a backdoor prescription, observing the language of the concept while violating the intent. Another might be "Don't fail to have job descriptions and a performance reward system for all staff."

The board's first and broadest staff means policy position is a simple constraint on executive authority: "The chief executive may neither cause nor allow any organizational practice that is imprudent or unethical." This sentiment is so obvious; why should the board have to dignify it as policy? There are two reasons for beginning at such a simple level. First, this position is the source from which all further constraints spring. It is the beginning. As further policies are built on this foundation, it will become increasingly important to maintain simplicity or, at least, clear connections with simplicity. In addition, as we must learn again and again, organizations attain excellence by doing the simple things well.

Second, approaching constraints from the broadest perspective, regardless of how simplistic this appears, ensures that the board can never, through oversight, leave a policy vacuum. Although this type of "backup" policy may be broader (allow more room for interpretation) than the board would like, it makes it impossible for an issue not to be covered by board policy at some level. If the extent of reasonable latitude under a constraint of, say, "imprudence" is greater than the board desires, then it needs to create further policy. But at no time will there be a lack of policy. In organizations where this principle of logical containment is not followed, executives or boards continually find issues not covered by board policy. Consequently, forceful staff action may be bottlenecked or staff members may take an unnecessary risk or miss an opportunity while the policy hole is being plugged.

Conventional, prescriptive policy development on staff means requires that the board foresee all possible actions and create policies targeted at those actions. This approach characteristically generates a great deal of unnecessary committee work. Perfect foresight is, of course, impossible, and such an approach leads to patchwork policymaking. This approach also ensures that the board forever remains a step or two behind staff, for staff operations continually generate new specifics.

Optimal policymaking produces neither a long list of disjointed pieces nor a mere restatement of approved staff documents. It produces a fabric of values that, no matter how thin, effectively blankets all possibilities. Creating this fabric with respect to executive means must begin with the broadest proscription. Without this broad statement there is no all-inclusive point of departure for further, more detailed explicit board constraints.

CEOs know there are limits on staff behavior but ordinarily have to make assumptions about what those limits are. While CEOs develop some skills in mind reading, they often miss the mark, occasionally becoming ex-CEOs in the process. So CEOs in traditional governance can either ask repeatedly for board sanction of this or that with each concrete plan or activity and all changes thereto (thereby drawing the board into the intricacies of staff means) or, just to be cautious, impose more limitations on staff action than the board would have intended. Unnecessary constraint often lowers performance, a consequence the board surely does not want. A constraint lowers performance by raising cost or lowering product quantity; nothing is free, including constraints.

Making Board Policies *the Board's* Policies

For integrity of governance, the board must generate policies from its own values, not parrot them from staff values. A side effect of traditional patchwork policymaking is that staff members are forced repeatedly to ask the board for approvals. When the board approves what the staff has submitted, it buys into the values that underlie the approved material, thereby embracing an unspecified number of undebated and unwritten policies that it had not intended to enunciate. That is, the embedded values—to the extent the board even noticed them—may be acceptable to the board, but the board's own values would not have caused them to be laid down as a requirement. In the governance design presented here, the board adopts only policies for which its values dictate a need. Board policies are not passed to please staff, even the CEO. The CEO is already empowered to make decisions, as long as they are consistent with the board's policies. The CEO is unlikely to request that the board restrict executive latitude further. Because he or she is already empowered, such a request would clearly indicate that the CEO is merely using the board to avoid making a decision.

Despite the churning commotion of implementation, a board's ethics and prudence standards tend to remain constant. When written into policy, the board's standards serve as an anchor for all staff action. There is room for staff to move around when tossed about in stormy weather, but there is not so much room that the staff loses its bearings or strays from what the board holds the organization out to be. Like an anchor, good policymaking is not complicated; its simplicity is why it works. Staff must be given a free hand to do what they know how to do but should not be either stranded or exposed by the board's failure to define boundaries.

Boards can provide this leadership only if they are not subjected to the same short-term pressures that operate on staff. If the board is tossed in the same stormy seas as the staff, it will have difficulty seeing past the next wave, much less to the horizon. The stability of a relaxed governance arena allows the board to ride above the fray fairly unperturbed. The board saves its energy for the more contemplative struggle about underlying values. A board that is more hurried than contemplative has probably fallen into staff-level issues and ceased to govern.

Let's go back to the global Executive Limitation policy. Having prohibited only unethical and imprudent behavior, the board may worry that its brush has been a little too broad. Any staff practice that fits within a reasonable interpretation of this range must be considered acceptable. A *reasonable interpretation* in this usage is akin to the "prudent person" test common in the law. A reasonable interpretation is one that can be demonstrated to the board as one that a reasonable person might make, given the same policy wording. If the majority of board members feel that practices that pass the reasonable interpretation test are still not acceptable, it is their policy that is in error, for it was not written to be as constraining as the board intends. Consequently, the board must further define and narrow the existing policy. As might be surmised, I have never found a board that did not wish to constrict the acceptable latitude further, beyond the global level.

Transforming Worries into Policies

The broadest constraint (prohibiting imprudent and unethical behavior) applies without differentiation to all areas of organizational activity. When creating policy beyond this general proscription, the board will doubtless apply its caution more to some subjects than to others; that is why moving to the next lower level takes the form of addressing specific aspects of the organization. Thus, policy not only drops to a lower level but begins to differentiate among organizational topics.

Subjects differentiated for further constraint could be seen as specific "worry areas." The most common worry areas in which policy is written to further define unethical and imprudent behavior involve financial condition, personnel, treatment of clients, compensation, asset protection, and budgeting. Addressing each of these subjects (1) affords board members the opportunity to agree on what is unacceptable; (2) sends the executive a clear message about what must be avoided, an explicitness that most executives find refreshing, albeit less manipulable; (3) enables the board to streamline future monitoring because it has established criteria against which to measure performance; and (4) enables the board to codify its anxieties and, consequently, to relax.

In conceiving these policies, the board should not focus just on current worries. A board should create Executive Limitations policies that cover the entire range of unpalatable circumstances. What a board would find unpalatable is not a function of recent events, though heightened sensitivity to one or another condition might be. Reactive policymaking takes responsive action at the time of a crisis, but this indicates that the board's leadership is driven by circumstances rather than by ideals. The idea is to design a system for whatever the future holds, not just to fix today's or yesterday's problems. When it is free from immediate concerns, the board uncovers values that have not theretofore surfaced, values that will be relevant to events as yet unforeseen. Still, the safety net effect of the logical containment principle saves the board from having to be perfect in its comprehensiveness.

Listening to worries voiced by board members helps the board establish Executive Limitations policies that are specific to the organization. One member of an Arizona board wondered aloud how disruptive it would be if the CEO were to be unexpectedly lost. The others were persuaded that this was a legitimate board worry. Converting that worry into an Executive Limitations policy resulted in immediate relaxation about the problem. The board adopted a policy requiring that the CEO never have fewer than two senior staff substantially familiar with board and executive officer activities. The majority of the board members felt that this policy provided all the emergency preparedness needed. The policy fit their values, precluded further worry, and was stated in two sentences.

WANT MORE? **2**

It is important that policies represent the values of the board that establishes them. Policies are not chosen from a catalogue, issued by a government agency, enunciated by staff, derived by consultants, or taken from books. Policies are personal to the board.

Typical Executive Limitations Topics

Because Executive Limitations policies spring from a board's sense of prudence and ethics, they are more likely than other categories of policy to resemble the policies of other boards using this model. Prudence and ethics are relatively common across boards, more so than ends. The following list is not specifically recommended, but does illustrate a few common Executive Limitations policy titles.

Vendor relations	A "floor" for their fair treatment
Asset protection	Unacceptable risk and treatment of fixed and liquid assets

Indebtedness	Limits on circumstances in which the executive could allow the organization to incur debt
Financial condition	Conditions of financial jeopardy to be avoided
Budgeting	Characteristics unacceptable in budgeting
Compensation and benefits	Characteristics not tolerated in administering wages and salaries

All Executive Limitations policies are messages from the board to its CEO. They are not messages from the board to staff, for the CEO is the only staff member to whom the board gives directions. (My assumption, for simplicity of explanation, is that there is a CEO, though having a CEO is not required in order to use the Policy Governance model. Without one, however, the board's executive delegation is to multiple points instead of one—a much harder task.) Further, the policies do not give the CEO power to do this or that. They take power or latitude away ("You may not . . . "). The CEO has whatever power the board does not withhold: the board is saying, "Go till we say stop" rather than "Stop till we say go."

To illustrate three Executive Limitations areas, let us look at board concerns with respect to financial management and personnel administration. In traditional governance, the financial concern is usually expressed in two ways: monthly reports on the actual financial condition of the organization and annual inspection of budget. In traditional governance, the personnel concern is manifested in approval of personnel "policies."

Financial Condition Policy

Boards put great stock in monthly or quarterly financial reports. Yet a substantial number of board members do not understand these reports. Even in boards comprising persons competent at analyzing financial statements, it is uncommon for the board to know as a body what it deems unapprovable. Such a situation makes the importance of the approval process questionable and repeatedly invites discussion about financial details. Actually, even if the standards were clear to everyone, approval of a financial report would still be simply an acknowledgment that the data exist, that the preceding month or quarter actually took place.

In converting to Policy Governance, boards are usually unwilling to let the standard rest solely on so broad a proscription as avoiding imprudence. That is because some practices or conditions might not be imprudent in the general sense but are outside what a

WANT MORE?

3

given board is willing to countenance. To adopt a policy that further defines the acceptable boundaries of ongoing financial conditions, the board must discuss and debate those circumstances it finds unacceptable, ones that have a smaller range of reasonable interpretation than simply avoiding imprudence. Financial condition is a wavering phenomenon; most of its squiggles are of no consequence. Some aspects, however, are worrisome or even frightening.

Ordinarily, the top level within this policy requires that the financial condition never result in financial jeopardy or expenditures at odds with any priorities expressed by the board in regard to results or beneficiaries. Beneath this broad proscription, foremost among the several considerations is usually that spending never exceed revenues (or some more finely tuned relationship appropriate to the circumstances). If the organization has the ability to borrow funds or has reserves, the prohibition might limit the amount of indebtedness or withdrawals from reserves, or it might prohibit indebtedness or withdrawal except under specified conditions. Moreover, that an executive has not spent more than has been received might be a rather hollow datum if expenses have been put off and revenues rushed into the reporting period. Further, shifts of wealth hidden within the overall numbers may obscure important financial jeopardies such as a decreasing ratio of current assets to current liabilities. Fine-tuning the policy language can address these points and, at the same time, enhance the board's appreciation of issues of financial jeopardy.

The board must discuss and understand these and related issues in order to create a financial condition policy. In the short run, as much value is derived from the new level of understanding as from the policy itself. A board can use expert counsel in producing such a policy, as long as the expert does not create the policy. The expert should help board members attain a more complete understanding. The understanding supplies data on which board members' values about risk, safety, conservatism, brinkmanship, and so forth can operate. The aggregated and debated board values create the policy. For most boards, the list of unacceptable conditions thus derived is more complete and more systematic than the items it would have routinely inspected using the standard approval method. In addition to being more complete, the subsequent monitoring of financial statements requires far less time than many boards and finance committees traditionally spend.

The board of Second Harvest Food Bank of East Central Indiana expressed the limits of financial management acceptability in its policy "Financial Condition and Activities" (Exhibit 5.1), based on criteria that the board considered to be conditions of jeopardy. The board felt it could accept any reasonable definition of "timely manner" in criterion 3, though another board might need to restrict the range by using words such as "within the discount period or thirty days, whichever is earlier" with respect to the debt portion of the criterion.

Of course, an additional Executive Limitations policy that is specifically focused on investments would be needed by an organization with a sizable endowment. A simple form of this policy, useful even for boards with more modest reserves, might merely instruct that the CEO not invest or hold operating capital in insecure investments, including uninsured checking accounts and bonds of less than AA rating, or in non-interest-bearing accounts, except

**Exhibit 5.1. Second Harvest Food Bank
of East Central Indiana, Anderson, Indiana
Executive Limitations Policy
"Financial Condition and Activities"**

With respect to the actual, ongoing financial condition and activities,
the CEO shall not cause or allow the development of fiscal jeopardy
or a material deviation of actual expenditures from board priorities
established in Ends policies. Further, without limiting the scope of the
foregoing by this enumeration, he or she shall not:

1. Expend more funds in the fiscal year to date than had been actually
   received in the previous fiscal year.

2. Use the board reserve fund.

3. Fail to settle payroll and debts in a timely manner.

4. Allow tax payments or other government-ordered payments or filings
   to be overdue or inaccurately filed.

5. Acquire, encumber or dispose of real property.

6. Fail to aggressively pursue receivables after a reasonable grace period.

---

where necessary to facilitate ease in operational transactions. Having policy control over investments is normally better than having
board members on an investment committee make investment decisions, according to investment adviser John Guy (1992, 1995).

Budget Policy

A financial condition policy establishes the boundaries of the acceptable ongoing financial status—that is, the condition that is often
referred to by the shorthand term *actual* (actual financial position as
opposed to expected position). Boards can go further and establish
which characteristics of financial *intentions* would not be acceptable.
Financial intentions, or financial planning, take the form of a budget and, often, numerous budget adjustments during a year.

Most nonprofit and public boards consider the budget approval
process sacrosanct. To suggest that board budget approval might not

be a necessary element of financial stewardship runs against a firmly held belief, one so firm that some board members contend that no regularly occurring board activity is as important as budget approval. The reason given is that the board must have control over the budget because of the board's fiduciary responsibility. In addition, some say that the budget is the most important policy document the board passes.

Both contentions are somewhat correct. The board must have control over that for which it is accountable. And the budget does, albeit usually implicitly, represent much of what is important to an organization—its aims, its risks, its conservatism. Neither argument, however, dictates *how* a board should control a budget and the budget's policy implications. The starting questions for any board are "What is it about the budget that we wish to control?" and "If we were never to see a budget, what specific conditions would we worry about?"

A budget concerns events that have not yet occurred. It is a plan. Like all plans, it makes suppositions, conveys intentions, and designs process or flow. It is a rather special plan inasmuch as it is denominated in money. Most budgets, moreover, are line-item budgets rather than program budgets or result-package budgets, so from a governance perspective, they illustrate some of the less meaningful aspects of financial planning. For example, the expected cost for a certain outcome is of central interest when a board debates its Ends policies. How much the group insurance component of support staff compensation is expected to be has less intrinsic value.

What is it that the board wishes to control? If the board had to list every possible dollar figure and ratio in the budget, it would give up and go home! Only the most compulsive board members want to know the budget for stationery, much less control it. In fact, there are very few aspects of a budget that responsible boards need to control. Boards want and need control over certain budgetary characteristics to fulfill their legal and ownership responsibilities. Few boards have any idea what these characteristics are.

To fine-tune its fiduciary responsibility, a board must decide which aspects of the budget to control. If the board has been checking these budgetary characteristics all along, jotting them down will take but a few moments. If the board finds it cannot readily do this, there is reason to question what the detailed budget approval process has been seeking. What, in fact, was approved? Is it possible that the admittedly high principle of fiduciary responsibility has been used to justify a process that is less effective than board members thought? In my years of watching budget approvals, I have concluded that this is exactly what goes on.

Enlightenment is nearly inescapable when a board sets out to codify its worries about financial planning. What would worry board members about a budget? What would cause them not to approve a budget? The important features begin to stand out, and the less important ones recede. The vast array of figures becomes less intimidating for nonfinancial people. Financial people are afforded the opportunity to connect their technical expertise with their wisdom. It is on the wisdom level that they meet the other board members; they are no longer strangers divided by a language barrier.

On this journey, the board gets serious about the meaning of fiduciary responsibility. This responsibility does not mean controlling the number of phone lines, but it does mean controlling the ability to pay the bills. It does not mean controlling out-of-state (or out-of-province) travel, but it does mean controlling the conservatism with which revenues are projected. Or are those issues the wrong ones? Debate ensues. Values about risk, brinkmanship, probity, judiciousness, proportions of effort, and so forth begin to receive more attention than more mundane factors. And throughout, the process is disciplined by a progression from big questions to small ones, as it should be in all policy creation.

As with all other Executive Limitations policies, the message is directed to the CEO and is one of limitation, not empowerment. The CEO is already empowered by the "go till we say stop" system of delegation. What he or she needs to know are the limits of power, the acceptable latitude in exercising it. The CEO must ponder these questions: "How liberal may I be in counting chickens prior to their hatching (projecting revenues)? How low may I let the ratio of current assets to current liabilities slip and still maintain intended levels of results? How much may I dip into reserves when pinched for cash? To what extent may I meet cash-flow necessities by shifting money temporarily among special-purpose funds?" These and other value questions arise during financial planning, whether for next month or next year. Agile, empowered management can address these choices within board values far more effectively than a board can.

An additional bonus of the executive limitations approach is the policy's applicability to *all* financial planning—that is, the plans for next month and next year and all the replanning that occurs in the real world of constant change. An organization rarely has one budget for a year. As conditions shift and assumptions fail to pan out, it may have many. Every budget alteration made by the CEO, no matter how many there are, must meet the test of the board's budget policy. CEOs can respect the stability of this type of board leadership. The only fixed aspects of budgets, then, are the policies on which they are based and the certainty that specifics will be endlessly altered.

Most boards that I have helped through this process have had a hard time coming up with more than half a page of budgeting constraints. What message does this send? All those years of painstaking budget approvals by the board, not to mention finance committee time, resulted in half a page of unacceptable conditions. The approval process had always gone far beyond checking for unacceptable conditions. Having no policy that delineated the unacceptable conditions, the board foraged about wherever individual interests and fears directed them. Moreover, this painstaking scrutiny seldom resulted in material change to the submitted budgets and not infrequently overlooked dangerous conditions until it was almost too late.

Boards are accountable for budgets, but not more accountable than they are for what the organization accomplishes in actual results for people per dollar. Budgets are simply not the board's most important job. Directing what good is done for which people and at what cost is its most important job. Missing the mark with respect to ends even by a small percentage costs the world far more than most budgetary errors. Gwendolyn Calvert Baker, executive director for the national board of the YWCA, found that when you deal with financial planning this way, "The program drives your budget; your budget doesn't drive your program."

The board of the State Employees Credit Union created a policy (Exhibit 5.2) to control the credit union's budgeting. Item 1 of the numbered parts implies that one important assessment of a budget is determining that it avoids the financial jeopardies already set forth in the organization's financial condition and activities policy.

Exhibit 5.2. State Employees Credit Union, Lansing, Michigan Executive Limitations Policy "Financial Planning/Budgeting"

Financial planning for any fiscal year or the remaining part of any fiscal year shall not deviate materially from Board's Ends priorities, risk fiscal jeopardy, or fail to be derived from a multi-year plan.

Further, without limiting the scope of the foregoing by this enumeration, the CEO shall not plan in a manner that:

1. Risks the organization incurring those situations or conditions described as unacceptable in the Board's policy Financial Condition and Activities.

2. Fails to include credible projection of revenues and expenses, separation of capital and operational items, liquidity, and disclosure of planning assumptions.

3. Provides less for Board prerogatives during the year than is set forth in the Cost of Governance policy.

As complicated as budgeting is for a complex organization, the governance of budgeting need not be.

Personnel Policy

When nonprofit (as opposed to, say, public school system) boards are asked to show their policies, they produce their personnel "policies." It is ironic that the one document in which the word *policy* is almost always misused is the most frequent example of board policy that comes to mind. The question for boards, beyond the broader proscription against being unethical or imprudent, is "What is it about dealings with personnel that we need to control?" The answer is anything that a reasonable person might consider ethical or prudent but that the board does not want to have happen.

The board of the Orchard Country Day School decided that secretive decision processes, which it found unacceptable, constituted mistreatment that might slip by as acceptable under the broad "don't be unethical" rule. Another board decided the same about any prejudice toward an employee who has filed a grievance. Most boards have decided to omit references to sex, race, and age discrimination in jurisdictions where the law covers these items. Violation of the law is so patently a case of imprudent behavior that no additional words need be wasted. But a board that believes that the law does not go far enough could increase the constraint beyond the law's protection.

The board does have a personnel policy under the Policy Governance model, but it is unlikely to be more than a page long. The previous board personnel policy manual becomes the property of the CEO, to change as he or she sees fit (limited, of course, by policy). Similarly, the board does not decide remuneration of the CEO's subordinates but likely has a policy that limits the CEO's compensation decisions. Exhibits 5.3 and 5.4 display such policies.

**Exhibit 5.3. Tennessee Managed Care, Nashville, Tennessee
Executive Limitations Policy
"Treatment of Staff"**

With respect to treatment of paid and volunteer staff, the chief executive may not cause or allow conditions which are inhumane, unfair, or undignified. Further, without limiting the scope of the foregoing, he or she shall not:

1. Discriminate among employees on other than clearly job-related, individual performance or qualifications.

2. Fail to take reasonable steps to protect staff from unsafe or unhealthy conditions.

3. Withhold from staff a due-process grievance procedure, able to be used without bias.

4. Fail to acquaint staff with their rights under this policy.

**Exhibit 5.4. Mennonite Mutual Aid, Goshen, Indiana
Executive Limitations Policy
"Compensation and Benefits"**

With respect to employment, compensation, and benefits to employees, consultants, contract workers, and volunteers, the CEO shall not cause or allow jeopardy to fiscal integrity or constituency image. Further, without limiting the scope of the foregoing, he or she shall not:

1. Change his or her own compensation and benefits.

2. Promise or imply permanent or guaranteed employment.

3. Establish or change retirement benefits so as to cause unpredictable or inequitable situations, including those that:

   A. Incur unfunded liabilities.

   B. Provide less than a basic level of benefits to all full-time employees.

   C. Allow any employee to lose benefits already accrued from any prior plan.

Range of Executive Limitations Policies

In Executive Limitations policies, different boards have varying things to say, both in volume and in restrictiveness. One board may find another's policies too restrictive or irresponsibly loose. To my knowledge, there is no "right" level or "right" content, but it is critical that in any specific organization, the CEO and board always know precisely what the marching orders are at all times.

Most boards will rely on a number of policy topics, such as the three just discussed, but the full list of policies will differ from board to board within the same type of organization and will certainly differ from one type of organization to another. An international development agency will have policies different from those of a family planning service. Boards of county commissioners, libraries, chambers of commerce, and trade or professional associations will all differ, though they are subject to the same principles.

The policy "Communication and Support to the Board" from the board of Miracle Hill Ministries, Greenville, South Carolina, shown in Exhibit 5.5, illustrates the way many Policy Governance boards choose to ensure that they receive sufficient information and assistance. A board could, of course, establish a secretariat separate from operational staff, but that is rarely necessary.

WANT MORE?

4

Still, a part-time board needs to have considerable informational and infrastructure help to make its task possible. And while it relies on that help, it must never become subservient to or steered by its helpers.

Protection of organizational assets is an issue for all boards that, like all staff means issues, can be addressed through an appropriate Executive Limitations policy. Exhibit 5.6 shows how Yavapai College in Prescott, Arizona, worded its asset protection policy. This policy would work for most organizations; however, the board of a financial institution would likely have another policy to limit the CEO's authority with respect to investments.

Exhibit 5.5. Miracle Hill Ministries, Greenville, South Carolina Executive Limitations Policy
"Communication and Support to the Board"

The President/CEO shall not permit the board to be uninformed or unsupported in its work. Further, without limiting the scope of the foregoing by this enumeration, he or she shall not:

1. Neglect to submit monitoring data required by the board (see policy on Monitoring President/CEO Performance) in a timely, accurate and understandable fashion, directly addressing provisions of board policies being monitored.

2. Let the board be unaware of relevant trends, anticipated adverse media coverage, material external and internal changes, particularly changes in the assumptions upon which any board policy has been previously established.

3. Fail to advise the board if, in the President/CEO's opinion, the board is not in compliance with its own policies on Governance Process and Board/Staff Linkage, particularly in the case of board behavior which is detrimental to the work relationship between the board and the President/CEO.

4. Fail to marshal for the board as many staff and external points of view, issues and options as needed for fully informed board choices.

5. Present information in unnecessarily complex or lengthy form or in a form that fails to differentiate among information of three types: monitoring, decision preparation, and incidental.

6. Fail to provide a mechanism for official board, officer or committee communications.

7. Fail to deal with the board as a whole except when (a) fulfilling individual requests for information or (b) responding to officers or committees duly charged by the board.

8. Fail to report in a timely manner an actual or anticipated noncompliance with any policy of the board.

9. Fail to supply for the consent agenda all items delegated to the President/CEO yet required by law or contract to be board-approved, along with the monitoring assurance pertaining thereto.

**Exhibit 5.6. Yavapai College, Prescott, Arizona
Executive Limitations Policy
"Asset Protection"**

The President shall not allow corporate assets to be unprotected, inadequately maintained, or unnecessarily risked.

Without limiting the scope of the foregoing by this enumeration, the President shall not:

1. Fail to insure against fire, theft and casualty losses to the full extent of current replacement value and against liability losses incurred by the College itself, its Board members, and its employees, consultants and agents in an amount usually carried by comparable organizations.

2. Allow unbonded personnel access to material amounts of funds.

3. Subject the College plant and equipment to improper wear and tear or insufficient maintenance.

4. Unnecessarily or willfully expose the College, its Board or staff to claims of liability.

5. Fail to protect intellectual property, information and files from loss or significant damage or willfully violate the intellectual property rights of others.

6. Receive, process or disburse funds under controls which are insufficient to meet the Board-approved auditor's standards.

7. Invest or hold operating capital in unsecured instruments, including uninsured checking or saving accounts or bonds having less than an AA rating at any time, or in non-interest-bearing accounts except when necessary to facilitate ease in operational transactions.

8. Endanger the College's public image or credibility, particularly in ways that would hinder the accomplishment of its Ends.

In practice, most boards get by with fewer than ten Executive Limitations policies. These tend to average less than a page in length. But the vessel is adjustable, allowing as much restriction or freedom as a board feels is right. Boards must realize, however, that no matter how narrow a policy is intended to be, there is still room for interpretation. The CEO's job is largely one of making those interpretations as he or she delegates tasks to others. Unless the board itself wishes to do the organization's work, this will always be the case. Interpretation is so integral to the nature of management that one could describe a manager's job as translation from one level of abstraction to another.

Consequently, it is never legitimate to complain that board policy with respect to the CEO and staff is fuzzy, open to interpretation, or general. Board debate must turn on the *degree* of fuzziness, interpretive range, and generality. A board member who feels that certain policy language allows too great a range of interpretation is obligated to argue for language that narrows the range. The member only detracts from his or her good argument if he or she complains, in effect, that policy should not allow any range. It is in studious management of the generalities that a board enhances both its contributions and those of staff.

Board and staff need as much freedom as possible to perform. The board is responsible for creating the future, not minding the shop. Chait and Taylor (1989) bemoaned the fact that so much of boards' time is "frittered away on operations" (p. 45), mired in minutiae, and thus unavailable for policy and strategy. "Rather than do more, boards would be better advised to demand more" (p. 52). The staff needs freedom from the board's friendly intrusions to do its work. The board cheats the organization's potential achievement if it constrains too much; it risks cheating standards of acceptable conduct if it constrains too little. Proactively setting relatively few limits for the CEO increases the freedom of both the board and the CEO (Barth, 1992).

Summary of Delegation with Ends and Executive Limitations

Figure 5.1 illustrates how board expectations need to be established for an organization. I will assume that there is a CEO, but, in any event, the board's instructions are to the operating organization. The principle of decreasing ranges of delegated authority (Chapter Three), along with the positive nature of ends versus the negative nature of executive limitations (Chapters Four and Five), when combined, produce a set of directives.

Figure 5.1. Policy Control of Target and Barriers

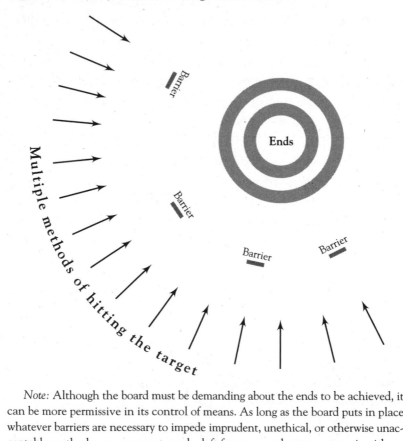

Note: Although the board must be demanding about the ends to be achieved, it can be more permissive in its control of means. As long as the board puts in place whatever barriers are necessary to impede imprudent, unethical, or otherwise unacceptable methods, management can be left free to use whatever means it wishes.

In Figure 5.1, the ends are depicted as an archery target toward which the CEO, using broad prerogatives, aims in any way that he or she sees fit. Of course, the CEO's prerogatives are not unlimited; the barriers that represent Executive Limitations policies block various paths toward the ends. One effect of this type of delegation is that both board and CEO are very clear about what the target is and what the barriers are. Another effect is that vast areas of CEO prerogatives remain open to staff creativity and innovation. The board does not prescribe executive means. If it did, those prescriptions would show up in this drawing as windows through which the CEO must shoot, thereby shutting off many possible and potentially pioneering methods.

The concepts of ends and executive limitations are displayed in another way in Figure 5.2. The many letters represent uncountable staff activities, decisions, situations, circumstances, and methods—in short, all the non-ends, operational aspects of the organization. The board does not delve into these aspects as individuals, committees, or the full board. The board needs to control non-ends aspects, of course, but the control takes the form of providing the sides and spout of a funnel. The sides stand for the limits of acceptability, beyond which the organization would exceed its authority. The spout symbolizes the required effect of all those uncountable staff means: producing the right results for the right people at the right cost—that is, ends.

Many persons find one or the other of these visualizations helpful for keeping the concepts in mind. These sketches can be altered to demonstrate the adjustable size of board prescriptions and proscriptions. In Figure 5.1, the central ring of the target can be larger or smaller, representing more broadly or more narrowly defined ends; each barrier can be wider or narrower, representing more or less blocking of executive prerogatives. In Figure 5.2, the sides can be closer together or farther apart, signifying a narrower or wider range of acceptability; the spout can be more or less restricted, signifying more or less tightly defined ends.

Figure 5.2. Policy Control of Activities and Outputs

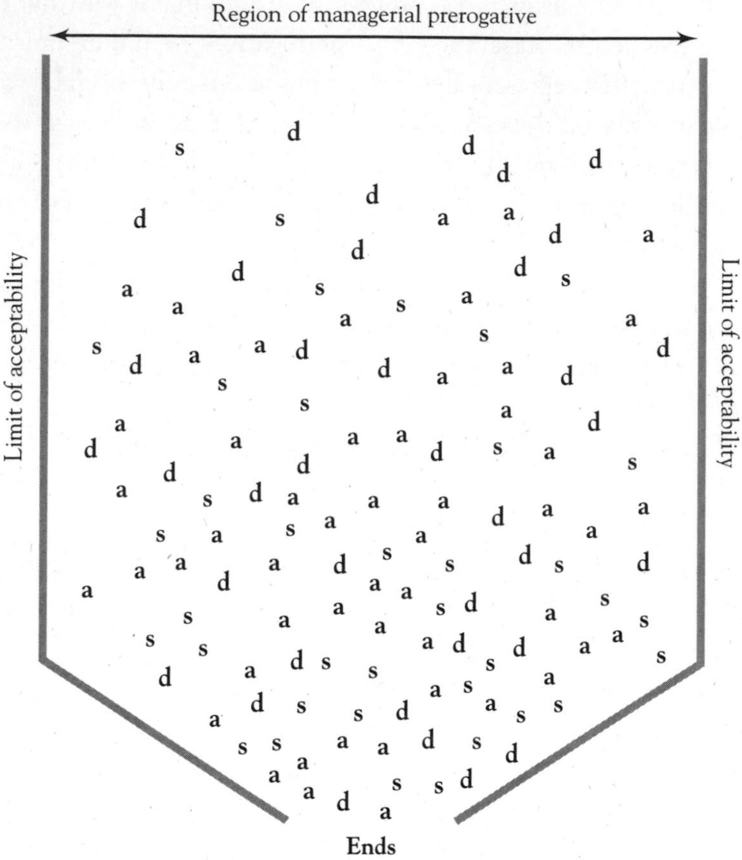

Note: The board is freed from concern or involvement in the situations (s), activities (a), and decisions (d) of management as long as it is clear about the limits of acceptability and the ends to be achieved. Failing to produce the prescribed ends or acting outside the limits of acceptability invoke a board response, but actions consonant with board criteria do not.

Executive Limitations Policies on the Policy Circle

Let me again remind you of the policy circle shown in Figure 3.3. Figure 5.3 illustrates how a given board might have filled in the outer levels of the quadrant depicting staff means. Each board, of course, will choose a different level of detail at which to stop,

Figure 5.3. Executive Limitations Policies Completed

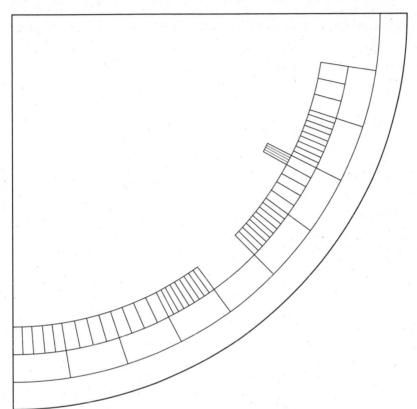

Note: The completed Executive Limitations policies cover all possible board worries about management means because they begin at the broadest level (which covers everything) and extend to the desired level of specificity. At this point, the board feels it is safe to say that the CEO is authorized to select any management means that are not prohibited by a reasonable interpretation of these policies.

beyond which the CEO is allowed to make any reasonable inter-pretation. The number of policies and their depth in Figure 5.3 are not intended to portray the right depth or number of policies but are only one example among many possibilities. Moreover, whatever the depth, number, and content of board policies, the board retains the right to change them whenever its wisdom so dictates.

Next Chapter

We have examined the brevity and great leverage of Executive Limitations policies, which are established to ensure that staff action is neither imprudent nor unethical. Delegation that is so simple yet so powerful, however, assumes a certain kind of relationship between governance and management. In Chapter Six, I turn my attention to the relationship between the board and its CEO.

WANT MORE?

Further Reading

1. Carver, J. "Why Should the Board Use Negative Wording About the Staff's Means?" *Board Leadership*, 2002n, no. 61.

2. Carver, J. "Dealing with the Board's First-Order and Second-Order Worries: Borrowing Trouble Effectively." *Board Leadership*, 2003f, no. 66.

   Oliver, C. "The Board and Risk." *The Bottom Line, the Independent Voice for Canada's Accounting and Financial Professionals*, Oct. 2002a.

   Carver, J. "Free Your Board and Staff Through Executive Limitations." *Board Leadership*, 1992f, no. 4. Reprinted in J. Carver, *John Carver on Board Leadership*. San Francisco: Jossey-Bass, 2002.

   Carver, J. "Running Afoul of Governance." *Board Leadership*, 1993p, no. 7. Reprinted in J. Carver, *John Carver on Board Leadership*. San Francisco: Jossey-Bass, 2002.

3. Carver, J. "Redefining the Board's Role in Fiscal Planning." *Nonprofit Management and Leadership*, 1991c, 2(2), 177–192. Reprinted in J. Carver, *John Carver on Board Leadership*. San Francisco: Jossey-Bass, 2002.

   Carver, J. *Three Steps to Fiduciary Responsibility*. The CarverGuide Series on Effective Board Governance, no. 3. San Francisco: Jossey-Bass, 1996t.

Carver, J., and Oliver, C. "Financial Oversight Reform—The Missing Link." *Chartered Financial Analyst* (Institute of Chartered Financial Analysts of India), Dec. 2002e, 8(12), 31–33.

Oliver, C. "Getting Off Lightly." *The Bottom Line, the Independent Voice of Canada's Accounting and Financial Professionals*, May 2002c, *18*(6), 11.

Carver, J. "Crafting Policy to Guide Your Organization's Budget." *Board Leadership*, 1993b, no. 6. Reprinted in J. Carver, *John Carver on Board Leadership*. San Francisco: Jossey-Bass, 2002.

Carver, J. "Crafting Policy to Safeguard Your Organization's Actual Fiscal Condition." *Board Leadership*, 1993c, no. 6. Reprinted in J. Carver, *John Carver on Board Leadership*. San Francisco: Jossey-Bass, 2002.

Carver, J. "Fiduciary Responsibility." *Board Leadership*, 1993f, no. 6. Reprinted in J. Carver, *John Carver on Board Leadership*. San Francisco: Jossey-Bass, 2002.

Carver, J. "Making Informed Fiscal Policy." *Board Leadership*, 1993j, no. 6. Reprinted in J. Carver, *John Carver on Board Leadership*. San Francisco: Jossey-Bass, 2002.

4. Carver, J. "Does Your Board Need Its Own Dedicated Support Staff?" *Nonprofit World*, Mar.–Apr. 2000a, *18*(2), 6–7.

Carver, J. "CEOs! Guiding Your Board Toward Better Governance." *Board Leadership*, 1997e, no. 29. Reprinted in J. Carver, *John Carver on Board Leadership*. San Francisco: Jossey-Bass, 2002.

Strong Boards Need Strong Executives
The Board-Executive Relationship

No single relationship in the organization is as important as that between the board and its CEO. That relationship, well conceived, can set the stage for effective governance and management. However, probably no single relationship is as easily misconstrued or has such dire potential consequences.

It is often said that the most important task of a board is the choice of a CEO. Although the choice is surely important, establishing an effective relationship is just as important. Many good CEOs have been rendered ineffective as a result of a poor relationship with their board. Many poor CEOs have been allowed to remain because of an inadequately designed relationship with their board. The relationship I mean is not the interpersonal, social sort but the structured affiliation of related jobs.

To describe an effective relationship, we must attend to the board's job, the CEO's job, and the connection between them. In this chapter, the focus is on the CEO's job and the link between board and CEO. Board policies on empowerment of staff and the nature of staff accountability in Policy Governance constitute a category called *Board-Management Delegation*. In this chapter, I begin with a definition of the CEO role and the nature of the accountability and empowerment it implies. Then I deal with the kind of information the board needs for responsible oversight of the CEO and what this has to do with the CEO's performance evaluation. I end by discussing how to keep the roles of board and CEO separate and complementary.

Defining a CEO

Except for a few unique functions of the board, almost all organizational activities are performed by staff. Even in relatively small organizations, the sheer volume of staff activity would overwhelm a part-time board. Furthermore, the myriad interrelationships among separate functions in an organization frequently awe even a full-time staff.

Boards ordinarily choose to coordinate these intricate parts by employing a CEO to put all the pieces in place. More than a mere coordinator, a CEO is accountable for making all the parts come together in an acceptable whole. While it is possible for a board to link to executive action without a CEO, it makes the job of delegation—both giving instructions and tracing accountability—far more complicated. With a CEO, the board is able to govern by dealing conceptually only with the whole and officially only with the CEO. As the board's bridge to the staff, the CEO has a role more distinct than merely lead staff member. A powerfully designed CEO position is a key to board excellence. It enables a board to avoid the intricacies and short-term focus of staff management and to work exclusively on the holistic, long-term focus of governance.

WANT MORE?

1

Many nonprofit and public organizations have chronic problems with the CEO function, either because it is overpowered or because it is underpowered. In either event, many of the benefits of having a CEO can be lost, as well as much of the board's opportunity for excellence. If a strong CEO causes a board to be weak or if a strong board causes a CEO to be weak, the role has been ill designed. Many boards unwittingly invite their CEOs to be either manipulators or Milquetoasts.

The policy of the Garden City Community College board titled "Delegation to the President" (Exhibit 6.1) expresses the method in which power is passed. (This is not their global policy in this category. Their global policy, like many others', simply states that the single official link between board and staff is the chief executive, titled *president*.) Pay particular attention to point 6, wherein the board as a body has limited the rights of its own members as individuals to commandeer resources through seemingly benign requests for information. This provision is clearly consistent with a strict interpretation of the "one voice" philosophy—that is, that boards must speak as one, not as individual members.

WANT MORE?

2

Situating the CEO Role Within the Organization

Understanding how to design an effective CEO function requires us first to look beyond the distraction of titles and, second, to grasp the peculiar organizational phenomenon of cumulative responsibility.

The traditions of various pursuits bring with them preferred CEO titles, among them *superintendent, executive vice president, city manager, administrator, headmaster, county executive, president, secretary general*, and *executive director*. In recent years, there has been a trend among some nonprofit agencies to switch from *executive director* to *president*. The reasons given are "to be more businesslike" or "to adopt the corporate model." When this name change occurs without a change in functions, only the cosmetics have been affected. The title itself has no managerial relevance; the function is what is important. *Chief executive officer*, sometimes used as a title, is used here to refer to the CEO function, regardless of job title.

The CEO function can be vested either in the top staff person or in the board chair, although the latter option is "rife with ambiguity and complexity" (Lorsch and MacIver, 1989, p. 94). There is a long corporate tradition of having one person both chair the board and be CEO, though this tradition has reversed in the United Kingdom. Historically, in business corporations, however, entrepreneurs gathered boards around them as their enterprises grew. Even large,

Exhibit 6.1. Garden City Community College, Garden City, Kansas Board-Management Delegation Policy "Delegation to the President"

All board authority delegated to staff is delegated through the president so that all authority and accountability of staff—as far as the board is concerned—is considered to be the authority and accountability of the president.

1. The board will direct the president to achieve certain results for certain recipients, at a certain cost through the establishment of Ends policies. The board will limit the latitude the president may exercise in practices, methods, conduct, and other "means" through the establishment of Executive Limitations policies.

2. As long as the president uses any reasonable interpretation of the board's Ends and Executive Limitations policies, the president is authorized to establish all further policies, make all decisions, take all actions, establish all practices, and develop all activities.

3. The board may change its Ends and Executive Limitations policies, thereby shifting the boundary between board and president domains. By doing so, the board changes the latitude given to the president. So long as any particular delegation is in place, the board members will respect and support the president's choices.

4. Only decisions of the board acting as a body are binding upon the president.

5. Decisions or instructions of individual board members, officers, or committees are not binding on the president except in rare circumstances when the board has specifically authorized such exercise of authority.

6. In the case of board members or committees requesting information or assistance without board authorization, the president can refuse such requests that require—in the president's judgment—a material amount of staff time or funds or are disruptive.

publicly held corporations often operate with a friendly circle cen-
tering on the chair-CEO combination. Standard practice or not,
some have long recognized the conflict of interest this method pre-

WANT MORE?

3

sents (Geneen, 1984). More recently, a number of corporate governance writers have pointed out the vast difference
between the roles and the difficulty of one person fulfilling
them both simultaneously. A more extensive argument for separate
roles in Policy Governance terms is made in my book (coauthored
with Caroline Oliver) *Corporate Boards That Create Value*.

Clearly, nonprofit and public organizations are best served when
they vest the chair function and the CEO function in separate persons. The CEO holds final authority "outside of the broad powers
held by the board. To invest this final authority in the hands of a
part-time board member would seem inappropriate" (Fram, 1986).
Regardless of the board's choice in positioning the CEO function,
it is necessary for managerial integrity that a board clearly use one
method or the other and not wander back and forth, with the top
staff person sometimes reporting to the board chair and sometimes
not. If the top paid executive must get the approval of the board
chair or is seen as being supervised by the board chair, then the
board chair is the de facto CEO.

Some boards state in their bylaws that the board chairperson is
CEO yet operate as if the paid executive performs that role. On the
other hand, some boards clearly state that their paid executive is
CEO but allow the board chairperson to play that role as he or she
sees fit. Such caprice in a critical relationship is damaging to an
effective board-staff linkage. Still other boards hold the executive
responsible to the board treasurer, the chairperson, and several committees (most notably, the executive committee). Such a situation
gravely confounds the relationship. A board-CEO relationship is
weakened when it is allowed to become an officers/committees/
board–CEO relationship.

For board and CEO peace of mind, it is very important to define
the board and CEO functions as simply as possible. The CEO's only

accountability should be to the board as a body, not to officers of the board nor to board committees. This prescription does not prevent interaction between the CEO and committees or individuals as long as the CEO is instructed and judged only by the board as a whole. Board process and structure must be in harmony with that wholeness.

Being held accountable to the full board for organizational performance is a distinct characteristic of the CEO function. That accountability is an accumulation of responsibilities in the staff. Upward accumulation of responsibility is a key phenomenon in describing the executive's job, the board's job, and the relationship between board and non-CEO staff.

Accountability as Cumulative Responsibility

Each individual is responsible for his or her own behavior. When individuals come together in organizations, they are still fully responsible for their own behavior. Supervisors, too, are responsible for their own personal contributions and compliance, but they are also responsible for the behavior of their subordinates. Supervisors have, then, two kinds of responsibility: direct or personal responsibility, similar to that of any other individual, and cumulative responsibility, which accrues upward from the bottom of the organization.

In designing hierarchical relationships, jobs, and performance evaluation, boards must treat these two types of responsibility in different ways. I assign the word *accountability* to the responsibility that accumulates upward. Therefore, each manager is *responsible* for his or her own job contributions and compliance and is also *accountable* for the total contributions and compliance of his or her team, however extensive that team might be. (These words are open to other definitions, of course, but this distinction will be the one used in this text and typically in other Policy Governance writings.) The accountability burden increases as one goes up the organizational ladder, though responsibility may not. In other words, the personal job responsibility of the CEO may not be more difficult than that of the manager of word processing, but the CEO is encumbered with far more accountability.

From the board's point of view, the important lesson is that *the board's relationship with the CEO be formed by the accountability of the CEO position, not its responsibility.* In other words, the board need not be concerned with what job responsibilities fall to the CEO. The board's concern is confined to what it holds the CEO accountable for.

By the definitions just given, the CEO is accountable for no less than the entire product and behavior of the organization. That means everything except the board and its functions. And the CEO is accountable to the board as a body. This seems straightforward enough, but consider the implications:

The board has only one employee. For most official purposes, the board has only one employee, the CEO. The CEO has all the rest. If something goes wrong in the organization (for example, a failure in producing ends or a violation of the board's executive limitations), there is only one person at whom the board can point. The CEO is no less accountable to the board for the actions of the most distantly removed staff member than for his or her own direct actions. Everything is part of the CEO's accountability package. The board needs no official connection with staff members except at the CEO's behest.

The CEO's work is immaterial. The CEO is accountable for seeing that the entire enterprise meets board expectations. His or her personal work is only a single component of that performance. The
WANT MORE? working job description of a CEO (what he or she actually contributes personally) is not for the board to decide and certainly not for the board to use in evaluating CEO performance. The skills sought in a CEO are those associated not with responsibility but with accountability. For example, grant writing, plant maintenance, and accounting are not the point. Executive

job design, leadership, strategic organization, and setting a climate of creative achievement are.

Board members and the CEO are colleagues. The relationship between the CEO and any individual board member is collegial, not hierarchical. Because the CEO is accountable only to the full board and because no board member has individual authority, the CEO and board members are equals. The relationship between the CEO and the board chairperson should be one of supportive peers as well. They are not hierarchically related, because to be so would shift the CEO function to the chairperson.

The job of the CEO is to work whatever magic it takes to ensure an acceptable amount, type, and targeting of benefits in prudent and ethical ways. To shoulder this much accountability, a strong CEO is needed. Some boards are reluctant to empower the CEO to this extent. Their reasons vary from being unwilling to let go of the strings on decision making to being unwilling to burden CEO and staff with such momentous decisions. But if the board delegates less authority, it must constantly forsake strategic leadership to make tactical decisions.

Leadership is being cheated in either case. As for burdening staff, in most cases, staff members work no more in making decisions than they already do in *almost* making decisions—for example, in writing recommendations or providing support to board committees. Staff members will not perceive the right to make choices as a weight but as an energizing boost. Jane H. Adams, executive director of the California Park & Recreation Society, Sacramento, states that the model "has empowered staff tremendously" and results in "a greater sense of accountability for staff as well."

Boards would do well to discard the traditional distinction of "day-to-day management" in describing the CEO's purview. Does this imply that the board's job is "month-to-month"? If so, both the board and CEO are working dangerously close to their noses. The board should be looking years ahead, and the CEO should usually look ahead almost as far, except perhaps in quite small organizations. Day-to-day management is not the CEO's task; even when meant symbolically, this description misleads more than helps.

The CEO role is sufficiently different from that of both board and staff that the common two-role relationship between governance and operations (board-staff) would be better conceived as a three-role phenomenon (board-CEO-staff). In a formal sense, the CEO role insulates the staff from the board and the board from the staff. However, the insulation does not rigidly prohibit contact between board and staff members. On the contrary, those very human connections are never problematic if the formal roles are clear. The rule is merely that the board can never direct or judge staff performance, though it may impose as many requirements on its CEO as it deems fitting.

Because of its summative nature, a list of CEO job contributions (not job activities) is the simplest in an organization: the CEO is accountable to the board of directors for (1) achieving Ends policies and (2) not violating Executive Limitations policies.

This is the long and the short of the job. The CEO neither takes over board prerogatives nor stands meekly aside while the board does staff work. The CEO position is as invested in having a strong board as in having a free hand. It is a function that, being strong, can afford to bid both board and staff to grow.

This highly focused CEO job description is true only when the board does its job. The board's desires must be clear to both board members and the CEO. As many CEOs have discovered, if you do not know what the board wants, it may be impossible to please it. The reverse is also true. Boards that lack standards and systematic monitoring are not displeased when they should be.

Monitoring Executive Performance

With the board operating at arm's length from operations and delegating so much authority to the CEO, how can it know that its directives are being followed? Boards receive much information, only some of which is for monitoring purposes. Boards commonly fail to distinguish among classes of information and, thus, cloud the question of monitoring. It is helpful to separate information into three types.

Types of Information

Decision information. Decision information is information the board receives to aid it in making decisions—for example, to select a budget policy from among alternative positions, to decide on an approach to use for the governing process itself, or to establish the qualities it desires in a new CEO. This type of information is used solely to make board decisions. It is not judgmental. It is prospective in that it looks to the future.

Monitoring information. Monitoring information is used to gauge whether previous board directions found in Ends and Executive Limitations policies have been satisfied. It is judgmental. It is retrospective in that it always looks to the past. Good monitoring information is a systematic survey of performance against criteria. In being aimed at specific criteria, it is more like a rifle shot than a shotgun blast. It does not demand "Tell us everything" but requests "Tell us this, this, and that."

Incidental information. Information that is used neither to make decisions nor to monitor falls into the incidental information category because it has no governance utility. It often masquerades as monitoring information. Thus, boards may hear staff reports, read lengthy documents on activities, or even scrutinize performance, but lack criteria against which to judge the information received. Such conscientious activity creates the illusion that the board is effectively monitoring performance. Even the revered monthly or quarterly financial report stands indicted here. To the extent that the criteria against which the financial report is judged are not obvious, it yields incidental rather than monitoring information. Boards do, indeed, get smarter in a scattered kind of way, but they wallow in information rather than use it to monitor. I have found that the majority of information received by boards is of this type.

A common board member folly is to want to "know everything that is going on." Boards can be dragged through tiring information because a few members think it is their duty and therefore subject the entire board to their specific list of operational interests. Although this thirst can never be quenched, their boards consequently do review and dabble in much staff activity. Ironically, spending so much time in this impossible attempt to learn all that is going on interferes with really knowing how their organizations are doing. First, boards that are awash in staff material have little time to create the policies at the outset that will serve as criteria. Second, even if boards had such policies, the endless stream of data is largely immaterial to a focused, rigorous comparison of performance against criteria. Flailing in irrelevant information can be raised to an art form by committee reports and show-and-tell agendas.

WANT MORE?

5

But all this is not to say there is something wrong with incidental information. In itself, it is harmless and can even help board members get a personal feel for the organization. The grave trap in incidental information is that the board may delude itself that the need to do rigorous monitoring has thus been satisfied.

Criteria for Monitoring

Monitoring is often used to mean "following along" or "watching." We might monitor the room temperature, enemy troop movements, or the status of proposed legislation. Those are legitimate uses of the word. But in Policy Governance, *monitoring* can never mean "following along," however attentively. In Policy Governance, the word *monitoring* always means a comparison of reality to policy. In other words, if there is no stated expectation, there can be no monitoring. Hence, as an example, the typical board's review of financial statements does not rise to the level of Policy Governance monitoring because data are not being compared to previously stated board expectations.

Good monitoring is necessary if a board is to relax about the present and get on with the future. Preestablished criteria are required for good monitoring. Setting criteria ahead of time is so critical to good governance that I will dwell for a moment on why criteria are necessary and then on how setting criteria in a two-step process prior to monitoring taps board wisdom more effectively than simply letting criteria emerge while reviewing a document.

First, preestablished criteria save board time. Each act of judging will take more people and more time if the criteria are unclear. Boards can rush through the process with little real inspection, of course, but if rubber-stamping is to be avoided, each judging action will consume material board time. Very little more time is needed to establish the range of acceptability, after which assessing performance or plans is an easy task of comparison with these preestablished criteria. The real work is at the front end; savings accrue thereafter. The board avoids the continuing start-from-scratch approval struggle that exists when criteria are unstated.

Second, criteria save staff time. Time is lost when staff proposals are based on considerations later found to be unacceptable. In many cases, boards so routinely approve staff plans and reports that rejection is not a realistic worry. Even under such rubber-stamp conditions, staff time is often spent dressing up the report or proposal to ensure that the ritual is smooth. A great deal of ingratiating manipulation of boards has been known to occur during this process.

Third, board judgment of managerial performance is simply not fair without criteria. Many CEOs have received unearned harsh judgment from boards whose values became clear only after executive initiative had been taken. Such boards find it easier and safer to shoot down staff action than to struggle with and declare their own values at the outset.

Fourth, a board does a far more creditable job of judging staff performance if it does so in two distinct steps rather than one. In the common one-step approach, a board judges without preestablished criteria; individual board members use idiosyncratic criteria and share their yes-or-no responses; and totaling all the yes-or-no responses yields an official board action. Such a vote records the summary of individual judgments against individual criteria. From such a process, it is tricky to infer the board's aggregate values. Group judgment on the exact criteria cannot be gleaned from mere recounting of comments and arguments because the criteria so inferred merely constitute a laundry list of individual expectations. In other words, after an approval, no one knows what the unstated, relevant criteria were!

A two-step process leads to a far better product. Board members debate and decide at the outset the group values that will be codified in Ends and Executive Limitations policies. The only judgment that takes place in monitoring is whether actual performance matches a reasonable interpretation of the preestablished criteria. Each board judgment is no longer a new ball game but a continuation of a clarifying process in which board values are increasingly well represented in policy language. Monitoring is simpler because the value issues have already been resolved in the creation of the policy. Comparing monitoring information against the policy can then be made into a rather mechanical, routinized process. With monitoring thus systematized, the board can be more certain that monitoring is diligent, even without squeaky wheels or crises to compel its attention. Such systematic assurance that things are not going awry is less likely to be incomplete due to board fatigue or distraction, is more fair to all concerned, is more likely to engage the board in an appropriate level of thinking, and, conversely, is far less likely to engage board members in trivia.

Incorporating the Reasonable Interpretation Rule

Monitoring, then, is the systematic, data-based determination by the board that organizational performance complies with a reasonable interpretation of prestated board expectations. Those expectations are expressed in the board's Ends and Executive Limitations policies. In this text, I will not dignify the scattered, non-criteria-based process of conventional board operation with the term *monitoring*, so when I use the word, the reader can be sure

I mean the rigorous, data-based, policy-driven process of Policy Governance.

Monitoring, then, has two distinct components. First, the CEO must demonstrate to the board that he or she has used a reasonable interpretation of the board's policies. Second, the CEO must provide evidence that the interpretation has been fulfilled. So the justification of the CEO's interpretation is an essential component of monitoring. The monitoring information can be found by the board to be unsatisfactory based either on an interpretation the reasonableness of which is not demonstrated or on data about performance that are not convincing.

WANT MORE?

6

Incidentally, it is recommended that the board make its decision about the reasonableness of the CEO's interpretations at the time of monitoring rather than earlier. Although this may seem counterintuitive, there are a number of reasons for a board to avoid what would amount to a prior approval of interpretations. The rationale is spelled out in *Reinventing Your Board* (Carver and Carver, 1997c; revised edition scheduled for 2006), which includes a more step-by-step explanation of this and other implementation practicalities.

Although the specifics of monitoring reports are dealt with more extensively in *Reinventing Your Board*, the format of reporting simply follows the logic. In a clear sequence and as briefly as possible, the CEO (1) repeats the words of the relevant subsection of board policy (for board members' convenience), (2) gives the board his or her interpretation along with the reason the board should find it reasonable, then (3) cites data to verify that the interpretation has been fulfilled. Omitting any one of these components makes it difficult or impossible for board members to know whether a reasonable interpretation of board expectations has been met. Obviously, this kind of criterion-specific, data-based reporting is vastly different from the typical submission of standardized reports.

Improper monitoring can prove the downfall of a board's commitment to use Policy Governance correctly. But done according to the rules laid down here, it yields fairness, rigor, and board freedom from the rambling attempts typically used to ensure executive accountability. "If some traditional boards think Policy Governance does not provide staff accountability, just speak with our executive director about the monitoring reports that must be submitted to the board," invited the board president of the North Bay (Ontario) and District Association for Community Living, Robert Fetterly. The pointedness of monitoring in Policy Governance reveals most traditional board monitoring as little more than wandering around in the presence of data or personal assurances.

Methods of Monitoring

If the board adopts the discipline of monitoring only what it has already addressed in policy, its anxiety will drive it to develop all the policies needed. "If you haven't said how it ought to be, don't ask how it is" describes the principle that forces a board to monitor instead of meander. The board can then monitor each policy however frequently it desires by one or more of three methods:

1. *Executive report*. The CEO makes available a report that directly addresses the policy being monitored. Unlike the common type of staff report, it is geared to a specific board policy. Monitoring of the financial condition of an organization, for example, would not manifest as the standard balance sheet and income statement. It would, instead, go point by point through the unacceptable actions and circumstances spelled out in the board's policy on financial condition. Because the report relates so directly to policy language, no additional explanation is needed. Staff compliance or violation should be evident at a glance. It is the CEO's responsibility to produce data that enable a majority of the board to feel reasonably assured of adequate performance.

2. *External audit*. The board selects an external resource to measure staff compliance with respect to a specific policy. It is important that the external party assess performance against the CEO's interpretation of the board's policy. If the external person judges

against his or her own standards, the resulting assessment confounds monitoring and decision information. Financial auditors are the most common example of this method, but external audits need not be confined to financial issues.

3. *Direct inspection.* The board assigns one or more board members to check compliance with a specific policy. Infrequently, the board as a whole might perform this inspection. Direct inspection might require an on-site visit or inspection of a staff document. This monitoring method should not be used unless the board role and discipline are in excellent order, lest it deteriorate into meddling. Board members involved have no authority to direct anyone, nor may they make judgments on any basis but the literal policy.

The "Monitoring Executive Director Performance" policy shown in Exhibit 6.2 was produced by the board of Missions Resource Network, headquartered in Bedford, Texas, to ensure systematic assessment of the organization's performance. Note that the board chose to monitor their Financial Condition and Activities policy with two separate methods and frequencies. The board had not completed its Ends category of policies when this policy was created, so point 4 in their policy shows monitoring scheduled only for Executive Limitations policies. Ends policies will be added to this list as they develop.

The CEO's Evaluation

The CEO's only job is to make everything come out right! That translates into achieving the board's Ends policies and not violating its Executive Limitations policies. This is exactly what the board expects of the organization as a total entity. Organization performance and CEO performance are the same. Evaluation of one is evaluation of the other. Accountability can be gravely damaged when the two are viewed differently.

Monitoring organizational and executive performance is a continual process. The board may wish to punctuate this continuity

Exhibit 6.2. Missions Resource Network, Bedford, Texas Board-Management Delegation Policy "Monitoring Executive Director Performance"

Systematic and rigorous monitoring of Executive Director job performance will be solely against the only expected Executive Director job outputs: organizational accomplishment of board policies on Ends and organizational operation within the boundaries established in board policies on Executive Limitations.

Accordingly:

1. Monitoring is simply to determine the degree to which board policies are being met. Information that does not do this will not be considered to be monitoring information.

2. The board will acquire monitoring data by one or more of three methods:

   A. by internal report, in which the Executive Director discloses compliance information, along with his or her justification for the reasonableness of interpretation;

   B. by external report, in which an external, disinterested third party selected by the board assesses compliance with board policies, augmented with the Executive Director's justification for the reasonableness of his or her interpretation; and

   C. by direct board inspection, in which a designated member or members of the board assess compliance with policy, with access to the Executive Director's justification for the reasonableness of his or her interpretation.

3. In every case, the standard for compliance shall be *any reasonable interpretation* by the Executive Director of the board policy being monitored. The board is the final arbiter of reasonableness, but will always judge with a "reasonable person" test rather than with interpretations favored by board members or by the board as a whole.

4. All policies that instruct the Executive Director will be monitored at a frequency and by a method chosen by the board. The board can monitor any policy at any time by any method, but will ordinarily depend on a routine schedule.

(cont'd)

**Exhibit 6.2. Missions Resource Network, Bedford, Texas
Board-Management Delegation Policy
"Monitoring Executive Director Performance," Cont'd**

Policy	Method	Frequency
Treatment of Beneficiaries	Internal	Annually (September)
Treatment of Donors	Internal	Annually (September)
Treatment of Staff	Internal	Annually (September)
Financial Planning and Budgeting	Internal	Quarterly (end of quarter)
Financial Condition and Activities	Internal	Monthly (end of month)
	External	Annually (end of year)
Asset Protection	Internal	Annually (September)
Endowed Funds	Internal	Quarterly (end of quarter)
Emergency Executive Succession	Internal	Annually (September)
Compensation and Benefits	Internal	Annually (September)
Communication and Support to the Board	Direct inspection	Annually (September)
Ends Focus of Grants or Contracts	Internal	Annually (September)

with an annual CEO performance appraisal, even though a case can be made that the regular monitoring system *is* the CEO's evaluation. Periodically summing all the intervening monitoring judgments into a formal CEO evaluation is fine as long as the board understands that the ongoing monitoring is even more important and certainly exerts the greatest effect on organizational performance. Periodic evaluations are no more than summaries of the ongoing evaluation, since adding other criteria at the annual appraisal would be both unfair and managerially sloppy.

There are three common ways in which boards add superfluous evaluative criteria. First, some boards allow unstated expectations to be part of the evaluation. These are criteria that the board might have chosen to include in its policies but did not. If a single board member is doing the evaluation, these unstated expectations might well be those of that board member alone. Second, one of the many generic personnel evaluation forms that can always be found in circulation might be used. Third, CEO performance might be compared against personal objectives that the CEO himself or herself originally proposed. In this case, the board is inappropriately judging its CEO against his or her criteria rather than the board's. These three extraneous standards of performance seriously weaken the powerful synonymity between board policies and CEO accountability.

Any forms developed for CEO appraisal must reflect the single source of evaluative data. I have seen school boards create citizen forces to design a superintendent evaluation, an action that is irresponsible to the public as well as to the CEO. If the boards did their job, such games with evaluation would be unnecessary. The only relevant questions are the following: What did we charge the organization to accomplish? What did we prohibit the organization from doing? How did the organization do against only those criteria? The answers to those questions constitute the CEO's evaluation. The board should seek public help to create policy criteria at the outset but not to bail the board out for not having done its job in the first place.

The importance of limiting CEO evaluation to the criteria represented by board policies on ends and executive limitations is so great as to merit repetition. It is common for boards to indulge their (or their CEO's) need to assess CEO skills and personality. To

WANT MORE?

7

be sure, CEOs, like anyone else, have areas that need improvement. It is to their benefit for them to seek the help of knowledgeable advisers and to continue their education and development. But if, commendably, they do so and ends are not achieved or executive limitations not observed, why should they earn points for self-improvement efforts? On the other hand, if they do no self-development but achieve the ends and observe the executive limitations, why should they be penalized? The purpose of evaluating the CEO is not to become the CEO's coach. In fact, it is best for the board not to think of itself as evaluating the CEO at all. It should evaluate the organization based on relevant board policies and pin that evaluation on the CEO.

Evaluating the CEO seeks to ensure that board values are truly in place. The great utility in CEO performance appraisal derives from its being integrated with the board's policy fabric and with the concept of accountability—that is, cumulative responsibility. Because of this integral dependence on preestablished criteria, it is impossible for the board to evaluate the CEO when its own job has not been done.

Keeping the Roles Separate

Without a clear difference in job contributions, the board becomes staff one step removed. It is not unusual for a board to see its job as perched on top of staff jobs. It's no wonder, then, that boards have problems distinguishing their decision areas from those of their CEOs! The effective board relationship with an executive is one that recognizes that the jobs of board and executive are truly separate. Effectiveness calls for two strong, totally different responsibilities. Either party trying to do the other's job interferes with effective operation. It is not the board's task to save the CEO from the responsibilities of that job, nor is it the CEO's task to save the board from the responsibilities of governing. Further, it must always remain clear who works for whom. The board can respect, even revere, the CEO's skills, commitment, and leadership yet never slip subtly into acting as if the board works for him or her.

Two commonplace events in the board-CEO relationship deserve a closer look, each representing a clouding of role distinction: (1) executive recommendations to the board and (2) board involvement in executive plans and practices.

Recommendations by the Executive

Boards often wait for executive recommendations before they make a move. Some even believe that to do otherwise is either foolhardy or a repudiation of the CEO. As long as boards deal predominantly with staff-level material and decisions, their instincts about this matter are correct. It would be improper for the board to make such decisions on its own. But if we clear all staff issues from the board's agenda and are left with only those that truly belong to the board, the scenario changes significantly. Now the same behavior shows up as the ostensible leaders waiting for the CEO to tell them what to do next. What the CEO wants the board to do may be of interest and may even have some legitimate influence, but it is surely not the driving force of good governance.

Current practice is a confounding, then, of two errors. First, boards deal so predominantly with low-level issues that the CEO's not having a controlling influence would be foolish. Second, boards often avoid confronting genuine governance decisions by falling back on executive recommendations. When it comes to the long-term, visionary, strategic import of an organization, asking the CEO, "What do you want us to decide?" is not the language of leaders.

To help the board develop more integrity in leading, the CEO would do better not to bring the board any executive decisions. And for governance decisions, he or she can assist the board most not by making recommendations but by helping to develop policy options and their various implications. The CEO might also make spokespeople available to the board for the various policy alternatives. In this manner, the board's choice is truly the board's choice—a substantive involvement with not a hint of rubber-stamping. The vitality of the process engages the board at an appropriate level. Board members become more aware of the important currents affecting the organization's fortunes and future. Members leave the board meeting knowing they have been doing the board's rather than the staff's work. This more alive and meaningful board work will inevitably have a salutary effect on the quality of management.

Intrusions by the Board

Making staff decisions trivializes the board's job, disempowers staff and interferes with their investment in their work, and reduces the degree to which the CEO can be held accountable for outcomes.

Boards make staff-level decisions through any number of single motions: to hire someone, to award the painting contract to a certain contractor, to change a certain personnel rule, to switch funds from one budget line to another, to purchase a certain computer system, to purchase new tires for the van, and so on to a level far below strategic leadership. Boards are often inexplicably unwilling to allow their CEOs to make decisions that are competently and routinely handled by many persons in their daily lives. I have seen boards entrust a multimillion-dollar organization to a CEO, then prohibit that person from making expenditures greater than $25,000!

Exhibit 6.3 illustrates some concrete actions in which a board should engage and some in which it should not. Decision authority that is retained versus that which is delegated is roughly equivalent to the common terms *hands on* and *hands off*, though the board must safeguard its authority over both. *Hands on* and *hands off* also correspond to the definitions of *responsibility* and *accountability* that were explained earlier in this chapter.

In addition to the approval process discussed in Chapter Three, boards also intrude into management by trying to help or advise staff in operational areas. Whether given by individuals, committees, or the whole board, advice to staff from the governors often is confused with direction. In such cases, staff members have to exercise their diplomatic skills to maintain social graces while safeguarding the integrity of delegation. Therefore, when board members volunteer to do jobs for which the CEO is accountable, it is mandatory that they come under the control of the CEO. The board may not responsibly allow individual members to jeopardize an unambiguous board-staff role distinction.

WANT MORE?

8

Exhibit 6.3. Hands-On Versus Hands-Off Tasks for the Board

Hands On!

Examples of What the Board Should Do Hands On

- Set the board's work plan and agenda for the year and for each meeting

- Determine board training and development needs

- Attend to discipline in board attendance, following bylaws and other self-imposed rules

- Become expert in governance

- Meet with and gather wisdom from the ownership

- Establish the limits of the CEO's authority to budget, administer finances and compensation, establish programs, and otherwise manage the organization

- Establish the results, recipients, and acceptable costs of those results that justify the organization's existence

- Examine monitoring data and determine whether the organization has achieved a reasonable interpretation of board-stated criteria

Hands Off!

Examples of What the Board and Its CGO* Should Keep Hands Off

- Establish services, programs, curricula, or budgets

- Approve the CEO's personnel, program, or budgetary plans

- Render any judgments or assessments of staff activity for which no previous board expectations have been stated

- Determine staff development needs, terminations, or promotions

- Design staff jobs or instruct any staff member subordinate to the CEO (except when the CEO has assigned a staff member to some board function)

- Decide on the organizational chart and staffing requirements

- Establish committees to advise or help staff

*The term CGO, introduced in Chapter Three, is roughly equivalent to chair.

Not only the CEO but other staff members are eager to make decisions and to perform. As individuals, they, like the CEO, are not hierarchically related to individual board members. Nonetheless, it would be naïve to maintain that the disparity in social power that sometimes exists between board members and staff members can be entirely overlooked, although organizational culture can minimize and often even eliminate its effects. Taking explicit care in the definition of roles makes it possible for anyone to talk with or elicit wisdom from anyone with no harmful effects on the chain of command. People operate better when they are not bound by rigid channels of human contact. Having the right kinds of rules enables the board to get the most out of staff without forgoing the very human need for free communication.

The board has a stake in obtaining the most return on what a CEO costs. Return on CEO is greatest when the CEO's decision power is used to the fullest—bounded, of course, by the board's interpretation of its own accountability. It is in the board's interest to have a powerful CEO. But the board would be irresponsible if it allowed even dazzling CEO decision making to take the organization in a direction the board did not desire or to foster activity the board considered unethical or imprudent. If a board establishes the ends it wants and the

 WANT MORE? means it does not want, it optimizes both CEO power and board power simultaneously. The board's confidence increases as its fatigue decreases. The CEO's freedom to make decisions increases as the limitations on that freedom are made explicit. The concept of return on CEO becomes, by extension, return on personnel, which is usually the largest single outlay of nonprofit and public resources. Even a minor improvement in this return benefits ends accomplishment in one year more than most boards have contributed by involvement in details in their entire history.

Mutual Expectations

The board and its CEO constitute a leadership team. Their contributions are formally separable. When clearly differentiated, the two roles can be supportive and respectful of each other. John Fitzpatrick, trustee for the Austin (Texas) Independent School District, speaks of "a stable Board-Superintendent relationship . . . an ideal structure and vehicle to enable our Board, District and staff to be effective." As in sports, the team functions only as long as the positions are clearly defined at the outset.

Teamwork is not the blurring of responsibilities into an undifferentiated mass. The foremost expectation of mutual support is that each person remain true to his or her peculiar responsibility. The CEO must be able to rely on the board to confront and resolve issues of governance while respectfully staying out of management. The board must be able to rely on the CEO to confront and resolve issues of management while respectfully staying out of governance. Policy Governance, according to Jacques Gerards, CEO of the Dutch Association of Governors in Health Care, Zoetermeer, The Netherlands, "gives governing bodies and CEOs a clear insight in their mutual relationship and in their distinct responsibilities."

Each can reasonably expect the other to exhibit leadership. If the board's job is well designed, board leadership is simply a matter of fulfilling that job with the vision and integrity of servant-leadership. But the quality of the design is paramount. Vision, values, and strategic mentality must be integral to the position. The CEO's leadership has two components. The CEO must influence an organizational culture in which the organization's impacts on the world are at least up to board expectations. In addition, though it should not be a requirement of his or her job, the CEO has the opportunity to influence the board toward greater integrity and capability for strategic leadership. Pressing, cajoling, and even embarrassing a board toward greater integrity are far greater gifts than pressing, cajoling, and embarrassing it toward specific content recommendations—that is, getting the board to give the CEO what he or she wants. It is difficult for a CEO to do the latter without sacrificing the former. A leader will choose the former path.

The board has the right to expect performance, honesty, and straightforwardness from its CEO. Boards can at times be under-standing about performance deficiencies but should never bend an inch on integrity. The CEO has the right to expect the board to make the rules clear and then play by them. He or she has the right to expect the board to speak with one voice, despite the massive currents that flow within the board's constituencies. And the CEO has the right to expect the board to get its own job done. Frank Branca, Chairman of the board of directors of Digital Federal Credit Union in Marlborough, Massachusetts, believes that his board's use of Policy Governance "has allowed our Board and Management to optimize [those] individual and collective responsibilities."

Policy Governance was not designed for CEOs' benefit (nor, for that matter, board members' comfort) but for the effective exercise of owners' authority over that which they own. Nevertheless, CEOs who want to perform, who have no need to control the boards they work for, and who are not put off by the accountability that comes with real decision making have much to gain from Policy Gover-nance. Not only are they given genuine chief executive authority, but they are protected against the unnecessary risks that poor governance frequently imposes. CEOs' careers have been damaged by failing to please a board that does not speak with one voice. They have been subject to criticism—sometimes publicly—from board members based on individual members' criteria that were never agreed to by the board as a whole. They have been unfairly evaluated on expectations that the whole board agrees on but never actually stated. They have been abandoned to ownership condemnation, even though the board's position should be between the ownership and the CEO. Their managerial skills have frequently been stultified by boards that are determined to have committees on every important managerial issue. When great authority is wielded with an inadequate process, good people can cause much injury. Boards composed of kind and generous individuals can, as official groups, be unkind and hurtful.

The Management Sequence

This text is concerned with the theory and practice of governance, not management. There is no need here, then, to trace in detail what occurs between the creation of Ends and Executive Limitations policies and the board's receipt of monitoring data on those policies. In brief, the normal sequence for a management whose board is using Policy Governance is as follows: The first step is that the CEO, using whatever resources are available (frequently other staff or outside experts), arrives at an interpretation of the policies he or she is confident can be shown to be reasonable. The CEO then assigns the accomplishment of parts of the task to various staff, using delegation skills that are normal in management. As time goes by, the CEO sees to any coaching, discipline, reassignments, or other midcourse corrections deemed necessary. As the time for monitoring approaches, the CEO sees to it that credible data are gathered to present to the board. In fact, the CEO might well have done interim monitoring not for the board but for internal purposes. The board is involved only at the beginning and the end of this chain of events.

Board-Management Delegation Policies on the Policy Circle

Let me again remind you of the policy circle shown in Figure 3.3. Figure 6.1 illustrates how a given board might have filled in the outer levels of the quadrant depicting the governance-management interface. Each board, of course, will choose a different level of detail at which to stop, beyond which the CGO is allowed to make any reasonable interpretation. The number of policies and their depth in Figure 6.1 are not intended to portray the right depth or number of policies but are only one example among many possibilities. Moreover, whatever the depth, number, and content of board policies, the board retains the right to change them whenever its wisdom so dictates.

Figure 6.1. Board-Management Delegation Policies Completed

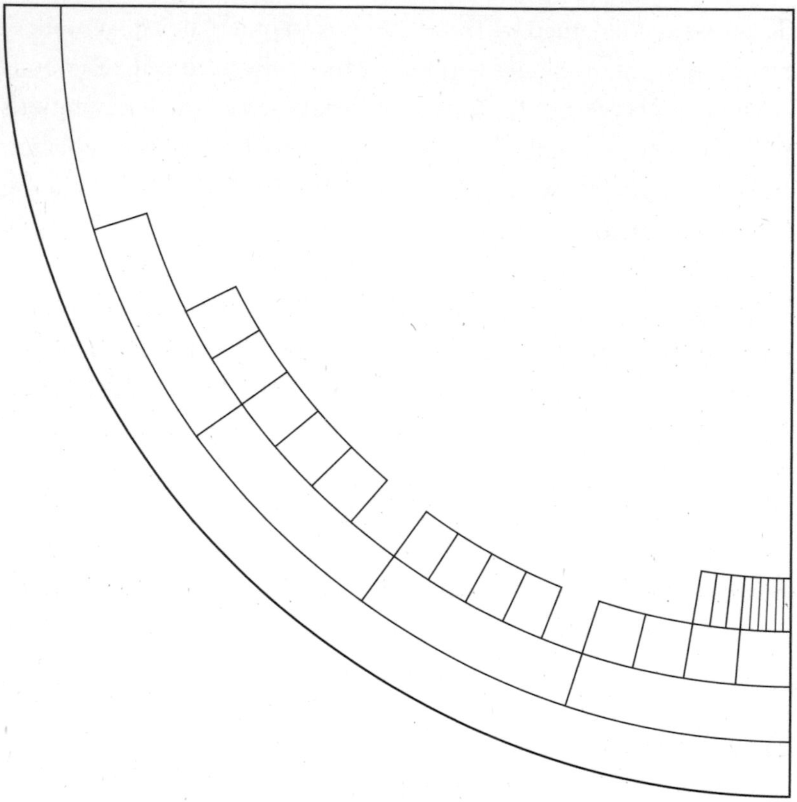

Note: The board has established its Board-Management Delegation policies deeply enough that any decisions or choices made by a delegatee will be acceptable to the board if they are a reasonable interpretation of the broader statements. Thus, the board can now safely delegate all further decisions in this category.

Next Chapter

Getting the board's job done is the theme of this entire book. In Chapter Seven, however, I focus more on ownership accountability, job description, and discipline of an effective board. These constitute the subject matter of the fourth and final category of board policies, Governance Process.

WANT MORE?

Further Reading

1. Carver, J. "Title Versus Function: The Policy Governance Definition of a CEO." *Board Leadership*, 2002k, no. 59.

   Carver, J., and Carver, M. "The CEO's Role in Policy Governance." *Board Leadership*, 2000, no. 48.

   Carver, J. "Separating Chair and CEO Roles with Smoke and Mirrors." *Board Leadership*, 2003p, no. 68.

   Carver, M. "What Is a CEO?" *Association*, June–July 1998c, *15*(4), 18–20.

   Carver, J. "Do You Really Have a CEO?" *Board Leadership*, 1996g, no. 26. Reprinted in J. Carver, *John Carver on Board Leadership*. San Francisco: Jossey-Bass, 2002.

   Carver, J., and Carver, M. M. *The CEO Role Under Policy Governance*. The CarverGuide Series on Effective Board Governance, no. 12. San Francisco: Jossey-Bass, 1997a.

   Raso, C. "Two People in the CEO Role: Can It Work?" *Board Leadership*, 2000, no. 48.

   Carver, M. "FAQ: When a Policy Governance Board Hires a New CEO, What Are Some Important Dos and Don'ts to Remember During the Hiring Process and the New CEO's Early Weeks?" *Board Leadership*, 2004c, no. 74.

2. Carver, J. "Creating a Single Voice: The Prerequisite to Board Leadership." *Board Leadership*, 1992a, no. 2, pp. 1–5. Reprinted in J. Carver, *John Carver on Board Leadership*. San Francisco: Jossey-Bass, 2002.

3. Carver, J., and Oliver, C. *Corporate Boards That Create Value: Governing Company Performance from the Boardroom*. San Francisco: Jossey-Bass, 2002c.

   Carver, J. "The New Chairman: A Chief Governance Officer (CGO) for Tomorrow's Board." *Institute of Corporate Directors Newsletter*, Aug. 2003m, no. 109, pp. 1–2.

Dayton, K. N. *Governance Is Governance*. Washington, D.C.: Independent Sector, 1987.

Lorsch, J. W., and MacIver, E. *Pawns or Potentates: The Reality of America's Corporate Boards*. Boston: Harvard Business School, 1989.

Leighton, D.S.R., and Thain, D. H. *Making Boards Work: What Directors Must Do to Make Canadian Boards Effective*. Whitby, Canada: McGraw-Hill Ryerson, 1997.

Cadbury, A. "The Corporate Governance Agenda." *Corporate Governance: An International Review*, 2000, 8(1), 10.

Carver, J. "Should Your CEO Be a Board Member?" *Board Leadership*, 1996r, no. 26. Reprinted in J. Carver, *John Carver on Board Leadership*. San Francisco: Jossey-Bass, 2002.

Cadbury, A. *The Company Chairman*. Hemel Hempstead, Hertsfordshire, U.K.: Director Books, 1995.

Cadbury, A. *Corporate Governance and Chairmanship: A Personal View*. Oxford: Oxford University Press, 2002a.

4. Carver, J. "The CEO's Objectives Are Not Proper Board Business." *Board Leadership*, 1995c, no. 20. Reprinted in J. Carver, *John Carver on Board Leadership*. San Francisco: Jossey-Bass, 2002.

5. Carver, J. "What If Board Members 'Just Want to Know' About Some Aspect of Operations?" *Board Leadership*, 2003v, no. 65.

   Carver, J. "What If the Committee Chair Just Wants to Know?" *Board Leadership*, 1997o, no. 29. Reprinted in J. Carver, *John Carver on Board Leadership*. San Francisco: Jossey-Bass, 2002.

6. Conduff, M., and Paszkiewicz, D. "A 'Reasonable Interpretation of Ends': What Exactly Does It Mean?" *Board Leadership*, 2001, no. 54.

   Carver, J. "Why Only the CEO Can Interpret the Board's Ends and Executive Limitations Policies." *Board Leadership*, 1999k, no. 46. Reprinted in J. Carver, *John Carver on Board Leadership*. San Francisco: Jossey-Bass, 2002.

7. Moore, J. "Meaningful Monitoring: The Board's View." *Board Leadership*, 2001b, no. 54.

Moore, J. "Meaningful Monitoring." *Board Leadership*, 2001a, no. 53.

Carver, J. "The Mechanics of Direct Inspection Monitoring." *Board Leadership*, 1998m, no. 39. Reprinted in J. Carver, *John Carver on Board Leadership*. San Francisco: Jossey-Bass, 2002.

Carver, J. "Board Access to the Internal Auditor." *Board Leadership*, 2003a, no. 68.

Carver, J. "One Board Fails to Follow Its Own Monitoring Policy and Courts Fiscal Disaster." *Board Leadership*, 1994g, no. 14. Reprinted in J. Carver, *John Carver on Board Leadership*. San Francisco: Jossey-Bass, 2002.

Carver, J. "Handling Complaints: Using Negative Feedback to Strengthen Board Policy." *Board Leadership*, 1993h, no. 8.

Carver, J. "Putting CEO Evaluation in Perspective." *Board Leadership*, 1996p, no. 26. Reprinted in J. Carver, *John Carver on Board Leadership*. San Francisco: Jossey-Bass, 2002.

Carver, J. "Getting It Right from the Start: The CEO's Job Description." *Board Leadership*, 1996j, no. 26. Reprinted in J. Carver, *John Carver on Board Leadership*. San Francisco: Jossey-Bass, 2002.

Carver, J. "Off Limits: What Not to Do in Your CEO Evaluations." *Board Leadership*, 1996m, no. 26. Reprinted in J. Carver, *John Carver on Board Leadership*. San Francisco: Jossey-Bass, 2002.

Carver, J. "A Simple Matter of Comparison: Monitoring Fiscal Management in Your Organization." *Board Leadership*, 1993q, no. 6. Reprinted in J. Carver, *John Carver on Board Leadership*. San Francisco: Jossey-Bass, 2002.

8. Carver, J. "It's Not the Board's Role to Act as Management Consultant to the CEO." *Board Leadership*, 2000c, no. 49.

Carver, J. "Board Members as Amateur CEOs." *Board Leadership*, 2001a, no. 53. Reprinted in J. Carver, *John Carver on Board Leadership*. San Francisco: Jossey-Bass, 2002.

Carver, J. "How Can Staff Know That Board Advice Is Not Actually Veiled Instruction?" *Board Leadership*, 2001g, no. 59.

Carver, J. "The Trap of Answering Your CEO's Request for More Guidance." *Board Leadership*, 2003t, no. 66.

Carver, J. "When Board Members Act as Staff Advisors." *Board Leadership*, 1992o, no. 9. Reprinted in J. Carver, *John Carver on Board Leadership*. San Francisco: Jossey-Bass, 2002.

Swanson, A. "Who's in Charge Here? Board of Directors and Staff—The Division of Responsibility." *Nonprofit World*, 1986, 4(4), 14–18.

Carver, J. "Policy Governance Is Not a 'Hands Off' Model." *Board Leadership*, 1995j, no. 19. Reprinted in J. Carver, *John Carver on Board Leadership*. San Francisco: Jossey-Bass, 2002.

9. Carver, J. "FAQ: Doesn't Policy Governance Require Too Much Confidence in the CEO?" *Board Leadership*, 2003g, no. 68.

Carver, M. "FAQ: It Worries Me That in the Policy Governance System, the Board Gives a Huge Amount of Authority to the CEO. What Makes This OK?" *Board Leadership*, 2004b, no. 73.

Carver, J. "Does Policy Governance Give Too Much Authority to the CEO?" *Board Leadership*, 2001e, no. 55. Reprinted in J. Carver, *John Carver on Board Leadership*. San Francisco: Jossey-Bass, 2002.

The Board's Responsibility for Itself

Governing Oneself Precedes Governing Others

The subject of this book, of course, is the redesign of the board job. How a board decides organizational results, how it controls operations, and how it relates to staff reveal much about its job design. It still remains for the board to deal explicitly with how it governs its own process, including a job description through which the board can discipline its time and action. Surely, a board that cannot govern itself cannot hope to govern an organization. Perspectives on the governing task itself are codified in the Governance Process category of policies. In Chapter Eight, I deal with officers and committees—in other words, the subdivisions of board labor; in this chapter, I address the board's accountability as a whole.

I begin by introducing the concept of ownership, the source from which board accountability derives. I then fix the onus of responsibility for good governance on the governors themselves. Next, I recognize the dynamics that affect the individual board members' ability to fulfill their responsibility as a group. I then present management of board process as a natural outgrowth of the board's products. Finally, I set forth a board job description, along with a commentary on board work beyond policymaking.

The Moral Ownership

Stakeholders in a nonprofit or public organization may be clients, students, patients, staff, taxpayers, donors, neighbors, general citizenry, peer agencies, suppliers, and others. The board could be said to be accountable to all these groups, and certainly these groups all have some type of ownership in the organization. But the special class of stakeholders I call *owners* are those on whose behalf the board has any responsibility to others. This narrower concept of ownership encompasses only those stakeholders who are situated as stockholders in an equity corporation are.

WANT MORE?
1

Ownership as a special concept constitutes the origin of board accountability. The concept of ownership saves the owners—the special group of people who give the organization its legitimacy—from being lost in the general array of stakeholders. Surely the members of a trade association have a different order of ownership than, say, vendors or even staff members that work for the association. For a city council, the city's population occupies a position different from that of other stakeholders.

Various stakeholder groups may overlap, and, in some cases, two groups may comprise the same people. The ownership of an antique auto club is made up of club members; the beneficiaries of the club are the same people. The ownership of a community mental health center is the community at large; the beneficiaries constitute a portion of that community. The ownership of a public school system is the population of the school district; the beneficiaries are the students. Moreover, in the last two cases, the staffs of these institutions are members of the community at large and, therefore, also owners. Owners may be a group that is either larger or smaller than the group of beneficiaries. Even when the same people are involved, the organization's differing responsibilities to the several constituencies are kept straight by separating the concepts.

WANT MORE?
2

Ownership and *trusteeship*, as I use those terms, are only occasionally legal realities. It is the social obligation of trusteeship, whether or not it is codified in law or contract, that concerns us here. Moral rather than legal ownership is the basis on which a board determines its accountability. When law requires a membership (a legal ownership) in what is not basically a membership organization, the board must determine whether the moral ownership is a larger body that extends far beyond the bounds of the formal membership. (Law in some jurisdictions requires a nonprofit organization to have a membership, typically to elect a board. Unlike a genuine membership in a trade association or a professional society, this membership is frequently a cobbled-together handful of interested persons or even staff. The law in these cases is satisfied, but the Policy Governance meaning of *ownership* is not.) The more board members agree on whose behalf they are serving, the more powerful their role as board members will feel.

Let me digress for a moment. The legal issues in agency theory are familiar to every lawyer. When one person (the agent) acts on behalf of another (the principal), it is unlikely if not impossible for the agent to completely ignore his or her own interests. Hence, the problem of agency is that the interest of the principal rarely surmounts all self-interest of the agent. The relationship between a

WANT MORE?

3

large body of people and a smaller group authorized to act on their behalf is equally familiar to political scientists. The Policy Governance model was unwittingly founded on concepts first described by philosophers who were addressing the social contract among real humans that creates an incorporeal entity we have come to call the *state*. We who would be thorough students of governance have much to learn from Rousseau, Hume, and Mill.

The composition of the moral ownership that I propose can be obvious, as it is for a city council, or it can be obscure, as it is for a public radio station. Are the owners regular listeners, donors, everyone in the listening area, or all classical music buffs? For organizations that receive government and foundation grants, it is important that the grantor not be seen as the owner. Ownership is not merely paying the bills, although this may be a factor. Grantors are usually best seen as high-volume customers with whom the organization makes a deal. It can choose not to make the deal. No such choice is available to the board concerning its ownership; the rightful owners do not lose their status because the board wishes to ignore it. The test for ownership is not with whom the board makes a deal but whom the board has no moral right not to recognize.

The board is ordinarily a subset of the ownership, acting as a trustee on the owners' behalf. *The board's trust relationship with owners supersedes its relationship with staff*. The primacy of this relationship is easy to forget when the stream of board activity and the high visibility of organizational personnel pull the board staffward. Boards learn to speak staff language, use staff acronyms, and become involved in internal organizational issues. This understandable, intense identification with staff detracts from their being trusteeship-driven. It occurs at the expense of interaction with the owners and resolution of the owners' complex interests. The mechanisms of board work must be designed to remind the board that its rightful identity is with the owners, not with the staff.

There are boards that are themselves the entire ownership. Consider, for example, an equity corporation (usually a small one) in which all investors are on the board. The nonprofit equivalent would be a board that makes no pretense of representing anyone but itself. It presents itself to the public as no more than a small group that has its own agenda, but one that lawfully conforms to not-for-profit statutes. Such a board would undoubtedly be self-perpetuating (though not all self-perpetuating boards would be in this class), maintaining justifiably absolute control over its membership and its prerogatives. I mention this kind of ownership-board equivalence simply because it does exist but not because it is common. Board members should carefully examine their status before judging themselves to be such a board.

The Board's Responsibility for Board Performance

Board members, not staff, are trustees in a moral sense for the ownership and, consequently, must bear initial responsibility for the integrity of governance. "He that would govern others, first should be the master of himself" (Massinger, 1979). The board is responsible for its own development, its own job design, its own discipline, and its own performance. Before any discussion of board process to improve governance, this responsibility must be clear to board and staff alike. Primary responsibility for board development does not rest in the CEO, staff, funding bodies, or government. These other parties doubtless have an interest in better governance. They may even seize the opportunity to affect governance quality. But they are not where responsibility for governance resides.

Only responsible stewardship can justify a board's considerable authority. Board members who do not choose to accept this breadth of responsibility should resign. If they do not, it is the responsibility of other board members to structure a board development system in which such persons are, if not "converted," eliminated from the board. Being warm, willing to attend meetings, inclined to donate money, and interested in the organizational subject matter do not constitute responsible board membership. These characteristics are desirable but far from sufficient.

It is inviting to rely on the CEO to motivate a board. This scenario frequently extends further than the provision of an occasional motivational "fix." It may extend as far as spoon-feeding. No matter how well the CEO tells the board what to do and when to do it, governance cannot be excellent under these conditions. Going through the motions, even the "right" motions, is fake leadership that transforms a CEO into a baby-sitter. Only a deluded board waits for its CEO to make it a good board.

Under these conditions, public-spirited and ethical CEOs prod the board to do and say what they think a responsible governing body should do and say. With time, observers of such a situation may question the need for the board to be responsible: "If everything turns out well, what is the fuss? Getting the board to be truly responsible may be pedantic and perhaps unrealistic. After all, board members frequently are just volunteers; how can a part-time, outside group of largely nonprofessionals presume to tell a professional or technical staff what to do?" This litany impedes any further inclination to motivate leaders to lead.

The preceding unhappy scenario is the best-case scenario! What if the CEO is not public-spirited and ethical? The improprieties resulting from lackadaisical governance are easy to imagine. I have observed boards whose laissez-faire rubber-stamping came to an abrupt end upon discovery of misconduct. Most nonprofit boards are too private or too small for public embarrassment to be a realistic threat, but they must endure their own awareness of having been asleep at the throttle. Their failure may have been not in misjudging a specific issue but simply in not having realized that the throttle belonged to them. The debacles at Enron, WorldCom, and other corporations are prime examples of the failure of governance that are familiar to anyone who reads a newspaper.

Boards are responsible for their attendance, discipline, governance methods, development, agendas, and ability to envision the future. Others can help. Surely the CEO should even be required to help. Helpers, however, can only assist a body that has assumed full responsibility for itself; helpers can only marginally compensate when ostensibly responsible parties are not taking responsibility.

The board of the Ohio College of Podiatric Medicine has set the standards to be met in the conduct of board affairs (Exhibit 7.1). Notice how the board makes clear that it, not its staff, is responsible for the board's governance performance.

Diversity and Dynamics

As a board sets out to fulfill its trusteeship, its most immediate responsibility is to deal with the implications of being a group. Individuals must understand their individual obligations and how those aggregate into a group obligation. Indeed, the hurdle of moving to true group responsibility can easily keep a board from attending to critical duties. Boards are fraught with extensive interpersonal dynamics, like any other group of human beings. People differ in

Exhibit 7.1. Ohio College of Podiatric Medicine, Cleveland Governance Process Policy "Governing Style"

The board will govern with an emphasis on (a) outward vision rather than an internal preoccupation, (b) strategic leadership more than administrative detail, (c) clear distinction of board and chief executive roles, (d) collective rather than individual decisions, (e) future rather than past or present, and (f) proactivity rather than reactivity. The board will:

1. Deliberate in many voices, but govern in one.

2. Cultivate a sense of group responsibility. The board, not the staff, will be responsible for excellence in governing. The board will be an initiator of policy, not merely a reactor to staff initiatives. The board will use the expertise of individual members to enhance the ability of the board as a body, rather than to substitute the individual judgments for the board's values.

3. Direct, control and inspire the organization through the careful establishment of broad written policies reflecting the board's values and perspectives. The board's major focus will be on the intended long term impacts outside the operating organization, not on the administrative or programmatic means of attaining those effects.

4. Enforce upon itself whatever discipline is needed to govern with excellence. Discipline will apply to matters such as attendance, preparation for meetings, policymaking principles, respect of roles, and ensuring the continuity of governance capability. Continual board development will include orientation of new members in the board's governance process and periodic board discussion of process improvement. The board will allow no officer, individual or committee of the board to hinder or be an excuse for not fulfilling its commitments.

5. Monitor and discuss the board's process and performance at each meeting. Self-monitoring will include comparison of board activity and discipline to policies in the Governance Process and Board-Staff Linkage categories.

their comfort with confrontation, in their ability to express feelings, and in the personal defenses they bring to an interaction. People differ in fears, hopes, optimism, and excitement, all of which contribute to the interpersonal aspects of board operation. These aspects exist quite apart from models, rational structures, and job designs.

This book does not set out to deal directly with the interpersonal dynamics of governing groups. The abundant and useful literature on small-group process obviates the need for such discussion here. I do, however, recognize the powerful influence that interpersonal processes have on governance. Indeed, I have seen interpersonal dysfunction completely block a number of boards from proceeding into successful implementation after initially embracing the Policy

WANT MORE?

4

Governance model. Most of all, I want to persuade the reader that taking time to design a sound board process, before the process becomes personalized, is the greatest safeguard against the debilitating effects of unfortunate interpersonal dynamics. The only other preventive measure that comes close is to ensure that all board members are intelligent, communicative, assertive, and mentally healthy! Alas, even emotionally together Renaissance people cannot compensate for an inadequate governance process. The most extensive study of the interaction of corporate board members was authored by Leblanc and Gillies (2005).

Designing areas of board job performance carefully will profoundly channel the interpersonal process of a board. For example, job design influences the types of conflict that will be experienced and members' decision whether to follow a commonly proclaimed discipline or their individual discipline. Diversity is directed toward some areas and muted or eliminated in others. Clarifying tasks and off-limits topics helps to depersonalize subsequent struggles over the appropriateness of an issue for board discussion.

A sound, codified board process can ameliorate jockeying for power, individuals' controlling the group through negativism, and the digressions into unrelated topics. Dealing with the dysfunctional behavior of a board member is far more difficult if the board has not previously determined what constitutes appropriate behavior. This proposition is quite helpful in dealing with the occasional renegade board member. Without board-developed guidelines, the matter will be considered a clash between personalities, and the issue of acceptable board behavior becomes lost in ill feelings.

The board of Glendale Elementary School District No. 40 showed unusual character in adopting "Board Members' Code of Conduct I" (Exhibit 7.2). (This board has a separate "Code of Conduct II" policy for the usual conflict-of-interest provisions.) As a group, the elected board members determined to protect the school system from themselves as individuals, a commendable and bold action. Many elected boards I've dealt with recoil from getting tough with themselves simply because, as independently elected officials, they have no authority over one another. This board decided to find a way.

Effectively dealing with even appropriate diversity requires a discussion of process prior to the occurrence of specific disagreements. Diversity must somehow be funneled into a single position. Not all ideas can prevail, and if members approach disputes personally, there will be winners and losers. Simple compromise is not necessarily a responsible solution; either of two very different approaches may be far better than a compromise between them. The challenge can be sidestepped by delaying decisions or by squelching dissent as being too painful, too impolite, or too impolitic. Indecisiveness and unanimous votes often result from the desire to avoid confrontation.

As the family members did in *Who's Afraid of Virginia Woolf?* (Albee, 1962), boards sometimes deliberate on inconsequential issues to avoid dealing with a difficult, unspoken issue. What appears to be a preoccupation with trivia may be fear of confronting the larger issues in a group setting. Small wonder; we are not very good at confronting central issues, even as individuals. Moreover, board members deprived of trivia might not know how to spend their time. A board member once asked me in all sincerity, "What

**Exhibit 7.2. Glendale Elementary School
District No. 40, Glendale, Arizona
Governance Process Policy
"Board Members' Code of Conduct I"**

The public is represented by the school board acting as a body.
Consequently, the school system is answerable to the board as a body,
not to individual board members. The board fails to be accountable to
the public if it allows any breach in this principle. Therefore, individual
board members are committed to proper use of their authority and to
decorum consistent with maintaining the integrity and discipline of
board leadership.

1. While the board as a body cannot exercise authority over individual
   board members, the board is responsible for the organization's exposure to members acting as individuals. To that end, the board can
   exercise authority over the superintendent's response to individual
   members and can enumerate its expectations for individual member
   discipline.

   A. While the board expects individual members to be given common
      courtesy, it does not require the superintendent and staff to heed
      any individual member's opinions or instructions.

   B. Regardless of any individual member's dissent from a decision of
      the board, he or she must support that the superintendent is
      bound by directions given by the board as a whole.

2. Individual board members may not attempt to exercise authority over
   the organization unless explicitly set forth in board policies.

   A. Individual members' interactions with the superintendent or staff
      must recognize that individual members have no authority over
      staff or to insert themselves into staff operations. (Nothing con-
      tained in section 2.a is intended to restrict or discourage normal
      and open communication between the governing board, staff and
      community.)

      i.   No board member can place himself or herself between staff
           members in their disputes or negotiations.

      ii. No board member can serve on staff committees, engage in
           solving staff problems, or interpret anything to staff.

Exhibit 7.2. Glendale Elementary School
District No. 40, Glendale, Arizona
Governance Process Policy
"Board Members' Code of Conduct I," Cont'd

---

      iii. No individual board member may be in the schools except
          a) when engaged in organized board visitation or monitoring
          of system performance, b) after notifying appropriate staff, and
          c) when fulfilling a role distinct from being a board member,
          such as parent or invited volunteer.

B. Although all members are obligated to register differences of opinion on board issues at the board level as passionately as desired, individual members may not direct their differences of opinion to staff in a manner which would create dissension or polarization in the organization or undermine a decision of the board majority.

C. Members' interactions with public, press, or other entities must recognize that individuals have no authority to speak for the board unless specifically authorized by the board.

D. Members will not individually render judgments of superintendent of staff performance apart from compliance with board policies as monitored by the board as a body.

---

would be left for the board to do if detailed review and approval of staff plans and procedures became unnecessary? If we do not do staff work, what will we do?" This organization had for years avoided a searching exploration of its purpose. The board continued to hide behind the manufactured busyness and apparent conscientiousness of its demanding, staff-driven agenda.

    Another way to escape confrontation with diversity is to use board committees, heavily assisted by staff, to make recommendations. Operating largely from CEO recommendations is a similar dodge. Conflicts among board members are thus avoided, as is any questioning that might be interpreted as lack of faith in the CEO. Instead of judiciously resolving differences, the board ignores them or smooths them over. Rather than eliciting and embracing their differences, board members are embarrassed or even frightened by them. This is a pity, particularly for boards that represent the public, for such differences partly define what it means to be public.

When boards choose to recognize and handle differences, they find that they need a mutually agreed-upon system to keep the group on task. Without a good system, personality becomes the dominant characteristic of any confrontation. Our points of departure may be ideas, but interactions can easily deteriorate into issues of feelings and control. As people form alliances and experience personal power, the person who expresses an idea becomes more important than the idea. And feeling rebuffed or vindicated may become more important than judging the merit of the idea.

Governing can thus be shaped by personalities rather than issues. Overpoliteness and power-based confrontation, seemingly opposite, both spring from valuing personal aspects more than the issues. Once the calm surface has been broken, interpersonal dynamics that squelch dissent transform into personal confrontation. The opportunity to develop productive confrontation centered on issues dies, people get hurt, and the governance experience leaves a bad taste. If the system is poor, even well-meaning people bore or bite each other to death.

The chairperson bears a peculiar responsibility with respect to board process; however, more cogent to this discussion, the entire board cannot avoid its share of responsibility. In other words, the existence of a chairperson does not relieve other board members from their duty to contribute to the integrity of the process. If the board as a whole does not accept responsibility for board process, the best the chairperson can achieve is superficial discipline. As Jerry Kerr of Nepean, Ontario, puts it, "It is everyone's obligation to make meetings work, even those who are not in charge."

One way in which the board can initiate good process is by creating explicit policies concerning the topic within the Governance Process category. The chairperson can then maintain the process by referring to board policy, which is easier than invoking disciplinary measures on the basis of his or her individual sense of what should be. Board members expect too much of the chairperson when they ask him or her to save the board from being held hostage by its most controlling member. Each member has the right to want to run things or never to budge. But as a body, the board does not have the right to allow individual proclivities to destroy the process.

The board of Three Rivers Area Hospital determined a cycle of board business that guarantees board education, linkage with the board's ownership, and other functions. The board's expression is shown in Exhibit 7.3.

A process that is explicitly designed can produce a discipline controlled by the will of the board rather than by individual inclinations or exigencies of the immediate dynamics. When board process is derived from the job to be done, it will be aptly shaped by the planned products. There always lurks the danger that the products of governance will turn out to be merely the random after-effects of an unplanned process.

Board Products: A Job Description

Construction of Governance Process policies begins with consideration of the board's overall reason for existence, because the ultimate test of process is whether this reason is fulfilled. The board's megaproduct (as opposed to that of the organization) is the bridge built between those to whom the board is accountable and those who are accountable to the board.

An effective board process, then, must start by clarifying the specific contributions of this bridge between owners and producers. Before we can design board process intelligently, we must ascertain what the board exists to accomplish; form follows function. Appropriate practices are determined on the basis of the accomplishments expected. The board's job description is thus the central factor in the board's process.

Conventional job descriptions are detailed lists of job activities. Their emphasis is on job means rather than job products. I use a

Exhibit 7.3. Three Rivers Area Hospital, Three Rivers, Michigan Governance Process Policy "Agenda Planning"

To accomplish its tasks with a governance style consistent with board policies, the board will follow an annual agenda which (a) completes a re-exploration of Ends policies annually and (b) continually improves board performance through board education and enriched input and deliberation.

1. The cycle will conclude each year on the last day of September so that administrative planning and budgeting can be based on accomplishing a one year segment of the board's most recent statement of long term Ends.

2. The cycle will start with the board's development of its agenda for the next year.

    A. Consultations with selected groups in the ownership or other methods of gaining ownership input will be determined and arranged in the first quarter, to be held during the balance of the year.

    B. Governance education and education related to Ends determination (e.g. presentations by futurists, demographers, advocacy groups, staff, etc.) will be arranged in the first quarter, to be held during the balance of the year.

3. Throughout the year, the board will attend to consent agenda items* as expeditiously as possible.

4. CEO monitoring will be included on the agenda if monitoring reports show policy violations, or if policy criteria are to be debated.

5. CEO remuneration will be decided after a review of monitoring reports that corresponds with the anniversary date of the CEO.

*Chapter Ten explains the concept of consent agendas.

more powerful, succinct format that omits activities and focuses on why activities take place—the intended outcomes. This method, convincingly advocated by Reddin (1971), yields a job description that, in effect, states the value added by the position. How is the organization different because this job exists? What does this job contribute? In describing job contributions, I speak of job *products* simply to keep before us at all times the output aspect of work rather than the activity.

Boards can contribute any number of products to an organization. Only three products cannot be delegated, and this irreducible trio applies to all governing boards. The board's role as a bridge between ownership and staff produces three mandatory products.

Core Board Products

The board must contribute whatever legitimate link the organization has with its ownership. Thus, the board's first direct product is the organization's *linkage to the ownership.*

The board's second direct product is *explicit governing policies.* These policies should be the ones I describe as Ends, Executive Limitations, Board-Management Delegation, and Governance Process policies, developed in each case to whatever level of detail the board chooses. The policies are designed to cover fiduciary responsibilities, risk, priorities, and, generally, all board and organizational activity.

Finally, the board is obliged to ensure the staff's fidelity to the board's policies. If the CEO continually fails to fulfill these explicit expectations, the board itself is culpable. The board has no choice but to take the necessary remedial steps. The board's third direct product is *assurance of organizational performance.*

These three undelegable job contributions are the unique responsibilities of a governing board; only the governing body can contribute these products. The board may add other products to this list, but it cannot shorten it and still govern responsibly.

Optional Board Products

Although all other contributions to the organization beyond the core three may be delegated to the CEO, it does not necessarily follow that the board should delegate them. The most common additional board products involve fundraising and legislative action.

Should a board be responsible for fundraising? The answer depends on the kind of organization and its circumstances. From the perspective of governance concepts per se, one can only say that fundraising may be either delegated or retained, at the board's discretion. If a board assumes this responsibility, it should define its fundraising product well enough that there is no confusion between staff and board responsibilities. Fundraising is an activity, not a result. Using results language forces the board to confront the task it has taken on as opposed to its expectations of staff. Does the board merely make philanthropic contacts and leave to the staff the

 WANT MORE? responsibility for actually producing the money? Or is the board responsible for achieving the funding goal itself? Or is the board's direct responsibility something other than either of these two options? Wasteful conflict about the roles of the board (or its fundraising committee) and the CEO (or the CEO's director of development) can be reduced or perhaps avoided by defining the job in terms of the expected result rather than the means used to attain that result.

With respect to legislative action, the same points apply. Does the board wish to assume responsibility for legislative strategy? For network notification? For "personal presence" at hearings? Remember, too, that board members can offer themselves as volunteers under staff direction without complicating the board's job itself. For example, the board might hold the CEO accountable for certain legislative impact but promise to supply board members as informed volunteers to participate in testimony under the CEO's direction. With this approach, there is no need to add legislative results to the board's job, for achievement would then be the CEO's responsibility. Yet board members are still providing a valuable contribution as volunteers in the management effort. It must always remain clear who has authority and responsibility for the strategy and mechanics necessary to achieve the legislative results. In this instance, the CEO is in charge, even though board members are involved. Board members work for the CEO, or the CEO's designee, when engaged in activities for which the board holds its CEO accountable.

Whatever the board decides about assuming more than the basic three responsibility areas, the matter must be made explicit and all further board activities must be made consonant. Because the three core areas cannot be delegated, it is important that they be given primacy. No board should add items unless it is sure that its allegiance to the first three will not be diluted.

Some might say that fundraising is the chief responsibility, even the raison d'être, of a board. I disagree. Fundraising by the board may be critical to a given organization, but it is more important that the organization be worth raising funds for. That worth is what the three areas of basic governance are designed to ensure. I do not mean to denigrate board fundraising in cases in which the board has

WANT MORE?

6

made sure the organization is worth the donors' money. To the contrary, I applaud it and hold both the skills and the dedication involved with great respect. There is no reason that a board cannot attend quite well to the basic three products plus fundraising, but this wholeness is ill served by lopsided attention to fundraising as the chief board responsibility.

The Basic Board Job Description

The irreducible minimum contributions of governance are restated below. Note that these constitute the board's specific job responsibility, but if accomplished, they ensure the board's overall accountability as well, using the definitions discussed in Chapter Six. This responsibility/accountability aspect of managerial job design saves the board from acting as if everything is its job. The board creates a limited responsibility list but constructs it so that the board's accountability for the total is not circumvented in the name of simplicity. Here is a summary of the board's job products:

1. *Linkage to the ownership.* The board acts in trusteeship for its ownership and serves as the legitimizing connection between this base and the organization.

2. *Explicit governing policies.* The values of the whole organization are encompassed by the board's explicit enunciation and proper categorization of broad policies.

3. *Assurance of satisfactory organizational performance.* Although the board is not responsible for carrying out the staff's job, it must ensure that the staff as a total body meets the criteria the board has set. In this way, its accountability for that performance is fulfilled.

Each of these three products is a job output, not a job activity, though any number of attendant activities are implied. The board job, however, is neither built on activities nor evaluated on the completion of activities. Within each area of responsibility, the board can set objectives to guide its short-term work. Although the board need not set objectives for staff work, it surely must for its own work.

The board of the International Policy Governance Association enumerated its job products in a policy titled "Board Job Description" (Exhibit 7.4). Optional outputs were considered and not chosen, so there are only three parts, expressed carefully as values added rather than activities. The Board-Management Delegation category appears here as "Board-Executive Function Relationship," an immaterial variation in the category name. The third value added is what in some management literature has been called a linking pin. Its effect is that the board is not successful unless management is successful.

Exhibit 7.4. International Policy Governance Association Governance Process Policy "Board Job Description"

Specific job outputs of the board, as an informed agent of the ownership, are those that ensure appropriate organizational performance. Accordingly, the board has direct responsibility to produce:

1. The link between the ownership and the operational organization.

2. Written governing policies which address the broadest levels of all organizational decisions and situations.

    2.1. *Ends:* Organizational products, impacts, benefits, outcomes, recipients, and their relative worth (what good for which recipients at what cost).

    2.2. *Executive Limitations:* Constraints on executive authority, which establish the prudence and ethics boundaries within which all executive activity and decisions must take place.

    2.3. *Governance Process:* Specification of how the board conceives, carries out and monitors its own task.

    2.4. *Board-Executive Function Relationship:* How power is delegated and its proper use monitored; the authority and accountability of the CEO.

3. Assurance of successful organizational performance.

The Board's Hands-On Work

The three job products are intended to capture the reason the board exists. In organizations in which the board wishes to add more outputs to its basic three, the additional job products must be reflected in the job description. In any case, subsequent board work is channeled into activities designed to fulfill these intended outcomes. Previous chapters have dealt with the principles and actions pertinent to job products 2 and 3. Let us now consider some aspects and activities of job product 1 and briefly note the work involved when the board adds areas.

Direct Work: Linkage with the Ownership

The identity of ownership and perhaps the favored channels for connecting with it are deliberated and then set forth in the Governance Process category of board policies. That explication is, like all policymaking, a verbal undertaking. Making the linkage real, however, is likely to require action.

The board should continually struggle to define and link with its ownership. It should do so with the same vigor that it would if the owners were organized and looking over the board's shoulder. "'Community' ownership," Ewell (1986) wrote of hospitals, "is not clearly defined, and the community does not voice its opinions or require reports on hospital performance as rigorously as industry shareholders do." It is only in rare cases that such owners are organized. In the case of nonprofit organizations, it is even likely that most owners have no idea that they are owners. Any ownership voice that becomes audible is doubtless the voice of but one segment of ownership. Although the board owes that segment its ear, it owes the silent segments the recognition that one group does not

WANT MORE?

7

represent all. Elected boards seem particularly vulnerable to the error of listening to segments as if they were the whole. I have seen city councils, library boards, school boards, and utility commissions be unintentionally unjust to owners who were not vociferous. Allowing lengthy floor time for a few faction spokespersons makes boards feel democratic but may cheat the broader mandate. Linkage to the ownership requires a more affirmative outreach than holding open meetings and entertaining spokespeople from the floor. Lee Combs, vice president of the Adams 12 Five Star Schools board in Thornton, Colorado, has credited Policy Governance with "[focusing] the board's efforts on listening to the community, defining what the community wants and doesn't want comprehensively."

Linkage with the ownership can be viewed as attitudinal, statistical, and personal. The first, simplest level of obligation encompasses attitude: board members behave with the belief that they are moral trustees for the owners. This intention establishes a frame of mind that, while not particularly schooled, at least leads the board to appropriate considerations and loyalties when resolving value issues. At the second level, the board gathers statistical evidence of the owners' concerns, needs, demands, and fears. Techniques include surveys, interviews by third parties, and statistical data. The third level is more personal; it engages board members in direct contact with owners and owners' representatives. Interviews, focus groups, public forums, invited presentations at board meetings, dialogue with other boards or public officials, and other intimate exchanges might be employed.

Maintaining the attitude of linkage may require no overt action. Developing a board that is informed with respect to the pure data on ownership and its desires may require no more than study. But the third level, personal contact, requires overt action by board members. They must go forth, sit and listen, make conversation, and struggle with communication. The board may choose to take these actions as a whole, in committees, or as individuals.

The board's status as a subset of the ownership is a built-in mechanism of linkage. Board members do not constitute a random subset, however; they are selected because they can best fulfill the trust of governance. Because nonrandomness is a factor, boards must ensure that the selection process does not impair the most visible connection to ownership—personal similarity. Persons similar to the ownership in race, income level, geographic location, gender, and other characteristics are obviously connected to the ownership. But it is unwise for even a meticulously representative board to consider its

WANT MORE?

8

ownership linkage thus discharged. Whether a black person can represent blacks or a woman can represent women is questionable. The superficial characteristics indicate only that specific groups have not been excluded, not that they are adequately represented. Tokenism might suffice for the former, but only an adequate, ongoing linkage to ownership will ensure the latter.

A board can take any number of steps to attain the diversity it wants in board membership. The board of Heifer Project International expressed its intent in its Governance Process policy titled "Board Inclusivity," shown in Exhibit 7.5.

The board can delegate responsibility for parts of the linkage task to committees or individual members. A committee might meet with a focus group or a delegation from the ownership in partial fulfillment of a board objective relating to the quality of linkage. The board's objective on linkage should be clear, as should any limits on the activities involved and the expected time for completion. In other words, the usual elements of delegation apply to a board's assignment of tasks to subgroups. The board has the option of delegating to a committee or to an officer, just as it can delegate to the CEO, but delegation to board members is a more slippery process. Because the board has much better control over tasks delegated to the CEO than those given to board members due to the

Exhibit 7.5. Heifer Project International, Little Rock, Arkansas Governance Process Policy
"Board Inclusivity"

The board should represent a variety of backgrounds as well as various segments of the HPI community, including women and different minority and ethnic groups that will reflect the vision and understanding of HPI's mission.

In this spirit, the board will:

1. Encourage nominating bodies to nominate people from diverse backgrounds, including persons from protected groups, as representatives on the HPI board.

2. Encourage diverse representation on all task forces, committees, subsidiary boards, and other groups that may be formed.

3. Recruit persons from diverse backgrounds for "at-large" positions on the HPI board.

---

clear hierarchical relationship between the board and the CEO, it is propitious to keep the board's self-delegations to a minimum. The more there are, the more care must be taken to ensure that the objectives are actually achieved and that there is no overlap with tasks for which the CEO is accountable.

One way for boards to link with the ownership is to connect with other organs of their ownership. In communities, many boards claim to speak on behalf of the general public. Yet boards in the same community often have virtually no dialogue with each other. Their staffs may interact, but at the governance level, there is virtually no systematic interaction. Were they more attentive to their linkage with ownership, boards would realize that they have much to discuss with one another inasmuch as they have overlapping, if not identical, ownerships. For community boards that truly see themselves as wedded to the larger context, over 25 percent of board effort spent dealing with other boards would not be out of line. The cross section of community leadership thus linked holds the promise of making a real difference in the fabric of a community.

Direct Work: Optional Responsibilities

If philanthropic funding, public image, legislative impact, or other delegable performance areas are made board responsibilities, the board must organize itself to perform. The board has the option of operating as a whole, in committees, or through individual assignments. In any event, it becomes the responsibility of the board, not the staff, to develop and use whatever means are necessary. If the board wants the staff to carry out and be responsible for the outcome of a specific task, then that task should not be part of the board's job. Policy control by the board will suffice. To the extent that a board adds direct responsibility areas to its job, the situation increasingly approaches that of the workgroup board mentioned in Chapter One. The risk of diluting attention to the core governance responsibilities also grows accordingly, as does the risk of confusing board and CEO roles.

The optional areas of responsibility listed in the preceding paragraph benefit from a rich literature concerning ways to organize for optimal performance. I do not presume to add to that body of knowledge here, except to point out how important it is that the board clarify the tasks it has assumed. Taking on an activity is not rigorous enough. The board's responsibility in any of these areas is not activity—however busy and impressive—but results. It is both more powerful and more incisive to define the responsibility in results terminology at the outset.

Governance Process Policies on the Policy Circle

Once more, I remind you of the policy circle shown in Figure 3.3. Figure 7.1 illustrates how a given board might have filled in the outer levels of the quadrant depicting the board's own role, responsibilities, discipline, and mechanics. Each board, of course, will choose a different level of detail at which to stop, the point beyond which the chair (or other board member or committee if so stated by the board) is allowed to make any reasonable interpretation. The number of policies and their depth in Figure 7.1 are not intended to portray the right depth or number of policies but are only one example among many possibilities. Moreover, whatever the depth, number, and content of board policies, the board retains the right to change them whenever its wisdom so dictates.

Next Chapter

In the organization of board work, officers and committees emerge as official subdivisions of the whole board. Strategic leadership is best served when this division of labor does not jeopardize the board's wholeness or confound its linkage with management. Particular attention is given to the principles of board committees and to the chair's role, as well as his or her more accurate title, *chief governance officer*. In Chapter Eight, I discuss roles and rules for a board's officers and committees.

Figure 7.1. Governance Process Policies Completed

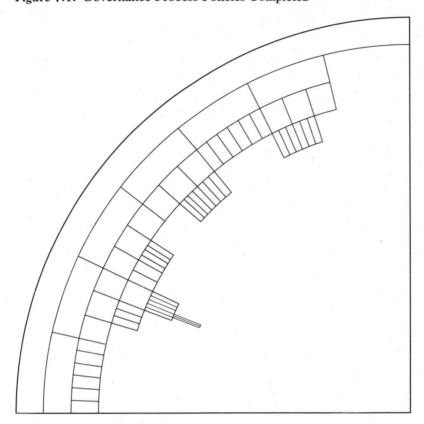

Note: The board has established its Governance Process policies deeply enough that any decisions or choices made by a delegatee will be acceptable to the board if they are a reasonable interpretation of the broader statements. Thus, the board can now safely delegate all further decisions in this category.

WANT MORE?

Further Reading

1. Carver, J. "Understanding the Special Board-Ownership Relationship." *Board Leadership*, 1995n, no. 18. Reprinted in J. Carver, *John Carver on Board Leadership*. San Francisco: Jossey-Bass, 2002.

Carver, J. "Ownership." *Board Leadership*, 1995h, no. 18. Reprinted in J. Carver, *John Carver on Board Leadership*. San Francisco: Jossey-Bass, 2002.

Carver, J. "Can a Board Establish Ends Policies Without Identifying Its Owners First?" *Board Leadership*, 1999a, no. 41.

Oliver, C. "He Who Pays the Piper Calls the Tune." *Board Leadership*, 2001b, no. 57.

Carver, J. "Thoughts on Owners and Other Stakeholders." *Board Leadership*, 2003r, no. 68.

Carver, J. "Determining Who Your Owners Are." *Board Leadership*, 1995e, no. 18. Reprinted in J. Carver, *John Carver on Board Leadership*. San Francisco: Jossey-Bass, 2002.

Carver, J. "When Owners and Customers Are the Same People." *Board Leadership*, 2000k, no. 47.

Carver, J. "Clarifying the Distinction Between Owners and Customers." *Board Leadership*, 2001d, no. 55.

Carver, J. "When Customers Are Owners: The Confusion of Dual Board Hats." *Nonprofit World*, 1992p, *10*(4), 11–15. Reprinted in J. Carver, *John Carver on Board Leadership*. San Francisco: Jossey-Bass, 2002.

2. Carver, J. "Understanding the Special Board-Ownership Relationship." *Board Leadership*, 1995n, no. 18. Reprinted in J. Carver, *John Carver on Board Leadership*. San Francisco: Jossey-Bass, 2002.

Carver, J. "When Owners Are Customers: The Confusion of Dual Board Hats." *Nonprofit World*, 1992p, *10*(4), 11–15. Reprinted in J. Carver, *John Carver on Board Leadership*. San Francisco: Jossey-Bass, 2002.

3. Mill, J. S. *Considerations on Representative Government*. New York: Harper, 1867.

Wolfe, J. *An Introduction to Political Philosophy*. Oxford, U.K.: Oxford University Press, 1996.

Rousseau, J. J. "Discourse on Political Economy." In J. J. Rousseau, *Jean-Jacques Rousseau: The Social Contract* (C. Betts, trans.). Oxford, U.K.: Oxford University Press, 1999. (Originally published 1758.)

Rousseau, J. J. *Jean-Jacques Rousseau: The Social Contract* (C. Betts, trans.). Oxford, U.K.: Oxford University Press, 1999. (Originally published 1762.)

Hume, D. *Philosophical Essays on Morals, Literature, and Politics.* Washington, D.C.: Duffy, 1817.

Carver, J. "A Theory of Governing the Public's Business." *Public Management* (Great Britain), Mar. 2001n, *3*(1), 53–71. Reprinted in J. Carver, *John Carver on Board Leadership.* San Francisco: Jossey-Bass, 2002.

4. Carver, J. "Bullies on the Board." *Board Leadership,* 1998d, no. 36.

Oliver, C. "Boards Behaving Badly." *Board Leadership,* 2000a, no. 51.

Oliver, C. "Cultivating Good Board Manners." *Board Leadership,* 2000c, no. 52.

Oliver, C. "Getting Personal." *Board Leadership,* 2001a, no. 55.

Oliver, C. "Developing Group Discipline." *Board Leadership,* 2003b, no. 68.

Oliver, C. "In the Minority." *Board Leadership,* 2003d, no. 65.

Carver, J. "The CEO and the Renegade Board Member." *Nonprofit World,* 1991a, *9*(6), 14–17.

Oliver, C. "Do unto Others: Cultivating Good Board Manners." *Association and Meeting Management Directory.* Winnipeg, Canada: August Communications, 2003c.

Carver, J. "Planning the Board's Conduct." *Board Leadership,* 1993m, no. 10. Reprinted in J. Carver, *John Carver on Board Leadership.* San Francisco: Jossey-Bass, 2002.

Carver, J. "When the Founding Parent Stays on the Board." *Board Leadership,* 1997s, no. 31. Reprinted in J. Carver, *John Carver on Board Leadership.* San Francisco: Jossey-Bass, 2002.

Carver, J. "A Team of Equals." *Board Leadership,* 1995m, no. 19. Reprinted in J. Carver, *John Carver on Board Leadership.* San Francisco: Jossey-Bass, 2002.

Carver, J. "Owning Your Agenda: A Long-Term View Is the Key to Taking Charge." *Board Leadership,* 1993k, no. 7. Reprinted in

J. Carver, *John Carver on Board Leadership*. San Francisco: Jossey-Bass, 2002g.

Carver, J. "Policy Governance Is Not a 'Hands Off' Model." *Board Leadership*, 1995j, no. 19. Reprinted in J. Carver, *John Carver on Board Leadership*. San Francisco: Jossey-Bass, 2002.

Leblanc, R., and Gillies, J. *Inside the Boardroom: How Boards Really Work and the Coming Revolution in Corporate Governance*. Mississauga, Ontario, Canada: Wiley, 2005.

5. Carver, J., and Carver, M. "How to Tell Board Means from Staff Means." *Board Leadership*, 2004, no. 73.

Carver, M. "Governance Isn't Ceremonial; It's a Real Job Requiring Real Skills." *Board Leadership*, 1997, no. 31.

Carver, J. "Crafting the Board Job Description." *Board Leadership*, 1993d, no. 10. Reprinted in J. Carver, *John Carver on Board Leadership*. San Francisco: Jossey-Bass, 2002.

6. Carver, J. "Give, Get, or Get Off?" *Contributions*, Sept.–Oct. 1998g, 12(5), 8–12.

Carver, J. *"Board Members as Fundraisers, Advisors, and Lobbyists."* The CarverGuide Series on Effective Board Governance, no. 11. San Francisco: Jossey-Bass, 1997b.

Carver, J. "Giving, Getting, and Governing: Finding a Place for Fundraising Among the Responsibilities of Leadership." *Board Leadership*, 1993g, no. 7. Reprinted in J. Carver, *John Carver on Board Leadership*. San Francisco: Jossey-Bass, 2002.

7. Mogensen, S. "The Big Picture: Policy Governance and Democracy." *Board Leadership*, 2003, no. 70.

Carver, J. "What Can Boards Do to Ensure That They Are Providing Full Representation of an Organization's Ownership?" *Board Leadership*, 1999i, no. 43.

Oliver, C. "When Owners Don't Agree." *Board Leadership*, 2003g, no. 70.

Oliver, C. "Understanding and Linking with the Moral Ownership of Your Organization." *Board Leadership*, 1999, no. 44.

Moore, J. "Linking with Owners: The Dos and Don'ts." *Board Leadership*, 1999, no. 46.

Kradel, E. "Just How Should Boards Communicate with Owners?" *Board Leadership*, 1999, no. 45.

Carver, J. "Connecting with the Ownership." *Board Leadership*, 1995d, no. 18. Reprinted in J. Carver, *John Carver on Board Leadership*. San Francisco: Jossey-Bass, 2002.

8. Tremaine, L. "Finding Unity and Strength Through Board Diversity." *Board Leadership*, 1999, no. 43.

Carver, J. "Achieving Meaningful Diversity in the Boardroom." *Board Leadership*, 1993a, no. 8. Reprinted in *Board Leadership*, 1999, no. 43, and in J. Carver, *John Carver on Board Leadership*. San Francisco: Jossey-Bass, 2002.

Carver, J., and Carver, M. M. *Making Diversity Meaningful in the Boardroom*. The CarverGuide Series on Effective Board Governance, no. 9. San Francisco: Jossey-Bass, 1997b.

Officers and Committees

The Chief Governance Officer and Other Divisions of Board Labor

Officers and committees are the mechanisms by which a board partitions its governance job. Establishing officers and committees is a delicate undertaking because subdivisions endanger board wholeness. Preservation of one-voice governance and integrity of board-to-CEO delegation are both threatened.

In this chapter, I address the problems and principles involved in establishing officers and then committees, introducing the role of chief governance officer (CGO). In each case, I examine the topic with respect to three factors: minimalism, protection of the CEO role (the role, not the person), and board holism. Finally, I comment on typical committees in light of Policy Governance principles.

Officers

I assume that the board has decided to name its organization's top paid executive as CEO. Further, to simplify this discussion, I will not consider the CEO to be a board officer. Commonly, boards establish the chair, vice chair, secretary, and treasurer, though it is not rare to find more than one vice chair and a chair-elect.

Minimalism

Structure is best kept to the minimum necessary to accomplish the task. Establishing more officers than needed increases complexity with no compensating gain. Consequently, a board should start with the minimum number of officers required by law and add more only as they are needed. In many jurisdictions, nonprofit boards can get by with two officers: a chairperson and a secretary.

From the minimalist standpoint, it is often hard to justify more officers. The office of vice chairperson usually exists only so that someone is readily available to fill in for an absent chairperson; however, a board can simply rotate temporary chairing duties in the absence of the chairperson. The treasurer is an unnecessary office in organizations that have a CEO. The CEO can, in many jurisdictions, double as secretary. The point I wish to make here, however, is not which officers are justified but that establishing the fewest officers required by the task will result in clearer rules and a smoother process.

Distinguishing the Chief Governance Officer from the Chief Executive Officer

Frequently, there is ambiguity between two important leadership roles. The board's leader for its own process is commonly called *chairperson, chairman, chairwoman*, simply *chair, president*, or other variations. The board's chosen leader for the operational organization is commonly called *executive director, secretary general, general secretary, general manager, superintendent, city manager, president* (again!), or other variations. In each case, a role is to be played that underlies the confusing variety of titles used. The top managerial role is normally thought of—and has been regularly referred to in previous chapters—as *chief executive officer*, abbreviated CEO.

There has, however, been no generic name for the leader of governance, the officer whose role it is to keep governance in order, the primus inter pares on the board. So when the title *president* is used, we have no idea which role is referred to. *Chairman* raises obvious gender problems, while *chairperson* and *chairwoman* seem awkward. *Chair* is innocuous but seemingly inanimate. And because the role of this person in Policy Governance goes far beyond simply chairing a meeting, it is not even fully descriptive of the job. Moreover, in the majority of U.S. and Canadian equity corporations, the management and governance leadership roles are combined in one person. Consequently, the words *chairman* and CEO are so wedded that

WANT MORE?

1

most of the distinction is lost not only in function but verbally as well. In order to have a generic term specifically and exclusively for the role of board leader that is as simple and as accurately descriptive as possible, I have introduced the expression *chief governance officer*, abbreviated CGO.

Consequently, henceforth in this text, I will refer to the CGO rather than *chair, chairman, chairwoman*, or *chairperson*. To avoid a possible source of confusion, let me add that the title of CGO as used in this book refers to the *real* chief of the governance process, not the executive position that is sometimes given that title in American corporations. Such a misunderstanding of the concept implied by the title is not surprising, given the baffling state of corporate governance in this age.

The CGO is the leader of the board's process on behalf of the board. He or she is not the board's boss. He or she is not the CEO's superior. The CGO, basically, sees to it that the board gets its job

WANT MORE?

2

done as the board has defined that job. As displayed in Figure 3.4, the CGO's decision authority rests *within* the board's, even though the board charges the CGO with keeping its own discipline in order. The CGO is a perfect illustration of Robert Greenleaf's servant-leader.

Protection of the CEO Role

Accountability works best when delegation is traceable, unitary, and balanced. For delegation to be traceable, each link from superior to subordinate must be clear to all parties. To be unitary, assignment of responsibility to and subsequent evaluation of any person must occur through a single channel rather than multiple channels. If the boss is a board, the principle of unity requires that the entire group speak as one, to preserve the single channel. To be balanced, the CEO must be answerable for that over which he or she has been given authority, but for no more.

If the CEO must answer to one voice only, no individual board officer can have any authority over the CEO or other staff. Board member Dawn Oparah of Peachtree City, Georgia, states, "We will deliberate in many voices but govern in one." Most violations of this principle involve the CGO or treasurer, each of whom has been known to assume authority over staff functions. The board-CEO connection is interrupted as much by an officer who assumes individual authority over the CEO as by any other board member who does so. The executive either works for the board as a whole or does not.

If the CGO has no authority over the CEO, who tells the CEO what the board expects? The board does. When the board speaks with one voice in explicit statements, what can the CGO legitimately add? If the CGO presumes to represent the board to management, he or she either is acting unnecessarily (if nothing is added) or abusing authority (if something is added). Moreover, an executive who is obliged to acquiesce to what the CGO adds is now (1) working for the CGO alone and can no longer be called CEO (because the CGO is now acting as CEO) or (2) working for both board and CGO, which is untenable because it is not unitary.

A similar flaw in delegation is commonly found in the treasurer's role. A board holds its CEO accountable for financial integrity. The CEO is given commensurate authority to do whatever is necessary (establish financial methods, keep records, adjust budgets) to maintain whatever level of financial safety the board finds acceptable. Yet more than half of the sets of bylaws I have encountered state that the treasurer of the board is charged with the books of account, disbursement, and a host of other financial management activities.

If the treasurer is responsible, then an integral part of management accountability has been taken from the CEO. The case can be made that the CEO role, thus dismembered, no longer exists. Does the treasurer have the authority to carry out this role? If not, then responsibility and authority are not matched. If so, does that mean the treasurer has authority over financial staff and perhaps over the CEO? Does the CEO then work for the treasurer as well as for the board? On the other hand, if the CEO is the one account-able to the board for financial probity, how can the bylaws assign the job to the treasurer?

The office of treasurer in such an organization is like a vestigial organ. It may have been needed when the organization was so small that the board treasurer truly did fulfill that financial function. Or perhaps that never was the case, but legal counsel inserted a boil-erplate provision in the bylaws, despite its meaninglessness. In any event, boards, executives, and staff financial officers across the land wade through wasteful nonsense every month, pretending that the treasurer role makes sense.

I often encounter the following process. The staff financial offi-cer and CEO confer with the treasurer prior to a board meeting. At the meeting, the freshly briefed treasurer recapitulates what he or she has been told. The treasurer looks informed, and the board feels secure because the ritual continues. Substituting finance commit-tee for treasurer in this scenario does not make the pretense any more reasonable.

Some boards slightly alter the treasurer issue by creating assistant treasurers who are staff members involved in finance. In this version, bylaws give the treasurer the usual overstated responsibilities but allow the treasurer to delegate any number of them to assistants. Now there is delegation from a board officer not only to the osten-sible CEO but also to the CEO's subordinates. Just who is responsi-ble for what and to whom in these convoluted circumstances?

The truth is, in the presence of a CEO, there is no role for a board treasurer that is both necessary and legitimate. If an unnec-essary role is manufactured, great care must be taken that it be legit-imate. One reasonable, albeit still manufactured role would be to monitor financial performance; however, this role is illegitimate if the treasurer monitors financial performance against criteria other than those set forth in the board's policies. And when the board's criteria are clear and when monitoring information precisely answers to these criteria, an expert interpreter is rarely needed.

Board Holism

A holistic board is a single organizational position and must officially behave as one. Board officers exist to help the board do its job, not as powers unto themselves. For the minimum two officer positions, I suggest the following job descriptions, stated in the job product style:

> *Chief governance officer:* Responsible for the integrity of board process
>
> *Secretary:* Responsible for the integrity of board documents

These job responsibilities serve the wholeness of governance. They do not interfere with unitary delegation to the CEO. The CGO is not responsible for the functioning of the organization nor for the quality of the CEO. The CGO is responsible for the functioning of the board, which ordinarily proves to be job enough! Using the board job description from Chapter Seven, the CGO can trust that if the board works well, CEO performance will follow.

If the CGO's job product is integrity of board process, selection of a CGO should be based on ability to achieve that output. The CGO's job requires skilled handling of group process and an ability to lead a group fairly but firmly, to confront and even to welcome its diversity, and to adhere to board-stated rules for board conduct. Boards should take great care to choose CGOs who can develop the leadership that often lies dormant in the group. Rather than foisting a heavy-handed discipline on board members, a good CGO incites the board to generate all the rules it needs out of its own wisdom. The CGO merely calls forth the board's own statements of discipline when needed, as if he or she has no choice but to deal with the group in the way the group itself has decreed. The David M greeting card sentiment penned by Monica Sicile to describe friends aptly describes good CGOs as well: "Friends sing your song when you forget the words." A good CGO

WANT MORE?

3

demonstrates the optimum combination of discipline and group responsibility when, with as much affection as firmness, he or she confronts the board with its own song.

The quality of governance often depends on the skill of the chairing party. The better the board, the more judiciously it chooses a CGO; but ironically, the more responsible the board is as a group, the less the CGO makes a difference in the near term. Boards belittle governance when they choose CGOs on the basis of length of service or availability. It is better to obtain a good leader who can invest three hours a month than a marginal leader who has thirty hours to give. Many a CEO has seethed under a CGO who had time to spare.

It is essential to remember that the CGO works for the board, not the reverse. Therefore, if the CGO interferes with the board's getting its job done well, the board has no one to blame but itself. So the importance of the CGO's job is not that it wields the topmost authority in the organization but that it is needed by the board to assist the board's wielding of that topmost authority. That being the case, I still wish to emphasize that the CGO is a central figure in the governance process. The Policy Governance model not only equips the board for excellent governance but also enables the CGO to do his or her job well. In Northern Ireland, Brian Acheson, who is chairman of the board at Castlereagh College, Belfast, attests to this, saying that " [I] found that I had an approach for dealing with everything required of me: planning the annual cycle of business, discharging probity and process obligations, engaging members in purposeful consideration of organizational priorities, and responding to unforeseen events. It is my first term in office, but I feel like an experienced pro." Policy Governance requires more decision making of a CGO than that involved in simply chairing meetings, but it also offers a valuable blueprint for the rest of this vital job.

The board of the American Institutes of Research has a policy that outlines the board chair's job (Exhibit 8.1) in terms of values added and authority to take action.

**Exhibit 8.1. American Institutes of Research, Washington, D.C.
Governance Process Policy
"Board Chair Job Description"**

The Chair of the Board is a specially empowered member of the Board, the chief governance officer, whose role is to assure the integrity of the Board's process and, secondarily, to occasionally represent the Board to outside parties.

1. The assigned result of the Chair's job is that the Board behaves consistently with its own rules and those legitimately imposed upon it from outside the organization.

   A. Meeting discussion content will be on those issues that, according to Board policy, belong to the Board to decide or to monitor.

   B. Information that is neither for monitoring performance nor for Board decisions will be avoided or minimized and always noted as such.

   C. Deliberation will be fair, open, and thorough, but also timely, orderly, and kept to the point.

2. The authority of the Chair consists in making decisions that fall within topics covered by Board policies on Governance Process and Board-CEO Linkage, with the exception of (a) employment or termination of a CEO, and (b) where the Board specifically delegates portions of this authority to others. The Chair is authorized to use any reasonable interpretation of the provisions in these policies.

   A. The Chair is empowered to chair Board meetings with all the commonly accepted power of that position, such as ruling and recognizing.

   B. The Chair has no authority to make decisions about policies created by the Board within Ends and Executive Limitations policy areas. Therefore, the Chair has no authority to supervise or direct the CEO.

   C. The Chair may represent the Board to outside parties in announcing Board-stated positions and in stating Chair decisions and interpretations within the area delegated to her or him.

   D. The Chair may delegate this authority, but remains accountable for its use.

The CGO's responsibility to board holism extends to his or her ex officio role with the public and press. When interviewed, the CGO does not have the authority to venture beyond what the board has actually said. "Representing the board" means stating only what the board has stated, unless the board has specifically granted further authority. One workable way to carry out this function is to apply the same delegation principle applied to the CEO, except within the Governance Process and Board-Management Delegation policy categories. This approach allows the CGO to make decisions about board process and mechanics as well as specifics of the delegation and monitoring process so long as she or he is within the board's broader pronouncements on these topics. The CGO cannot, however, interpret Ends and Executive Limitations. To do so would be to instruct staff and, thereby, to be in conflict with the authority the board has given to the CEO. These distinctions are shown graphically in Figure 3.4, in which separate domains are assigned to CGO and CEO.

While the CGO is guardian of what the board is doing, the secretary is guardian of what the board has done. If the secretary's job product is "integrity of board documents," selection of a secretary should be based on ability to make that contribution. Responsible for no one else's behavior but his or her own, the secretary need only be compulsive about correctness, accuracy, and appearance. The secretary's job may have little to do with taking minutes but will have much to do with the official record of process and actions. He or she certifies the evidence of board action, including board policies and minutes.

The "Board Job Description" policy of the International Policy Governance Association (Exhibit 7.4) states the job outputs that would constitute the board's connecting owner values (item 1) through to managerial performance (item 3). The intervening board output (item 2) is the explicit clarification of decisions in the four policy categories already described.

Minutes constitute the most basic record of board action. Even the all-important board policies cannot be shown to have been created or altered except through the authority of the minutes. What any board "says" includes only those statements passed in an official process. Detailed, narrative minutes (more than what the board has *officially* said) are unnecessary and detract from the board's unitary voice, as well as loading the record with material of negligible official significance. In long minutes, it is almost impossible for the writer to render an unbiased record of the board conversation. If the minutes are wrong, someone has been misrepresented; if they are right, it does not matter, because only official motions that are passed represent board action. A record of official motions and any statements that individual members specifically wish the record to show suffice for minutes in almost any board situation.

Committees

Board committees are to help get the board's job done, not to help with the staff's job. Like officers, committees should be established with due care for minimalism, preservation of the CEO role, and holism. Have no more committees than absolutely needed. Do not compromise the clear accountability linkage between the board and its CEO. Disturb board wholeness as little as possible.

Minimalism

Traditionally, we speak of boards and committees in the same breath. Boards are supposed to have committees, aren't they? Some boards have told me that they determined their size on the basis of how many members were needed for committees! And these were governing boards with nothing to do but govern; they did not need or use committees to make up for lack of staff. Committees can serve a useful function, but the propitious path is to start with no committees and add them only when they are clearly needed.

Even then, the choice to establish committees, no matter how intelligently made, is not simply a decision about ideal structure. There are no right committees to have, no list of correct subdivisions for getting a job done. None of the common committees is indispensable—not even audit or compensation committees, despite recent changes in corporate governance practices. Subdividing the board to get a job done is the personal preference of board members at the time. A particular mixture of persons may work better or worse in subgroups, depending on the members' personal characteristics.

Protection of the CEO Role

Board committees are established to aid the process of governance, not management. This simple rule safeguards the board-CEO accountability relationship. When board committees are assigned tasks that make them oversee, become involved in, or advise on management functions, it becomes less clear who is in charge of these activities. Personnel, executive, and finance committees are habitual offenders. The CEO role deteriorates as a result of these committees' well-intended interference. The board's ability to hold the CEO accountable deteriorates apace.

Unfortunately, many board committees are actually designed to be involved in staff-level issues. This is bound to occur when the boards themselves are involved below their level. The problem seems even greater in committees than in full boards because of the belief that committees should be involved in details and because of the traditional committee assignments.

Level of Work

It is widely accepted that committees should delve into more detail than the board as a whole. To boards that insist on acting on staff-level issues, forming a subgroup to work through the details may well make sense. But to the extent that boards extricate themselves from staff work to do board work, this need evaporates. If the committee is to help the board do its proper work, working at the lower level is neither appropriate nor helpful.

Board committees should work at the board's level, not below it. With respect to policymaking, the best contribution a committee can make is to prepare board-level policy issues for board deliberation. With respect to the nonpolicymaking aspects of a board's job (for example, linkage to ownership or fundraising), committees may deal with details, though even then not in areas that have been delegated to staff.

Topics

Just as board policy types need not reflect management divisions of labor or administrative categories, there is no reason for boards to form subgroups based on administrative categories. When boards create committees with titles that duplicate staff functions, those committees can be expected to drift into staff work. Personnel committees automatically work at the staff personnel officer level. Finance committees usually slip into a comparable trap. Committees dealing with specific staff programs will likely find themselves dealing with staff-level management issues concerning those programs.

When a board committee works at the staff level, the crisp board-CEO-staff chain of accountability disintegrates. Look at the relationship between the committee and affected staff. For whom does the staff work—the committee or the CEO? If the staff works for the CEO, then it cannot take direction from the committee (otherwise, the CEO can hardly be held accountable for the outcome); yet such direction, more or less subtle, does take place. If the staff works for the committee, then there is no true CEO because the board has chosen to delegate to staff through more than one channel.

Some boards protest that such committees exist only to advise staff, thereby making good use of the special skills of board members. But advice to staff by committees—or even by the full board—is suspect. Although offering advice (as opposed to giving instructions) may be a committee's honest intention, the staff members are seldom so sure. Boards may easily overlook the lack of clarity, but staffs rarely escape its consequences. Staff members are loath to treat committee input as they would true advice—that is, advice with no strings attached.

What does one do with advice from the boss? If it is merely advice rather than a directive, there is no obligation to pay attention. If it is merely advice, advisees are within their rights to dispense with one set of advisers and select another or no one. If it is merely advice, the staff members may, by not attending meetings or reading reports, effectively disband the committee. If it is merely advice, the board will not think ill of its staff for these rebuffs. If the board has made ends and executive limitations clear, evaluation of staff members—even informal evaluations—on the basis of their acceptance of advice is not only superfluous but pernicious.

Advisory mechanisms should be totally within the control of advisees. Staff members who want advice should obtain it however they deem best and from anyone they choose. Staff may ask board members for advice, as long as all parties understand the advice given is informative, not directive. Board members can advise freely as long as that counsel is not misconstrued as subtle orders. Establishing formal board committees to advise staff, however, is not only unnecessary but damaging. Susan McGillicuddy, elected trustee in Meridian Township, Michigan, was pleased that "our staff now don't have needless and duplicative subcommittee meetings and have been the backbone [of] our achievements."

Policy Governance rules for committees hinge on committees' origin rather than their composition. So a board committee belongs to the board and a staff committee to the staff, regardless of who is on the committee. Therefore, a board committee of both board and **WANT MORE?** staff composition would follow board committee rules and guard against slipping into staff-level issues. Board committees need never relate directly with staff except to gather intelligence for use in subsequent board deliberations or for board-authorized staff support.

Board Holism

No common practice so threatens board wholeness as the traditional approach to committee work. Let us consider how committees' work can be useful to a board at minimal cost to its unity.

Traditionally, boards with a great many decisions to make have found it natural to divide their labor. Several committees working simultaneously can digest and form solutions for several times as many problems as can the board working as a whole. Each committee works as a board in microcosm, studying, debating, formulating, and finally arriving at a course of action and recommendations for adoption by the board.

What does a board do with recommendations originating from its several committees? It can review each committee's entire process so that all board members understand and participate in the problem-solving experience; however, to do so would unnecessarily duplicate committee work and, in fact, obviate the need for committee work. So, by and large, committee recommendations are accepted. To avoid feeling like rubber stamps, board members may ask a few questions and put the committee on the spot before they give approval. Most board members accept that they do not know as much about issues handled by committees of which they are not a part. Unless there is reason to believe the committee is incompetent or biased, they accept the recommendations.

In reality, then, the board does not aggregate its values across a wide range of governance topics. It aggregates the values within committees on one topic at a time: the values of Liza, Erin, and Hannah about personnel; the values of Rachael, Martin, and Richard about finance; the values of Terry, Buckley, Tanya, and Jennifer about programs, and on and on. On the surface, the board is fulfilling its obligation to speak with one voice, but in fact, except for a relatively perfunctory approval vote, there is no board. There is only a group of congenial miniboards, inappropriately importing into governance a method that would be quite rational in a workgroup.

A governing board's responsibility is to create an integrated set of values that, taken together, cradle or encompass the nature of organization. Proper governance is not a piecemeal endeavor. Whole-board decision making tends to illuminate the dark corners where staff or individual board members can exercise undue power by pushing an idiosyncratic agenda. *The only way a board can create unified policies is to do so as a whole body.* Fortunately, when a board attends to the larger policy issues and refrains from prescribing executive methods, its job becomes manageable and the board can make decisions as a whole. The quality of the policies thus created reflects the value coloration of the entire governing body across all topics.

Consequently, board committees, when they are needed to assist the board in decision making, should do preboard work, not subboard work. They may work on matters before the board does, but at the board level. They should not work below the board level—in other words, at staff level. But if bringing a recommendation to the board does not support board holism, then what is effective "preboard" work? In boards that govern by policy, most committee work relates to board decisions about policy. A minor part of board work is doing rather than saying, and in these "doing" instances, committees can be used to accomplish an objective as long as their work does not overlap with that of the CEO.

Examples of "doing" jobs for a board committee might be choosing a venue for the annual meeting or designing a training program for board members. This kind of doing, because it is restricted to functions that belong solely to the board, causes no role conflict with the CEO. For this discussion, however, I consider only what committees can do to help boards create policy.

If a board is to deliberate and adopt a policy position, it will do a better job if several options are available. Having only one option is a flaw inherent in the recommendation practice. The availability of several alternatives, however, will not necessarily lead to an intelligent choice unless the board is aware of the implications of each option. In other words, the board needs to know the choices and the consequences of these choices. Only then can it ponder, debate, and vote intelligently.

A useful preboard job product of a committee is just such a recounting of policy alternatives and their implications. To produce alternatives and implications for the board, the committee must proceed through several careful steps. Assume that some problem, opportunity, or situation has arisen. The matter may have been assigned to the committee by the board or the committee may have come across it in the course of related work.

The committee's first task is to clarify just what the board-level issue is. Determining the appropriate question makes it possible to search for optional answers. The committee must be certain that it is addressing the correct issue, for it is not uncommon to spend prodigious time probing the wrong issues. Issues are incorrect when they belong to someone else or when they have been inadequately formulated—for example, when an issue has been stated at an inappropriate breadth. The committee then seeks alternative policy wording available to the board in answer to the issue. Next, the committee investigates the implications of each policy option in terms of cost, public relations, productivity, and other factors.

Relevant implications will shape how the emerging policy is formulated, so they must be approached thoughtfully. Staff may be called to assist, not in selecting a course of action but in ensuring that available options and important implications have not been omitted. External help may prove useful as well; the board's auditing firm, for example, may have helpful input regarding implications for specific financial options under consideration. The committee's product, then, consists of policy options and their implications.

Board members discuss, persuade, and vote. There is no committee choice to rubber-stamp, nor does the board redo what the committee has already done. No recommendation is necessary. (The committee may express its preferred option, but doing so would be of little utility.) In this process, the committee's job and the board's job are sequential and separate. Because all board members know the relevant implications of each option, a member not on the authoring committee is just as capable of casting an informed vote as anyone on that committee. Using a clearly presented survey of options and implications, then, the board makes a choice as a board.

Remember that boards that govern by policy need not deal with a flurry of never-ending details and low-level issues. They have the time to make fewer, though broader, decisions reflectively. Though they deal with massive value conflicts, these are not boards that react to every staff crisis or that feel nothing should go on that they do not know about. Boards that govern by policy can afford adequate preparation and wide-ranging board consideration of strategic interests.

The Bissell Centre board's policy on committees (Exhibit 8.2) protects the executive director's relationship with the board. Note that the policy attempts to prevent committees from becoming overly identified with any single area of organization, a common cause of the unofficial, topic-specific "miniboards" that some boards, unfortunately, allow to develop.

My approach to the policy role of board committees places a high value on action by the whole board. It values board-integrated oversight of large issues more than participation of segments of the board in narrow slices of the organization. With this approach, the bromide "real work takes place in committees" no longer holds true. The board meeting is the place of action. It is not the place for ritual voting or for carrying out the unnecessary business that clutters most board agendas. It is where leaders come together to make leadership decisions.

Legitimate Committees

If board committees should not be tied conceptually or physically to the specific divisions of staff labor and staff topics, to what should they be related? Which committees might a board use? Recall that the policymaking job is divided into four discrete categories. One option might be to structure committees around these categories.

One committee does preparatory work for board choices about ends, a second prepares for choices about executive limitations, a third prepares for policies about governance process, and a final one prepares for policies on board-management delegation. Since the

Exhibit 8.2. Bissell Centre of Edmonton, Alberta, Canada Governance Process Policy "Committee Principles"

The board may, from time to time, establish committees to help carry out its responsibilities. To preserve board holism, committees will be used sparingly, only when other methods have been deemed inadequate. Committees will be used so as to minimally interfere with the wholeness of the board's job.

1. Board committees may not speak or act for the board except when formally given such authority for specific and time-limited purposes. Such authority will be carefully stated in order not to conflict with authority delegated to the Executive Director.

2. Board committees are to help the board do its job, not to help the staff do its job. Committees will assist the board chiefly by preparing policy alternatives and implications for board deliberation. Board committees are not to be created by the board to advise staff.

3. If a board committee is used to monitor organizational performance in a given area, the same committee will not have helped the board create policy in that area. This is to prevent committee identification with organizational parts rather than the whole.

4. Board committees cannot exercise authority over staff, and in keeping with the board's focus on the future, board committees will ordinarily have no direct dealings with current staff operations. Further, the board will not impede its direct delegation to the Executive Director by requiring approval of a board committee before an executive action.

---

categories are exhaustive, the committee topics are exhaustive. If ad hoc rather than standing committees are desired, committees can be established whenever a special need arises, then disbanded. In either case, the nature of preboard work would be the same. When proper principles for committee work are maintained, the actual structuring is of less import. The structure may change as the board's need for subgroups evolves.

Comments on Traditional Committees

The approach to board committees that I have presented here differs substantially from conventional wisdom. To underscore this model's departure from governance as usual, let us look at several frequently encountered committees in light of the new concepts.

Personnel committees. There is no justification for standing personnel committees. After assisting the board on one or two policies, personnel committees have no place to go but into staff work. The board of an organization with a CEO never has a managerially legitimate reason to establish a personnel committee. But what about hiring a new CEO and handling grievances? If these tasks are so frequent as to require a standing committee, the board has a problem that will not be addressed by the establishment of a committee.

Executive committees. Executive committees are typically used to make board decisions between board meetings, an authority infrequently bestowed on any other board committee. Consequently, an executive committee tends to become the real board within the board, with debilitating effects on holism. An insider-outsider division among board members is not an uncommon result; the executive committee "becomes the 'in' group of the board, with a corresponding loss of interest and attention of other trustees" (Haskins, 1972, p. 12). If the board is of a manageable size, an executive committee as usually defined is not needed; however, circumstances peculiar to a given board may unavoidably impose a large board size, and an executive committee may be necessary in order to get business done. This necessity may arise, for example, due to the cost of assembling a large, geographically dispersed board.

When not established because of board size, an executive committee ordinarily arises because of a lack of clarity in the board's delegation of authority to the CEO. Thus, executive committees (1) assume prerogatives that should be left to the board, (2) make or approve executive decisions that should be left to the CEO, or (3) do both. In other words, executive committees that are authorized to act must take power from the board or from the CEO or both, thus weakening the central authority structure. When board meetings are as frequent as monthly, establishing an executive committee to make board decisions between meetings is specious. Board decisions will not arise that often if the board is proactive and delegates properly.

Program committees. If the program committee is involved in staff implementation decisions, it can be dropped with no loss. But if it prepares board-level issues for discussion, then it is in order. Program committees can be legitimate, as I described earlier, doing pre-board work with respect to ends. Most program committees I have encountered, however, are involved in program means rather than program ends, relating their work directly to current and near-term staff operations, and thus are inappropriate.

Finance committees. There is scant justification for finance committees, which are much like personnel committees. They can assist the board in developing a very few Executive Limitations policies on financial matters. After that, they have no place to go but into staff work. Sometimes, legitimate board work in fundraising is assigned to a finance committee, though the two functions are vastly different. In such cases, it would be better to rename the committee (calling it, for example, a *development committee*), so as not to invite it into inappropriate activity. With adequate financial Executive Limitations policies and the pointed, systematic monitoring described in Chapter Six, boards with CEOs have no need for finance committees.

If, however, the board has retained the function of safeguarding endowment or reserve funds, then an executive governance committee (to use the term previously introduced) might well be used to carry out that task. In this case, the board job description would include a fourth value added by the board's work—for example, "safety and return of reserve funds"; otherwise, the board would have no direct responsibility that could be delegated to a committee.

Nominating committees. The nominating committee exists not to help the board create policy but to help it replenish itself or its officers. This committee is a proper governance committee and is the only board committee that may need to be described and empowered in the bylaws, particularly if it is a membership committee (rather than a board committee) that selects nominees for the board.

Traditionally, committees and officers are often used to monitor staff performance. Chapter Six argues for monitoring organizational performance only against the criteria formulated by board policies. If the criteria exist and monitoring takes place as described, the need for committees or officers to monitor is all but eliminated. Need for a subgroup is often a sign that criteria have not been set forth or have not been set forth clearly. If monitoring reports are precisely aimed at the policies being monitored, boards can end the wasteful practice of using board time in meetings to determine whether criteria have been met. Officers and committees can then cease their unnecessary work and attend wholeheartedly to helping the board put its strategic leadership in order.

Next Chapter

Codifying board values and processes is a necessary element in enabling board leadership to be all it can be. Chapter Two makes a case for governing by policy, but using a new approach to that task. Subsequent chapters describe four categories of board policies along with implications of the new approach for the board as a whole, board officers, and board committees. Real-life policies are presented in the foregoing chapters to illustrate discrete policy topics. In the next chapter, I demonstrate the flow of policy creation from the global level toward more detailed levels—that is, how policies are developed through a number of graduated levels.

WANT MORE?

Further Reading

1. Carver, J. "The Case for a 'CGO.'" *Board Leadership*, 2001c, no. 56.

   Carver, J., and Oliver, C. "The Case for a CGO" (Appendix B). *Corporate Boards That Create Value*. San Francisco: Jossey-Bass, 2002b.

2. Carver, J. "The Unique Double Servant-Leadership Role of the Board Chairperson." In L. C. Spears and M. Lawrence (eds.), *Practicing Servant Leadership: Succeeding Through Trust, Bravery, and Forgiveness*. San Francisco: Jossey-Bass, 2004i.

3. Carver, J. "Reining in a Runaway Chair." *Board Leadership*, 1998o, no. 38. Reprinted in J. Carver, *John Carver on Board Leadership*. San Francisco: Jossey-Bass, 2002.

   Carver, J. "Who Sets the Board Agenda?" *Board Leadership*, 1999j, no. 41.

   Carver, J. "Separating Chair and CEO Roles with Smoke and Mirrors." *Board Leadership*, 2003p, no. 68.

   Carver, J. *The Unique Double Servant-Leadership Role of the Board Chairperson*. Voices of Servant-Leadership Series, no. 2. Indianapolis, Ind.: Greenleaf Center for Servant-Leadership, Feb. 1999h.

   Oliver, C. "A Debatable Alliance." *Board Leadership*, 2005b, no. 77.

   Carver, J. *The Chairperson's Role as Servant-Leader to the Board*. The CarverGuide Series on Effective Board Governance, no. 3. San Francisco: Jossey-Bass, 1996d.

   Carver, J. "A Few Tips for the Chairperson." *Board Leadership*, 1992c, no. 3, p. 6. Reprinted in J. Carver, *John Carver on Board Leadership*. San Francisco: Jossey-Bass, 2002.

   Carver, J. "Sometimes You Have to Fire Your Chair." *Board Leadership*, 1996s, no. 28. Reprinted in J. Carver, *John Carver on Board Leadership*. San Francisco: Jossey-Bass, 2002.

4. Carver, J. "Committee Mania Among City Councils." *Board Leadership*, 2003c, no. 68.

Carver, J. "Rethinking the Executive Committee." *Board Leadership*, 2000h, no. 52.

Carver, J. "Board Committees: Essential and Non-Essential." *Contributions*, July–Aug. 1998b, *12*(4), 20, 35.

Oliver, C. "The Strange World of Audit Committees." *Ivey Business Journal* (University of Western Ontario), Mar.–Apr. 2003e, *67*(4), 1–4. (Also available as reprint no. 9B03TB09 at www.iveybusinessjournal.com.)

Carver, J. "The Executive Committee: Turning a Governance Liability into an Asset." *Board Leadership*, 1994c, no. 14. Reprinted in J. Carver, *John Carver on Board Leadership*. San Francisco: Jossey-Bass, 2002.

Carver, J. "What If the Committee Chair Just Wants to Know?" *Board Leadership*, 1997o, no. 29. Reprinted in J. Carver, *John Carver on Board Leadership*. San Francisco: Jossey-Bass, 2002.

9

Policy Development by Levels
Adding Details Judiciously

In Policy Governance, policies are neither monolithic documents nor rhetorical masterpieces. They are statements that are carefully assembled level by level. The concept of policy levels has already been explained as a spectrum from the most inclusive, global statements to the most specific, focused ones. Policies created in this way have a distinctive architecture—an outline format in which the preamble carries the most global meaning, with narrower statements appearing under it and further outline subparts cascading when necessary to fulfill the policy's intent.

The Crucial Difference Between Levels and Lists

To make proper use of the concept of policy levels, the board must understand how levels differ from lists. It is so common as to be ubiquitous in governance publications to list the decisions the board is to make alongside the decisions management is to make. Because there is an appealing simplicity to dividing the labor in this way, few question it. Sometimes the lists go a bit further, displaying columns in which a checkmark indicates whether a certain document or decision is decided by the board, recommended by the CEO and approved by the board, decided jointly by board and CEO, or decided by the CEO. Of course, division of authority between board and management is done entirely differently in Policy Governance.

Policy Governance recognizes that the board is accountable for everything and therefore, in the absence of clear delegation, must decide everything. But delegation is not a matter of choosing up which burdens will be borne by whom. Between equals, that method would suffice. For example, as equals, you and I might agree on your accomplishing this part of the total tasks while I achieve the other part. If we are related by hierarchy, however, you in the higher position are still accountable for what you give to me to do in my lower position. In other words, not only are all jobs yours prior to your delegating to me, but accountability for them remains yours even after you've delegated to me. You cannot delegate an obligation you did not personally start off having. Thus, in dividing tasks, the board is delegating; the board and CEO are not "choosing up."

Policy Governance deals with this matter by viewing delegation as a series of decreasingly enveloping layers. The board begins with all authority and direct responsibility. It can never rid itself of any of the total accountability imposed by that fact. But it can make decisions at the greatest breadth of the accountability, assigning lower levels to management. To preserve its accountability, the board must demand (not request or hope) that management use the authority thus delegated so that all its smaller decisions remain within the board's broader ones. In other words, the board's decisions are all-enveloping when made and remain all-enveloping as organizational activities proceed.

This concept works as long as the board very carefully confines itself to the most enveloping decisions (represented in Policy Governance as the broadest policies) and drops into less enveloping ones *only one level at a time*. However many levels of decisions the board makes will form an unbroken blanket of decisions that contain all other decisions by delegatees. This blanket covers every possible organizational action, decision, situation, or achievement—the "logical containment" feature of Policy Governance that was discussed in Chapter Three.

Mechanically, these board decisions take the outline form I have shown in exhibits throughout the text. Within each policy, there may or may not be lists, but such lists are *always* within a single level of policymaking. Moreover, this approach is incompatible with the "board approves budget" kind of checklist. Why? A budget is made up of many different levels of decisions, from a broad one about the relationship to be maintained between revenues and expenses to a narrow one about whether hiring cleaning staff is preferred to contracting with a cleaning company. In the budget format, not only can the board not address the broadest levels of decisions, but the levels are not even distinctly displayed. One can't tell which aspects of budget the board will decide and which ones it is content to allow management to decide. Budget approval is but one illustration of how the authorship of decisions is frequently ambiguous in traditional decision-making systems.

It was the Policy Governance model's unique and clarifying approach to distinguishing governance and management decisions that first attracted the attention of the Office of Company Secretary of British Petroleum in 1995, the Australian Department of Defense in 2000, and others along the way. This feature of the model, according to Monica van der Hoff-Israël, general manager of the National Project Implementing Lump Sum Financing in Dutch Primary Education, provides "absolute clarity to all parties in organizations about who deals with what."

The fact that the board moves from broader decisions to narrower ones helps in knowing which issues are appropriate for the board's agenda. As shown in Figure 9.1, issues that are slightly narrower than ones already committed to board policy are appropriate, because the board always has the right to move toward greater detail. But narrower issues than that are not appropriate for board decisions, because deciding those smaller issues would involve

Figure 9.1. Appropriateness of Issues for Board Decision Making

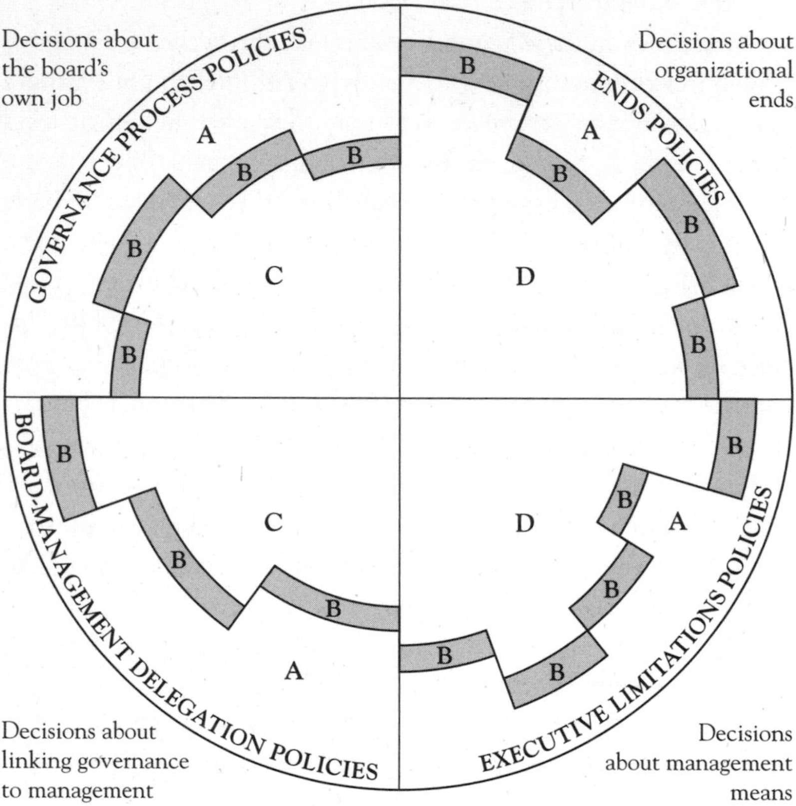

Decisions about the board's own job

GOVERNANCE PROCESS POLICIES

Decisions about organizational ends

ENDS POLICIES

BOARD-MANAGEMENT DELEGATION POLICIES

Decisions about linking governance to management

EXECUTIVE LIMITATIONS POLICIES

Decisions about management means

Note: The policy circle from previous chapters is marked here with board decisions already made and adopted in policy language (A); decisions at a level currently the prerogative of the CGO or CEO but proper for the board to make if it wishes to narrow the range of authorized interpretation (B); decisions at a level currently delegated to the CGO (C) or CEO (D) that are *inappropriate* for the board to make.

leaping over intervening broader issues. Not only does jumping levels destroy the wholeness of the purview delegated to CGO or CEO, but it eliminates a natural safeguard against the board's unnecessarily dipping into a bits-and-pieces style of decision making in which the board makes decisions about whatever issues happen to catch its attention.

Of course, issues in the real world pop up randomly, not organized and classified according to the neat Policy Governance categories of type and level. Boards must learn how to "abstract up" to broader issues that envelop or contain the more specific one that has burst to members' attention. For example, if the board is worried about late-working employees going to their cars in a dark parking lot, it would abstract that concern up to its value about endangering staff in any way. The next level above that one might be the board's value about

WANT MORE? prudence and ethics with regard to staff in general, but it is
likely to have already covered that broad issue. Having thus abstracted up a little too far, the board would then come down just a little and discuss policy that would deal with the highest form of the issue it has not yet addressed (general endangerment). It might or might not choose to adopt such a policy addition. This approach minimizes the volume of board decisions and ensures that decisions driven by specifics do not leave cracks between the roles.

Form and Function

To demonstrate the sequence in which levels of policy are created, in this section, I display a series of policies developed by real boards.

Ground Rules

Because of the verbal nature of the board's task, the use and even the arrangement of words are important factors in governing. Here are a few ground rules for developing and displaying the board's words.

Participation and voting. The board can invite anyone to partic-ipate in its task of policy creation. Staff members, outside experts, persons from other boards, or anyone that the board feels can help it make wiser choices is free to play a role in debate. Although it is important for the board to be open about this phase, it is just as im-portant for it to guard its own right to make the choice. Anyone can participate, but only the board will vote.

Decision information. In Chapter Six, I described the differences among information for decisions, information for monitoring, and information for incidental purposes. As the board prepares to create policy, its single-minded focus should be on decision information. Decision information is of whatever nature and comes from whatever source the board finds appropriate. For example, ends decisions might require demographic data, needs assessment data, owner testimony, staff input concerning operational capabilities and costs, and information about what has been possible in similar organizations.

Boards developing Executive Limitations policies might call for information from financial, risk management, or other experts. These experts are in a position to understand what can go wrong and, therefore, what to prohibit by policy. Because such outside experts may be accustomed to traditional governance, they may need to learn relevant aspects of Policy Governance before they can help effectively. One straightforward approach is to ask the expert, "If you were on this board—not in charge of the staff function that manages this issue—what would you be worried might happen?"

Board-Management Delegation and Governance Process policy development are directly related to the board's own means. Adopting a fully developed conceptual model of the board's job will help the board answer many questions in these areas. Gathering information about how other organizations function within that model may also be a useful exercise.

Everything in its place. When the board creates policy, it does so within one of the four categories of board policy: Ends, Executive Limitations, Board-Management Delegation, or Governance Process. Policy is not to be created that either (1) falls outside these categories or (2) crosses these categories. Either flaw would reveal that the board is not rigorously defining its task. Any legitimate single governance issue can only be in one of the categories, not several. Furthermore, board members will often need to translate the organizational issue they want to address to a higher level ("abstract up") before dealing with it. Normally, policy issues are not generated from events in an organization but rather from the board's studied consideration of its leadership task. Thus, the board would usually create policy proactively, but on infrequent occasions it might do so in reaction to considerations it had overlooked until it was stimulated by some current event.

Proceeding from the top down. A board addresses policy issues by beginning at the global level and only proceeding to more detailed levels after the top level is complete; the written policies reflect this progression. Thus, a policy may consist of only a single sentence. Or it may consist of the single sentence that forms a preamble, followed by one or more statements (which I've designated with numbers), each of which either stands alone or is followed by further indented substatements (designated with letters). Theoretically, there is no limit to how far this sequence can go. Pragmatically, the limit is encountered rather quickly, for as the board goes into greater detail, the workload involved—carefully gathering information on all options, then debating and voting at each step—grows geometrically.

Meticulous care. Because board policy has an extensive multiplier effect, it must be created with care and exactitude. The board's policymaking process needs to be akin to a commercial airline pilot's filing a careful flight plan rather than deciding routes as the mood strikes him or her along the way. A well-designed policy is a lever that multiplies the board's effort, providing immense power. Archimedes said that if he had a lever long enough and a place to stand, he could move the earth. Due to its power, well-designed policymaking imposes a burden of precision greater than most boards are accustomed to.

Format

The format of the policies shown in this chapter demonstrate the hierarchical structure in which the broadest principles are voiced first, while those addressing a greater level of detail come later, in order from broadest to narrowest. This physical layout of board policies follows from the theory of expressing board values from larger to smaller. This format can help boards create clear, adequate organizational policies. It encourages a way of thinking about organizational concerns from the top down, starting with large issues, working down through smaller ones, and leaving the rest of the decision-making field free. In this free field, the CEO can make choices about ends and means and the CGO can make decisions about how the board operates and how the mechanisms of board-management linkage work. Let's look at how language is shaped into policies that leave only the amount of ambiguity the board intends.

Examples of Policy Expansion

I will demonstrate the sequence of expansion from a global policy to ones of greater detail, first in Ends, then in Executive Limitations. I will assume that the board has decided to use serial numbers for organizing its policies. A serial number approach is a matter of convention, one chosen to make policy designations simpler to handle. In the scheme used here, the prefix indicates the policy category. Quite arbitrarily, 1 indicates Ends and 2 indicates Executive Limitations (although it is not shown in this illustration, 3 might indicate Board-Management Delegation and 4, Governance Process). Therefore, the most global Ends policy is numbered 1.0 and the most global Executive Limitations policy is 2.0. This numbering system is not a matter of Policy Governance principle but of board convenience.

As the board expands policies in each category, it assigns decimal suffixes. A policy just a bit more narrow than the broadest Ends policy might be 1.1, while another policy that is no more narrow but on a separate subtopic might be 1.2. Regarding policy maintenance, I suggest adding a letter suffix to subsequent versions as amendments occur. Quick checks of board members' board books can then ascertain whether everyone has the most current policies.

Ends Policy Development

To illustrate the sequence of policy growth, Exhibit 9.1 shows where a progression of Ends policy development began for the board of LifeStream Services, located in Yorktown, Indiana. Another board or, indeed, this same board in ten years might aim the organization toward very different ends. The rule, remember, is that the CEO is empowered to use any reasonable interpretation of the board's words.

LifeStream Services did not create titles for their policies. Other boards may choose to use titles for each. The matter is cosmetic, since the title itself carries no weight as policy direction. The global Ends policy is often called "Purpose," "Mission," "Basic Purpose," "Macro-Ends," or another title chosen by the board. Only the substance of the policy matters.

If the board had stopped at the global level of Ends policy development shown in policy number 1.0 (Exhibit 9.1), it would have left open a wide range of CEO prerogatives, indeed—not only about the cost of results but about the nature of the results themselves! The board is obligated to accept as successful any achievement that can be considered a reasonable interpretation of the board's policy language.

Policy number 1.1 (Exhibit 9.2) shows that the board decided to augment its broad language. The board must have felt that not doing so would leave an untenably wide range of choice to the CEO. Note that the numbered parts are parallel issues, each a level of abstraction below the statement that stood alone before but has

Exhibit 9.1. LifeStream Services, Yorktown, Indiana
Global Ends Policy
Policy No. 1.0

Older and disabled persons in the LifeStream service area will live secure, productive, and independent lives at a cost to LifeStream comparable with similar organizations.

Exhibit 9.2. LifeStream Services, Yorktown, Indiana
Global Ends Policy Extended to a Second Level
Policy No. 1.1

Older and disabled persons in the LifeStream service area will live secure, productive, and independent lives at a cost to LifeStream comparable with similar organizations.

1. Communities will demonstrate that they value aging.

2. Community members will have knowledge and skills to prepare for a secure and healthy old age.

3. Older and frail persons will have resources to maximize their quality of life.

now become a preamble. This board has not taken the opportunity to give a sense of its priorities among these second-level ends statements. Having not done so, the acceptable priorities are any reasonable interpretation of priorities the CEO wishes to use. The LifeStream board, however, decided not to stop at the second level but to go still further.

As to format, the board could simply continue the outlining format on the same page, putting more material under the three second-level items found in Exhibit 9.2. That is certainly workable, but for ease in handling the policy documents, boards have usually found separate sheets preferable. Choosing this format, the LifeStream board went to separate pages to extend their policies to a third level. On each of these added pages, the lowest level of the previous policy becomes the preamble of a policy dealing with only one subtopic. LifeStream's separate-page method is displayed in Exhibits 9.3, 9.4, and 9.5.

Of course, the LifeStream board could have gone into even further detail, but it chose not to. Why? Because it felt that at the level of detail reached in Exhibits 9.3, 9.4, and 9.5, any reasonable interpretation the CEO might use would be acceptable. In making such policies, the depth and content will vary from board to board. The only constants are the principles of governance that are followed

Exhibit 9.3. LifeStream Services, Yorktown, Indiana
Second-Level Ends Policy Extended to a Third Level
Policy No. 1.2

Communities will demonstrate that they value aging.

1. Community environments will be functioning for the aging.

2. Community resources will be allocated appropriately to meet needs of the aging.

3. The community will recognize the contributions of older persons.

4. Communities will involve older persons in decision-making.

Exhibit 9.4. LifeStream Services, Yorktown, Indiana
Second-Level Ends Policy Extended to a Third Level
Policy No. 1.3

Community members will have knowledge and skills to prepare for a secure and healthy old age.

1. At risk seniors and persons with disabilities will have knowledge, skills, and resources to successfully remain in the home of their choice.

2. Caregivers will have knowledge, skills, strengths, and resources to successfully cope with caring for a loved one at home.

3. Older persons will have the knowledge and skills to effectively use the legal and law enforcement systems.

Exhibit 9.5. LifeStream Services, Yorktown, Indiana
Second-Level Ends Policy Extended to a Third Level
Policy No. 1.4

Older and frail persons will have resources to maximize their quality of life.

1. Seniors and older persons with disabilities will have improved nutritional health.

2. Older and disabled persons will be satisfied with their social, emotional, and spiritual well-being.

through every step, including the commitment to stop at the point at which any reasonable interpretation is acceptable.

Executive Limitations Policy Development

Executive Limitations policies begin with a prohibition that is broad enough to cover all possible circumstances and activities that the board would find unacceptable. After that point, Executive Limitations policies follow the same path of development as the one just shown for Ends policies. It all starts by couching the global statement carefully, perhaps as in policy number 2.0 (Exhibit 9.6) of Unnamed Pension Fund. (I am obliged to protect the anonymity of the board that adopted this policy.) While the board can stop at this level if it is willing to accept any reasonable interpretation of these words by the CEO, it would be extremely rare for a board to do so.

Exhibit 9.7 illustrates policy number 2.1, an extension of the global policy into the second level, focusing on the board's limit of acceptability as it relates to preservation of capital. Policy number 2.1. is a topic-specific detail that constitutes a level just under global policy number 2.0. The board has made the clerical choice to separate this policy from the global policy shown in Exhibit 9.6 instead of

Exhibit 9.6. Unnamed Pension Fund
Executive Limitations Policy
Policy No. 2.0: "Global Executive Limitations"

The CEO shall not cause or allow transactions, activities, circumstances, or decisions in or about the organization to be imprudent, unlawful, or in violation of commonly accepted business and professional ethics.

Exhibit 9.7. Unnamed Pension Fund
Executive Limitations Policy
Policy No. 2.1: "Preservation of Capital"

The CEO may not fail to preserve capital investment and investment returns sufficient to secure statutory payments and ancillary benefits to pension system participants over the long term.

---

displaying it as a subpart of that policy. As always, the board could have stopped at this level of detail, if it had been willing to allow its CEO to use any reasonable interpretation of this narrower policy.

The board of Unnamed Pension Fund chose to extend its policy from the second level into two further proscriptions at the third level. The original policy number 2.1 was augmented to include a further level on the same topic. Exhibit 9.8 shows how the policy looked at this stage. But deciding not to stop at this point, the board went into still further detail (the fourth level) on the same topic, yielding the policy in Exhibit 9.9. (Because the board was amending its policy no. 2.1, the subsequent amended policies were numbered 2.1a and 2.1b.)

During the development of the policy's final depth and content, there was disagreement among board members about both the depth and the content at each level. But the policy represents what the board officially adopted, so the CEO can be assured that he or she need not be concerned about what individual board members thought. He or she will be judged based only on what the board finally adopted. The opinions of dissenting members have been heard, but only by their board colleagues, not by the CEO.

As with Ends policies, the board can augment any of the Executive Limitations policies, as long as the addition (1) proceeds from the global policy (2.0) and (2) moves toward more detail only one

Exhibit 9.8. Unnamed Pension Fund
Executive Limitations Policy
Policy No. 2.1a: "Preservation of Capital"

The CEO may not fail to preserve capital investment and investment returns sufficient to secure statutory payments and ancillary benefits to pension system participants over the long term. Further, without limiting the scope of the foregoing by this enumeration, the CEO shall not:

1. Allow asset allocation that varies materially from that consistent with full funding of future benefits as described in Ends policies.

2. Fail to maximize investment earnings within asset classes.

**Exhibit 9.9. Unnamed Pension Fund
Executive Limitations Policy
Policy No. 2.1b: "Preservation of Capital"**

The CEO may not fail to preserve capital investment and investment returns sufficient to secure statutory payments and ancillary benefits to pension system participants over the long term. Further, without limiting the scope of the foregoing by this enumeration, the CEO shall not:

1. Allow asset allocation that varies materially from that consistent with full funding of future benefits as described in Ends policies. Varying materially is further described as:

   A. In US Equities, variance from a target of 40% by more than plus or minus 2

   B. In International Equities, variance from a target of 15% by more than plus or minus 2

   C. In US Fixed Income, variance from a target of 30% by more than plus or minus 4

   D. In Real Estate, variance from a target of 14% by more than plus or minus 2

   E. In Cash, variance from a target of 1% by more than plus 2 or minus 1

   F. In Venture Capital and other classes not otherwise specified in this policy, variance from a target of 0% by more than plus 1

2. Fail to maximize investment earnings within asset classes. Failure to maximize is further defined as

   A. In US Equities, failure to meet or exceed Standard & Poor's Super Composite Index by 50 basis points

   B. In International Equities, failure to meet or exceed MSCI All Country World Ex-US Index by 100 basis points

   C. In US Fixed Income, failure to meet or exceed Salomon Smith Barney Broad Investment Grade Index by 50 basis points

   D. In Real Estate, failure to meet or exceed PERS Custom Real Estate Index by 100 basis points

   E. In Cash, failure to meet or exceed Three Month US Treasury Bill by 10 basis points

level at a time. The same discipline applies to policies in the Board-Management Delegation and Governance Process categories. They expand in exactly the same way, so I will only describe them rather than display examples of the policy expansion.

Board-Management Delegation Policy Development

In like manner, the board policy that sets the stage for the governance-management relationship is a global statement. The global policy (let's call it 3.0) would probably establish that the official connecting link from governance to operations is a single chief executive officer, titled however the board chooses. (The CEO's title is immaterial, but the nature of the job is crucial.) Further policy development might add definition to the method of delegation and the method of monitoring performance. Some examples are shown in Chapter Six. Remember that the CGO is granted the authority—and with it the obligation—to interpret and further fulfill the board's words in this category.

Governance Process Policy Development

This category, dealing as it does with the board's own job, begins with a global description of the purpose and role (let's call that policy number 4.0). The global level is likely to focus on the board's key role as a link in the chain of command (the chain of moral authority) between owners and operators.

Further policy expansion in governance process is likely to address the board's commitment to a certain discipline in its operations, the precise values added by the board's activities, a code of conduct, and so forth. Some examples are shown in Chapters Seven and Eight. The CGO is granted the authority—and with it the obligation—to interpret and further fulfill the board's words in this category as well.

The Importance of Format

Policy architecture goes beyond the merely cosmetic. It is an important device, a "terraced" policy format that keeps clear at all times how broadly and how narrowly the board has expressed itself on various topics. It follows, then, that the process of developing policies of this sort is itself an important skill of board leadership. For example, because a multilevel policy is the concrete manifestation of the theoretical broad-to-narrow mapping of a board's values, the board should know how to avoid skipping levels. There must be content at every level. It is not a level of policy, for example, to simply introduce the next lower level. If it does this, the board fools itself by masking that it has actually jumped a level and has forfeited the ability to find out that the lower levels might not be necessary at all. I will leave this more advanced topic of policy writing to the explanations in *Reinventing Your Board* (Carver and Carver, 1997c; second, revised edition, 2006), which guides a board through the step-by-step sequence of arriving at its own tailored versions of policies.

The Continuing State of Policies on the Policy Circle

In earlier chapters, I used the policy circle to illustrate the relationship of the four categories of policies and multiple levels of policies. When the board has addressed each category to the depth at which it is disposed to accept any reasonable interpretation of those policies, the board has built a small body of policies that express all the board's relevant values. The resultant body of policies "surround" all other decisions, situations, and activities, goals, objectives, and plans, as depicted in Figure 3.4. Of course, the depth of policies shown in Figure 3.4 is not intended to portray the right depth, but is only one example among many possibilities.

Next Chapter

After designing a technical framework to meet the governance challenge, a board must confront the hard part: making it work with real human beings in real situations. Too often, board dreams are shaped, constrained, and thwarted by meandering, crowded, and pressing agendas. Board dreams, unhappily, are too often regulated, if not determined, by their agendas. In Chapter Ten, I will consider how governing board members can ensure that their agendas and discussions serve their dreams.

WANT MORE?

Further Reading

1. Carver, J. "Abstracting Up: Discovering the Big Issues Among the Trivia." *Board Leadership*, 1994a, no. 15. Reprinted in J. Carver, *John Carver on Board Leadership*. San Francisco: Jossey-Bass, 2002.

10

Making Meetings Meaningful

Creating the Future More Than Reviewing the Past

In striving for excellence and struggling to conserve time, boards are compelled to use their energy and talent more precisely. The central resource in governance is the wisdom with which board members enter the boardroom. Eliciting this wisdom on the right issues, at the right time, and in the right form is not easy. Crowded agendas, scattered discussions, and all the familiar weaknesses of group behavior conspire against the efficient use of board energy.

Like the parent of a two-year-old, the governing board knows it has power but never quite feels truly in charge. Because of inadequate information, the changing rules of external authorities, a staff that is more knowledgeable than the board about organizational activities, and time constraints, the board may appear to be the seat of organizational power in theory more than in fact. The traditional mechanisms that are intended to help board members feel they are more on top of things and more involved can themselves drive boards even further afield.

In this chapter, I look at how it is possible to accomplish a large job, one built almost entirely on the use of words, in a small amount of time. I then discuss the care a board must exercise in selecting subject matter, especially in instances in which outside expectations dictate poor use of board time. Next, I explore the formal, planned use of board time as manifested in agendas. Having dealt with economy

in the use of time, I turn to the central goal of board discussion—
transforming diverse voices into a single voice. I end the chapter
with a brief consideration of board meetings conducted according
to the Policy Governance model.

Managing a Talking Job

Even though governance consists almost entirely of talking and
leaving action to others, boards have precious little time in which
to do their job. Even a liberal average of six hours per month yields
less than two regular work weeks in an entire year. There is little
room for inappropriate or wasteful activity when a year's
governing must take place in such scant time. Even in small
organizations, the number of possible items for learning, discussion, and decision is far greater than the available time will
allow. Just because a topic is important is not reason enough to deal
with it; there are too many important topics.

WANT MORE? 1

To further complicate the use of time, each board member has
favorite interests to explore or points to make. On large boards,
enabling all members to have their say can slow the process to a
crawl. It is not uncommon for boards to adopt unstated strategies
that deny members this right, not because anyone seeks to throttle
them but because giving members this leeway consumes too much
time. As conventional board agendas are wide open to topics of staff
means, board actions can easily become a laundry list of individual
members' operational interests.

Boards fall prey to the same clean-the-desk syndrome that afflicts
individuals. In the face of overwhelming choices among competing
and profound values, it is attractive to fall back on doing menial work.
For an individual, that may entail nothing more harmful than the
diversion of cleaning his or her desk; for a board, it is likely to mean
dabbling in details. Damaged delegation aside, the distraction robs
the board of precious time, the more so because boards are able to
convince themselves that such diversions constitute being involved.

There are always staff members who are eager to use board time for show-and-tell. Diversion is particularly inviting because the topic seems legitimate. Staffs are proud of their work and want to talk about it. Attracting praise or even notice from the board can be very rewarding. Tradition fails to warn boards that faithfully listening to staff reports may not be governance at all.

External authorities demand board time. They do so sometimes for legitimate reasons but often because of a dysfunctional construction of governance. An example is the raft of inappropriate actions demanded of local school boards by legislatures and of many private social service agencies by their certifying bodies. For public and nonprofit boards receiving public money, the lawfully required wastes of time not only plunder the resource of board talent but also jeopardize the tenuous psychology of strategic thinking.

WANT MORE?

2

In the few hours that remain after such diversions, a board's expression of visionary leadership is thoroughly unlikely. Tradition, time, and available diversions are stacked against real leadership. "Surely," observes Gene Royer, speaking of boards of education, "our forebears . . . did not envision our taking on all these combined chores and cramming them into a two-hour meeting once or twice a month" (Royer, 1996b, p. 61). This budget needs to be approved. This grant must be signed and sent right away. Financial reports are to be reviewed. A roof needs to be repaired. An aspect of the group insurance needs to be changed. Staff cost-of-living increments and merit raises must be sanctioned. Time's up. Perhaps we can get around to strategic leadership next year. A surfeit of insistent demands makes a mockery of boards' yearning for the long view.

Choosing the Issues

The board's job is a verbal task. The school board coaches no basketball teams. The county commission constructs no bridges. The hospital board cures no patients. The symphony board conducts no music. The board's job is not to coach, construct, cure, or conduct.

The board talks. Debating, clarifying, and enunciating values are talking tasks.

Words are the board's tools. When the job is one of words, there must be discipline in the talking. That discipline involves what is talked about, how the talking occurs, and when it is done. It is not acceptable to talk about any issue that might come up. It is not acceptable to talk about an issue in whatever way is desired. It is not acceptable to talk about an issue at an inappropriate time. Boards, as trustees for the interests of others, have no more right to converse randomly than employed lathe operators have to cut whatever piece of metal strikes their fancy. When boards wander aimlessly, they are as negligent as the professional shortstop who decides that right field is a nicer place to be today. Boards cannot simply address any topic in any way they wish at the moment and hope to excel.

Screening Form Before Content

Screening issues prior to board discussion brings process criteria to bear on board meetings. Boards can resolve the question "What will we allow ourselves to talk about?" before specific issues arise and their enthusiastic sponsors obscure the discipline that could have been exercised. Michael Brandau, a former member of the Beaufort County Board of Education in Beaufort, South Carolina, observed that it is important for board members to "understand the powerful tools the Policy Governance model provides" and "the commitment and discipline the model requires." The board needs to address the matter of its discipline in a Governance Process policy. Instituting such a policy enables a board to judge an issue against criteria for appropriateness before including it on the board's agenda. It is important that no one start speaking to the content of the issue before dealing with its form.

The first screening question is "What category does this issue fall into?" Is it an issue of intended effects in the world? An executive means issue? An issue of the governance job itself? Or an issue of board-executive linkage? Answering this screening question concretely labels the issue as one of ends, executive limitations, governance process, or board-management delegation.

The second screening question is "Whose issue is it?" If the issue belongs to this organization at all, it should be clearly owned by either the board or the CEO. If the issue belongs to a staff member other than the CEO, as far as the board is concerned, it belongs to the CEO. So the question before the board is, simply, "Is this issue yours or mine?" Finding that an issue is "yours *and* mine" bespeaks unclear criteria or an issue whose phrasing needs to be untangled. Beware of "shared responsibility"; *shared* likely means *shirked* and almost certainly means *sloppy*. In a good system, there are no orphan issues. They all belong somewhere.

The third screening question is "What has the board already said in this category, and how is the issue at hand related?" This question looks not only at the content of existing board policy but at the breadth or level of that policy. Content is inspected to determine (1) whether the board has already dealt with the issue and, if so, in what way and (2) whether the issue at hand is several levels of abstraction below current board policy or simply the next level lower. If the board has already addressed the matter, then the only relevant question is whether the board wishes to change what has already been said. If the issue at hand is several levels below the current board policy level, the task is to reframe the issue (underscoring, once more, the useful skill of abstracting up) so that it is conceptually adjacent to previous policy.

One way to do this is to ask, "What is the broadest way to address this issue so that it is still at a lower level than the board policy we already have?" Having answered that question, the board should ask, "Will that suffice to deal with our concern?" If not, the board repeats the process. For example, let's say that the board has a policy prohibiting the CEO from paying staff compensation that is "materially greater than the market rate." This policy would fall just below, or would be "conceptually adjacent" to, the broadest policy of the Executive Limitations category: "Allow no practice or circumstance that is unethical or imprudent."

Let us assume that a board member expresses concern that "market" can mean the local or national market or a special segment, such as the professional market. Perhaps there is a worry that with respect to clerical salaries, political problems will arise if the organization is out of line with local governmental scales. Although the board member does not want to limit the CEO to the local market in seeking people to fill positions, the member is convinced that *market* is unacceptably broad in light of this political worry. A majority of the board may feel comfortable with the level of proscription that has already been set forth. If a vote reveals that the majority is satisfied, then there is no issue. If a majority agrees with our concerned member, the compensation policy might be amended to read, "No compensation may materially exceed the rate that is customarily paid in the applicable market. Local units of government will constitute the market for job classifications that local governments employ." The board would have, in effect, extended policy to a lower, more detailed level, although the policy is still only two sentences long.

These screening checks take surprisingly little time if the board uses the configuration of categories and levels described in previous chapters. The registry of all board policies creates a values map, which the board uses to navigate through the otherwise confusing array of established and potential policy issues. Determining the placement of any organizational issue with respect to other issues and with respect to board and CEO territories is made relatively easy.

It is out of order for board members to talk about content before the form is settled. The obvious reason is that much time could be wasted by board members' waxing eloquent on an issue the board should not be deciding anyway. And if the board ends up deciding that options and implications are needed for informed deliberation, it would be out of order to begin problem solving before these data have been developed, perhaps by a committee.

Being Ready for Discussion

The need to obtain adequate data before creating policy can be a reasonable cause of delay. There is a danger in waiting, however. Boards, like individuals, have a tendency to put off doing an acceptable job on something and instead wait forever in order to do it perfectly. Complete information is rarely available, so boards, like all managers, must learn to take action with incomplete data. The peculiar situation in this case, however, is that the option to put off making policy is often an illusion. A board cannot wait until later to create policy, for even as it waits, the existing policy—albeit perhaps unstated—is in effect. A board can delay changing a policy, but it cannot delay the organization's having one.

Executive action continues whether or not the values on which it is based are stated. If those actions are consonant with a previously stated board policy, they can legitimately remain unchanged until the board alters the policy. If the board does not mind that, then a delay causes no harm. If, however, the board is not happy with certain actions, even though they are consonant with the old policy, a delay merely prolongs the period in which such actions must be deemed acceptable. In such cases, the board may adopt a tentative policy that approximates a "final" board position. Although this policy may change soon, it is fully official until then.

Although rapid policy development can be achieved with sufficiently capable consulting, Miriam Carver and I explain a step-by-step, do-it-yourself method in our book *Reinventing Your Board* (Carver and Carver, 1997c; revised edition scheduled for 2006). Policies developed in this way normally need no more subsequent revision than policies that have taken much longer to develop. In fact, policies formulated after months of work are, in some ways, worse. Boards are reluctant to alter policies that have taken them so long to develop! So the more quickly developed policies are just as good and, as it turns out, more flexible. Once board members grasp the idea of policies as values, they are able to turn their worries and intentions into governing documents with little difficulty.

Rubber-Stamping Responsibly

It is hard to find champions for rubber-stamping. It enjoys de facto popularity while enduring rhetorical derision. Rubber-stamping is the relatively automatic approval of another's plan or performance. Exactly what that means, however, is not as clear as it might appear at first.

For example, if a board believes that whom department directors hire as their secretary is staff business, it follows that the board should not be involved in the hiring. Most persons would not consider such delegation to be rubber-stamping. If for some external reason—let's say the law requires it—employment of secretaries must be sanctioned by the board, then it follows that the board will be asked to approve a hiring decision. What if the board feels as it did before? Would the board now be rubber-stamping if it approved the new hires without debate and, in fact, without even reading the names? Most persons would call this rubber-stamping. But the same degree of governance responsibility was exercised in each scenario.

Even good delegation appears to be rubber-stamping when the delegated action passes across the agenda. School board agendas would shrink if the boards delegated sensibly. Antiquated, ill-devised laws and tradition require that unnecessary items be on the agenda. Because those items are on the agenda, school boards feel compelled to probe and publicly comment on a great deal of trivia, even though doing so makes no managerial sense. But not to do so might subject them to ill-informed charges of rubber-stamping.

When board members have an uncomfortable feeling that they are rubber-stamping, they dig in and study the offending issue, ask questions, and stimulate discussion. Such behavior is conscientious and is often the wise response, but not always. Sometimes, the more effective, system-improving response would be to question why the issue is on the board agenda. Certain items on the agenda should be rubber-stamped because the right to make the decision in question ought to be the CEO's. The revealing question is how a CEO decision gets on the agenda in the first place.

Tradition and Law

Tradition brings personnel procedures, budgets, plans, and program designs to the board for approval in most organizations. In some organizations, the list extends to hiring, job descriptions, organizational design, and even more mundane matters. These practices are often demanded by accrediting bodies because these bodies are merely following tradition themselves. Some states require that boards of agencies funded by state money approve all payment vouchers. Local governmental boards, such as city councils, county supervisors, and school boards, must conduct extensive reviews of staff operations. Both tradition and law embody a meat-ax approach to accountability: to ensure order, virtually all staff activity must be passed before the board to be belabored and blessed, even when the activity has already occurred! This myopic version of accountability justifies disproportionate attention to financial and legal jeopardies at the expense of program outputs. It serves accountants and attorneys who would avoid jeopardy far more than it serves dreamers, creators, and leaders who would add value to the world. This kind of accountability sways boards into spending more time looking over their shoulder than over the horizon.

Mindless rubber-stamping of true board prerogatives is a dereliction of duty. Rubber-stamping of decisions that should be management prerogatives is not. Management prerogatives are whatever means the CEO chooses in order to accomplish a reasonable interpretation of board-dictated ends that are within a reasonable interpretation of board-dictated executive limitations. If the CEO is within these boundaries, then what reason would the board have for not approving? Disapproval would mean that the board did not construct its boundaries in a serious way in the first place. On the other hand, if disapproval is not seriously considered, why is board time needed for approval?

When board approval is imposed externally, the board is justified in intentionally rubber-stamping. That is, it can go ahead and approve as it is required to do (rubber-stamp) and move on. If the board has truly done its homework and is fully convinced that its responsibility has been faithfully discharged, it need not take the approval seriously, for it is merely an empty formality.

WANT MORE?

3

This tactic is similar to the consent agenda that many public boards use to speed routine items. It differs in two ways: (1) its origin and (2) the mechanics and meaning of removing items. Conventional consent agendas are intended to isolate routine, noncontroversial actions so that less board time is consumed. The consent agenda suggested here has nothing to do with the controversiality of an issue or with its routineness. It concerns prior delegation and might more accurately be termed an *automatic approval agenda*.

Issues placed on the CEO's automatic approval agenda are among the many decisions that the board has already determined are in the CEO's domain. They may not be routine and they may be controversial, but they are not board decisions. Any item calling for board judgment, such as making a policy decision or determining that monitoring data are acceptable, would never be on such a frankly pro forma agenda. Unlike conventional consent agenda items, these items may not be moved from the special agenda to the regular agenda at a single board member's request. They are on the automatic approval list not to save time but because the board has made a conscious decision that these items should not come to the board at all. They have shown up as board business only because some authority to whom the board is beholden has said they must. Therefore, no single board member can have the right to undelegate the matter—that is, to have the item moved from the special to the regular agenda. The board as a whole, of course, does have that right.

Finally, a word about rubber-stamping that is done to coddle executive indecisiveness. There are CEOs who do not want the responsibility of decision making. To such CEOs, a tradition that transfers their responsibility to the board is quite comforting. They enjoy hiding behind "but it was the board's decision." Boards collude with these CEOs, thinking that it is kindhearted to let them off the hook on "hot" decisions. It is sloppy management design to differentiate board and CEO decisions on the basis of the CEO's preference. This practice contributes to diffusion of roles rather than to clarity. If the CEO does not or cannot make decisions, the board has good reason to question whether it has the right CEO. As a rule, the board need never make a decision solely because the CEO does not want to make it. When the CEO is not both enabled and expected to make CEO decisions, the board is wasting a powerful tool and much of its own valuable time.

Planning the Agenda

Boards must continually struggle with agenda content: "What do we have to do at this meeting?" There is an element of passivity in this statement, a hint that boards will put on the agenda whatever the exigencies of their world puts there for them. The spokesperson for those pressing circumstances is most often the CEO. And as some hapless boards have discovered too late, he or she who is the oracle through whom the gods speak to the board assumes a commanding position even without malevolent intentions.

It is common for boards to defer to their CEO on agenda sequence and content. To the extent that a board is needlessly entangled in staff practices, it is compelled to get its signals from persons intimately familiar with staff issues and timetables. Boards become so dependent on their staff to fill agendas that many would find themselves adrift without such guidance. "Of course," they say, "our CEO provides most of our agenda content, because she or he is the one who knows what is going on around here." The problem is circular: boards are trapped in staff-level issues and therefore need staff input as to what those issues are. Staff members are called on to generate board agendas, and therefore board agendas are composed chiefly of staff-level material. Through these actions, the board's job is defined as reviewer of staff material, not creator of board material. In fact "board material" traditionally comes to consist largely of staff material to be reviewed. In these circumstances, board and staff lose sight of just what a board issue looks like.

WANT MORE?
4

Tying Agendas to the Long Term

Boards are often subject to a zigzag phenomenon in agenda content. Without staff guidance, the problem is usually worse. More than we would like to admit, agendas are developed around rituals, reactions to immediate stressors, or last-minute approvals for external consumption. Suppose a board has carefully eliminated business it does not need to do. It has disposed of meaningless actions and has sufficiently empowered the CEO to save it from staff decisions. Yet it is still faced with the concrete, real-time problem of the next meeting's agenda. The board cannot fall back and have the staff supply enough items to keep it busy. The leaders cannot ask the followers to tell them what their job is.

Yet board work need not come to a screeching halt. When confronted with an ambiguous or bewildering task, we need only retire to the next higher level of thought to get our bearings. If we lose our way on wooded paths, we can reestablish confidence by hovering over the forest for a few moments. What we cannot do physically, we can do mentally. The board that wishes to be in charge of its own job needs to hover a while, to shift its attention from the immediate agenda to the year's agenda and, if that is insufficient, to the perpetual agenda.

The perpetual agenda comprises the basic board job contributions and any optional ones the board has added. These outputs belong to the board; they are not merely a summation of staff work. This perpetual agenda was discussed in Chapter Seven as a board job description. To gain control over its own agenda (so that the outcome will truly be the board's agenda, not the staff's agenda), the board must begin with the nature of governance itself. What does this board exist to contribute?

Remember that the unique and continuing contributions of the board—its perpetual agenda—include (1) linkage with ownership, (2) explicit governing policies, and (3) assurance of organizational performance. A board looking for a starting place would do well to begin with the second contribution, creating policies in all four categories. Linkage with the ownership should be undertaken only after the board has established and expressed—in a Governance Process policy—who the ownership is and how the connection will be made. Executive performance cannot be ensured before Board-Management Delegation, Executive Limitations, and Ends policies are established, as these policies contain the delegation, monitoring, and performance criteria.

In short, the board should get most of its policies in order before undertaking any other task. The perpetual agenda provides a starting place from which the board can plan major board work in the immediate future. Hence, the perpetual agenda leads to a more specific, time-framed agenda that is neither long-term nor short-term. The most useful time segment for planning board meeting agendas is often about one year.

The board establishes objectives for the ensuing year within each of its responsibility areas. The board might determine to forge a dialogue with other boards or to enhance communication with its ownership through public or private media. It might improve policy integrity through more systematic inclusion of financial experts or dissenting programmatic viewpoints. It can upgrade its assurance of organizational performance by making the monitoring system more rigorous or less costly. If the board has adopted other contribution areas, such as securing philanthropic funds, it can set objectives for these responsibilities. To maintain consistency, these board intentions are built into an expansion of the board's job description policy and sometimes incorporated in a separate policy (as shown in Exhibit 7.3), in either case in the Governance Process category. That is, all of the board's objectives are kept in the policy framework as are other board decisions.

Establishing board objectives for the midterm, then, yields a sequence of single-meeting agendas and between-meeting work. Weekly, monthly, or quarterly meetings are thus integrally derived from the larger process. Officer or committee expectations are drawn from the same schedule. Note that the board's annual establishment of the agenda, though open to staff input, is not staff-dependent. Because of this, the board is able to move two steps forward in terms of taking responsibility: not only does it produce answers without executive ventriloquism, but it generates the questions as well and, hence, exhibits a significantly greater level of leadership.

This approach to agenda setting makes three major contributions to rational board process. First, it avoids the zigzag agendas set from meeting to meeting. Second, the board is in greater control of its own agenda and not dependent on its CEO to tell it what to do each time. Third, the rightfully dominant board concern with ends is less likely to be lost in a sea of lesser issues.

Ends Justify the Meetings

I have found that policies in all categories except Ends are rather stable. The global Ends policy may hold relatively still, but explication of beneficiaries, benefits, and cost or priorities at lower levels seems to require change often enough to warrant continual attention.

For the board, one eye should be on customer-equivalents and one on ownership. In other words, one outcome of a good governance system is that the governors are free to concentrate on ends and on those on whose behalf ends are decided and pursued. (For city councils and professional or trade associations, these may be the same people.) Relative value stability in other policy areas and the strategic importance of ends lead the board to work on two compelling concerns each year: (1) "How can we connect with even more integrity with those on whose behalf we serve?" and (2) "Given new information, new wisdom, or new possibilities, what good for which people at what cost should we strive to achieve in the years ahead?" In other words, the majority of board energy is expended on the first element of its job (linkage with ownership) and the first part of the second element (policies concerning ends).

Although improvement in ownership linkage need not be constrained by specific time periods, specifying ends is frequently tied to time-sensitive staff actions such as writing budgets and planning programs. Ends work is therefore subject to more punctuations in the flow of time. Because the board's ends work is strongly tied to administrative time lines, for most boards, the annual agenda is best constructed around a yearly cycle of exploring and restating Ends policies.

The board selects an external event to which the organization directs itself. For some, this is the budget submission date of the major funder. For others, it may be the annual meeting of the membership, the start of a financial year, or the completion of an election cycle. In any event, the date selected is when executive planning must either go into effect or be publicly announced.

To give the CEO ample time to prepare for that deadline, the board's annual update of all Ends policies is set two or three months earlier. To update, the board restudies its global and all subsidiary Ends policies in light of new information and, possibly, new dreams. Then, working backward from the due date, the board calculates a year of agendas to lead it to that point. It uses the same technique to establish completion dates for committee tasks, should the use of committees be needed. Other board needs can be and are considered, but the central organizing factor is the never-ending focus on Ends policies.

The board plans its dialogue with other representatives of the ownership (other boards, councils, and commissions), examines its assumptions about environmental factors, and structures discussion of the implications of these activities with the CEO and other staff. The board may entertain speakers on competing viewpoints or on the division of social labor among the various organizations in the area. Board-to-board dialogue and other work designed to enlighten the board as it refines its vision may require more time than the board has. Or too much leadership influence may be needed to bring other boards along. At any rate, the work is sufficient enough that in the first year, a board probably will not accomplish all of these steps. Several annual cycles will be required before the board comes near its potential in visionary leadership.

Board members cannot go through this process, particularly early on, without stumbling. But it is much more defensible when the board stumbles in tackling big issues rather than small ones. The leadership involved in persuading boards to converse seriously about the effects they are seeking for their beneficiaries is a breakthrough itself. Even small successes are a giant leap from poring over budget lines or probing into sick leave procedures.

After the annual changes or reconfirmation of the Ends policies, the CEO begins to plan. The CEO embodies the first year's portion of the board's long-range vision in a programmatic plan and budget. In doing so, the CEO must adhere to all applicable board policies. The board is not responsible for this balancing act; the CEO is. Except for its normal monitoring, the board's annual work is completed when it reconfirms the Ends policies.

In summary, the board begins to gain control over its agenda when it accepts total responsibility for the agenda. Individual meeting agendas are derived from the larger picture of the board's goals for the midterm. These midterm goals are derived from the board's perpetual agenda, which, you will remember, equals the board's job description. The board governs according to a plan instead of shooting from the hip, thus avoiding the floundering that invites a res-

cue by its CEO. The board moves further from a short-term mentality by tying most of its activity to the challenge of guiding the
organization for the long term. Board time is to be spent largely on
creating the future. The regular agenda is designed to develop strategic vision, not by inserting an orphan agenda item (or even a retreat) on strategic planning but by being formed around and infused
with a long-range mentality.

Getting Started

The first year's agenda involves a great deal of start-up activity. For
example, no matter how long an organization has been in existence,
its board may well find that few true policies exist. Most preexisting policies are either staff documents improperly elevated to governance status or actual policies generated from staff, not board
values. Moreover, the board will likely have conceived of its job as
a collection of traditional activities rather than outputs. It is important to recognize the magnitude of the change in concepts and
behaviors that is needed in order for a board to embark on the path
of Policy Governance.

Gaining Commitment

The first step is to gain board members' commitment to strive
toward the new model. This involves discussing the model itself and
the changes that it portends. It is important to include the CEO in
the process and, as far as possible, to optimize all variables that will
affect the board's subsequent success. When the decision to pursue
Policy Governance is made, it should be captured in Governance
Process policies that are similar to the "Governing Style" and
"Board Job Description" policies shown in Chapter Seven (Exhibits
7.1 and 7.4, respectively).

Because this massive alteration of roles and rules will be so pivotal, as much consensus as possible is called for. The board will be
leading in a new order, inviting all the hurdles and detractors that

Machiavelli warned of. This decision, like all policy decisions, should not be delayed until full agreement is reached. Practices of the past need not cast the deciding vote. Moreover, board discussion should lead not only to a choice as firm as if it had been unanimous but to a clear understanding that all members are obligated to help make the resulting changes successful.

Following a Sequence

In most cases, the board should write policy before either linking with ownership or ensuring CEO performance. These latter tasks are better defined as the policies are established. If this means a number of policies need to be revised later, so be it.

A board may wish to review all of its old policies to see what it can translate into the new format, but this course of action takes far more time to organize and results in a poorer product than starting from scratch does. It is at this stage that boards come to realize how inadequate traditional policymaking is, even when done well. The confounding of means prescriptions, activities, results, high- and low-level values, single-event (nonpolicy) decisions, and violations of good delegation principles in previous documents often constitute a Gordian knot. Cutting through the knot by creating the board's new Policy Governance policies instead of trying to untie the knot and save individual policy strands is invariably the best option.

I should point out that the board policies created under Policy Governance make previous board documents (except bylaws) unnecessary. It would be dysfunctional for the board to establish new policies and keep the old board documents as well. Boards that adopt

WANT MORE?

5

Policy Governance invariably had budgets, personnel "policies," strategic plans, and other documents that work well in management but are inappropriate as governance documents. Typically, however, they do not disappear but instead become documents belonging to management. It is as if the board makes a gift to the CEO of its old documents, freeing the CEO to use them, not use them, or change them as he or she sees fit.

In building policies from scratch, the board should proceed according to the principles given in Chapter Three and illustrated in Chapter Nine: it should start "thin" in all categories and then carefully extend policies to include more levels of detail. This is best done with the help of a consultant who has advanced training in Policy Governance.

Managing the Transition

The process of creating new board policies takes from several months to a year or longer, depending on the board's commitment, agility, fear, and reluctance to make the necessary changes. If the board is guided by consultants who are fully trained in the Policy Governance model, all or most of the foregoing policies, except Ends, can be developed in two days. Adjusting previous board and CEO patterns of behavior takes longer.

During the transition, it is important to balance the need to maintain momentum with the need for the entire board's involvement and understanding. The longer the transition takes, the more likely it is that the changeover will not be completed, for the momentum to overcome old ways suffers. Staff can play an important role while the board retrains itself. The CEO should take care not to bring the board material that is inappropriate for its new role. Furthermore, the CEO must actually use the power that the board delegates. With the new policies in place, monitoring under the new regimen should start immediately, both to quell board worries and to convince board and CEO that the board stands behind its new rules.

At this point, boards usually have to struggle to remain focused on criteria-based reports rather than on the familiar standardized reports. It is easier to think about familiar reports (balance sheet, overdue accounts list) than the new criteria for which disclosure data are to be received. During the transition, boards often experience something like withdrawal symptoms in giving up their old traditional role. Accustomed more or less to flying by the seat of their pants, boards must learn in this early period to be comfortable

WANT MORE?

6

with more sophisticated systems. A jumbo jet cannot be flown using the cockpit technology of a crop duster.

E Pluribus Unum

Whatever the agenda content, the central interpersonal challenge the board faces is to convert divergent views into a single official view. It is as important for the board to have multiple minds as it is for it to have a single voice. To weaken the multiplicity of viewpoints would be to rob the board of the richness of its wisdom. To weaken the unity of voice would be to rob the board of its opportunity for effectiveness. On any issue, the board must elicit as much divergence as possible and then resolve it into a single position.

Pursuing *Pluribus*

Divergence occurs without prompting on many boards. On others, members must be given explicit permission and perhaps overt stimulation to diverge. A Policy Governance board is so focused on the

WANT MORE?

7

group exercise of responsibility and integrity that it is easy to overlook the importance of selecting and informing individual board members. This group of persons needs not only proper characteristics but proper preparation. Prospective and new board members particularly can benefit from being carefully informed of what is expected of them as individuals.

The Policy Governance case for racial, ethnic, philosophical, and gender diversity is based not on superficial political correctness but on the diversity present in the population the board represents. Because the board is a microcosm of the ownership, the need for diversity is driven by representational integrity. Each board should assess the composition of the ownership, determine what aspects of diversity are relevant, and, to the extent that the board can affect its own makeup, incorporate that thinking in the selection of future board members.

Even if all current board members are in perfect agreement on everything, the board should still discuss and adopt a policy that fosters and manages diversity. The discussion and the resulting policy will help ensure that board culture supports diversity. Are dissenters looked upon askance? Is it socially safe to disagree? The CGO should assertively pursue differing viewpoints. The behavioral message needs to be that disagreement not only is tolerated but is necessary to the health of the process. Furthermore, a board can reach outside to seek opposing viewpoints. The board should be so eager to widen its lens that it imports adversaries to invigorate the process!

Thus, the board is perceived as a forum of churning debate and exposure, an exciting place. This debate and exposure, of course, must concern the big questions rather than the small ones, the results rather than the methods. This is definitely not staff work, though staff members will undoubtedly have ideas to contribute. In fact, involving both board and staff here causes no problem. As long as roles are clearly defined, the board can invite staff to join in the fun. The board is not being pulled downward to staff-level concerns; rather, the staff members are being stretched upward to board-level concerns, though as guests in the process, not as its masters. As thinking, caring human beings, staff members have much to contribute to the dialogue, and everyone profits by their being invited to do so.

Pursuing diversity has implications for the practice of CEO recommendations. As I have already discussed, most nonprofit and many public boards unquestioningly use CEO recommendations as a point of departure for board action. In fact, boards often do not depart very far from this starting place. In the approach presented here, the CEO is a participant and may well include staff in the board's process. But he or she does so to provide a variety of viewpoints, not to support some prepackaged CEO recommendation. Staff input into the governance process does not need to be homogenized by the CEO if the input is about appropriate board issues. When the board does its job and allows and requires the CEO to do his or her job, exciting opportunities for bigness open up.

Ultimately Reaching *Unum*

Where do we go with all this richness? It is used chiefly to increase awareness, to decrease smallness (choosing furniture will not have the same allure for board members that it once did), to reveal new ways of looking at the world, and to sharpen the issues. This richness helps boards pose new, more penetrating questions. It guarantees that boards will henceforth operate a step ahead of staff rather than a dependent step behind. Boards stop trying to be the final authority and become instead the initial authority.

This healthy, provocative divergence still must be reduced to a single official position. Disagreement is best resolved from the conceptual top down. In other words, the board should elicit agreement first on the broadest position. For example, it would be much easier to get a majority to support "Human beings deserve a high quality of life" than "Business should be allowed to fail because more efficient economies increase overall quality of life." The larger the question, the more likely it is that differences can be resolved. This is one reason that the policymaking process recommended in this book starts with the broadest application. It is not that the broadest level is without controversy but that (1) it must be resolved, in any event, before the board deals with subsidiary issues and (2) it probably will be affected by fewer wide swings in board values.

Note that this approach requires the articulation of policy levels discussed in Chapter Three and developed further in Chapter Nine. That is, the board should not debate a page of undifferentiated priorities. It should debate the very brief global ends formulation first, then the next level of issues, then the next. Running them all together makes wise translation from diversity almost impossible. Even single-policy statements can have at least a couple of levels, the first represented in the preamble and the others in the body of the policy. Should the amount of diversity require it, the board can resolve the preamble level first, then work on the parts one at a time. This process is only slightly slower, and it is a far more accurate way of turning board values into hard copy. Furthermore, policies produced in this highly articulated outline form are easier to modify later through precisely targeted amendments.

Making the policy decision, in the final analysis, means taking a vote, thereby declaring a position to be official. Consensus, if honestly achieved, is certainly workable, but requiring a consensus before taking action is a prescription for either mediocrity or dishonesty. Koontz (1967) felt that the tradition of unanimity poses a major danger to board effectiveness wherein vociferous members can "tyrannize the majority" (p. 54). After the vote is taken, the official pronouncement must be as firm as if there had been no disagreement at all. Healthy governance requires that board members agree up front that any position resulting from a fair process is and rightfully should be the position of the board. This agreement on process should be embodied as a policy in the Governance Process category. Individual freedom of opinion, however, need not be sacrificed. There is no reason that the members of a board should pretend they agree on content after the vote when they did not before. But they should agree on and support procedural integrity. Supporting the process only when one wins the vote is not supporting the process.

In fact, recurring unanimous votes are suspect. All persons on a board may agree on a given issue. But if the voting record of a board is regularly or predominantly one of unanimous votes, we must ask whether dissent is being squelched or suspect that the issues are simply not important enough to disagree about. Either possibility calls for an examination of board process. Brian O'Connell, former executive director of Independent Sector, contends that boards try too hard for harmony and compromise. He welcomes occasional split votes, finding it better to have split votes—and even charged debate—than to water everything down so it becomes mush that offends nobody but that nobody gets very excited about, either.

Collecting Board Wisdom

Nonprofit and public boards generally are not good specimens of institutional memory. Some individual board members have a long memory of the organization's traditions and evolution. Some long-term staff members carry similar memories. But the board as a body may have a hard time remembering deliberations of only a few years ago. Staffs often wonder if such an entity as a board really exists, except in the most ephemeral way.

Turnover has much to do with this, but there is more to it. I have seen boards behave as if they did not have responsibility for previous board positions. The board as an organizational position goes on, regardless of individual turnover. An individual person becomes, upon induction, a part of a body that has existed for some time. The body's obligations and commitments do not change just because the new person has joined. The new member mounts a moving train, not one that leaves the station just as the last passenger gets on board.

Turnover and short memory are good reasons to use an explicit, brief policymaking approach. With succinct policies, the board's values are accessible, allowing new members to catch up more quickly. They know what their board stands for and which of its positions they disagree with. They get on board more quickly because they are not befuddled for two years before they understand what is going on. Institutional memory may still be foggy, but the accumulated value positions are not. Board values at their current stage of evolution can be found in a few pages. The vessel for better institutional memory is in place.

When explicit policies have been produced over a long period, an organizational "value history" is retrievable from the sequence of amendments. As opposed to sequences of events and personalities (the "story history"), value histories trace shifts in the organization's values over time. This type of documentation provides a sense of history without binding anyone to tradition.

Consider the collection of values in everyday situations. In the conduct of board meetings, a great deal is said but not seized. I see little to recommend the standard narrative minutes with all their detail, but I do commend the practice of capturing apparent consensus, majority feelings, or unresolved conflicts as they emerge randomly in discussion. Much wisdom is often expressed and has no place to go. Unless the comments are directly related to a policy under consideration at that moment, spontaneous board sentiments are lost.

I once consulted with an elected public board that developed most of a policy on the disposal of surplus real estate while they bantered during a break. They did not realize they had set forth the elements of a useful policy until I showed them my notes on the informal discussion. Such gems can be collected through a simple mechanism that does not detract from the topic at hand. The board secretary might persuade certain members to stay alert for such commentary. These positions can simply be noted for later review, for further focusing, and perhaps for consideration as policy or a change in existing policy.

If several board members are frightened by a news report of another organization's bad fortune and express their fear during a board meeting, what should be done? The board goes to the policy manual. Does policy address the worry? If not, how can it be made to do so? If policy does address the worry, is the monitoring system working? If it is working, does it assess performance closely enough or frequently enough to allow the board to relax? This step-by-step sequence not only diminishes board anxiety but results in a stronger policy position. Jacqueline Jackson of Palo Alto, California, calls this the "heartburn strategy: I determine what's bothering me, see if the policy covers it, put it in writing." When resolving the problem, the board must remain focused on the policies.

With a well-designed system, the board that takes care of its policies finds that the policies take care of it. Truly, making the policy system work is the way to make a board work. If worries are not dealt with forthrightly and in the self-correcting manner just narrated, they destroy the system, bottleneck board and staff, and crowd out time for ends development that is already critically short. Handled well, worries provide an opportunity to reconfirm that the system works and that expressing fears is a healthy part of the process.

The Character of Meetings

Let us consider how this process looks and feels. Perhaps the most obvious characteristic of this process is a short agenda (in number of items). Instead of facing a plethora of issues, the board encounters a much shorter list, although the issues are deeper. The board comes to see a lengthy agenda as a sign that something is wrong.

Attendance is high. Board meetings are not considered optional. Members attend because the meetings are interesting and they feel that they can accomplish something. There is an atmosphere of bigness and acceptance of diversity; the board is a forum to embrace diversity, not to homogenize it. Yet there also exists a businesslike awareness that the board is a deciding body, not a debating society. Meetings are worth board members' time. The members may have less exposure to interesting staff operations, but this loss is more than replaced by the active stream of contacts and issues generated from the ownership. At the forefront of the board's mentality is whether the dream is big enough, focused enough, visionary enough. There

WANT MORE?

8

is a refreshing conception of the board as part of a family of boards that form an inspiring stratum of leaders. Agendas and discussions increasingly reflect the realization that the organization's ends are integral to the larger context. In short, the board *lives* strategic leadership. I might not go so far as to match the ebullience of "RevLovejoy," a clergyperson and participant in the Web-based Policy Governance Forum, who said that under Policy Governance, "Board meetings are like some sort of foretaste of the kingdom," though I've truly felt inspired by boards that exemplify the sort of meaningful interaction I've described.

Next Chapter

The essentials of Policy Governance have now been covered. Chapter Eleven provides both challenges and counsel for attaining and maintaining successful strategic leadership on a governing board. A number of strategies are presented; the first few are old friends to us all, but they are couched in principles of the new governance.

WANT MORE?

Further Reading

1. Carver, J. "Just How Long Should Board Meetings Be?" *Board Leadership*, 1992j, no. 1, p. 6.

   Carver, J. "One Board Learns How Polling Moves Meetings Along." *Board Leadership*, 1994h, no. 13.

   Carver, J. *Planning Better Board Meetings*. The CarverGuide Series on Effective Board Governance, no. 5. San Francisco: Jossey-Bass, 1996n.

   Carver, J. "The Secret to Productive Board Meetings." *Contributions*, Mar.–Apr. 1998p, *12*(2), 20, 22.

   Oliver, C. "The Mighty Meeting." *Board Leadership*, 2004, no. 75.

   Carver, J. "Is Your Board in a Rut? Shake Up Your Routine." *Board Leadership*, 1992i, no. 4. Reprinted in J. Carver, *John Carver on Board Leadership*. San Francisco: Jossey-Bass, 2002.

2. Carver, J. "Protecting Governance from Law, Funders, and Accreditors." *Board Leadership*, 1994j, no. 11, pp. 1–5. Reprinted in *John Carver on Board Leadership*. San Francisco: Jossey-Bass, 2002.

   Hyatt, J., and Charney, B. "Sarbanes-Oxley: Reconciling Legal Compliance with Good Governance." *Board Leadership*, 2005c, no. 79.

3. Carver, J. "The Consent Agenda and Responsible Rubber Stamping." *Board Leadership*, 1998e, no. 38. Reprinted in J. Carver, *John Carver on Board Leadership*. San Francisco: Jossey-Bass, 2002.

4. Carver, J. "Owning Your Agenda: A Long-Term View Is the Key to Taking Charge." *Board Leadership*, 1993k, no. 7. Reprinted in J. Carver, *John Carver on Board Leadership*. San Francisco: Jossey-Bass, 2002.

Carver, J. "Who Sets the Board Agenda?" *Board Leadership*, 1999j, no. 41.

Carver, J. "The Consent Agenda and Responsible Rubber Stamping." *Board Leadership*, 1998e, no. 38. Reprinted in J. Carver, *John Carver on Board Leadership*. San Francisco: Jossey-Bass, 2002.

5. Carver, J. "What Happens to Conventional Documents Under Policy Governance?" *Board Leadership*, 1995o, no. 21. Reprinted in J. Carver, *John Carver on Board Leadership*. San Francisco: Jossey-Bass, 2002.

6. Carver, J. "Nine Steps to Implementing Policy Governance." *Board Leadership*, 1999d, no. 41. Reprinted in J. Carver, *John Carver on Board Leadership*. San Francisco: Jossey-Bass, 2002.

Carver, J., and Carver, M. M. *Reinventing Your Board: A Step-by-Step Guide to Implementing Policy Governance*. San Francisco: Jossey-Bass, 1997c.

Loucks, R. "Surviving the Transition: Igniting the Passion." *Board Leadership*, 2002, no. 59.

Lemieux, R. "Making the Commitment to Policy Governance." *Board Leadership*, 1999, no. 41.

7. Carver, J., and Carver, M. M. *Your Roles and Responsibilities as a Board Member*. The CarverGuide Series on Effective Board Governance, no. 2. San Francisco: Jossey-Bass, 1996b.

8. Carver, J. "The Secret to Productive Board Meetings." *Contributions*, Mar.–Apr. 1998p, *12*(2), 20, 22.

Carver, J. "Just How Long Should Board Meetings Be?" *Board Leadership*, 1992j, no. 1, p. 6.

Carver, J. *Planning Better Board Meetings*. The CarverGuide Series on Effective Board Governance, no. 5. San Francisco: Jossey-Bass, 1996n.

Carver, J. "One Board Learns How Polling Moves Meetings Along." *Board Leadership,* 1994h, no. 13.

Carver, J. "Is Your Board in a Rut? Shake Up Your Routine." *Board Leadership,* 1992i, no. 4. Reprinted in J. Carver, *John Carver on Board Leadership.* San Francisco: Jossey-Bass, 2002.

Maintaining Board Leadership

Staying on Track and Institutionalizing Excellence

I n this chapter, I synthesize more than summarize. The following strategies cut across various aspects of the Policy Governance model and challenge board members to move from paradigm to performance.

Be Obsessed with Effects for People

It seems obvious that the board's primary concern should be the benefits for people. But in the usual routine, programs, projects, activities, and methods demand so much attention that boards virtually neglect the benefits for people that justify the organization's existence in the first place! The never-ending struggle with organizational ends, according to Richard J. Peckham, formerly of the Kansas State Board of Education, "ought to consume us." That goal is claimed by John Fitzpatrick, a trustee of the Austin (Texas) Independent School District, who says, "the board is 100 percent focused on academic achievement and student success."

Don't Ponder Ends, Attack Them

"Passion, commitment, and fire for what we are doing must start at this table," pleads Donna Chavez, commissioner for the elected park district in Naperville, Illinois. Being obsessed with ends demands that the board tackle the difficult questions by mobilizing board time, mechanics, and concern around what good is to be done for which people at what cost. The board cannot forget these questions, even for one meeting.

All other policy categories are easy compared to this one; they are more quickly resolved and stable for longer periods. Adequate development of ends requires a long-term commitment. The board will forever be involved with ends issues; the struggle is never completed.

The rigorous focus of this process opens up new insights into what the proper ends should be. To make Ends policies about poverty in a community action agency, the board is forced to develop a new understanding of the nature and perpetuation of poverty. To make Ends policies for a public school system, the board must become more sophisticated about the skills needed for personal and social success in the world to come. To make Ends policies for a Third World development agency, the board must learn about the nuances of development and underdevelopment. The protocols of debate must enable deliberation on the questions as well as the answers. New questions will emerge over time and transform the degree and substance of the wisdom itself.

Moving mountains an inch often appears less active than moving molehills a mile. Boards that would be strategic leaders must move at a more deliberate pace than their staff, but on issues that are far more momentous. The leadership must keep the dream out in front so that board members always see mundane things like budgets and audits in the context of the overall effects that they have convened to achieve. This mentality is best achieved when no board meeting goes by without a debate or presentation on some facet of the ends development process. The central reason for board meetings, after all, is to define what difference the organization should make in the world.

Invigorate the Ends Debate

There is no more exciting topic than ends. An ends dialogue that is boring should be considered a symptom of poorly designed ends work. Apathy is easily avoided; a quick antidote is no further away than the staff. Even a small staff will harbor divergent, enthusiastically held ideas about the priority of outcomes. Encourage staff to develop arguments for competing viewpoints. Invite them to be passionate as well as coldly analytical.

Beyond the staff are even more sources of divergence. Some constituents do not believe your organization should exist at all. Listen to them. If your organization is in the public eye, there will doubtless be factions that think your priorities are all wrong. These factions do not agree with each other, and much can be gained from their debate. Rather than avoiding dispute, elicit it. The board should be the forum for public debate in its chosen area. It is, as the Rhode Island Board of Regents agreed to be, the "boiling cauldron" of whatever controversy is afoot.

Of course, none of these invigorating avenues is available if the board neglects to foster acceptance of diversity within its own membership. The board must value, even crave disagreement within its ranks if it expects to be comfortable with the lively dissent outside. A board that believes it must vote as a block in order for its pronouncements to carry weight fails to signal that its one voice always grows from and in spite of diversity. Strategic leadership is big enough to embrace diversity and wise enough to be enriched by it.

Divergence is not the only source of richness in the ends dialogue. Much of the vigor comes from allowing leaders to dream. In the short term, there is scant room for dreaming, for one must choose between being taken seriously and being visionary. In the long term, however, leadership cannot afford to overlook the wisdom of dreams, even the wisdom of playful dreaming. Vision that bounds higher than the barriers that confine us often springs from earnest playfulness.

Drive an Ownership Ends Dialogue Beyond the Boardroom

The board derives its identity and legitimacy from its ownership. Some ownerships (such as the general public) are broad enough to have trusteeship vested in multiple boards. Board service to the ownership need not be confined to the specific organization being governed. The board may well reach out to other organs of owner-ship—that is, other boards. In this extended arena, strategic lead-ership can have a momentous effect. Bringing the ends dialogue to the community of boards not only provides leadership to the whole but infuses the organization as well. It is more exciting and far-sighted to be part of an exciting and farsighted whole.

It is important that interboard dialogue focus on the results that each board pursues in the interests of the shared ownership. Orga-nizations commonly meet on more operational issues, an undertak-

WANT MORE?
1

ing that is appropriate for staffs, not boards. Boards could profit from discourse on their respective ends and the com-munity-related issues they have uncovered in deciding them. Does the sum of their ends accomplish the aggregate outcome that this cross section of leaders would want? Leaders in such an interaction feel a closeness with the abstract ownership that often eludes them in their separate board meetings. Their minds are stretched beyond their familiar home boardroom.

Don't Be Seduced by Cost Control

The quality of organizational results is best served by devoting unswerving attention to greater effectiveness, not to ever more stringent cost control. "An obsession with cost reduction produces narrowness of vision. . . . It actually hurts as much as helps," argues

WANT MORE?
2

Skinner (1986). Crosby (1979, 1984) and Deming (1986) forcefully maintain that costs will decrease when quality increases, although focusing on the reduction of costs does not increase quality. The concept of quality used by these authors concerns fulfilling customer requirements with minimal waste, unlike the more purely provider-oriented use of the word *quality* that is typical in many nonprofit and public agencies. It is not that cost reduction itself is bad but that the real issue is *return*—that is, results per unit cost.

Dare to Be Bigger Than Yourself

Demand daring. Bring the bigness of invigorated debate into the boardroom. The board's concerns need never be small again, for there will be neither time nor toleration for smallness. A conscious strategy is necessary because it is so easy to be more aware of the immediate and near at hand than the unbounded, distant horizons. Board members may arrive as individuals with all the problems of their day, but when they assemble around the table, they can truly transform themselves into architects of the future.

Keep Trusteeship Up Front

Trusteeship carries compelling obligations that are obvious to public boards that operate in the limelight. But not-so-public boards, which operate as if in trusteeship for the public, are not always known by that public. As a busy public, we do not run around to oversee those who operate in our name, though many a beleaguered

WANT MORE?

3

school board or city council may think otherwise. Social service and hospital boards operating as nonprofit, private corporations still see themselves as owned by the public, a public who often forgets that it is an owner. For such boards, there is less public pressure, though there is a greater moral challenge. How does a board act as an agent for principals who are unaware of the relationship? The board that would exercise leadership cannot avoid confronting the problem. If it is to be more than an academic consideration, the nature of trusteeship must be a frequent board topic. The formulation of the issue that I've found most incisive is that of Robert Greenleaf's servant-leadership.

Lead Leaders

With respect to the staff, it is pivotal that the board not only lead but lead leaders. Bigness must be passed on. Leading leaders calls for a mentality that allows others to make decisions. The board should never give the message, by trying to intervene in every potential mistake, that to err is unacceptable. Emphasizing the avoidance of errors rather than the creation of breakthroughs propagates not leaders but followers. It encourages not decision makers but bureaucrats. Leading leaders requires tolerance of risk, because leaders do not remain in the safe, old ruts. They try and sometimes fail.

One approach is to view governance as empowerment. The board passes power to others and expects them to use it as assertively and creatively as they dare. Dorothy I. Mitstifer, executive director of Kappa Omicron Nu Honor Society, East Lansing, Michigan, calls it "unleashing my creativity as a CEO." The board will have both the circumspection and the mechanism to empower the organization to work toward a specific goal (the impelling criteria of ends) within specific limits (the boundaries on means). The amount of risk is thereby controllable. Empowerment is not carte blanche, for delegation need not dissipate into abdication.

Furthermore, the board's ability to keep its own eye on the horizon is prodded by mental bigness in the executive staff. Having leaders work for us is a gift, indeed, for they ally themselves with that which is big in us, save us from distracting side issues, and urge us on toward still greater leadership.

Respect Your Words

If saying what you mean and meaning what you say is difficult for individuals, the task is even more formidable for a group. Boards have a tendency to write words that quickly become disjointed from their authors, as if the speakers and the spoken are unrelated. Some new board members are delayed in getting up to speed because it takes time to learn where all the relevant words are to be found and, after locating them, to learn which words mean something and which do not.

One solution is to use fewer words. When a board's verbal product is voluminous, there is no way that board members can fully

embrace it. It is common for public school board policies to be several centimeters thick. When a board has that many policies, for
practical purposes of governing it has no policies at all. It is far better that a board generate few words after much thought than many

WANT MORE?
4

words after little thought. Part of the problem arises, of
course, when the board acts as if it must approve or adopt
all staff documents. Most nonprofit boards should get ner-
vous when their total official paperwork increases beyond fifty pages.
There is nothing magic in this number, and it may not apply to all
boards, but the minimalist sentiment should be the same in all cases.

The second greatest source of volume is duplication. Stating the
same board value or perspective in different places increases the volume. There is less need to read carefully, because the material will
probably be repeated. The words at hand, therefore, lose some importance. Board utterances cast in the format of traditional administrative topics restate or imply the same values repetitively, for
relatively few values run across all topics. Perversely, if the values
are only implied rather than expressed explicitly, in repetition they
may be weakened rather than reinforced. Voluminous words,
reliance on inference, inconsistency, or any factor that weakens the
clarity of board values in their written form impairs the ability to
speak with one voice. A greater volume of board words makes board
values less clear.

When the board's policies are explicit, concise, and nonrepeti-
tive, it is necessary to observe them scrupulously. Maintaining the
integrity of board documents, and hence the integrity of the board's
word, requires that the board never violate its policies nor create
conflicting policies. This mandate would seem too obvious to state,
but it is regularly ignored. It occurs when the board creates policy
and then lays it aside, as if once done it may be forgotten.

Because existing board values can always be found in the single
repository of board policies, a board that is mindful of its integrity
would never consider a new action without relating it to existing
policies. Living closely with the policies enables any interpolicy

conflict to be cleared up in the normal course of business. The policies thereby evolve as a consistent expression of board values. Not only are they consistent, but they increase in quality, for the monitoring process reveals finer points or new information with which the board can hone its language still further.

Hence, every contemplated board action is pressed against the record of what the board has already said. The compendium of policies will be short and explicit enough for this to be done easily, so the board need not be a collection of librarians and lawyers. To ensure the continuing fidelity and usefulness of these policies over time, the board must constantly use them, or it will surely lose them.

Finally, a board's respect for its policy language can be heightened by cosmetics. Board policies, in this model, constitute a document as condensed as it is consequential. Presenting these few policies in a way that reflects their critical importance helps the board keep their importance in perspective. Therefore, the essential governance declarations should not be typed on plain paper or photocopied. Use special printed forms with color, if possible, and the organization's logo. Make them look like the momentous, center-stage statements they are.

Invest in Selection and Training

Performers—whether humans or machines—can perform only up to their capability. That capability can be diminished or improved, so it is a commodity that deserves care. The concept of investment is crucial, for the board can choose to see training as a troublesome

WANT MORE?
5

cost or as an opportunity to reap a return. If sophisticated and experienced board members find training an offensive concept, then find another word for it. But by no means should any board think it has skills that never fade, for even perfect board members have much to learn and relearn about teamwork and the exercise of group authority.

Recruit Those Who Can and Will Govern

Raw material makes a difference. If the board is able to select its own new members, it should start with a well-deliberated set

WANT MORE?
6

of qualifications. If the members are selected by others, whenever possible, the board should enlist the appointing authorities to use the board's desired qualifications. Aggressive recruiting involves not only selling prospective members on board membership but excluding those who do not fulfill the requirements.

Entrusting recruitment to a nominating committee can be useful, but integrity is maintained only if the board as a body has decided what types of people it desires. Too often, nominating committees are left completely to their own judgment. They cannot help but develop implicit criteria, but they rarely develop explicit criteria prior to becoming entangled in the personality-loaded interactions of recruiting. Even if they were to use a two-step process (a good idea if the board defaults), the board will not have been party to a matter that is critical to future board performance.

If the nominating committee has board-stated qualifications in hand (recorded as a Governance Process policy), it can render better service. The board should phrase its committee charge (also in the Governance Process category) so that finding the right people is given greater priority than filling vacancies. Boards "don't do a very good job of assessing prospective board members," says Edward Able, executive director of the American Association of Museums. Many boards have the wrong people on them. Indeed, boards would do well to tolerate a few empty seats instead of rushing to fill them. Recruiting would be more diligent if it were made known that membership on this board is an honor. After all, the board is selecting those who will bear the privilege and burden of trusteeship. With a more rationally defined board job, the California Park & Recreation Society, Sacramento, saw "an increase in the number of members who wish to serve on the board, as the board is now seen as doing 'important work,'" according to executive director Jane H. Adams.

What qualifications are important? These vary, of course, but with governance construed as I have described in this text, a few universal characteristics logically follow. Naturally, we all want Renaissance people, but to be more realistic and specific, we must start with the job to be done, so we begin by consulting the Governance Process policies on the board job description and style of governing. Members need to have the understanding, skills, and willingness to contribute to the governance task that the board has so carefully set forth. To promote the degree of strategic leadership championed in these pages, five qualifications, among others, are necessary.

1. *Commitment to the ownership and to the organization's specific area of endeavor.* As agents of the organization's ownership, board members must be committed to that trust. Commitment to the ends as currently stated is important, though less so, for ends are a continuing creation of the board itself. Therefore, fidelity to those in whose name ends are created is more essential than fidelity to the current wording.

2. *Propensity for thinking in terms of systems and context.* Some people focus quickly on parts. Whatever the relationship of whole to part might be, these persons more readily focus on the part itself for inspection, discussion, and decision. Such persons, with all good intentions, place distractions, if not massive roadblocks, in the way of strategic leadership. Prospective members who are more comfortable with parts have a valuable gift, but one that can more usefully be shared as a volunteer adviser to staff than as a board member. The board needs members who are cybernetically aware, drawn naturally to the harmony of the whole.

3. *Ability and eagerness to deal with values, vision, and the long term.* The board members who make the best contributions are those who have a natural propensity for looking not only beyond the stream of single events but beyond systems to the values on which they are

based. It is only a small step from divining today's values as they currently are to planning tomorrow's values as they should be. What stronger argument can be made that a board member's greatest gift to enterprise is educing, weighing, challenging, and frequently fighting over values?

4. *Ability to participate assertively in deliberation.* Productive board deliberation depends on bringing the foregoing characteristics to the governance struggle. Boards are overly tolerant of members who fail to share their capacities in a way that enhances the deliberative process. It is not enough to have the potential to be a good board member; the potential must be manifested through participation.

5. *Willingness to delegate, to allow others to make decisions.* Board members, with respect to one another, must be able to share power in the group process and, with respect to staff, must be able to delegate. Board members who are loath to delegate will impair the board's leadership by constantly bringing small issues up for consideration. They will impair staff by denying them the opportunity to grow.

Some prospective members are required to attend board meetings prior to assuming membership. Others are chosen from a pool of persons who are already familiar with board operations. These are useful tactics. At a minimum, a board should determine that a prospective member understands the board's governance model, bylaws, policies, current condition, and suspending issues. Frankly, a prospective member who fails to ask about such things is probably not a good candidate. Selection of the most qualified members deserves careful thought and design. *Qualified,* as is clear from the foregoing list, need not refer to academic credentials or high position. It need not relate to gender, color, or income. It is more likely to relate to grasp, mentality, connectedness, and commitment. As an assessment of past selection, consider this test: if fewer than half the board's members would make good chief governance officers, the selection needs improvement.

Prepare New Members and Old

Orienting new members can help institutionalize the board's governance process and prepare new members for immediate participation. Excellence can be lost simply through the influx of new members who have not agonized through the process of improvement. As they bring in their expectations about governance from other settings, they may cause a regression to the norm. Institutionalizing the hard-won process calls for helping new members understand the system of governance that has already been implemented by their colleagues. It is crucial that new members learn the principles of Policy Governance as quickly as possible. When this has been done, says Nash Williams, executive director of Southeast Georgia Regional Development Center in Waycross, "new board members can start making meaningful contributions almost immediately." Orientation is important enough to be a mandatory step rather than an optional exercise. The bylaws can require that a new member complete orientation prior to voting on any issue. That members who are ignorant of the organization are regularly given a voice in board decisions is an absurdity that only tradition can explain.

Continued education is needed by all board members, so orientation is merely one part of a larger commitment to having the necessary skills and insights for governance. Boards too infrequently invest in their own competence as much as good governance warrants. The board of Migrant/Immigration Shelter and Support in Owensboro, Kentucky, formulated a Governance Process policy committing the board to proper "knowledge, understanding, and skills" for all board members, new and old, in the service of what Tom Gregory (2003) calls "erosion prevention" (see Exhibit 11.1).

Part of the problem may lie in the word *orientation*, which may smack of learning where the lavatory, coffee pot, and desk supplies are located. Adequate preparation to shoulder the burden of strategic leadership requires something a bit more substantial. What is called for is *job training*, though that term may be offensive to

**Exhibit 11.1. Migrant/Immigrant Shelter
and Support, Owensboro, Kentucky
Governance Process Policy
"Preparedness for Leadership"**

The Board will ensure that the Board as a whole and each Board member
has the knowledge, understanding, and skills needed to function effectively and to reach the Board's intended outcomes. Accordingly:

1. The Board will schedule and participate in training and learning
   activities that equip the members to deal effectively with the opportunities, situations, problems, and responsibilities of their position.

2. As soon as practical after one or more new members are added to the
   Board, those new members will be trained in Policy Governance to a
   point where each new member can function well on the Board. The
   training also shall be made available to the other Board members and
   can be opened to the community. Ideally, multiple boards will coop-
   erate to sponsor joint training of new board members.

3. If a Board member does not obtain and maintain a level of knowledge, understanding, and skills needed to function as a productive
   Board member, and if that member is not carrying his or her fair
   share of the load, Board members shall remedy the situation as soon
   as possible with the cooperation of the deficient member. If reasonable remedial attempts fail, the Board, mindful of its obligations and
   responsibilities, will do what it appropriately can to replace the member or to have him or her replaced.

---

new members who are accomplished in their occupation or in
other board service. Whatever it is called, proper preparation of new
board members requires that they become thoroughly familiar with
the process and the current values of the board they are joining.

Present board members are the best persons to impart this training, though staff can certainly acquaint new board members with
operational matters. *Acquaint* is the operative word inasmuch as
new members' primary need is not for operational information.
Such information may help members form impressions of the whole

and even to ask good, board-relevant questions, but operational information is the domain of management, not of governance. No matter how well this information is presented and learned, it still will not equip the new member with the tools he or she needs to participate constructively in the board process. New member training must be built primarily around preparation for strategic leadership.

Carefully Manage Information and Knowledge

All jobs require those who perform them to continually update their skills and refurbish their understanding of the position. Turnover would perpetuate this need, even if it were capable of being met for all time for a given group of persons. Greater skills and understanding can often be obtained without the expenditure of dollars. If dollars are necessary, the outlay is best approached from the standpoint of investment rather than cost; instead of depicting training as an irritating cost, see it as an investment made for its expected return.

Consequently, return-on-investment criteria are applied. Although the return in terms of more effective governance will always be subjective because quantification is difficult, the idea is the same.

 WANT MORE? Boards learn that education per se is not the issue; it is education about the right things. Similarly, it is not just information that is the issue, but the right information. Moreover, decisions about board skill building and the supply of appropriate information would give appropriate consideration not only to the cost of training but to the cost of ignorance as well.

Because of its carefully structured separation of issues, Policy Governance is ready-made for the use of modern technology for process, record keeping, and displaying the status of issues at a given moment. Emergence of this capability—in effect, an Internet-based governance "secretariat"—is underway as this edition goes to press. Ray Tooley (2004) argued for a system that is instantaneously updated, "easily navigated from the broadest policy statement to the most detailed," with "current monitoring reports for each policy" (p. 7). Such a computerized system can enable task scheduling; historical access to board documents; management of board work between meetings; sharing of policies among boards of similar type; integration of multitiered organizations such as those with national, regional, and local boards; on-line voting; and audio and video con-

WANT MORE?

8

ferencing via the Internet. One beauty of such a system is that it not only makes using Policy Governance easier and, therefore, more likely to succeed, but can actually be a source of continuing education about the model due to its structure. Further, as Tooley says, "Time to get up to full Policy Governance speed is dramatically reduced" and "sustainability becomes much less of an issue" (p. 8).

Commit to Structured Practice

It has been observed that "boards rarely practice as a team. [Boards] meet to govern, not to rehearse" (Chait, Holland, and Taylor, 1996, p. 5). It is true that armies, rock bands, and football teams practice more frequently than they perform, while boards act as if practice is unnecessary. But for a board that is committed to the rigor of the Policy Governance model, practice is not only useful but crucial for maintaining skills. As situations arise that would otherwise be problems, the board must be able to use the model (or, more directly, the policies it has created by using the model) to reach a solution. Practicing skills will allow the board to maintain disciplined teamwork and prevent a few excited board members from taking the board off into top-of-the-head reactions.

Miriam Carver developed a structured practice methodology, which she and coauthor Bill Charney later published in a workbook,

WANT MORE?

9

that lays out a step-by-step series of rehearsals. Frequent use of this method will help a board not only maintain but elevate its governance skills. Frequent rehearsals during easy times makes it more likely that a board will stay the course during problematic times. Ian R. Horen, CEO of Painting and Decorating Contractors of America, St. Louis, accurately warns, "Preserving the concept of Policy Governance in an organization requires significant diligence. There is enormous temptation among the elected leadership to revert back to the abandoned structure and behaviors at the first sign" of difficulties.

Hence, Carver and Charney (2004) urge, "Since the point of rehearsal is to build board skill, practicing on a regular and frequent basis makes a good deal of sense, especially as board composition changes due to turnover. Accordingly, we suggest that boards set aside a brief period of time during each board meeting to solve a scenario presented either in this book or by a board member, staff member, or any interested party" (pp. 9–10). However, they caution, "governance rehearsal can be a meaningful concept only if the expectations and requirements of a governing board are clearly articulated. In other words, boards must rehearse in order to be effective, but unless there are established rules and expectations, *there is nothing to be rehearsed*" (p. 5; italics in original). I realize that boards, already pressed for time, will find it difficult to sustain such rehearsals. But devoting a relatively small amount of time to effective skill maintenance will pay for itself many times over.

Surmount the Conventional Wisdom

Until the prevailing understanding of governance changes, leaders must be aware of the deleterious influence of conventional wisdom. Current norms drag down boards that aspire to a higher standard. A board must continually overcome regressive pressures based in the general expectations people have of boards, the requirements foisted by funders and authorities, and even the well-intended advice of experts.

Influence of Those Who Expect

When observers see a board behaving atypically, they are surprised, maybe bewildered. Their discomfort with deviation has little to do with whether the departure from the norm is productive. When members of a national association watch their board or members of the public scrutinize an elected board, they may be confused, suspicious, and even angered if it does not behave in the way they expect.

In the public sector, the ownership's commitment to a better system is largely rhetorical. We do not petition our public boards to create more effective systems; we assail them for some small instance of implementation that offends us. So the board that would create a better system will find few committed supporters among the onlookers. A survey of what lobbyists lobby for would indicate which aspects of a system truly command our attention. We pursue fixes in regard to the element that concerns us, not more integrity in the process itself.

Rituals and symbols of responsible board behavior have grown over the years. Observers (not to mention board members themselves) have come to expect a responsible board to look a certain way: it approves budgets, monthly financial statements, and personnel "policies." It might adopt long-range plans, but these are expected to originate from staff recommendations for board reaction and revision. Observers have come to believe that boards that skip these steps are mere rubber stamps for staff wishes. They have seen occasional excesses and even disasters. So there is every reason to believe that boards who follow the prescribed route are responsible and those who do not are not. A board that forges new symbols does so at its own peril. The unmasking of empty symbols rarely receives as much attention as their absence.

Boldness and inclusion are keys to success in overcoming these impediments. Boldness is needed to do anything new against the pressure to conform. Inclusion of all relevant parties in the adventure helps to defuse opposition. In other words, the board can seek to include observers throughout its discussion of governance principles and during its adoption of a new model. Those included might be journalists, advocacy groups, unions, lawmakers, and any other relevant stakeholders.

Influence of Those Who Demand

Those who have power over the board constitute a special class of observers. Funding bodies, regulatory agencies, and lawmakers incorporate the conventional wisdom into their demands. After all, in the development of federal or state regulations, statutory language, association certification, and standards of accreditation, there has been little but traditional concepts of governance to guide the authors. Consequently, even vastly improved governance can run afoul of accreditation or law because of the improvements themselves. Mediocrity can pass tests that excellence fails. The board has an obligation to lawfulness, of course, but finding a way to preserve good governance while being lawful often requires creativity. Frequently, it requires legal counsel that is schooled in Policy Governance as well as in the law.

WANT MORE?
10

It is not uncommon for standard-setting bodies to be very prescriptive about what constitutes good governance. National associations might dictate that a local board have a certain set of committees, particular officers, or monthly meetings. Federal legislation and regulations might dictate that grantees meet similar requirements. Hospital accreditation may require the board to go through certain approval procedures. State laws require school boards to take action on a host of personnel and expenditure matters.

Often, little can be done aside from implementing the consent (automatic approval) agenda suggested in Chapter Ten. If possible, a board would be well advised to interact with funders, regulators, and accreditors in a manner that takes those parties' perceptions of threat to their authority into account as compassionately as possible. Sometimes it is possible to maintain a good governance model while giving the controllers what they are looking for—that is, evidence that they are in control and will not be viewed as lax by those who evaluate them. Enrolling them in the board's adventure in governance innovation may be one approach.

WANT MORE?
11

Another may be to proceed through the ritual behaviors expected but not take them seriously.

Influence of Those Who Help

Vast experience and expertise are accessible in the literature and from educators and consultants. Competent help can be obtained on strategic planning, financial oversight, fundraising, endowment building, administrative controls, audits, bylaws, corporate restructuring, and on and on. As part of their ongoing education as well as for specific issues that arise, boards should avail themselves of this body of knowledge, but very cautiously.

Because much expertise and many helpful formats have been developed within the conventional governance framework, the board must be a wise consumer. Texts, academic courses, and advice from consultants are likely to be topic-specific. The board needs assistance with its peculiar conceptual segment of budget, personnel, or planning activities, not with all budget, personnel, or planning activities. The board's role can be more easily confused than helped when the board becomes smarter about administrative or programmatic topics in their entirety, because the board can expend a great deal of energy on learning how to do the wrong things better.

The challenge facing boards is how to take advantage of accumulated knowledge yet reframe that wisdom so that it contributes to better governance within a conceptually useful model, not simply to more information within an impaired model. Some helpers can adapt to this challenge quite well, but boards should not expect adaptation to be either automatic or voluntary. A conceptual struggle might be involved, not to mention a little ego. Staff members, for example, may find that their training advice is not as useful to a board that is fulfilling an appropriate role. Although staff members may have expertise in many areas, governance is not typically one of these areas. To adapt their expertise to what the board needs to learn, staff must have an understanding of advanced governance.

That understanding is not so widespread that boards can expect to find it easily, even in skilled educators and consultants.

Help helpers to be helpful by querying them about competing value issues in the area under discussion. Rather than seeking their recommendation as to what a selected value might be, draw them out on the range of value alternatives available and what they see as the implications of options within that range. Implications are not only the predictable consequences but also the industry averages with regard to others' experience in making certain choices.

Particularly with regard to developing Executive Limitations policies, helpers can bring a great deal to a board's struggle to set the ranges within which staff members are allowed to act. They can assist the board in discovering, debating, and deciding what the conditions of jeopardy might be in, say, financial condition or personnel management. On these two topics, accountants and labor lawyers can be extremely enlightening if their counsel is taken in a way that relates to the board's proper role in such matters. Do not expect accountants or attorneys to know the proper board role, for they, too, will be operating from the conventional view. Following the raw advice of an accountant or attorney can, indeed, result in poor governance. The use of consultants has always been an important skill; good consultees are made, not born.

Make Self-Evaluation a Regular Event

There is no possibility of a board's governing with excellence in the absence of regular and rigorous self-evaluation. Like evaluation of

WANT MORE?

12

organizational performance, board self-evaluation should be against preestablished criteria. In Policy Governance, those criteria are embedded in Governance Process and Board-Management Linkage policies, for they set out how the board will function, the discipline it will follow, and the products it will produce. So while organizational performance evaluation tests organizational behavior and achievement, self-evaluation tests board behavior and achievement.

Exhibit 11.2 shows the "Monitoring Governance Process Policies" policy adopted by the publicly elected board of Adams 12 Five Star Schools in Thornton, Colorado. The Adams 12 board policy illustrates clearly the connection between Governance Process policies and regular board self-evaluation. Notice that the board recognizes that its CGO (in this case, the president) is empowered to

Exhibit 11.2. Adams 12 Five Star Schools, Thornton, Colorado Governance Process Policy
"Monitoring Governance Process Policies"

Systematic monitoring of the Board's adherence to Governance Process Policies will be against the policies themselves. Accordingly:

1. Monitoring is simply to determine the degree to which the Board is adhering to Governance Process policies.

2. Monitoring data will be acquired by three methods: (a) by direct Board inspection, in which a designated member or members of the Board assess compliance with the appropriate policy criteria, (b) by DSIT, in which a designated member or members of the committee assess compliance with the appropriate policy criteria, and (c) by external report, in which an external, disinterested third party selected by the Board assesses compliance with Board Governance Process policies.

3. In every case, the standard for compliance shall be *any reasonable President interpretation* of the Board policy being monitored. The Board is final arbiter of reasonableness, but will always judge with a "reasonable person" test rather than with interpretations favored by Board members or by the Board as a whole.

4. All policies will be monitored at a frequency and by a method chosen by the Board. The Board can monitor any policy at any time by any method, but will ordinarily depend on the attached monitoring report schedule.

Note: The monitoring schedule to which the policy refers has been omitted.

determine any reasonable interpretation he or she chooses for all Governance Process policies (including, incidentally, this one). The policy makes obvious that a board's self-evaluation has much in common with the board's evaluation of executive performance: they are both mandatory; they are both ongoing rather than sporadic or infrequent activities; and they both use preestablished criteria.

For self-evaluation to have practical effect, it must be frequent. In fact, frequent crude evaluations have a far greater effect than infrequent precise ones. For that reason, boards should devote at least a brief amount of time in each meeting to evaluating whether they are on course. An annual, more meticulous evaluation may be used as well, but it will not have as great an effect on ongoing board performance. In no event should board self-evaluation be a matter of downloading some generic form from the Internet.

Perpetually Redefine Quality

Just as the board's work on Ends policies is a perpetual task, so is its pursuit of excellence in the governing process itself. The definition of quality never stands still. What constitutes quality governance grows as we do, yet always remains a little beyond our grasp. The constancy of change can be unsettling. Ferguson (1980) said that it is not change itself so much as "that place in between we fear. It's like being between trapezes. It is Linus when his blanket is in the dryer. There is nothing to hold onto."

One solution is to give up the chase and settle for the status quo. A second is to continue the pursuit at the cost of feeling not good enough all along the way. The first trap is always present in human events. The temptation to settle for the norm is strong in public and nonprofit organizations because they are not forced to show results per dollar. The second trap is well known to people who learn fast and continually. They have only to look back a little to see the last thing they did that, in light of the new learning, now looks unwise. Their standards of wisdom and quality move forward, and advancing standards can be an unspoken indictment of the past. Hence, in addition to the direct cost of working toward higher ideals, there is a psychic discomfort that accompanies continual improvement.

View the Past as Inspiration, Not Impediment

Continual improvement can be viewed as harsh treatment of tradition. However, organizations with long histories can cherish their past without being beaten into inactivity by it. Organizational history, particularly a value history rather than a narrative history, can serve the purposes of renewal and recommitment by reminding members of what the organization represents. Traditions are a gift from the past, not a chain to the past. They are not to be discarded but to be built upon. Glendora Putnam, chairperson of the national board of the YWCA, spoke of her board as "moving ahead against long and revered traditions." When tradition boxes us in and mindlessly determines who we are, it is no longer to be revered but must be escaped. The board is, after all, creating tomorrow's traditions with the actions it takes today. Leadership compels us to be truer to tomorrow than to yesterday.

Pursue Excellence Rather Than Solving Problems

Commitment to excellence produces change that is more creative than reactive. Institute change to grow closer to an ever-receding standard of quality. Such change is not characteristically driven by problems. It is not problem solving as much as it is ideal creating. It aims to fill the gap between what is and what can be more than it seeks to escape what has been. It is a solution of the future rather than the past.

"If it ain't broke, don't fix it" loses its charm as a guiding principle because it delays improvement until it is necessary to move. Imai (1986) points out that if we do not fix the "unbroken," someone else will—with predictable market advantage. Peters (1988, p. 3) has altered the old bromide to, "If it ain't broke, you just haven't looked hard enough." For "broke" may be a property not of the thing itself but of its sufficiency in our ever-changing world. What was not broken comes to seem broken simply by virtue of new expectations and new possibilities.

Realize That Good Begets Better and Clarity Begets Trust

The easiest and best time to improve is when things are already going well. Incorporating better systems is gentler when it is not perceived as disciplining an errant member or as initiating a power struggle. When problems are rampant, almost any correction will be personalized. Thus, systematic monitoring of executive performance is best installed when the board and its CEO have a trusting, respectful relationship. Otherwise it will be perceived as punitive.

Ironically, with proper systems in place, the clarity of roles and expectations generates trust, perhaps in the way good fences make good neighbors. In situations in which there is low trust between a

WANT MORE? board and its management, the first area in which to pursue improvement is not in the trust itself but in clarity and transparency. The former is akin to pushing a hose instead of pulling it. If the board pursue the latter option, better governance yields and preserves trust.

Use the Policies Continually

The policies constructed according to the Policy Governance model are intended to answer every governance question or to point the way to the answer. This means that when unforeseen challenges arise, the board should go first to its policies. It means that when board-staff issues come up, the board should go first to its policies.

WANT MORE? Shooting from the hip is a natural but wasteful and dysfunctional reaction. I have seen boards act like pilots who use their instruments as long as the weather is good but abandon them when the weather turns bad, just when they are needed most. Regular rehearsals when things are going well, using an activity from *The Board Member's Playbook* (Carver and Charney, 2004) or a similar exercise of the board's choosing, will go far to prepare the board for intelligent action in times of crisis.

Never Forget That Governance is a Means

This book and, indeed, the Policy Governance model are dedicated to professionalizing governance—that is, basing its practices and rules on sound theory. Because of that underlying conceptual coherence, careless use of the model yields no model at all in the same way that *almost* using a technical tool correctly converts it to expensive junk. Yet a board must also realize that as important as the tool is, it is only a tool.

The organization does not exist for the purpose of being governed. So boards must learn to treat governance like they'd treat their car. The automobile is designed to work well when properly used and carefully maintained, but obsession with it need not displace getting to desired destinations. I have seen boards take more time in never-ending struggles about whether to follow this Policy Governance rule or

WANT MORE?

15

that than they spend accomplishing the purpose for which the rules were invented. Research would be useful on this point, but my experience is that such wasteful obsession is due either to variations in board members' understanding of the model or to resistance among board members to sticking with *any* consistent system. The former is self-explanatory. The latter leads to constant bickering about whether to follow the rules unswervingly. It is as if the board has chosen to buy PCs, but a few members cause unceasing discussions about whether to buy Macintosh programs they like.

Remember That Excellence Begins in the Boardroom

Boards can be successful strategic leaders if they nurture their group responsibility. That responsibility must be accepted by every board member, not just officers. All members must participate in the dis-

WANT MORE?

16

cipline and productivity of the group. All members must be willing to challenge and urge one another on to big dreams, lucid values, and fidelity to their trusteeship. All members must cherish diversity as well as an unambiguous, single board position derived from diversity. All members must strive for accountability in the board's job, confident that if quality dwells in the boardroom, the rest of the organization will take care of itself. For in the long run, as surely as excellence ends with clients, patients, students, or other customers, it begins with governance.

Governing well is difficult, but the greatest difficulty may lie in shifting from old to new paradigms. "Just as managerial ability is distinct from technical expertise," says Elaine Sternberg (1994) in an apt comparison, "so the qualities needed for being a director are not the same as managerial skill" (p. 228). Successful strategic leadership demands powerful engagement with trusteeship, obsessive concern with results, enthusiastic empowerment of people, bigness in embracing the farsighted view, and the commitment to take a stand for dreams of tomorrow's human condition. Re-creating governance can generate a zestful new genre of strategic leadership in the boardroom, to be sure, but the effects go far beyond. Douglas K. Smith (1996) points out the compelling opportunity to provide leadership through modeling: "When leaders are learning and growing, everything about them communicates the same opportunity to other people. They're excited, they do things differently. One of the most profound—and unusual—experiences people can have on the job is to see their leaders grow" (p. 27).

Next Chapter

The strength of Policy Governance is that it is founded on theory rather than tacked together from one experience to another. *Theory* in this case means an integrated set of concepts and principles tied to external realities. But even a sound concept must prove itself in real performance, so the natural and relevant question is "Does it work?" Since the inception of the Policy Governance model in the mid-1970s, hundreds of thousands of board members and executives can answer in the affirmative, but their testimony is anecdotal, unquantified, and unavailable. Research is desperately needed to answer the question. In the next chapter, I review the problems of governance effectiveness research, which, at this point, is as primitive an art as governance itself.

WANT MORE?

Further Reading

1. Carver, J. "The Invisible Republic." *Board Leadership*, 2004e, no. 74.

   Carver, J. "Economic Development and Inter-Board Leadership." *Economic Development Review*, 1990b, 8(3), 24–28.

   Carver, J. "Policy Governance as a Social Contract." *Board Leadership*, 2000f, no. 50.

   Carver, J. "Leading, Following, and the Wisdom to Know the Difference." *Board Leadership*, 1998k, no. 36. Reprinted in J. Carver, *John Carver on Board Leadership*. San Francisco: Jossey-Bass, 2002.

   Carver, J. "Organizational Ends Are Always Meant to Create Shareholder Value." *Board Leadership*, 2002h, no. 63.

2. Carver, J. "Beware the Quality Fetish." *Board Leadership*, 1998a, no. 37. Reprinted in J. Carver, *John Carver on Board Leadership*. San Francisco: Jossey-Bass, 2002.

   Crosby, P. B. *Quality Is Free*. New York: McGraw-Hill, 1979.

   Crosby, P. B. *Quality Without Tears*. New York: McGraw-Hill, 1984.

   Deming, W. E. *Out of Crisis*. Cambridge: Center for Advanced Engineering Study, Massachusetts Institute of Technology, 1986.

3. Carver, J. *The Unique Double Servant-Leadership Role of the Board Chairperson*. Voices of Servant-Leadership Series, no. 2. Indianapolis, Ind.: Greenleaf Center for Servant-Leadership, Feb. 1999h.

   Greenleaf, R. K. *Servant Leadership: A Journey into the Nature of Legitimate Power and Greatness*. New York: Paulist Press, 1977.

   Greenleaf, R. K. *The Power of Servant Leadership*. (L. C. Spears, ed.). San Francisco: Berrett-Koehler, 1998a.

   Spears, L. C. (ed.) *Reflections on Leadership: How Robert K. Greenleaf's Theory of Servant Leadership Influenced Today's Top Management Thinkers*. New York: Wiley, 1995.

Spears, L. C., and Lawrence, M. (eds.). *Practicing Servant Leadership: Succeeding through Trust, Bravery, and Forgiveness*. San Francisco: Jossey-Bass, 2004.

Carver, J. "The Servant-Leadership Imperative in the Invisible Republic." Keynote address, Greenleaf Center for Servant-Leadership 14th Annual International Conference, Indianapolis, Ind., June 11, 2004g.

Carver, J. *The Unique Double Servant-Leadership Role of the Board Chairperson*. Voices of Servant-Leadership Series, no. 2. Indianapolis, Ind.: Greenleaf Center for Servant-Leadership, Feb. 1999h.

4. Oliver, C. "Uncovering the Value of the Right Word." *Board Leadership*, 2001c, no. 59.

Davis, G. "Policy Governance Demands That We Choose Our Words Carefully." *Board Leadership*, 2000, no. 49.

Carver, M. "Speaking with One Voice: Words to Use and Not to Use." *Nonprofit World*, July–Aug. 2000, *18*(4), 14–18.

Carver, M. "Governance Isn't Ceremonial: It's a Real Job Requiring Real Skills." *Board Leadership*, 1997, no. 31.

5. Carver, J. "If Your Board Isn't Worth the Cost of Competence, It Isn't Worth Much." *Board Leadership*, 1998i, no. 35.

Mogensen, S. "Sticking to the Process Without Getting Stuck." *Board Leadership*, 2004, no. 74.

6. Carver, J. "Filling Board Vacancies." *Board Leadership*, 2002c, no. 63.

Moore, J. "Policy Governance as a Value Investment: Succession Planning." *Board Leadership*, 2002b, no. 60.

Carver, J. "Does Your Board Drive Away Its Most Promising Members?" *Board Leadership*, 1998f, no. 35. Reprinted in J. Carver, *John Carver on Board Leadership*. San Francisco: Jossey-Bass, 2002.

Carver, J. "Recruiting Leaders: What to Look for in New Board Members." *Board Leadership*, 1996q, no. 23. Reprinted in J. Carver, *John Carver on Board Leadership*. San Francisco: Jossey-Bass, 2002.

Carver, M. "Governance Isn't Ceremonial; It's a Real Job Requiring Real Skills." *Board Leadership*, 1997, no. 31.

Carver, J., and Carver, M. "A Board Member's Approach to the Job." *Board Leadership*, 1999a, no. 46.

7. Moore, J. "A Governance Information System." *Board Leadership*, 2002a, no. 60.

Tooley, R. "Using Information Technology to Sustain Policy Governance." *Board Leadership*, 2004, no. 76.

8. Tooley, R. "Using Information Technology to Sustain Policy Governance." *Board Leadership*, 2004, no. 76.

9. Carver, M., and Charney, B. *The Board Member's Playbook: Using Policy Governance to Solve Problems, Make Decisions, and Build a Stronger Board*. San Francisco: Jossey-Bass, 2004.

Carver, M. "Governance Rehearsal: A New Tool." *Board Leadership*, 2003a, no. 68.

Charney, B., and Hyatt, J. "When Legal Counsel Is Uninformed." *Board Leadership*, 2005, no. 79.

10. Carver, J. "When Bad Laws Require Bad Governance." *Board Leadership*, 2000j, no. 50.

Hyatt, J., and Charney, B. "The Legal and Fiduciary Duties of Directors." *Board Leadership*, 2005a, no. 78.

Carver, J. "Policy Governance and the Law." *Board Leadership*, 2005c, no. 78.

Hyatt, J., and Charney, B. "Legal Concerns with Policy Governance." *Board Leadership*, 2005b, no. 78.

Carver, J. "The Contrast Between Accountability and Liability." *Board Leadership*, 2005a, no. 78.

Kelly, H. M. "Carver Policy Governance in Canada: A Lawyer's Defense." *Miller-Thompson Charities and Not-for-Profit Newsletter*, July 2003, pp. 7–8. Reprinted in *Board Leadership*, 2004, no. 71.

Hyatt, J., and Charney, B. "Sarbanes-Oxley: Reconciling Legal Compliance with Good Governance." *Board Leadership*, 2005c, no. 79.

Charney, B., and Hyatt, J. "When Legal Counsel Is Uninformed." *Board Leadership*, 2005, no. 79.

Carver, M. "Independent? From Whom?" *Board Leadership*, 2005, no. 79.

Carver, J. "Our Second Legal Issue." *Board Leadership*, 2005b, no. 79.

11. Carver. J. "What Should Government Funders Require of Nonprofit Governance?" *Board Leadership*, 2002m, no. 59.

Carver, J. "Recommendations to the West Virginia Legislative Oversight Commission on Education Accountability." Unpublished paper written for the West Virginia legislature, 1991b. Reprinted in J. Carver, *John Carver on Board Leadership*. San Francisco: Jossey-Bass, 2002.

Carver, J. "Protecting Governance from Law, Funders, and Accreditors." *Board Leadership*, 1994j, no. 11, pp. 1–5. Reprinted in J. Carver, *John Carver on Board Leadership*. San Francisco: Jossey-Bass, 2002.

Carver, J. "When Bad Governance Is Required." *Board Leadership*, 1996u, no. 24.

Oliver, C. "Policy Governance in the Regulatory Environment." Information sheet. Toronto: Canadian Society of Association Executives, 1998.

Carver, J. "Toward Coherent Governance." *The School Administrator*, Mar. 2000i, *57*(3), 6–10. Reprinted in J. Carver, *John Carver on Board Leadership*. San Francisco: Jossey-Bass, 2002.

Carver, J. "Partnership for Public Service: Accountability in the Social Service Delivery System." Unpublished paper written for the Ontario Ministry of Community and Social Services, 1992k. Reprinted in J. Carver, *John Carver on Board Leadership*. San Francisco: Jossey-Bass, 2002.

12. Carver, J. "Living Up to Your Own Expectations." *Board Leadership*, 1999c, no. 42.

Carver, J. "Living Up to Your Own Expectations: Implementing Self-Evaluation to Make a Difference in Your Organization." *Board Leadership*, 1993i, no. 10. Reprinted in J. Carver, *John Carver on Board Leadership*. San Francisco: Jossey-Bass, 2002.

Carver, J. "Redefining Board Self-Evaluation: The Key to Keeping on Track." *Board Leadership*, 1993n, no. 10. Reprinted in J. Carver, *John Carver on Board Leadership*. San Francisco: Jossey-Bass, 2002.

Carver, J. "Performance Reviews for Board Members." *Contributions*, Jan.–Feb. 1999e, *13*(1), 16, 19.

Oliver, C. "Creating Your Policy Governance Tool Kit." *Board Leadership*, 2000b, no. 50.

Conduff, M. "Sustaining Policy Governance." *Board Leadership*, 2000, no. 51.

Gregory, T. "Board Erosion Prevention." *Governing Excellence* (International Policy Governance Association), Winter 2003.

13. Carver, J. "The Importance of Trust in the Board-CEO Relationship." *Board Leadership*, 1992h, no. 3. Reprinted in J. Carver, *John Carver on Board Leadership*. San Francisco: Jossey-Bass, 2002.

14. Carver, J. "Handling Complaints: Using Negative Feedback to Strengthen Board Policy." *Board Leadership*, 1993h, no. 8.

Carver, J. "What to Do When Staff Take Complaints Directly to Board Members." *Board Leadership*, 1997q, no. 31. Reprinted in J. Carver, *John Carver on Board Leadership*. San Francisco: Jossey-Bass, 2002.

Carver, M., and Charney, B. *The Board Member's Playbook: Using Policy Governance to Solve Problems, Make Decisions, and Build a Stronger Board*. San Francisco: Jossey-Bass, 2004.

15. Carver, J. "The Governance Obsession Syndrome" *Board Leadership*, 2002d, no. 60.

16. Carver, J. "Group Responsibility—Requisite for Good Governance." *Board Leadership*, 1998h, no. 38.

Carver, J. "Protecting Board Integrity from the Renegade Board Member." *Board Leadership*, 1994i, no. 13. Reprinted in J. Carver, *John Carver on Board Leadership*. San Francisco: Jossey-Bass, 2002.

12

But Does It Work?

Criticisms, Effectiveness Research, and Model Consistency

What does research show about the effectiveness of Policy Governance? In a word, nothing. Research has not shown that boards using the Policy Governance system are more effective than boards that do not. In fact, research has little useful to say about the effectiveness of *any* approach to governance.

Compared with research in managerial and technical subjects, governance research continues in a primitive state despite the great increase in studies over the past couple of decades. With respect to answering the question posed by the title of this chapter, there are three major impediments that researchers will have to overcome:

- First, for research on the use of Policy Governance to be credible, researchers must be able to tell when a board is using the model and when it is not. That may seem a simple matter, but the research and commentary literature has no shortage of opinions and findings by persons who were unable to recognize Policy Governance when they saw it. For example, a CEO's claiming to have a Policy Governance board has mistakenly been assumed by researchers to mean the board actually followed the principles of the model.

- Second, and actually a greater problem, there is extensive confusion over just what governance is for. Unless we can agree on the purpose of governance, arguing whether one approach or another is more effective is futile. For example, purposes of raising funds, supplying volunteer labor, or fulfilling the owner-representa-tive purpose described in this book lead to entirely different defin-itions of effectiveness.

• Third, the utility of research findings about component parts of governance is diminished when the larger question of purpose is unsettled. For example, researching which personality types lead to smoother decision making or which committee arrangements lead to more board member satisfaction may or may not be useful on a board that is deciding about the wrong things or with board mem-bers who are on the board for all the wrong reasons.

Despite the vacuum of support from credible governance effec-tiveness research, the Policy Governance model has achieved ar-guably more widespread recognition than any other organized system of governance—worldwide and across a broad range of sec-tors and organization types. Because of the model's ubiquity, radical departure from traditional norms, and substantial claims, it clearly warrants informed criticism. But while there have been criticisms of the Policy Governance model, they are surprisingly infrequent in light of its reputation and uncompromising principles. Some, however, come up frequently and warrant a response.

Criticisms of Policy Governance

I will omit the most frequent kind of criticism—that which arises out of a misreading of the model itself. Among other misconcep-tions, it is common to hear that the model forbids committees; does

WANT MORE? not allow communication between individual board mem-
1 bers and staff; restricts board decision making to ends issues, thereby preventing a board from dealing with staff means; keeps the board from exercising its fiduciary responsibility; puts areas of organizational information out of reach; and bans public input (in the case of public organizations). None of these is accurate, of course, which an even cursory reading of this text demonstrates.

What gives rise to these sorts of misrepresentations is anybody's guess, but what is clear is that they are not comments on the model. The ones that follow are and are worthy of a reply.

One Size Can't Fit All

Chief among the criticisms is that Policy Governance is a one-size-fits-all approach to the board's job. Surely, boards are all different from one another. Their organizations are all different; the times in which they operate change; they vary in maturity; and jurisdictions differ one from another. These things are true, but they argue *for* a

WANT MORE? universal theory of governance, not against it. The role of
2 theory is to tie together the fundamental truths of the governance task wherever it appears and whatever its superficial characteristics. A fundamental study of governance asks the question "What can be said about the attributes of any governance role in any situation?" If nothing can be said—that is, if there are no universal truths—then the critics' doubts are proven true.

But even the critics do not believe their own criticism. They would all believe, for example, that every board should know what its job is. They would contend that any board that delegates away some of its authority is obligated to demand accountability for the way that authority is used. The list goes on, but notice that as such a list progresses, one is building a set of universal principles. If we can but tie them together into a coherent whole, we have a model—a model that is as universal as its parts. It will not be a model of a certain structure, certainly, but one of certain principles and concepts. And that is all the Policy Governance model is. My response to the complaint that Policy Governance is a one-size-fits-all approach is to say, "Thanks. It's about time."

The anatomy chart in your physician's office is a one-size-fits-all model. Chemistry is a one-size-fits-all model (despite the seeming dissimilarities in our experiences). In fact, all scientific theories are just that. One should not be surprised but, rather, should be gratified that a search for universal principles yields universal principles!

The best retort to this criticism is simply to ask, "Which parts of the model are irrational or undoable?" I have found that the reply to that question usually reveals misunderstanding about just what the model actually is.

Policy Governance Rules Are Too Rigid

Although there are fewer rules in Policy Governance than in the professions and occupations in which many board members serve, it is true that the rules that constitute the model are, in fact, inflexible. That characteristic follows from my attempt to reduce the necessary features of the model to the bare minimum, enabling a framework of rules that is as simple and short as possible. But reduction to the few rules that apply universally renders those minimal rules absolutely mandatory. Those who consider firm rules to be a shortcoming overlook that games, from checkers to football, consist of unbendable rules. In other words, rigidity in its place is not a bad thing, from sterilization procedures in surgery to things we do for fun.

Frequently, however, this criticism masks a very different objection—that the model requires unusual discipline, enough to stick to the rules even when personalities and habits entice a board to abandon them. These rules do call for more discipline than boards typically exhibit, but they require far less than board members frequently exercise in their chosen fields of work. Electricians, farmers, pilots, surgeons, architects, and equestrians, for example, must all abide by far more demanding rules of discipline than the Policy Governance model imposes.

Policy Governance Just Can't Be the One True Way

This criticism is absolutely correct. To my knowledge, no authoritative Policy Governance resource has ever maintained that the model is the only possible way or the only true way to govern. There undoubtedly are other paradigms of governance that would be just as universally applicable as Policy Governance, but they have not yet emerged. Surely the future will change that.

WANT MORE?

3

The Model Denigrates Measurement

The Policy Governance model bids boards to set suitably broad expectations with great regard for meaningfulness but with no regard for measurement. So it is true that boards need not pay attention to the management mantra "Set measurable objectives." But that is not due to belittling the role of measurement in any way. In

WANT MORE?
4

fact, the model is as adamant about measurement as was Franz Karl Achard, the eighteenth- and nineteenth-century German chemist, who said, "The philosopher who does not measure only plays, and differs from a child only in the nature of his game" (*Columbia Electronic Encyclopedia, 2003*). Setting expectations in the form of Ends and Executive Limitations policies in the broadest form that welcomes any reasonable management interpretation is necessary to allow optimal empowerment and use of management creativity and agility.

And while the Policy Governance board does not consider measurement at the policymaking stage, it is adamant about it during the monitoring phase. Monitoring data are expected to be just that—data—rather than simply assurances. And the data must be demonstrated to the board's satisfaction to be a credible operational definition of the board's original policy language. Measurement in Policy Governance, then, is enormously important, but it does not impose a burden on the board in its creation of policies.

Policy Governance Denigrates
or Discourages Board Fundraising

Simply put, it does not. The model concerns the proper governance of an organization, not the optional board engagements of fund-

WANT MORE?
5

raising, lobbying, or other contributions. These may be important, even critical board tasks in specific situations, but they are not generic to all boards and thus are not part of a universal theory of governance. In many types of organizations, fundraising is not even remotely related to the board's job. The Policy Governance treatment of the nonuniversal job elements that may show up for a given board dictates that the board consciously decide what those values added (job products) are to be and include them in its job description (see Exhibit 7.4 for an example). So the Policy Governance model does not discourage fundraising, lobbying, or contributing volunteer service. It simply puts such activities, should they be appropriate, in their proper place.

The Model Must Be Used in its Entirety

In a field in which systems thinking is rare, perhaps it should not be surprising that this kind of criticism comes up repeatedly. Armstrong (1998a, p. 14), for example, considered it a fault that "the model will work best only when adopted in its entirety." Well, *of course*. And one's watch works only when all the parts designed in are left inside the case. We have no problem using Ford parts in a Ford and Chevrolet parts in a Chevy, nor do we expect Mac programs to run on PCs. But where we are willing to accept mediocrity—such as in boards, as history seems to indicate—disarray and disjointedness are misguidedly granted the honorable word *eclecticism!*

WANT MORE?
6

The Model Doesn't Fit Our Organization

Any serious attempt to design for the future must challenge constraints of the past. How could fuel injection ever have been invented if engineers had been expected to construct all fuel-air devices to look like carburetors? Yet it is frequently heard that Policy Governance will not work in a given organization because it doesn't fit "the way we do things." Even academics fall into the same trap, making comments like "The type of [governance] model should fit the organization's characteristics" (Armstrong, 1998b, p. 13).

One might ask just what makes the organization's current characteristics the touchstone. If managers were tyrannical toward their subordinates, would humane personnel practices be rejected on the same basis? To judge any governance approach based on whether it conforms to present organizational practices is an outrage. Critics who treat the operational organization as the independent variable and the expression of owners' voices as the dependent variable are announcing where they see governance and, by extension, owners' prerogatives in the scheme of things.

This criticism illustrates the management-centered (rather than ownership-centered) way in which governance is typically approached. "The way we do things" is invariably the way management does things or the way the previous boards have done things. The model, remember, deals with the organization's obligation to its ownership and the board's role in mediating that accountability. It is not presumptuousness but common sense to say that governance practices should not be compelled to fit the organization but that *the organization should fit governance practices*. The duty, then, is to work out the most advanced governance practices despite contrary management or governance histories—and that undertaking needs a model, for it is obliged to be driven not by current board practices, by a board's past practices, or by administrative prerogatives.

The Model Is Based on a Traditional, Mechanistic, Top-Down View of Organizations

Policy Governance is unambiguously hierarchical, it is true. Those who own the organization are clearly in the most authoritative position. The board acts on their behalf and is, therefore, one step down. Authority can be granted by the board to the CEO, but not by the CEO to the board. The CEO acts on the board's behalf and is, therefore, another step down. Other staff may be empowered by the CEO, but not the reverse. These relative positions in the chain of command do not convey wisdom or worth, only levels of authority to match their accountability. Most staff understand that hierarchy is not only inevitable but justifiable. Those few who want an equal partnership with the board are seeking rights beyond their accountability. The challenge of hierarchy is not met by pretending it does not exist. The challenge is met by

WANT MORE?

7

making it as humane and empowering as possible, consistent with accountability and the principle of agency.

Policy and Administration Cannot Be So Cleanly Separated

As late as a couple of decades ago, governance writers and practitioners were still citing the difference between policy and administration as if there were a bright line between them. Of course, given the imprecise definitions used for those words, the idea was a gross oversimplification. When a degree of enlightenment illuminated the error, the same commentators could claim to be sophisticated when criticizing Policy Governance for reintroducing the old mistake. But Policy Governance does not claim that there is a universally applicable stopping point for board encroachment on management choices. In other words, Policy Governance doesn't dictate where

WANT MORE?
8

the line demarcating board and executive decision making should be drawn. Decisions are seen as occurring in sizes from largest to smallest, forming an unbroken continuum with no preset point where governance magically becomes management. Policy Governance only calls upon each board to clearly establish a dividing line for its own organization. While it is not possible to say for all organizations where that boundary should go, for any given board and its executive there is no excuse for it to be ambiguous. If a CEO tells the board, "My staff and I operate as a team," the board understands. If, however, a CEO says, "I can't tell the difference between my job and those of my staff," the board has reason to worry.

Policy Governance Curtails Board Involvement

The model not only allows but demands board involvement. It does not excuse board involvement, however, in whatever strikes board members' fancy. Governance is an authoritative job that requires at least as much discipline of the board as it does of the staff. Discipline means that what one is involved in is not a matter of whim or personal motivation but one of careful and respectful design. The model was not designed to make board members happy or to help them fill their time. It was designed to ensure that owners are properly, wisely, and farsightedly represented. That requires not just board involvement but board involvement in the right things in the right way.

Board Members Are Prevented from Talking with Staff

It is hard to know where this criticism comes from. In fact, the model makes it safer for board members and staff members to interact as they wish than does traditional governance. It does so by

WANT MORE?
9

making the rule very clear that nothing a board member says to a staff member has directive authority. The board must speak in a single authoritative voice. Further, if there is a CEO, then the board speaks authoritatively only to the CEO. The beauty is that making the rules and roles clear means that anyone can talk with anyone about anything without doing harm.

In addition, it is common in the practice of Policy Governance for a board to invite the CEO to bring staff members in so that the board can hear their ideas and glean their wisdom about questions under board consideration. The board is open to knowledge from all directions, even though it commands only through one careful channel. In this way, staff members can become part of the board's extensive input system.

Policy Governance Requires an Expert CEO and a Conflict-Free Board

It is true that the more competent, committed, and conflict-free the board members and executive are, the better Policy Governance—or any other approach—will work. However, if a board with an inadequate CEO moves to Policy Governance, its CEO will not be any more incompetent than before. In such situations, the board finds that it did not have a CEO to start with but had only a top clerk who was incorrectly called a CEO. But just as often, when given the opportunity to actually be a CEO, free of over-the-shoulder board behavior, many CEOs rise to the occasion. In any event, the greatest effect of Policy Governance is to make CEO adequacy or inadequacy too obvious to overlook.

As for conflict among board members, rather than the model failing to work, its clarity about CEO authority starting where board decisions leave off means that management is not left hanging just because the board has failed to make a decision. Moreover, because the CEO is not obliged to pay any attention to the board until it has officially spoken, intraboard conflict does not jeopardize management as it does in traditional governance. Under Policy Governance, intraboard conflict may be uncomfortable, but it does not delay the CEO in getting on with business.

Policy Governance is Just Theory

Because the model is designed with the purity of theory, it can be criticized for being "just theory." Yet having no underlying theory has always been the greatest weakness of governance, whether in corporate or nonprofit organizations. Governance practices do change some over time, but usually through what Thomas Kuhn calls "development by accumulation" (1996, p. 2). The utility of theory is that all aspects of an undertaking can be aligned in the most productive fashion. Having a technology of governance helps free boards from the domination of current personalities and the flukes of their specific history. Policy Governance is both a theory and a sophisticated operating system for board leadership.

WANT MORE?
10

Research Has Not Proven the Model to Be Effective

This is a good criticism and entirely accurate. On the other hand, it has little utility inasmuch as no approach to governance has been shown by research to be effective. Until research can catch up to the need, the only choice is between a conceptually coherent, theory-based approach that has not been proven effective by research and a tradition-based patchwork of practices that also has not been proven effective by research. The quandaries of governance research receive more detailed treatment later in the chapter.

How Much Policy Governance Is Required to Be Policy Governance?

The Policy Governance model is composed of concepts and principles that have been imported from governance knowledge that has been around for many years: the board speaks on behalf of others; it works best at the policy level; it has topmost authority in the orga-

WANT MORE?
11

nization; and its authority is vested in the group, not the individuals. A list of such universally accepted principles— though expressed for equity corporate boards—is shown in Exhibit 12.1. Those and other long-standing points are recognized and usually refined in the Policy Governance model. But it is important to note that a number of concepts and principles unique to

---

Exhibit 12.1. Universally Accepted Principles of Accountable Governance

- The board governs on behalf of all owners.
- The board is the highest authority in the company, below only the owners.
- The board is the initial authority in the company.
- The board is accountable for everything about the company.
- All authority and accountability is vested in the board as a group.
- Governance roles and executive roles have different purposes.
- Delegation should be maximized, short of risking the board's fulfillment of its accountability.
- Assessing board performance requires evaluation of both governance and management.

Source: Adapted from Carver and Oliver, 2002c, p. 8.

Policy Governance (for example, those that deal with the ends-means distinction and the graduation of decision sizes) were created in order to build upon and systematize that preexisting knowledge, making it into a conceptually coherent, powerful instrument for governing.

Assembled from borrowed concepts in addition to truly new ideas, the Policy Governance model as a new entity, then, constitutes a unique system that is intended to be *used as a system*. Even so, there are parts that can be lifted from the model and used by themselves. For example, a board can profitably take from the model just the principle of never evaluating its CEO except on criteria set forth ahead of time. For uncountable boards, that discipline alone would be an improvement. If a board takes from Policy Governance only that board instructions to staff will be from the group as a whole rather than from individual board members or committees, that would be an improvement. Any one of a number of elements of Policy Governance can bring welcome change to the average board, even if the model as a whole is not adopted.

On the other hand, these improvements—while they are to be admired and sought—do not transform the nature of governance. They are akin to repairing an old car by repairing fan belts, brakes, and dents. Those are improvements, to be sure, but they can never produce a new car. No matter how much one fixes a typewriter, it will never become a word processor. The intent of Policy Governance is not simply to bring a few improvements to boards; a far less radical and less disciplined approach can do that. The aim of Policy Governance is to create in the place of an old, tired, inadequate role one that is predisposed to and capable of visionary leadership, empowering delegation, and ironclad accountability. The title of this book is simply a mild statement of that goal.

So when the utility of Policy Governance is researched, it is important that it is really the practice of Policy Governance that is under scrutiny, not merely bits and pieces of it. Without competence to tell the difference, individuals' opinions and findings of formal research provide relatively meaningless conclusions. A mere cursory understanding of the model or unjustified reliance on others' claims to be using it have impeded useful commentary and research, producing conclusions useless to the question of governance effectiveness, yet widely quoted among academics who should know better.

So what are the essential elements of the model, in the absence of which one can be said to be borrowing from Policy Governance but not using it? After all, the use of the word *model* is not happenstance; used in its scientific rather than its structural sense, it means a system of integrated, interacting parts. As with a clock, removing one wheel may not spoil the clock's looks, but it seriously damages its ability to tell time. It becomes an ornament, not a clock. So in Policy Governance, which wheels would have to be in place to still have our "clock"? Here, adapted from previous publications, is a list of the minimum requirements:

1. The board connects its authority and accountability to those who morally (if not legally) own the organization—if such a class exists beyond the board itself—seeing its role as servant-leader to and for that group. *Owners*, as used in the Policy Governance model, are not all of the stakeholders but are only those who stand in a position corresponding to shareholders in an equity corporation. Therefore, staff and clients are not owners unless they independently qualify as such.

2. With the ownership above it and operational matters below it, a governing board forms a distinct link in the chain of command or moral authority. Its role is commander, not adviser. It exists to exercise that authority and properly empower others rather than to be management's consultant, ornament, instrument, or adversary. The board—not the staff—bears full and direct responsibility for the process and products of governance, just as it bears accountability for any authority and performance expectations delegated to others.

3. The board makes authoritative decisions directed toward management and toward itself, its individual members, and committees only as a total group. That is, the board's authority is a group authority rather than a collection of individual authorities.

4. The board defines in writing (a) the results, changes, or benefits that should come about for (b) specified recipients, beneficiaries, or other targeted groups, and (c) at what cost or relative priority for the various benefits or various beneficiaries. These are not all the possible benefits that may occur but are those that form the purpose of the organization, the achievement of which constitutes organizational success. Policy documents containing solely these decisions are categorized as *Ends* in the terminology of the Policy Governance model but can be called by whatever name a board chooses, as long as the concept is strictly preserved.

5. The board defines in writing the behaviors, values added, practices, disciplines, and conduct of the board itself and of the board's delegation and accountability relationship with its own subcomponents and with the executive part of the organization. Because these are non-ends decisions, they are called *board means* to distinguish them from ends and staff means. All board behaviors, decisions, and documents must be consistent with these pronouncements. In the terminology of the Policy Governance model, documents containing solely these decisions are categorized as *Governance Process* and *Board-Management Delegation* but can be called by whatever names a board chooses, as long as the concepts are strictly preserved.

6. The board makes decisions with respect to its staff's means decisions and actions only in a proscriptive way in order simultaneously (a) to avoid prescribing means and (b) to place off-limits those means that would be unacceptable *even if they work*. Policy documents containing solely these decisions are categorized as *Executive Limitations* in the terminology of the Policy Governance model but can be called by whatever name a board chooses, as long as the concept is strictly preserved.

7. The board's decisions in Ends, Governance Process, Board-Management Delegation, and Executive Limitations begin at the broadest, most inclusive level and, if necessary, continue into more detailed levels that narrow the interpretative range of higher levels, proceeding one articulated level at a time. These documents are exhaustive, replacing or obviating board expressions of mission, vision, philosophy, values, strategy, goals, and budget. They are called *policies* in the terminology of the Policy Governance model but can be called by whatever name a board chooses, as long as the concept is strictly preserved.

8. If the board chooses to delegate to management through a chief executive officer, it honors the exclusive authority and accountability of that role as the sole connector between governance and management. In any event, the board never delegates the same authority or responsibility to more than one point.

9. In delegating decisions beyond the ones recorded in board policies, the board grants the delegatee the right to use any reasonable interpretation of those policies. In the case of Ends and Executive Limitations, when a CEO exists, that delegatee is the CEO. In the case of Governance Process and Board-Management Delegation, that delegatee is the CGO (chief governance officer), except when the board has explicitly designated another board member or board committee.

10. The board monitors organizational performance solely through fair but systematic assessment of whether a reasonable interpretation of its Ends policies is being achieved within the boundaries set by a reasonable interpretation of its Executive Limitations policies. If there is a CEO, this assessment constitutes the CEO's evaluation.

Since the intent is for a board to use an integrated system, not just a collection of practices, particular attention should be paid to the statement in principle 5 that says, in effect, that whatever practices are not expressly mandated in these principles must be consistent with them. If an outside authority demands board actions that are inconsistent with Policy Governance, the board creatively uses the consent (automatic approval) agenda or another device in order to be lawful without compromising governance. Because these ten points have been condensed to a minimum yet encompass the complete range of governance behavior, a few further examples of specifics might be useful.

For example, if the board confuses owners with other stakeholders by accepting non-owner input as owner input, it violates principle 1. If a board relies on the CEO to create the board's agendas, it is violating principle 2. If a board directs that the organization offer certain services or programs, it violates principle 6. If a board's Executive Limitations policy prohibits the CEO from "failing to have written job descriptions for all staff," it is violating principle 6. If it maintains statements of vision, values, or goals separate from those embedded in properly constructed policies, it violates principle 7. If it allows a finance committee or a financially expert board member to make rules for financial management, it is violating principles 3 and 8. If a board evaluates or instructs persons who report to the CEO, it is violating principles 2 and 8. If a board judges CEO performance based on what the board meant by policy wording rather than by whether the CEO's interpretation of the wording is reasonable, it violates principle 9. If a board evaluates its CEO on anything other than the applicable policies, it violates principle 10. If the board fails to assess carefully the CEO's justification for the reasonableness of his or her interpretations, it violates principle 10. Of course, these are only examples. The point is that Policy Governance is a precision system that promises precision in governance only if used with precision.

So, contrary to much of the research done to date, let us assume that when researchers compare the practice of Policy Governance with other approaches to governance, they can actually tell whether or not Policy Governance is being practiced. But having achieved that level of discernment, researchers must then confront the really big question for research on the effectiveness of governance: just what *is* "board effectiveness"?

Research on the Effectiveness of Governance

Governance is a *social construct*; it does not appear in nature. Because it is a function created by human beings for a human purpose, the purpose can be whatever we say it is. Typically, the purpose of a construct is derived from the dynamics of realpolitik, the happenstances of history, or a considered philosophical position. In the first instance, interactional struggles of the day use the construct as a weapon in jockeying for power or advantage. For example, a CEO might want the board to be a fundraiser and apologist for staff; an intrusive board chair might want governance to be based on chair hegemony. In the second instance, the fact that governance has been conducted a certain way for a long time justifies its continuing along the same course; hence, governance is limited by "how everyone else is doing it" or "the way we've always done it."

In designing Policy Governance, I took the third path, that of basing the nature of governance in a philosophical position, then aligning all its parts and practices with that nature. The upside of this approach is conceptual integrity; the parts all make sense taken as a whole, and the total plays a defensible role in the larger human scheme of things. Another upside is that although board members all come with their own personal agendas, there is a common ground of rationality that is sufficiently compelling to shape a compromise on their process. The downside is that governance that is so carefully crafted is out of step with conventional wisdom and the experience of accomplished board members, requires unusual discipline, and can be frightening to executives who fear a board with self-determination.

Policy Governance begins with the proposition that boards exist to provide owners an authoritative voice in the organizations they

own. Boards may perform optional functions, but this is their raison d'être. That is, they exist to translate informed owners' wishes
into organizational performance. I say "informed" because owners
must rely on their owner representatives to distinguish the doable
from the undoable and to summarize and synthesize multiple owner
viewpoints.

I have contended that a board derives its moral authority from
and incurs its most salient accountability to some base of legitimacy
that, for lack of a better term, I call the *ownership*. Ownership in
this sense does not rest merely on a legal definition of holding title
but is best described as a *moral* ownership. For the board of an
antique auto club, the ownership is the membership of the club. For
a city council, the ownership is the population of the jurisdiction.
For an equity corporation, the ownership is the body of shareholders. For some types of organizations, putting a name on the identity
of owners is not as easy as in the foregoing instances. But even when
identifying the owners is difficult, the utility of the concept is not
diminished any more than identifying the runway when landing is
less important just because a fog obscures it.

In normal life, ownership is an easy concept. Assume that I am
about to buy a new vehicle. I ask you to help me with the question
"Which is more effective, a Jaguar or a Land Rover?" If you do not
know what I want the vehicle for, you would be unable to help me.
Your knowing what my neighbors, creditors, or friends (all important stakeholders) want would not suffice. Although I owe these
stakeholders ethical behavior and maybe even helpfulness, my ownership of the vehicle per se is not diluted by those obligations. Even
law, which surely can restrict my use of what I own, would cause no
one to say I don't own my vehicle just because it is not to be driven
above the speed limit. Curiously, some governance research puts all
stakeholders on an even footing by measuring governance effectiveness with respect to their approval. It is as if the ownership concept either does not exist or is immaterial. The difference between
stakeholders and owners is dealt with in Chapter Seven, so at this

point I am only moved to note that these researchers would never dilute the meaning of ownership with respect to their family car in the same way. Unless we know directly—or by a representative process—what owners want, macroeffectiveness research is severely handicapped or, at worst, even pointless. By *macroeffectiveness*, I mean the effectiveness of the organization as a whole in fulfilling its essential purpose. Microeffectiveness research can proceed without confronting that difficulty. For example, will double-entry bookkeeping produce more easily traceable records than single-entry? Will phonics or phonetics result in higher reading scores? What methods are associated with greater acquisition of revenues? Which board behaviors are linked to CEO job satisfaction? What board member personality types are associated with greater perceived ability to make decisions? Such research—for example, about which personal characteristics work best on a board—must take into account that it is contaminated by whatever ideas people have on what boards need and what they should be doing. Similarly, research about whether boards that have gone through training—any training—are more satisfied with their performance than ones that have not is contaminated by what board members think fulfills their role.

Those are not inconsequential questions, nor is the research on them meaningless, but they avoid the massive question of which governance practices fulfill the social construct of ensuring that owners' interests dominate and are fulfilled by the organization. So

WANT MORE?

12

while microeffectiveness research is clearly legitimate, the predominance of subsidiary questions in the research literature obscures the fact that the large question is yet to be addressed. More insidious, many such studies imply that effectiveness in governance is to be judged by whether board members are more fulfilled, challenged, or involved; the CEO is happier or the board is less meddlesome; the board raises more funds; grant revenues are increased; committees are active; or the board chair perceives the CEO to be meeting his or her objectives. It is a travesty that research by credible academics acts—without ill intent—to so trivialize the role of owner representatives.

At this writing, the most thorough of academic studies on governance effectiveness of which I am aware—the dissertation of Patricia Nobbie (2001)—while taking care to avoid the common trap of failing to discern whether Policy Governance is in fact being used, falls squarely into the other trap of treating a group of management characteristics as independent variables and governance methodology as the dependent variable. The Policy Governance model was not created to accomplish any of the internal management indices selected for comparison. (The model does provide a framework that enables a given board to require accomplishment of those things, but there was no indication the selected boards had any such intent.) To reiterate, the Policy Governance model was designed to ensure—borrowing the terminology of the International Policy Governance Association— *owner-accountable organizational performance*.

WANT MORE?
13

It is not uncommon for research claiming to be a study of governance effectiveness to see governance as a dependent variable and management as an independent variable. That is, researchers assume that we already know what good management is, so the only task before us is to find out what good governance is. Therefore, a researcher might try to hold management constant and then see what governance practices fit it well. But that is entirely backwards and exemplifies what is wrong with traditional governance thinking. If the role of governance is to translate owners' wishes into organizational performance, the real question is what approach to management best fulfills what governance requires of it. In other words, despite researchers' assumption, in an individual instance, we have no way of knowing what good management is until we know how well it produces the results authoritatively required of it.

Policy Governance calls for more than merely a different set of board operating rules; it calls for something deeper—the simple philosophical position that organizational effectiveness depends on what owners want their organization for. If a board is needed at all, governance operates between owners and the organization itself, with the task of discovering or summarizing what owners want, tempering that knowledge with whatever relevant intelligence is appropriate, and requiring an operating organization to produce it. With that in mind, it becomes clear that research must incorporate a more defensible concept of what governance is *for* before it can research what is best for boards to *do*.

WANT MORE?

14

Thus, the central and even foundational research inquiry is to find which governance practices are best able to convert a judicious summary of owners' intentions into organizational performance. The question is simple, but researching it is not. Even as late as 2005, when this edition is going to press, to my knowledge, credible research on that pivotal question *has never been done*.

Policy Governance and Excellence in Board Leadership

The Policy Governance model is founded in the same owner representative role that is expounded in the social contract philosophy of Jean-Jacques Rousseau. The attitude and commitment that is built into Policy Governance is consistent with Robert Greenleaf's concept of servant-leadership. I drew liberally from the management literature in instances in which it offers advice that is applicable to governance. The mechanics of Policy Governance are simply a concrete design for translating governance theory into excellent governance performance—the conversion of conceptual design into an operating system.

Yet I cannot say that using the model even with unrelenting precision will ensure excellent board leadership. Boards that are unwise will remain unwise when using Policy Governance. Boards that are uncaring will remain uncaring when using Policy Governance. Boards that are ill-intentioned will remain ill-intentioned when using Policy Governance. Boards that are unintelligent will remain unintelligent when using Policy Governance.

WANT MORE?

15

The model does not ensure sagacious, farsighted, humane decision making, even though it provides the most carefully crafted framework with which to govern an enterprise on behalf of others. Just as an automobile with all possible performance and safety features cannot cause sensible driving, Policy Governance neither relieves board members from the task of coming to grips with difficult choices nor protects them from bad decisions.

WANT MORE?

16

To use the car analogy once more, the board will have all the challenges of plotting a course and driving astutely, but at least it won't have to worry about the roadworthiness of the vehicle itself. Policy Governance is merely a vehicle for board leadership, not its embodiment.

The Policy Governance model *enables* wise and intelligent people to govern with excellence; it does not produce excellence. Only board members can do that.

WANT MORE?

Further Reading

1. Biery, R. M., and Kelly, H. M. "Industry Canada's Unjustified Criticism of Carver Policy Governance." CCCC *Bulletin*, 2003, no. 2, pp. 3–5.

   Charney, B. "'Messy Democracies': Should They Be Protected or Cleaned Up?" *Board Leadership*, 2003, no. 65.

   Oliver, C. "Questions and Answers About Good Governance." *Board Leadership*, 2002f, no. 63.

   Carver, J. "Policy Governance Won't Work Because . . . " *Board Leadership*, 1998n, no. 36. Reprinted in J. Carver, *John Carver on Board Leadership*. San Francisco: Jossey-Bass, 2002.

   Hough, A. *The Policy Governance Model: A Critical Examination.* Working paper no. CPNS6. Brisbane, Australia: Centre of Philanthropy and Nonprofit Studies, Queensland University of Technology, July 2002.

2. Carver, J. "'One Size Fits All': The Lingering Uninformed Complaint." *Board Leadership*, 2003n, no. 65.

   Murray, V. "Is Carver's Model Really the One Best Way?" *Front and Centre*, Sept. 1994, p. 11.

   Armstrong, R., and Shay, P. "Does the Carver Policy Governance Model Really Work?" *Front and Centre*, May 1998, pp. 13–14.

   Armstrong, R. "A Study in Paradoxes." *Association*, 1998, *15*(4), 13–14.

3. Murray, V. "Is Carver's Model Really the One Best Way?" *Front and Centre*, Sept. 1994, p. 11.

4. Carver, J. "Giving Measurement Its Due in Policy Governance." *Board Leadership*, 1997h, no. 30. Reprinted in J. Carver, *John Carver on Board Leadership*. San Francisco: Jossey-Bass, 2002.

5. Carver, J. *Board Members as Fundraisers, Advisors, and Lobbyists.* The CarverGuide Series on Effective Board Governance, no. 11. San Francisco: Jossey-Bass, 1997b.

   Carver, J. "Giving, Getting, and Governing: Finding a Place for Fundraising Among the Responsibilities of Leadership." *Board Leadership*, 1993g, no. 7. Reprinted in J. Carver, *John Carver on Board Leadership*. San Francisco: Jossey-Bass, 2002.

6. Armstrong, R., and Shay, P. "Does the Carver Policy Governance Model Really Work?" *Front and Centre*, May 1998, pp. 13–14.

   Carver, J. "Why Is Conceptual Wholeness So Difficult for Boards?" *Board Leadership*, 1998r, no. 39. Reprinted in J. Carver, *John Carver on Board Leadership*. San Francisco: Jossey-Bass, 2002.

7. Carver, J. "FAQ: Isn't the Hierarchical Nature of Policy Governance Out of Step with Modern Participative Organizational Styles?" *Board Leadership*, 2002b, no. 60.

   Carver, J. "Making Hierarchy Work: Exercising Appropriate Board Authority in the Service of Mission." *Board Leadership*, 1994e, no. 12. Reprinted in J. Carver, *John Carver on Board Leadership*. San Francisco: Jossey-Bass, 2002.

8. Carver, J. "Is There a Fundamental Difference Between Governance and Management?" *Boardroom*, Mar.–Apr. 2003i, *11*(2), 1, 7.

Carver, J. "Is There a Fundamental Difference Between Governance and Management?" *Board Leadership*, 2002f, no. 60.

Carver, J. "Boards Should Have Their Own Voice." *Board Leadership*, 1997d, no. 33. Reprinted in J. Carver, *John Carver on Board Leadership*. San Francisco: Jossey-Bass, 2002.

9. Carver, J. "FAQ: Does Policy Governance Prohibit Staff from Talking with Board Members?" *Board Leadership*, 2002a, no. 63.

10. Carver, J. "Why Is Conceptual Wholeness So Difficult for Boards?" *Board Leadership*, 1998r, no. 39. Reprinted in J. Carver, *John Carver on Board Leadership*. San Francisco: Jossey-Bass, 2002.

11. Carver, J. "How You Can Tell When Your Board Is *Not* Using Policy Governance." *Board Leadership*, 1996k, no. 25. Reprinted in J. Carver, *John Carver on Board Leadership*. San Francisco: Jossey-Bass, 2002.

Rogers, S. "Policy Governance Top Ten." *Board Leadership*, 2005, no. 77.

Mogensen, S. "What Are the Other Models?" *Board Leadership*, 2002, no. 64.

Oliver, C. "Policy Governance and Other Governance Models Compared." *Board Leadership*, 2002e, no. 64.

12. Brudney, J. L., and Murray, V. "The Nature and Impact of Changes in Boards of Directors of Canadian Not-for-Profit Organizations." Unpublished paper, 1996.

Murray, V., and Brudney, J. "Improving Nonprofit Boards: What Works and What Doesn't?" *Nonprofit World*, 1997, *15*(3), 11–16.

Murray, V., and Brudney, J. "Do Intentional Efforts to Improve Boards Really Work?" *Nonprofit Management and Leadership*, 1998a, *8*(4), 333–348.

Murray, V., and Brudney, J. L. "Letters to the Editor." *Nonprofit World*, 1998b, *16*(1), 4–5.

Armstrong, R., and Shay, P. "Does the Carver Policy Governance Model Really Work?" *Front and Centre*, May 1998, pp. 13–14.

Armstrong, R. "A Study in Paradoxes." *Association*, 1998, *15*(4), 13–14.

13. Nobbie, P. D. "Testing the Implementation, Board Performance, and Organizational Effectiveness of the Policy Governance Model in Nonprofit Boards of Directors." Unpublished doctoral dissertation, Department of Public Administration, University of Georgia, 2001.

Nobbie, P. D., and Brudney, J. L. "Testing the Implementation, Board Performance, and Organizational Effectiveness of the Policy Governance Model in Nonprofit Boards of Directors." *Nonprofit and Voluntary Sector Quarterly,* 2003, 32(4), 571–595.

Hough, A., McGregor-Lowndes, M., and Ryan, C. "Policy Governance: 'Yes, But Does It Work?'" *Corporate Governance Quarterly,* Summer 2005, pp. 25–29.

14. Carver, J. "Rethinking Governance Research: Do Good Boards Produce Effective Organizations?" Unpublished paper for the University of Georgia Institute for Nonprofit Organizations, Apr. 10, 2001k. Reprinted in J. Carver, *John Carver on Board Leadership.* San Francisco: Jossey-Bass, 2002.

Carver, J. "A New Basis for Governance Effectiveness Research." *Board Leadership,* 2003k, no. 67.

Carver, J. "Watch Out for Misleading Interpretations of Governance Research." *Board Leadership,* 1998q, no. 40. Reprinted in J. Carver, *John Carver on Board Leadership.* San Francisco: Jossey-Bass, 2002.

Smith, C. J. "Eight Colleges Implement Policy Governance." *Trustee Quarterly,* 1996, no. 1, pp. 8–10.

15. Carver, J. "The Unique Double Servant-Leadership Role of the Board Chairperson." In L. C. Spears and M. Lawrence (eds.), *Practicing Servant Leadership: Succeeding Through Trust, Bravery, and Forgiveness.* San Francisco: Jossey-Bass, 2004i.

Carver, J. "The Servant-Leadership Imperative in the Invisible Republic." Keynote address, Greenleaf Center for Servant-Leadership 14th Annual International Conference, Indianapolis, Ind., June 11, 2004g.

Greenleaf, R. K. *Servant Leadership: A Journey into the Nature of Legitimate Power and Greatness.* New York: Paulist Press, 1977.

Greenleaf, R. K. "Servant: Retrospect and Prospect." In R. K. Greenleaf, *The Power of Servant Leadership*. (L. C. Spears, ed.). San Francisco: Berrett-Koehler, 1998b.

Spears, L. C. (ed.). *Reflections on Leadership: How Robert K. Greenleaf's Theory of Servant Leadership Influenced Today's Top Management Thinkers*. New York: Wiley, 1995.

Spears, L. C., and Lawrence, M. (eds.). *Practicing Servant Leadership: Succeeding Through Trust, Bravery, and Forgiveness*. San Francisco: Jossey-Bass, 2004.

Rousseau, J. J. "Discourse on Political Economy." In J. J. Rousseau, *Jean-Jacques Rousseau: The Social Contract* (C. Betts, trans.). Oxford, U.K.: Oxford University Press, 1999. (Originally published 1758.)

Rousseau, J. J. *Jean-Jacques Rousseau: The Social Contract* (C. Betts, trans.). Oxford, U.K.: Oxford University Press, 1999. (Originally published 1762.)

Carver, J. "Policy Governance as a Social Contract." *Board Leadership*, 2000f, no. 50.

16. Carver, J. "Can Things Go Horribly Wrong for Boards That Use Policy Governance?" *Board Leadership*, 2001b, no. 56. Reprinted in J. Carver, *John Carver on Board Leadership*. San Francisco: Jossey-Bass, 2002.

Carver, J. "How Executive Limitations Policies Can Go Awry." *Board Leadership*, 2001h, no. 57.

Carver, J. "What to Do When All Your Policies Are in Place." *Board Leadership*, 1997p, no. 32. Reprinted in J. Carver, *John Carver on Board Leadership*. San Francisco: Jossey-Bass, 2002.

Resource A: Varieties of Policy Governance Applications

The model of governance set forth in this book was developed to be generic, applicable no matter where or what boards govern. It is meant to encompass most organizational variations comfortably within a general theory of governance. Adapting the model to profit-based corporations, which have not been the subject of this book, requires only recognition that shareholders constitute the "for whom" component of ends. Public and nonprofit boards face special circumstances that make adaptation appear difficult, but only in rare cases is it actually so.

I have had the opportunity to interact with board members from every populated continent. Naturally, those boards span vast cultural differences, yet the fundamental precepts of Policy Governance garner an enthusiastic response across the world. For example, I have worked with native North American groups, all of whom found the concepts culturally compatible.

Still, each organization likes to feel that it is different, as each has its own history and personality. It has been said that consultants think all organizations are alike, while organizations think they are all different. Even so, boards would do well to resist focusing prematurely on their peculiarities and look first to generic principles of strategic leadership in governance. These principles, rather than detracting from the uniqueness of an organization, make its distinctiveness possible.

So a board must deal with its peculiar conditions by first ignoring them. The peculiarities should be viewed through a framework of general principles. Amazingly, boards often find that they are not so different after all. The real payoff lies in their being able to apply powerful, generic principles even when they are lured by an illusory atypicality.

"Governance is governance is governance" may not be the whole truth, but it is not a bad place to start. Special circumstances do matter, but to deal with them effectively, a board must have a sound footing in the basics. In this appendix, I present a few examples of how the generic model applies to special situations. My intent is not to address all the varieties of organizations but only to comment on the applicability of Policy Governance to their board work. The categorizations that follow are merely for convenience; it is also not my intent to create fixed categories, for you will see that a given organization might be placed in several of the categories.

City Councils or Other Elected Boards

Four peculiar conditions apply to city councils: (1) council members are elected individually; (2) councils have police power or coercive authority over a geographic territory (not just over their own staff); (3) councils are tightly regulated by state or provincial law as to powers and methods; and (4) when an independently elected mayor serves statutorily as CEO, the board-CEO structure does not pertain because the council does not have authority over the mayor. In these cases, the relationship is more like that of the Congress and the president, each having separate powers.

When each member represents a separate constituency, working together for the whole can be difficult. Furthermore, electorates tend to expect officials to attend to the smallest of concerns rather than the sweeping, momentous ones. City councils have a particularly hard time distinguishing between owner concerns and customer concerns. A citizen is more likely to complain about a garbage collection incident or stop sign placement than about the city's long-term maintenance of infrastructure.

Police power gives the council authority over third parties and thus creates a unique area of governance statements beyond the four policy categories of the model: *ordinances*, or, in Canada and the United Kingdom, *bylaws*. State-prescribed structure and procedures sharply cramp councils' latitude in governance and delegation. Moreover, councils resort to hands-on control so frequently that their time is always overcommitted, which severely strains council members. In addition, a greater political consequence, as stated by Ron V. Houser of the City of Grande Prairie, Alberta, is that "society is often unable to attract the best candidates with the necessary vision and talents to lead . . . due to [the job's having been defined as requiring such exhausting] time and financial sacrifices."

WANT MORE?

1

These conditions make it difficult but not impossible to apply good governance principles. Condition 4 in the preceding list (an independently elected CEO) introduces a major difficulty in fully applying the model, for the CEO is more beholden to the electorate than to the board. Even then, however, a council can use some of the same policymaking principles. In the pure council-manager form, this problem does not arise. With only minor exceptions, then, Policy Governance is applicable to elected councils.

School Boards

Local boards of public education have one of the most difficult tasks among public and nonprofit bodies. They face four peculiar conditions: (1) individual board members are often elected; (2) school boards are tightly regulated by state or provincial authorities; (3) school boards preside in the public spotlight over an emotional topic; and (4) everyone thinks he or she is an expert because, after all, we all went to school. Condition 1 is similar to the first situation confronting city councils. One of the effects is that school board members often act in a way that politically satisfies individual consumers rather than with the discipline needed for good governance. Condition 2 is so oppressive that school boards are forced to misuse most of their time in trivial pursuits. Condition 3 intensifies condition 1 inasmuch as the emotional electorate can be unyielding and irrational. Condition 4 simply makes the job a little more difficult. The generic Policy Governance model, however, is thoroughly applicable to school boards.

WANT MORE?

2

Boards in State and Provincial Government

Peculiarities of state and provincial government boards range broadly because of the wide variety of statutes that have established and charged such boards. Boards of government departments, depending on the jurisdiction, have to deal with greater or less control by the executive authority and have greater or less independence from other organs of government. They also have varying degrees of authority over their respective CEOs and departments. Across these boards, the generic Policy Governance model ranges from largely to totally applicable. I mean to include in this category the quasi-governmental organizations charged by government with overseeing or disciplining professions or other practitioners. In Canada, for example, this category would include regulatory colleges and law societies, and in the United States, it would include licensing boards. What these boards have in common is their intimate relationship with legislatures and legislation. These bodies regularly confront a difficulty in deciding whether their ownership is the body politic or the professionals or practitioners being regulated.

WANT MORE?

3

When describing such boards' jobs, legislators have a tendency to write enabling statutes that confound powers, prescribed activities, and outputs. Because the conceptual framework used by such boards does not disentangle these managerially distinct concepts, much leadership potential is wasted. There often appears to be a subtle legislative intent that the board not truly govern, but just as often, the problem is simply naïve design. An example of poor design is the Georgia State Board of Education. The board has various types of approval authority over the state superintendent and the Georgia Department of Education, yet the superintendent is an independently elected official. It is no wonder that vehement conflicts arise with such a dysfunctional arrangement.

College and University Boards

Community colleges and, in the United Kingdom, colleges of further education have been far more influenced by Policy Governance than boards of universities. In any event, the principles of Policy Governance apply fully, though in many institutions, boards are confronted internally with shared governance, the apportionment of relatively equal power with faculty or a faculty senate. The Policy

WANT MORE?

4

Governance view of this arrangement is that the real owners of the institution are being shortchanged by the dilution of the general public's control. This comment in no way questions the importance of faculty or the critical tradition of academic freedom, for it is in the public's best interest to satisfy and preserve both. In addition, in many North American jurisdictions, boards are confronted externally with laws that require board seats for students, faculty, and administrators. The Policy Governance view of that requirement is that is arises from a poor understanding of the board as owner representative.

Parks Boards

In the United States, about half of parks boards are elected, and the other half are appointed. In other countries, practices vary. The job

WANT MORE?

5

in all cases, however, is practically identical. When parks boards are attached to municipal government, there is frequently considerable confusion as to whether the board has a governing or an advisory role. If it is advisory, confusion is often about whom it advises and about what.

Boards of Charities, Social Services, and Community Organizations

This category is extremely broad, ranging from small advocacy groups to large entities organized to provide social benefit. It is in this group that one is more likely to find boards with no staff or very minimal staff in which board members form all or much of the only workforce available. When that is the case, whether the board chooses to treat

WANT MORE?

6

one person as a chief executive officer is crucial to the way the model is implemented. The model offers a way for the board to carry out the governance portion of its task, enabling board members to be volunteer workers and volunteer governors simultaneously by keeping the rules of each role separate. But some organizations in this class are quite large either in revenues or in their effect—for example, the YMCA, the YWCA, family counseling providers, and local improvement groups.

Boards of Cooperatives and Credit Unions

Cooperatives are membership organizations wherein the members are customers and beneficiaries as well as owners. Policy Governance has been implemented in agricultural, retail food, and other types of co-ops. One of the challenges for co-op boards is the dis-

WANT MORE?

7

tinction between members' interests as owners and their interests as customers. In credit unions—a distinct type of co-op—boards have that hurdle but also have to determine that their organization exists for the difference it makes in members' lives rather than for profitable operation. Prudent financial operation is important in all cases, of course, but does not form the reason for existence and, therefore, is not an ends issue.

Library Boards

The role of libraries in Western culture has evolved from being book depositories to integrating societal connectivity and resource availability. Library boards have struggled with important social currents in order to adapt to changing times and expectations. Many have had a hard time turning their focus from internal concerns to the role of libraries in the cultural developments yet to come. Policy Governance can be an enabling technology for the needed leadership.

WANT MORE?
8

Foundation Boards

The only peculiarity of foundation boards (excluding "operating" foundations—those that are themselves primarily service providers rather than funders) is that they give away money rather than run their own programs. Thus, they are like relief agencies, the United Way, the Community Chest, and government funding agencies. The generic model is entirely applicable.

Church Boards

When the church board is actually the church's governing body, the model is totally applicable. When this is not the case (for example, in Catholic parishes), the variety of arrangements makes a single comment difficult. For example, some local church boards are merely advisory to a larger hierarchy, while others are advisory to the clergy, and some are in charge, but only of non-theological aspects of the church. In these latter cases, the generic model is only partially applicable, for the board does not have total governing authority over the enterprise. In churches in which there is no question about the authority of the board as member representative, granting CEO status to the religious leader in many cases results in a struggle, because many such leaders can conceive of themselves as teachers but not as executives.

WANT MORE?
9

Hospital Boards

Hospital boards have one peculiarity—the "third power" relationship with physicians. Doctors who are granted privileges to practice in a hospital constitute an organized body called the medical staff.

Unlike employed personnel, medical staff do not work for the board, though there may also be salaried physicians who do. The administrative and clinical people operating under the CEO do work for the board and often find themselves caught in the middle between board and medical staff. Occasionally, the medical staff is directly represented on the board. Even so, boards can completely apply the generic model, usually by treating the medical staff organization as a body advisory to the board on the quality of medical practice and practitioners, while still honoring a fully empowered CEO role.

WANT MORE?

10

The multicorporate systems in which hospitals are often involved may have an additional peculiarity. It is common to find a parent-subsidiary structure and roles that are artifacts of government payment schemes, not designs based on optimal health care delivery.

Boards of Associations or Federations of Organizations

In this configuration, otherwise separate organizations have formed another tier of organization, a separate corporation to which the constituent entities yield some of their powers for a common purpose. The peculiarity of the federation form lies in the nature of the ownership, which is ordinarily a membership composed of individual organizations. Like city councils, association boards have great difficulty distinguishing their members' ownership role from their customer role. Improved governance by the association board must be accompanied by greater buy-in from the broader group, because it is important for the membership to exercise control more responsibly—that is, to be responsible owners.

Because such groups often use the association to impose standards on themselves, individual organizations in the membership frequently try to make an end run around the association's mandates, placing the association staff in the middle. This phenomenon is particularly insidious when the person leading the end run is also a board member. Power struggles ensue and can deteriorate into bizarre entanglements. The ownership's reluctance to be governed, even by its own rules, is exposed. Association staffs often see member organizations as more provincial and less concerned with the esoteric issues. Constituent agencies see the association staff as out of control and may even suspect the staff of hoodwinking the asso-

WANT MORE?

11

ciation board. All manner of patchwork, politically motivated structure, and process can grow up around these problems, though none of them resolves the fundamental governance flaws that spawned them. The generic Policy Governance model is totally applicable.

Professional societies and other individual membership organizations follow the same general structure and are susceptible to similar interpersonal stresses. The difference is that instead of each member being an organization, each member is a person. Because such associations usually exist for the benefit of members, they are both customers and owners.

Holding Company and Subsidiary Boards

The arrangement of boards in parent-subsidiary situations is an upside-down version of the federation. In this case, the single central board owns the multiple boards. The holding company structure has long existed in the profit sector but is a relative newcomer to nonprofit organizations. Four peculiar conditions exist: (1) the ownership of subsidiaries usually comprises a single voting member,

WANT MORE?

12

the parent corporation; (2) there is often a direct supervisory link between the staff of the parent and the staff of the subsidiary, dysfunctionally bypassing the subsidiary board; (3) the chain of successive staffs and boards up through the hierarchy can become a channel of repetitive approvals, taking power away from the subsidiary boards; and (4) in some cases, the parent never intends the subsidiary board to govern and only wants it to provide legal window dressing. None of these conditions causes a problem in application of Policy Governance, and conditions 2 and 3 can be considerably improved by the application of better principles. The generic model is applicable, except when condition 4 exists, in which case the model must be adapted.

Civic Club and Homeowners' Association Boards

The peculiarity is the absence of staff, so these comments apply to any board that has no staff or almost no staff. The board members who can be rounded up are the only staff in sight. If the board remembers to wear its governance and workgroup hats separately, the only operational peculiarity lies in the nature of delegation. The board essentially delegates to subgroups of itself or to officers. For the governance portion of the board's job, the model is fully applicable, though not nearly as necessary as in larger organizations.

Advisory Boards

The roles an advisory body assumes depend solely on the person or group seeking advice. Therefore, the role of an advisory body is whatever someone needs and someone else agrees to perform. The Policy Governance model is partially applicable, but mainly for understanding the role of the real board or staff to which the advisory body is attached.

If they are advising the governing board, advisory boards or committees can most influentially advise about ends issues. To influence ends responsibly, a body must do virtually the same things it would do if it were to govern ends. In that sense, advisory groups can use precepts of the model to give counsel within the latitude available to the advisee. In many cases, advisory boards are merely collections of advisers, which means that many voices rather than one unified board voice are heard. In this role, neither group decisions nor formal meetings are necessary.

It is best that an advisory body advise only one advisee or level in the organization. An advisory body should be appointed by the person or group wanting advice, not an authority higher than the advisee. Moreover, an advisory body should not be allowed to develop an institutional inertia that resists dissolution. And if possible, it is best never to call an advisory body an advisory *board* instead of some other word less open to misinterpretation of its role.

Corporate Boards Organized for Profit

Because owners' intent in an equity corporation is likely to be their own monetary return on investment, ends are phrased in terms of monetary shareholder value instead of benefits for third parties. Consequently, even though equity corporations are ordinarily held to a less forgiving test of productivity than nonprofits or government, their ends are far easier to state. The largest problem with corporate board development is failure to see the board as a commander rather than as an adviser. The board comes to be just another department for the CEO to manage, until things go terribly wrong or until interpersonal stress disrupts the arrangement. The model presented in these pages, with only slight alteration, is completely applicable to the governance of business corporations; extensive treatment of Policy Governance in equity corporations is provided in *Corporate Boards That Create Value* (Carver and Oliver, 2002c).

WANT MORE?

13

In that book, Caroline Oliver and I point out that on one hand, equity corporate ends might be simpler than those in nonprofit and governmental organizations, but on the other hand, their ends can be more complicated than merely a statement of monetary return:

> In a company organized for profit, the results component
> of the ends relates ordinarily to the financial value that
> accrues to the company owners; that is, results are what
> is commonly referred to as *shareholder value*. However,

there can be variations. In some small start-up companies, for example, desired results may include working
independently with trusted partners in an exciting
field—plus satisfactory financial return. In some family-
owned companies, the value owners want is the satisfaction of having family members working together in the
same business—plus satisfactory financial return. [p. 63]

Large publicly traded corporations are quite likely not
only to focus on shareholder value alone as the company's ends but to rename this category *Shareholder
Value*. As a result of this straightforward focus, this category is often an extraordinarily brief one. [p. 142]

To the extent that corporate boards represent owners and hold
CEOs accountable, their need for better governance is as great as that
on nonprofit and public boards. Recent codes do improve transparency and trustworthy reporting, but a great gap remains between what
is called *shareholder democracy* and board practice. Monks has
been perhaps the foremost spokesperson about this failing.
Referring to Policy Governance as a competitive advantage
for British Petroleum, Booker (2004) claimed, "Policy Governance
can enhance the ability of corporations to compete in the market. [It]
should deliver ever greater and lasting returns to shareholders . . . BP
provides a case study of such an application. If you consider how our
business has been transformed in the last ten years I think that provides some comfort to any doubters."

WANT MORE?

14

Legislatures, Congresses, and Parliaments

Probably the most important structural difference for these "boards"
is that, as in some city governments, the CEO (governor, president,
prime minister, premier) is not subordinate to the board. In the ab-
sense of a hierarchical relationship out of which separate roles and

authority can be generated, legislative and executive powers are separated in chartering documents.

Still, an examination of legislative behavior, using principles of
board governance, is a tempting exercise. Controversy over micro-
management receives frequent attention, as do legislators' inves-
WANT MORE? tigative excursions into executive areas that are perceived
15 to have political appeal. Budgeting on an annual basis for
gargantuan agencies of government strains credulity, the
more so when compounded by the perennial lateness of the budget
process. The long-term mentality of government is severely hampered by such budget policy.

The inability of legislative groups to deal well with their own
members' individual impingements on the executive process (intervening in grants, influencing procurement) bespeaks an irresponsi-
bility of momentous proportions. In the United States, the Housing
and Urban Development and Keating Five scandals of the late
1980s and early 1990s were instances of congressional interference
that went too far even by Congress's lax standards.

By "coaxing, flattering and occasionally threatening federal agencies to meet constituent needs" at the rate of more than three mil-
lion cases each year (Kiernan, 1989), members of Congress "try to
solve the nation's problems one at a time" (Ralph Nader, cited in
Kiernan, 1989) rather than forcing self-correction in the systems that
produce these anomalies. In politically self-serving displays of power,
individual legislators damage (or, at best, fail to improve) effectiveness in the very systems their legislation created. Members of Congress were offended when a former Housing and Urban Development
administrator suggested that members use oversight power, instead,
to ensure proper administrative operation (Felton, 1989).

Former Senator Howard Baker (1989), speaking of the U.S. Congress as "a kind of national board of directors," said that that body
should represent the people on major policy decisions. Its calling is
"not to manage the federal establishment to the last detail. We have
an executive branch . . . to do that. Congress could do its job better

if it did less of it." Nevertheless, the most august of assemblies, shrouding actions in pomp, can do very silly things. Legislative traditions predate the development of twentieth-century management, so it is no surprise that legislative action often transpires as if principles of modern management had never been developed.

WANT MORE?

Further Reading

1. Oliver, C. (gen. ed.), with Conduff, M., Edsall, S., Gabanna, C., Loucks, R., Paszkiewicz, D., Raso, C., and Stier, L. *The Policy Governance Fieldbook: Practical Lessons, Tips, and Tools from the Experiences of Real-World Boards.* San Francisco: Jossey-Bass, 1999.

Carver, J. "A Theory of Governing the Public's Business." *Public Management* (Great Britain), Mar. 2001n, *3*(1), 53–71. Reprinted in J. Carver, *John Carver on Board Leadership.* San Francisco: Jossey-Bass, 2002.

Carver, J. "Policy Governance Views Citizens as Owners." *Nation's Cities Weekly,* Jan. 29, 1996o, p. 5.

Carver, J. "Governing the Community Organisation." *Community Management* (Australia), Mar. 1999b, *1*(1), 22–23.

Carver, J. "Redesigning Governance in the Cities." *Florida Municipal Record,* 1984c, *58,* 2–4.

Carver, M. "Transforming the Governance of Local Government." *IGNewsletter,* Nov. 2003, *12,* 4–5.

Carver, J. "A City Council Creates Ends Policies." *Board Leadership,* 1997f, no. 33. Reprinted in J. Carver, *John Carver on Board Leadership.* San Francisco: Jossey-Bass, 2002.

Carver, J. "Elected Boards: Meeting Their Special Challenge." *Board Leadership,* 1994b, no. 15. Reprinted in J. Carver, *John Carver on Board Leadership.* San Francisco: Jossey-Bass, 2002.

Carver, J. "Reinventing the Governance in City Government: The Next Frontier for City Councils." *Nation's Cities Weekly*, Jan. 27, 1997n, p. 10.

2. Royer, G. "Proactive About What?" *American School Board Journal*, 1996a, *183*(6), 34–39.

Royer, G. *School Board Leadership 2000: The Things Staff Didn't Tell You at Orientation*. Houston: Brockton, 1996b.

Carver, J. "Toward Coherent Governance." *The School Administrator*, Mar. 2000i, *57*(3), 6–10. Reprinted in J. Carver, *John Carver on Board Leadership*. San Francisco: Jossey-Bass, 2002.

Carver, J. "Remaking Governance: The Creator of 'Policy Governance' Challenges School Boards to Change." *American School Board Journal*, Mar. 2000g, *187*(3), 26–30. Reprinted in J. Carver, *John Carver on Board Leadership*. San Francisco: Jossey-Bass, 2002.

Carver, J. "New Means to an End." *Times Educational Supplement* (Great Britain), July 1, 1994f, p. 6. Reprinted in J. Carver, *John Carver on Board Leadership*. San Francisco: Jossey-Bass, 2002.

Carver, J. "A Public School Board Establishes Ends Policies." Board Leadership, 1997m, no. 32. Reprinted in J. Carver, *John Carver on Board Leadership*. San Francisco: Jossey-Bass, 2002.

Carver, J. "Toward Coherent Governance." *The School Administrator*, Mar. 2000i, *57*(3), 6–10. Reprinted in J. Carver, *John Carver on Board Leadership*. San Francisco: Jossey-Bass, 2002.

3. Carver, J. "If You Want It Done Right, Delegate It!" *Board Leadership*, 1997j, no. 29. Reprinted in J. Carver, *John Carver on Board Leadership*. San Francisco: Jossey-Bass, 2002.

Oliver, C. (gen. ed.), with Conduff, M., Edsall, S., Gabanna, C., Loucks, R., Paszkiewicz, D., Raso, C., and Stier, L. *The Policy Governance Fieldbook: Practical Lessons, Tips, and Tools from the Experiences of Real-World Boards*. San Francisco: Jossey-Bass, 1999.

Oliver, C. "Board Accountability in Highly Constrained Environments." *Board Leadership*, 2005a, no. 80.

4. Carver, J. "The Orphan Topic: Making Sense of the Governors' Dilemma." in *FEnow* (Association of Colleges, London), Spring 2003o, pp. 26–27.

Carver, J. *Reinventing Governance: Enabling a Revolution in Leadership for Community College Boards*. Washington, D.C.: Association of Community College Trustees, 1993o. Videotape.

Gregory, T. W. "How to Implement Policy Governance." *Trustee Quarterly*, 1996a, no. 1, pp. 5–6.

Gregory, T. W. "What Is Policy Governance?" *Trustee Quarterly*, 1996b, no. 1, pp. 3–4.

Carver, J., and Mayhew, M. M. *A New Vision for Board Leadership: Governing the Community College*. Washington, D.C.: Association of Community College Trustees, 1994.

Smith, C. J. "Eight Colleges Implement Policy Governance." *Trustee Quarterly*, 1996, no. 1, pp. 8–10.

5. Carver, J. *Governing Parks and Recreation: Board Strategic Leadership in a New Light*. Alexandria, Va.: National Recreation and Park Association, 1987. Videotape.

Carver, J. "Governing Parks and Recreation." *Parks and Recreation*, 1990c, 8(3), 24–28. Reprinted in J. Carver, *John Carver on Board Leadership*. San Francisco: Jossey-Bass, 2002.

6. Carver, J. "Board Accountability in the Modern Charity." *Solicitors' Journal* (Great Britain), Spring 1995a.

Oliver, C. "Best Practice Governance in Charities." *LawNow* (University of Alberta), Apr.–May 2003a, 27(5), 33–34.

Carver, M. "Governing the Child and Family-Serving Agency: Putting the Board in Charge." *Georgia Academy Journal*, Spring 1998b, 5(4), 8–11.

Carver, M. "Enabling Boards to Be Accountable for the Agency." In "Best Practices/Promising Practices" special section. *Georgia Academy Journal*, 6(2), 1998d, 10.

Carver, J. "A Community Board Struggles with the Cost of Its Results." *Board Leadership*, 1996e, no. 23. Reprinted in J. Carver, *John Carver on Board Leadership*. San Francisco: Jossey-Bass, 2002.

Carver, J. "Girl Scout Council Learns What Kind of Help Counts the Most." *Board Leadership*, 1992g, no. 1. Reprinted in J. Carver, *John Carver on Board Leadership*. San Francisco: Jossey-Bass, 2002.

Oliver, C. (gen. ed.), with Conduff, M., Edsall, S., Gabanna, C., Loucks, R., Paszkiewicz, D., Raso, C., and Stier, L. *The Policy Governance Fieldbook: Practical Lessons, Tips, and Tools from the Experiences of Real-World Boards*. San Francisco: Jossey-Bass, 1999.

7. Oliver, C. (gen. ed.), with Conduff, M., Edsall, S., Gabanna, C., Loucks, R., Paszkiewicz, D., Raso, C., and Stier, L. *The Policy Governance Fieldbook: Practical Lessons, Tips, and Tools from the Experiences of Real-World Boards*. San Francisco: Jossey-Bass, 1999.

Carver, J. "A New Job Design for Board Leadership." *Cooperative Business Journal*, May 2001j, *15*(4), 5, 9.

Carver, J. "A New Game Plan For Co-op Boards." *Cooperative Business Journal*, Apr. 2001i, *15*(3), 4.

Carver, J., and Carver, M. "Meeting the Challenge: Credit Union Survival Calls for Strong Governance and Strong Management." *Credit Union Management*, Apr. 1999d, *22*(4), 20–23.

Carver, J., and Carver, M. "Good to Go." *Credit Union Management*, June 1999c, *22*(6), 47–49.

Carver, J., and Carver, M. "A Finely Tuned Instrument." *Credit Union Management*, July 1999b, *22*(7), 54, 56.

8. Carver, J., and Carver, M. "Governing (Not Managing) the Library." *Indiana Libraries*, 1998, *17*(1), 8–10.

Carver, J. "Toward More Effective Library Boards." *Focus on Indiana Libraries*, 1981c, *35*(7–8), 8–11.

9. Carver, J., and Clemow, T. "Redeeming the Church Board." Unpublished paper, 1990.

Carver, J. "Ends and Means: Nurturing the Relationship Between a Congregation and Its Governing Body." *Practice of Ministry in Canada*, Feb. 1995f, *12*(1), 17–19.

Biery, R. M. "The Problem with Boards." *Christian Management Report*, Feb. 2003, pp. 15–18.

10. Moore, J. *Governance for Health System Trustees*. Ottawa, Canada: CHA Press, 2003.

Carver, J. "A Model for Strategic Leadership." *Hospital Trustee*, 1989a, *13*(4), 10–12.

Carver, J. "A Hospital Board Creates Ends Policies." *Board Leadership*, 1997i, no. 34. Reprinted in J. Carver, *John Carver on Board Leadership*. San Francisco: Jossey-Bass, 2002.

Carver, J. "To Focus on Shaping the Future, Many Hospital Boards Might Require a Radical Overhaul." *Health Management Quarterly*, Apr. 1994m, *16*(1), 7–10. Reprinted in J. Carver, *John Carver on Board Leadership*. San Francisco: Jossey-Bass, 2002.

Oliver, C. (gen. ed.), with Conduff, M., Edsall, S., Gabanna, C., Loucks, R., Paszkiewicz, D., Raso, C., and Stier, L. *The Policy Governance Fieldbook: Practical Lessons, Tips, and Tools from the Experiences of Real-World Boards*. San Francisco: Jossey-Bass, 1999.

11. Carver, J. "Families of Boards I: Federations." *Board Leadership*, 1996h, no. 25. Reprinted in J. Carver, *John Carver on Board Leadership*. San Francisco: Jossey-Bass, 2002.

Carver, J. "Reinventing Governance." *Association Management*, Aug. 1999g, *51*(8), 70–77. Reprinted in J. Carver, *John Carver on Board Leadership*. San Francisco: Jossey-Bass, 2002.

Carver, J. "Are Boards Searching for the Holy Grail?" *Association*, Dec. 1998–Jan. 1999, *16*(1), 27–29. Reprinted in J. Carver, *John Carver on Board Leadership*. San Francisco: Jossey-Bass, 2002.

Carver, J. "The Board of a Trade Association Establishes Its Ends Policies." *Board Leadership*, 1997c, no. 31. Reprinted in J. Carver, *John Carver on Board Leadership*. San Francisco: Jossey-Bass, 2002.

Oliver, C. "Keeping Tabs on the CEO." *Association Magazine*, Oct.–Nov. 2002d, *19*(6), 9–11.

Dalton, A. "What Happens When a Federation Board Adopts Policy Governance?" *Board Leadership*, 2000, no. 47.

Oliver, C. (gen. ed.), with Conduff, M., Edsall, S., Gabanna, C., Loucks, R., Paszkiewicz, D., Raso, C., and Stier, L. *The Policy Governance Fieldbook: Practical Lessons, Tips, and Tools from the Experiences of Real-World Boards*. San Francisco: Jossey-Bass, 1999.

Carver, J. "Lighting Candles or Cursing the Darkness." *Association*, Dec. 1995–Jan. 1996, pp. 14–15.

12. Carver, J. "Families of Boards II: Holding Companies." *Board Leadership*, 1996i, no. 27. Reprinted in J. Carver, *John Carver on Board Leadership*. San Francisco: Jossey-Bass, 2002.

Carver, J. "When Board Members Are the Only Staff in Sight." *Board Leadership*, 1993r, no. 9. Reprinted in J. Carver, *John Carver on Board Leadership*. San Francisco: Jossey-Bass, 2002, pp. 227–230.

13. Booker, J. "Applying Policy Governance Principles in the Business World." Paper presented to the International Policy Governance Association Conference, Indian Lakes, Illinois, June 12, 2004.

Carver, J. "Boards Should Add Value: But Which Value and to Whom?" *Institute of Corporate Directors Newsletter*, Jan. 2003b, no. 106, pp. 1, 2, 14.

Carver, J. "Shareholder Value Is *Not* the Problem: Corporate Misdeeds Cannot Be Blamed on Putting Shareholders First." *Institute of Corporate Directors Newsletter*, Mar. 2003q, no. 107, pp. 1–2.

Carver, J. "The Trap in Greater Board Activism: Investors Need More Governing, Not More Micromanaging." *Institute of Corporate Directors Newsletter*, May 2003s, no. 108, pp. 14–15.

Oliver, C. "What's Really Missing?" *Boardroom*, 2003f, *11*(1), 4, 7.

Carver, J. "Foreword." In P. Wallace and J. Zinkin, *Corporate Governance: Mastering Business in Asia*. Singapore: Wiley, 2005d.

Carver, J. "Corporate Governance Model from an Unexpected Source—Nonprofits." *The Corporate Board*, Mar.–Apr. 1997g, pp. 18–22. Reprinted in J. Carver, *John Carver on Board Leadership*. San Francisco: Jossey-Bass, 2002.

Carver, J., and Oliver, C. *Corporate Boards That Create Value: Governing Company Performance from the Boardroom*. San Francisco: Jossey-Bass, 2002c.

Carver, J., and Oliver, C. "Crafting a Theory of Governance." *Corporate Governance Review*, Oct.–Nov. 2002d, *14*(6), 10–13.

Carver, J. "The Opportunity for Re-Inventing Corporate Governance in Joint Venture Companies." *Corporate Governance—An International Review* (Great Britain), Jan. 2000e, 8(1), 75–80.

Carver, J. "Reinventing Corporate Governance—An Opportunity." *Boardroom*, July 1999f, 7(4), 1, 7.

Carver, J. "Leadership du conseil: 'The Policy Governance Model'" [Board leadership: The Policy Governance model]. *Gouvernance Revue Internationale* (Canada), Spring 2000d, *1*(1), 100–108. Reprinted under the title "A Theory of Corporate Governance: Finding a New Balance for Boards and Their CEOs" in J. Carver, *John Carver on Board Leadership*. San Francisco: Jossey-Bass, 2002.

Carver, J., and Oliver, C. "Financial Oversight Reform—The Missing Link." *Chartered Financial Analyst* (Institute of Chartered Financial Analysts of India), Dec. 2002e, 8(12), 31–33.

14. Monks, R.A.G. "Shareholder Activism: A Reality Check." *The Corporate Board*, 2001, *22*(129), 23–26.

Monks, R.A.G., and Minow, N. *Corporate Governance*. (3rd ed.) Oxford, U.K.: Blackwell, 2004.

15. Carver, J. "Building an Infrastructure of Governance in Eastern Europe." Paper for the governments of Czechoslovakia and Hungary, 1990a. Reprinted in J. Carver, *John Carver on Board Leadership*. San Francisco: Jossey-Bass, 2002.

Carver, J. "Seizing the Governance Opportunity for Central European NGOs." Paper presented at the National Forum of Bulgarian Foundations, Sophia, Bulgaria, Feb. 1992m. Reprinted in J. Carver, *John Carver on Board Leadership*. San Francisco: Jossey-Bass, 2002.

Carver, J. "Recommendations to the West Virginia Legislative Oversight Commission on Education Accountability." Unpublished paper written under contract with the West Virginia legislature, 1991b. Reprinted in J. Carver, *John Carver on Board Leadership*. San Francisco: Jossey-Bass, 2002.

Carver, J. "Partnership for Public Service: Accountability in the Social Service Delivery System." Unpublished paper written for the Ontario Ministry of Community and Social Services, 1992k. Reprinted in J. Carver, *John Carver on Board Leadership*. San Francisco: Jossey-Bass, 2002.

Mogensen, S. "The Big Picture: Policy Governance and Democracy." *Board Leadership*, 2003, no. 70.

Resource B: Bylaws

This book speaks more to the process and focus with which leaders can better lead than to the initial, enabling mechanism. Yet mechanics cannot be entirely ignored, even when one deals predominantly with principles and concepts. For all nonprofit and many public boards, bylaws establish the kind of organ that the board itself is to be. Bylaws, therefore, may help or hinder governance as conceived in these pages.

Bylaws are located in the middle of the hierarchy of documents, which it is helpful to visualize as three links of a chain. The topmost level is the *establishment document*, which, for nonprofit organizations, is articles of incorporation or letters patent and for public agencies is a statute or other governmental order or charter. This

WANT MORE? document creates an artificial person, a corporate entity. **1** The third and lowest level comprises *pronouncements of the governing body*; in Policy Governance, these would consist almost entirely of policies. The middle level is *bylaws*. Bylaws connect this artificial creature of the state to real human beings. These real beings, acting as a board, for practical purposes, become the artificial person called a *corporation*.

I offer the following guidelines concerning characteristics of the bylaws:

Length. Bylaws are best kept lean. Include only items that establish the basic structure and empowerment of the board and its members. Whatever can legitimately be put into policy should be omitted in the bylaws.

Membership. Not-for-profit statutes sometimes call for a "corporate membership" to which the board is accountable. The members are the nonprofit equivalent of stockholders. For many groups, such as chambers of commerce and service clubs, membership is a pragmatically useful concept. For others, such as community health clinics, membership is a confusing legal device. It is not comprehensive enough to be the moral ownership referred to in this text. Yet it is usually larger than the board and thus constitutes a separate body to be dealt with. Some organizations make use of membership in a ceremonial way, conducting annual meetings and board elections as a ritual. For most, however, it is best to nullify the membership in practice by simply constituting the board as the only membership, thus satisfying law and simplicity simultaneously.

Board size. With respect to board size, the simple rule is to justify any number over seven. There is nothing magic about this number, and I do not mean to suggest that it is the right number. However, as boards grow progressively beyond this size, they pay an increasing price in awkwardness, discipline failures, and unfocused energy. Large boards have more than their share of flaws. Such boards are easier to

WANT MORE?

2

manipulate. Members of large groups tend to assume less responsibility as individuals. Large boards have more difficulty setting meeting dates, deliberating about issues, and staying on task. Nason (1989), speaking of foundation boards, found that the feeling of unity, common purpose, involvement, participation, and responsibility for the organization is greater in smaller boards. But he also felt that the range of viewpoints and judiciousness of final consensus are enhanced by larger boards. Taking these opposing factors into account, I would promote as the guiding principle that a board should be no larger than the task of ownership linkage requires.

Quorum. Set the quorum no lower than 51 percent. A surprising number of nonprofit boards establish the quorum at one-third or, on rare occasions, even lower. They usually do so because of attendance problems and bitter experiences in not making the quorum. But a quorum set low is an open admission that attendance does not matter. A board would do better to struggle with expected

WANT MORE?
3

board member behavior than to hide the issue with a low quorum. Indeed, boards should discuss whether an entirely new approach to the quorum should be launched. Why not approach board attendance in the same way as staff's? No CEO would proudly claim that on most workdays, over 51 percent of his or her staff turns up for work.

Attendance. One way to deal with the quorum is to require attendance. Public boards have far fewer problems with attendance than nonprofit boards. In the latter, it is not uncommon to find an attendance requirement, but with two fatal flaws. The first error is recognizing a difference between excused and unexcused absences. In practice, there is no difference, for it is a rare board that can determine whether an excuse is good enough. So *excused* comes to be defined as notification that one will not be present. This fulfills the requirement for courtesy, not for attendance.

The second flaw is that termination of membership is not automatic but dependent on a vote. A motion must be made that Rosemarie or David be kicked off the board. No one wants to do that, so the attendance provision is not enforced. A workable, though slightly softened, provision can be written: "Any member absent from three meetings in succession or four meetings in any twelve-month period is automatically terminated. If such a member requests reinstatement within two months, the board may reinstate the seat, though this provision may not be used for any member more than once per term."

Officers. Keep the number of officers minimal, and describe their jobs in terms of output areas and authority. Unless the board chooses to name its chairperson as CEO, do not describe the chair's job in terms of a CEO role; for example, do not state that the chair has general supervision over the ostensible CEO or organization. It is important to describe the chair's job in a way that is consistent with the chief governance officer function described in this text. It would even be a good step to use *chief governance officer* as the title at the outset. If the organization is large enough to have a staff CEO, avoid having a treasurer unless it is demanded by law or standard setters. If a treasurer is a must, let the CEO also play that role. Consider having the CEO be secretary as well. There is no power in these roles when they are properly construed, so the board loses nothing but ambiguity.

Committees. If the bylaws are under the control of the board, there is no reason that any committee needs to be included. Committees can be dealt with in board policies. If, however, the bylaws are under the control of a membership, the membership can enshrine in bylaws whatever mechanisms it wishes. Of course, the board is the primary mechanism, but the membership may want to define a nominating committee with which it will select board members. I would caution against going as far as credit union institutions in establishing a special committee as a shadow board.

Staff. Bylaws are for the membership and the board, not for staff. All material relating to staff can be omitted.

Legal review. The bylaws constitute a legal document. Legal counsel should review any substantive changes. It is best that legal counsel not write the bylaws but only review the board's product. Lawyers are qualified to opine on the legality and risk exposure of bylaws but are not qualified to determine how the board wishes to be.

WANT MORE?

Further Reading

1. Carver, J. "Shaping up Your Bylaws." *Board Leadership*, 1995k, no. 20. Reprinted in J. Carver, *John Carver on Board Leadership*. San Francisco: Jossey-Bass, 2002.

2. Oliver, C. "Why Size Matters." *Board Leadership*, 2003, no. 67h.

   Carver, J. "Won't a Larger Board Mean There is Greater Diversity in Governance?" *Board Leadership*, 2004j, no. 73.

3. Carver, J. "Why Not Set Your Quorum Requirement at 100 Percent?" *Board Leadership*, 1998s, no. 37. Reprinted in J. Carver, *John Carver on Board Leadership*. San Francisco: Jossey-Bass, 2002.

   Carver, J. "Is Your Board Having Difficulty Reaching a Quorum?" *Board Leadership*, 1994d, no. 11.

Resource C: Glossary

A new paradigm necessarily introduces new concepts, ones that must be represented by words. Whether to use words already in general use or to underscore the switch from old to new with unfamiliar terms is not easily answered. Caroline Oliver and I expressed the issue in our book *Corporate Boards That Create Value* (Carver and Oliver, 2002, p. 123) this way: "To use familiar words for new concepts reduces the alien impression of the new, but risks contaminating the new concept with meanings carried over from the old. To use unfamiliar words for new concepts safeguards the new meaning, but at the expense of more jargon. Jargon, of course, is simply what we call the new terms before they become familiar. . . . This is a glossary, not the argument for these terms and definitions. Those arguments are presented in the text."

The following glossary borrows heavily from *Corporate Boards That Create Value* and from Miriam Carver's 2000 article in *Nonprofit World* entitled "Speaking with One Voice: Words to Use and Not to Use."

ACCOUNTABILITY, RESPONSIBILITY: These terms have various legitimate definitions. In Policy Governance, however, *responsibility* normally refers to a position's direct, hands-on obligation, whereas *accountability* refers to all the direct, hands-on obligations over which the position has purview and authority. That is, accountability is a summation of all the responsibilities of subordinates plus those of oneself. For example, the board is responsible for good policies and accountable for staff being treated with respect.

ANY REASONABLE INTERPRETATION: The authorization to take a superior at his or her word—that is, to follow instructions using whatever interpretation the subordinate chooses, so long as he or she can demonstrate that the interpretation is a reasonable one. The "any reasonable interpretation" rule is indispensable to optimal delegation.

BOARD (ADVISORY): A group with no authority except that granted to it by some authoritative position, such as the governing board or a staff member. (A staff member may grant authority only within his or her range of authorized prerogatives.) Due to the potential for confusion, it is best not to use the word *board* to designate advisory bodies.

BOARD (GOVERNING): A group of peers who have total accountability for an organization, along with total authority over it, normally on behalf of someone else.

BOARD MEANS: The areas of board decision making that are about the governance process itself, including the board's accountability and connection to owners, and the board's link to management. Decisions about board means are found in the Governance Process and Board-Management Delegation policy categories.

BOARD-MANAGEMENT DELEGATION POLICIES: The category of board policy in which the board states the nature and mechanics of the relationship between governance and management. This includes the methods of delegation and of evaluating performance.

CEO (CHIEF EXECUTIVE OFFICER): Usually titled *executive director, president, secretary general, general manager, superintendent,* or a similar designation, this position holds the top level of executive authority beneath the governing authority of the full board, regardless of his or her formal title. The CEO runs the organization with full authority to take action and make decisions about ends and staff means as long as they fulfill a reasonable interpretation of board policies in the Ends and Executive Limitations categories.

CGO (CHIEF GOVERNANCE OFFICER): Usually titled *chair, chairperson,* or *president,* the person who holds this position is "first among equals" on the board, with responsibility for ensuring that the board follows its own rules and those imposed by external authorities. The CGO, at the behest of the board, runs the board (but is not the boss of it), with full authority to take actions and make decisions about the board's means as long as they fulfill a reasonable interpretation of board policies in the Governance Process and Board-Management Delegation categories.

COMMITTEE (BOARD): A group established by the board to help with some aspect of the board's direct responsibilities. The composition of the group can be whatever the board decides is appropriate. It is a board committee by virtue of who creates it rather than its membership (for example, having staff members or other nonboard members on the committee does not prevent it from being a board committee).

COMMITTEE (STAFF): A group established by or under the CEO's authority. There is no effect on governance, nor is the board involved in the formation, charging, or termination of such a committee.

CONSENT AGENDA, AUTOMATIC APPROVAL AGENDA: A part of the board's agenda that includes decisions the board has delegated to the CEO but that an outside authority requires the board to make. This agenda merits an automatic approval unless monitoring data submitted with it reveals that the decisions are not consistent with the applicable board policy. Disapproval or removing an item from the agenda in order to discuss it, though perfectly acceptable in traditional governance, would in Policy Governance constitute inappropriate undelegating of a decision.

CONSTITUENTS: A term often used by elected boards that may indicate conflation of the roles of beneficiary and owner—roles that in Policy Governance must be kept distinct from one another, even if the roles are played by the same persons.

CUSTOMERS, CONSUMERS, BENEFICIARIES, RECIPIENTS: Interchangeable terms for the persons or populations for whom results are to occur. This "targeting" element of the ends concept can also be stated in terms of *students, patients, members,* or whatever word is applicable to the type of organization under consideration. This class can overlap ownership if the organization is one of self-service, such as a municipal government, trade association, or equity corporation. (In equity corporations, shareholders are both owners and the group that is intended to benefit. Therefore, the words *consumer* and *customer* can be misleading inasmuch as they are not ends phenomena in that setting.)

ENDS POLICIES: The category of board policy that sets forth the fundamental reason for an organization's existence in terms of the expected results for specified populations at some stated efficiency, cost, or priority among other results. The ends concept embraces the organization's intended effects on the world—not unintended ones, but those whose fulfillment constitutes one measure of CEO performance.

EXECUTIVE LIMITATIONS POLICIES: The board's proscriptions on the CEO's means that establish boundaries within which executive decision making can operate freely. By defining only what is unacceptable, these policies avoid telling management how to manage, thereby keeping the board from micromanaging or meddling.

GOALS AND OBJECTIVES: Terms that are very useful in management but problematic in governance in that they do not respect the ends-means differentiation and often do not respect the principle that decisions come in graduated sizes.

GOVERNANCE: The job of the governing board. Sometimes used by others—but not in this text—to include the entire top leadership structure, both board and executive. Governance exists to translate informed owners' wishes into organizational performance.

GOVERNANCE PROCESS POLICIES: The category of board policy in which the board deals with most of its own means, including the board's relationship with owners, its own process, its internal workings (committees, officers), and the discipline to which it is committed.

MANAGEMENT (OR STAFF) MEANS: All aspects (decisions and engagements) of management that are not ends. Largely, these include decisions about methods, conduct, ways of doing business, activities, programs, markets, products, and anything other than ends expectations and performance.

MEANS: All non-ends decisions and engagements of board or management. Virtually all decisions made in the organization and by its board are means decisions.

MISSION (OR MISSION STATEMENT): A widespread expression for both boards and management, but a confusing one for governance because in its common usage, it does not distinguish between ends and means. Some Policy Governance boards call their global Ends policy their *mission*—a practice that causes no problem as long as ends discipline is followed in its composition.

MODEL (GOVERNANCE): A conceptually coherent operating system or theory of the board's role, position, practice, and relationships. In Policy Governance, *model* is used where *paradigm* would also fit; it refers to the universal, generic principles and concepts of the board's job, upon which can be built practices and mechanics appropriate to a specific board's circumstances.

OWNERS, OWNERSHIP: The group on whose behalf the board governs. Ownership may be a legal issue (as in equity corporations or as implied in membership associations) or may not. For example, most community groups consider the community at large to be their ownership in a moral though not a legal sense. The board is owner representative, a concept unfamiliar to many nonprofits.

PLANNING: Making decisions about the future today, an important activity that can apply to both ends and means and both governance and management. Hence, while it is a useful word, it does not help in distinguishing the board's job from management's.

POLICY: A value or perspective that underlies action. In Policy Governance, board policies occur in four categories: Ends, Executive Limitations, Governance Process, and Board-Management Delegation. These four categories exhaust all possible board decisions. Each policy tends to be quite brief, and policies are always arranged in descending order of breadth.

POLICY CATEGORY: In Policy Governance, one of four defined topics in which board policies are grouped. The categories (see Policy) are chosen for their congruence with governance principles, not for their utility within management. They are derived by first separating ends and means, then separating the board's means from management means, then dividing the board's means into two parts for ease of use.

POLICY GOVERNANCE: The registered service mark held by John Carver that denotes a way of guiding governing boards toward fulfilling their accountability—specifically, a conceptual model composed of logically derived principles and concepts. In practice, the term refers to the entire conceptual model, which is a universal paradigm of governance. There are not various "policy governance" models but only one Policy Governance model.

POLICY LEVELS: The continuum of policy, starting at the broadest (open to most interpretation) and descending in sequential steps to the narrowest (open to the least interpretation). Board policies always begin at the broadest level and extend into more detailed levels until they reach the point at which the board can accept any reasonable interpretation of its words.

PROCEDURES: In Policy Governance, there is no need to distinguish policy from procedure, only a need to distinguish board documents from management documents. Board expressions in Policy Governance are in policy categories and policy format, even if in some instances they look like procedures. Whatever management chooses to call its documents is a management prerogative (unless limited by the board).

SERVANT-LEADERSHIP: Robert K. Greenleaf's conception that leadership should be informed and motivated by servanthood, as owner representatives and leaders cannot achieve excellence in the absence of the mentality of servant-leadership.

SPEAKING WITH ONE VOICE: Although boards should entertain and even seek as much diversity of opinion as practical, the only authoritative voice is that of the full board's decision. The board can change or abandon its official decision, but individual board members cannot.

STAKEHOLDERS: Anyone with a stake in the organization. This very broad category includes staff, vendors, neighbors, clients, board members, and so forth. The Policy Governance concept of ownership is a subset, not an equivalent of stakeholders.

Although the board has an accountability obligation to owners, it has an ethical obligation to stakeholders.

STRATEGY: Same as *planning*, except the word always has long-term, big-picture implications, which *planning* might not. Because it can apply to both ends and means and both governance and management, the term does not help in distinguishing the board's job from management's.

VALUES, BELIEFS: Positions of the board with regard to relative importance, ethics, obligations, assumptions, comparative merit, or utility. To the extent that these are relevant to governing, the Policy Governance model systematizes their expression according to whether they represent a board's philosophical position or an instruction to management. Separately stating these outside the policy framework indicates that the framework is not being used properly.

VISION OR VISION STATEMENT: See Mission; Values, beliefs.

References

Ackoff, R. *Creating the Corporate Future*. New York: Wiley, 1981.

Albee, E. *Who's Afraid of Virginia Woolf?* New York: Atheneum, 1962.

Argenti, J. *Your Organization: What Is It for? Challenging Traditional Organizational Aims*. London: McGraw-Hill Europe, 1993.

Armstrong, R. "A Study in Paradoxes." *Association*, 1998, *15*(4), 13–14.

Armstrong, R., and Shay, P. "Does the Carver Policy Governance Model Really Work?" *Front and Centre*, May 1998, pp. 13–14.

Baker, H. H., Jr. "Replace Congress with a 'Citizen Legislature.'" *Chicago Tribune*, June 16, 1989, sec. 1, p. 27.

Barth, N. "Clear Policy Statements Can Free You to Act Creatively." *Board Leadership*, 1992, no. 1, p. 8.

Biery, R. M. "The Problem with Boards." *Christian Management Report*, Feb. 2003, pp. 15–18.

Biery, R. M., and Kelly, H. M. "Industry Canada's Unjustified Criticism of Carver Policy Governance." *CCCC Bulletin*, 2003, no. 2, pp. 3–5.

Blumenthal, L. "Nonprofits Awakening to Need for Effective Boards." *Nonprofit Times*, 1988, *2*, 5–20.

Booker, J. "Applying Policy Governance Principles in the Business World." Paper presented to the International Policy Governance Association Conference, Indian Lakes, Illinois, June 12, 2004.

Brudney, J. L., and Murray, V. "The Nature and Impact of Changes in Boards of Directors of Canadian Not-for-Profit Organizations." Unpublished paper, 1996.

Buzan, T., and Buzan, B. *The Mind Map Book: How to Use Radiant Thinking to Maximize Your Brain's Untapped Potential*. New York: NAL/Dutton, 1994.

Cadbury, A. *The Company Chairman*. Hemel Hempstead, Hertsfordshire, U.K.: Director Books, 1995.

Cadbury, A. "The Corporate Governance Agenda." *Corporate Governance: An International Review*, 2000, 8(1), 10.

Cadbury, A. *Corporate Governance and Chairmanship: A Personal View*. Oxford: Oxford University Press, 2002a.

Cadbury, A. "Foreword." In J. Carver and C. Oliver, *Corporate Boards That Create Value: Governing Company Performance from the Boardroom*. San Francisco: Jossey-Bass, 2002b.

Cadbury, A. "Foreword." In J. Carver, *John Carver on Board Leadership: Selected Writings from the Creator of the World's Most Provocative and Systematic Governance Model*. San Francisco: Jossey-Bass, 2002c.

Carver, J. "The Director's Employment Contract as a Tool for Improved Governance." *Journal of Mental Health Administration*, 1979a, 6, 14–25.

Carver, J. "Profitability: Useful Fiction for Nonprofit Enterprise." *Administration in Mental Health*, 1979b, 7(1), 3–20.

Carver, J. *Business Leadership on Nonprofit Boards*. Board Monograph Series, no. 12. Washington, D.C.: National Association of Corporate Directors, 1980a.

Carver, J. "Toward a Technology of Governance." Unpublished paper, 1980b.

Carver, J. "Is America Ready for Self-Governance? The Third Sector." In D. Nachmias and A. Greer (eds.), *The Crisis of Authority: Citizen Boards and the Governance of Public and Private Agencies*. Milwaukee: Urban Research Center, University of Wisconsin, 1981a.

Carver, J. "The Market Surrogate Obligation of Public Sector Boards." *Journal of Mental Health Administration*, 1981b, 8, 42–45.

Carver, J. "Toward More Effective Library Boards." *Focus on Indiana Libraries*, 1981c, 35(7–8), 8–11.

Carver, J. "Leadership Through Boards, Councils, and Commissions: Creating the Future Through Better Governance." Paper presented at the annual meeting of the National Association of Community Leadership Organizations, Cleveland, Ohio, Sept. 19, 1983.

Carver, J. "Consulting with Boards of Human Service Agencies: Leverage for Organizational Effectiveness." *Consultation*, 1984a, 3(3), 27–39.

Carver, J. "Professional Challenges for an Emerging Community: The Challenge to Nonprofit Governance." Paper presented at the annual meeting of the Nonprofit Management Association, San Francisco, June 6–10, 1984b.

Carver, J. "Redesigning Governance in the Cities." *Florida Municipal Record*, 1984c, 58, 2–4.

Carver, J. *Strategic Leadership: New Principles for Boards, Councils, and Commissions.* San Francisco: Public Management Institute, 1985a. Audiotape.

Carver, J. *A Tested, Fresh Approach to Designing the Board's Job.* Milwaukee, Wis.: Family Service America, 1985b. Audiotape.

Carver, J. "Women on Governing Boards." Unpublished paper, 1985c.

Carver, J. "Boards as Cost Centers." Unpublished paper, 1986a.

Carver, J. *Eighteen Principles for Effective Leadership by the Board of Directors: An Introduction to the Technology of Governance for Nonprofit Organizations.* Monograph in an untitled series. Berkeley, Calif.: Center for Community Futures, 1986b.

Carver, J. *Nonprofit and Governmental Boards: New Design for Leadership.* Atlanta: Georgia Power Company, 1986c. Videotape.

Carver, J. *Governing Parks and Recreation: Board Strategic Leadership in a New Light.* Alexandria, Va.: National Recreation and Park Association, 1987. Videotape.

Carver, J. "Re-Inventing the Governing Board." *Access,* 1988a, *1*(1), 4–8.

Carver, J. "Vision, Values, and the Trivia Trap." *Florida Focus,* 1988b, *1*(2), 1–5.

Carver, J. "A Model for Strategic Leadership." *Hospital Trustee,* 1989a, *13*(4), 10–12.

Carver, J. "Re-Inventing the Board: Strategic Leadership for Public and Nonprofit Governance." Nationally broadcast video teleconference presentation. Athens: University of Georgia, 1989b.

Carver, J. "Building an Infrastructure of Governance in Eastern Europe." Paper for the governments of Czechoslovakia and Hungary, 1990a. Reprinted in J. Carver, *John Carver on Board Leadership.* San Francisco: Jossey-Bass, 2002.

Carver, J. "Economic Development and Inter-Board Leadership." *Economic Development Review,* 1990b, *8*(3), 24–28.

Carver, J. "Governing Parks and Recreation." *Parks and Recreation,* 1990c, *8*(3), 24–28. Reprinted in J. Carver, *John Carver on Board Leadership.* San Francisco: Jossey-Bass, 2002.

Carver, J. "The CEO and the Renegade Board Member." *Nonprofit World,* 1991a, *9*(6), 14–17.

Carver, J. "Recommendations to the West Virginia Legislative Oversight Commission on Education Accountability." Unpublished paper written for the West Virginia legislature, 1991b. Reprinted in J. Carver, *John Carver on Board Leadership.* San Francisco: Jossey-Bass, 2002.

Carver, J. "Redefining the Board's Role in Fiscal Planning." *Nonprofit Management and Leadership,* 1991c, *2*(2), 177–192. Reprinted in J. Carver, *John Carver on Board Leadership.* San Francisco: Jossey-Bass, 2002.

Carver, J. "Creating a Single Voice: The Prerequisite to Board Leadership." *Board Leadership*, 1992a, no. 2, pp. 1–5. Reprinted in J. Carver, *John Carver on Board Leadership*. San Francisco: Jossey-Bass, 2002.

Carver, J. *Empowering Boards for Leadership: Redefining Excellence in Governance.* San Francisco: Jossey-Bass, 1992b. Audiotape.

Carver, J. "A Few Tips for the Chairperson." *Board Leadership*, 1992c, no. 3, p. 6. Reprinted in J. Carver, *John Carver on Board Leadership*. San Francisco: Jossey-Bass, 2002.

Carver, J. "The Founding Parent Syndrome: Governing in the CEO's Shadow." *Nonprofit World*, 1992e, *10*(5), 14–16.

Carver, J. "Free Your Board and Staff Through Executive Limitations." *Board Leadership*, 1992f, no. 4. Reprinted in J. Carver, *John Carver on Board Leadership*. San Francisco: Jossey-Bass, 2002.

Carver, J. "Girl Scout Council Learns What Kind of Help Counts the Most." *Board Leadership*, 1992g, no. 1. Reprinted in J. Carver, *John Carver on Board Leadership*. San Francisco: Jossey-Bass, 2002.

Carver, J. "The Importance of Trust in the Board-CEO Relationship." *Board Leadership*, 1992h, no. 3. Reprinted in J. Carver, *John Carver on Board Leadership*. San Francisco: Jossey-Bass, 2002.

Carver, J. "Is Your Board in a Rut? Shake Up Your Routine." *Board Leadership*, 1992i, no. 4. Reprinted in J. Carver, *John Carver on Board Leadership*. San Francisco: Jossey-Bass, 2002.

Carver, J. "Just How Long Should Board Meetings Be?" *Board Leadership*, 1992j, no. 1, p. 6.

Carver, J. "Partnership for Public Service: Accountability in the Social Service Delivery System." Unpublished paper written for the Ontario Ministry of Community and Social Services, 1992k. Reprinted in J. Carver, *John Carver on Board Leadership*. San Francisco: Jossey-Bass, 2002.

Carver, J. "Seizing the Governance Opportunity for Central European NGOs." Paper presented at the National Forum of Bulgarian Foundations, Sophia, Bulgaria, Feb. 1992m. Reprinted in J. Carver, *John Carver on Board Leadership*. San Francisco: Jossey-Bass, 2002.

Carver, J. "When Board Members Act as Staff Advisors." *Board Leadership*, 1992o, no. 9. Reprinted in J. Carver, *John Carver on Board Leadership*. San Francisco: Jossey-Bass, 2002.

Carver, J. "When Owners Are Customers: The Confusion of Dual Board Hats." *Nonprofit World*, 1992p, *10*(4), 11–15. Reprinted in J. Carver, *John Carver on Board Leadership*. San Francisco: Jossey-Bass, 2002.

Carver, J. "Achieving Meaningful Diversity in the Boardroom." *Board Leadership*, 1993a, no. 8. Reprinted in *Board Leadership*, 1999, no. 43, and in J. Carver, *John Carver on Board Leadership*. San Francisco: Jossey-Bass, 2002.

Carver, J. "Crafting Policy to Guide Your Organization's Budget." *Board Leadership*, 1993b, no. 6. Reprinted in J. Carver, *John Carver on Board Leadership*. San Francisco: Jossey-Bass, 2002.

Carver, J. "Crafting Policy to Safeguard Your Organization's Actual Fiscal Condition." *Board Leadership*, 1993c, no. 6. Reprinted in J. Carver, *John Carver on Board Leadership*. San Francisco: Jossey-Bass, 2002.

Carver, J. "Crafting the Board Job Description." *Board Leadership*, 1993d, no. 10. Reprinted in J. Carver, *John Carver on Board Leadership*. San Francisco: Jossey-Bass, 2002.

Carver, J. "Evaluating the Mission Statement." *Board Leadership*, 1993e, no. 5. Reprinted in J. Carver, *John Carver on Board Leadership*. San Francisco: Jossey-Bass, 2002.

Carver, J. "Fiduciary Responsibility." *Board Leadership*, 1993f, no. 6. Reprinted in J. Carver, *John Carver on Board Leadership*. San Francisco: Jossey-Bass, 2002.

Carver, J. "Giving, Getting, and Governing: Finding a Place for Fundraising Among the Responsibilities of Leadership." *Board Leadership*, 1993g, no. 7. Reprinted in J. Carver, *John Carver on Board Leadership*. San Francisco: Jossey-Bass, 2002.

Carver, J. "Handling Complaints: Using Negative Feedback to Strengthen Board Policy." *Board Leadership*, 1993h, no. 8.

Carver, J. "Living Up to Your Own Expectations: Implementing Self-Evaluation to Make a Difference in Your Organization." *Board Leadership*, 1993i, no. 10. Reprinted in J. Carver, *John Carver on Board Leadership*. San Francisco: Jossey-Bass, 2002.

Carver, J. "Making Informed Fiscal Policy." *Board Leadership*, 1993j, no. 6. Reprinted in J. Carver, *John Carver on Board Leadership*. San Francisco: Jossey-Bass, 2002.

Carver, J. "Owning Your Agenda: A Long-Term View Is the Key to Taking Charge." *Board Leadership*, 1993k, no. 7. Reprinted in J. Carver, *John Carver on Board Leadership*. San Francisco: Jossey-Bass, 2002.

Carver, J. "Planning the Board's Conduct." *Board Leadership*, 1993m, no. 10. Reprinted in J. Carver, *John Carver on Board Leadership*. San Francisco: Jossey-Bass, 2002.

Carver, J. "Redefining Board Self-Evaluation: The Key to Keeping on Track." *Board Leadership*, 1993n, no. 10. Reprinted in J. Carver, *John Carver on Board Leadership*. San Francisco: Jossey-Bass, 2002.

Carver, J. *Reinventing Governance: Enabling a Revolution in Leadership for Community College Boards*. Washington, D.C.: Association of Community College Trustees, 1993o. Videotape.

Carver, J. "Running Afoul of Governance." *Board Leadership*, 1993p, no. 7. Reprinted in J. Carver, *John Carver on Board Leadership*. San Francisco: Jossey-Bass, 2002.

Carver, J. "A Simple Matter of Comparison: Monitoring Fiscal Management in Your Organization." *Board Leadership*, 1993q, no. 6. Reprinted in J. Carver, *John Carver on Board Leadership*. San Francisco: Jossey-Bass, 2002.

Carver, J. "When Board Members Are the Only Staff in Sight." *Board Leadership*, 1993r, no. 9, pp. 6–7. Reprinted in J. Carver, *John Carver on Board Leadership*. San Francisco: Jossey-Bass, 2002.

Carver, J. "Abstracting Up: Discovering the Big Issues Among the Trivia." *Board Leadership*, 1994a, no. 15. Reprinted in J. Carver, *John Carver on Board Leadership*. San Francisco: Jossey-Bass, 2002.

Carver, J. "Elected Boards: Meeting Their Special Challenge." *Board Leadership*, 1994b, no. 15. Reprinted in J. Carver, *John Carver on Board Leadership*. San Francisco: Jossey-Bass, 2002.

Carver, J. "The Executive Committee: Turning a Governance Liability into an Asset." *Board Leadership*, 1994c, no. 14. Reprinted in J. Carver, *John Carver on Board Leadership*. San Francisco: Jossey-Bass, 2002.

Carver, J. "Is Your Board Having Difficulty Reaching a Quorum?" *Board Leadership*, 1994d, no. 11.

Carver, J. "Making Hierarchy Work: Exercising Appropriate Board Authority in the Service of Mission." *Board Leadership*, 1994e, no. 12. Reprinted in J. Carver, *John Carver on Board Leadership*. San Francisco: Jossey-Bass, 2002.

Carver, J. "New Means to an End." *Times Educational Supplement* (Great Britain), July 1, 1994f, p. 6. Reprinted in J. Carver, *John Carver on Board Leadership*. San Francisco: Jossey-Bass, 2002.

Carver, J. "One Board Fails to Follow Its Own Monitoring Policy and Courts Fiscal Disaster." *Board Leadership*, 1994g, no. 14. Reprinted in J. Carver, *John Carver on Board Leadership*. San Francisco: Jossey-Bass, 2002.

Carver, J. "One Board Learns How Polling Moves Meetings Along." *Board Leadership*, 1994h, no. 13.

Carver, J. "Protecting Board Integrity from the Renegade Board Member." *Board Leadership*, 1994i, no. 13. Reprinted in J. Carver, *John Carver on Board Leadership*. San Francisco: Jossey-Bass, 2002.

Carver, J. "Protecting Governance from Law, Funders, and Accreditors." *Board Leadership*, 1994j, no. 11, pp. 1–5. Reprinted in J. Carver, *John Carver on Board Leadership*. San Francisco: Jossey-Bass, 2002.

Carver, J. "Tips for Creating Advisory Boards and Committees." *Board Leadership*, 1994k, no. 11. Reprinted in J. Carver, *John Carver on Board Leadership*. San Francisco: Jossey-Bass, 2002.

Carver, J. "To Focus on Shaping the Future, Many Hospital Boards Might Require a Radical Overhaul." *Health Management Quarterly*, Apr. 1994m, *16*(1), 7–10. Reprinted in J. Carver, *John Carver on Board Leadership*. San Francisco: Jossey-Bass, 2002.

Carver, J. "Board Accountability in the Modern Charity." *Solicitors' Journal* (Great Britain), Spring 1995a.

Carver, J. "Boards Lead Best When Services, Programs, and Curricula Are Transparent." *Board Leadership*, 1995b, no. 19. Reprinted in J. Carver, *John Carver on Board Leadership*. San Francisco: Jossey-Bass, 2002.

Carver, J. "The CEO's Objectives Are Not Proper Board Business." *Board Leadership*, 1995c, no. 20. Reprinted in J. Carver, *John Carver on Board Leadership*. San Francisco: Jossey-Bass, 2002.

Carver, J. "Connecting with the Ownership." *Board Leadership*, 1995d, no. 18. Reprinted in J. Carver, *John Carver on Board Leadership*. San Francisco: Jossey-Bass, 2002.

Carver, J. "Determining Who Your Owners Are." *Board Leadership*, 1995e, no. 18. Reprinted in J. Carver, *John Carver on Board Leadership*. San Francisco: Jossey-Bass, 2002.

Carver, J. "Ends and Means: Nurturing the Relationship Between a Congregation and Its Governing Body." *Practice of Ministry in Canada*, Feb. 1995f, *12*(1), 17–19.

Carver, J. "Governing in the Shadow of a Founder-CEO." *Board Leadership*, 1995g, no. 22. Reprinted in J. Carver, *John Carver on Board Leadership*. San Francisco: Jossey-Bass, 2002.

Carver, J. "Ownership." *Board Leadership*, 1995h, no. 18. Reprinted in J. Carver, *John Carver on Board Leadership*. San Francisco: Jossey-Bass, 2002.

Carver, J. "Policies 'R' Us." *Board Leadership*, 1995i, no. 20. Reprinted in J. Carver, *John Carver on Board Leadership*. San Francisco: Jossey-Bass, 2002.

Carver, J. "Policy Governance Is Not a 'Hands Off' Model." *Board Leadership*, 1995j, no. 19. Reprinted in J. Carver, *John Carver on Board Leadership*. San Francisco: Jossey-Bass, 2002.

Carver, J. "Shaping up Your Bylaws." *Board Leadership*, 1995k, no. 20. Reprinted in J. Carver, *John Carver on Board Leadership*. San Francisco: Jossey-Bass, 2002.

Carver, J. "A Team of Equals." *Board Leadership*, 1995m, no. 19. Reprinted in J. Carver, *John Carver on Board Leadership*. San Francisco: Jossey-Bass, 2002.

Carver, J. "Understanding the Special Board-Ownership Relationship." *Board Leadership*, 1995n, no. 18. Reprinted in J. Carver, *John Carver on Board Leadership*. San Francisco: Jossey-Bass, 2002.

Carver, J. "What Happens to Conventional Documents Under Policy Governance?" *Board Leadership*, 1995o, no. 21. Reprinted in J. Carver, *John Carver on Board Leadership*. San Francisco: Jossey-Bass, 2002.

Carver, J. "Who Is in Charge? Is Your Organization Too Staff-Driven? Too Volunteer-Driven?" *Board Leadership*, 1995p, no. 22. Reprinted in J. Carver, *John Carver on Board Leadership*. San Francisco: Jossey-Bass, 2002.

Carver, J. "Lighting Candles or Cursing the Darkness." *Association*, Dec. 1995–Jan. 1996, pp. 14–15.

Carver, J. "The 'Any Reasonable Interpretation' Rule: Leap of Faith or Sine Qua Non of Delegation?" *Board Leadership*, 1996a, no. 28. Reprinted in J. Carver, *John Carver on Board Leadership*. San Francisco: Jossey-Bass, 2002.

Carver, J. "Board Approval and Monitoring Are Very Different Actions." *Board Leadership*, 1996b, no. 24. Reprinted in J. Carver, *John Carver on Board Leadership*. San Francisco: Jossey-Bass, 2002.

Carver, J. "Boards Should Not Be the Final Authority but the Initial Authority." *Board Leadership*, 1996c, no. 23. Reprinted in J. Carver, *John Carver on Board Leadership*. San Francisco: Jossey-Bass, 2002.

Carver, J. *The Chairperson's Role as Servant-Leader to the Board*. The CarverGuide Series on Effective Board Governance, no. 3. San Francisco: Jossey-Bass, 1996d.

Carver, J. "A Community Board Struggles with the Cost of Its Results." *Board Leadership*, 1996e, no. 23. Reprinted in J. Carver, *John Carver on Board Leadership*. San Francisco: Jossey-Bass, 2002.

Carver, J. *Creating a Mission That Makes a Difference*. The CarverGuide Series on Effective Board Governance, no. 6. San Francisco: Jossey-Bass, 1996f.

Carver, J. "Do You Really Have a CEO?" *Board Leadership*, 1996g, no. 26. Reprinted in J. Carver, *John Carver on Board Leadership*. San Francisco: Jossey-Bass, 2002.

Carver, J. "Families of Boards I: Federations." *Board Leadership*, 1996h, no. 25. Reprinted in J. Carver, *John Carver on Board Leadership*. San Francisco: Jossey-Bass, 2002.

Carver, J. "Families of Boards II: Holding Companies." *Board Leadership*, 1996i, no. 27. Reprinted in J. Carver, *John Carver on Board Leadership*. San Francisco: Jossey-Bass, 2002.

Carver, J. "Getting It Right from the Start: The CEO's Job Description." *Board Leadership*, 1996j, no. 26. Reprinted in J. Carver, *John Carver on Board Leadership*. San Francisco: Jossey-Bass, 2002.

Carver, J. "How You Can Tell When Your Board Is *Not* Using Policy Governance." *Board Leadership*, 1996k, no. 25. Reprinted in J. Carver, *John Carver on Board Leadership*. San Francisco: Jossey-Bass, 2002.

Carver, J. "Off Limits: What Not to Do in Your CEO Evaluations." *Board Leadership*, 1996m, no. 26. Reprinted in J. Carver, *John Carver on Board Leadership*. San Francisco: Jossey-Bass, 2002.

Carver, J. *Planning Better Board Meetings*. The CarverGuide Series on Effective Board Governance, no. 5. San Francisco: Jossey-Bass, 1996n.

Carver, J. "Policy Governance Views Citizens as Owners." *Nation's Cities Weekly*, Jan. 29, 1996o, p. 5.

Carver, J. "Putting CEO Evaluation in Perspective." *Board Leadership*, 1996p, no. 26. Reprinted in J. Carver, *John Carver on Board Leadership*. San Francisco: Jossey-Bass, 2002.

Carver, J. "Recruiting Leaders: What to Look for in New Board Members." *Board Leadership*, 1996q, no. 23. Reprinted in J. Carver, *John Carver on Board Leadership*. San Francisco: Jossey-Bass, 2002.

Carver, J. "Should Your CEO Be a Board Member?" *Board Leadership*, 1996r, no. 26. Reprinted in J. Carver, *John Carver on Board Leadership*. San Francisco: Jossey-Bass, 2002.

Carver, J. "Sometimes You Have to Fire Your Chair." *Board Leadership*, 1996s, no. 28. Reprinted in J. Carver, *John Carver on Board Leadership*. San Francisco: Jossey-Bass, 2002.

Carver, J. *Three Steps to Fiduciary Responsibility*. The CarverGuide Series on Effective Board Governance, no. 3. San Francisco: Jossey-Bass, 1996t.

Carver, J. "When Bad Governance Is Required." *Board Leadership*, 1996u, no. 24.

Carver, J. "All Volunteers Can Be Good Board Members—Not!" *Board Leadership*, 1997a, no. 32.

Carver, J. *Board Members as Fundraisers, Advisors, and Lobbyists*. The CarverGuide Series on Effective Board Governance, no. 11. San Francisco: Jossey-Bass, 1997b.

Carver, J. "The Board of a Trade Association Establishes Its Ends Policies." *Board Leadership*, 1997c, no. 31. Reprinted in J. Carver, *John Carver on Board Leadership*. San Francisco: Jossey-Bass, 2002.

Carver, J. "Boards Should Have Their Own Voice." *Board Leadership*, 1997d, no. 33. Reprinted in J. Carver, *John Carver on Board Leadership*. San Francisco: Jossey-Bass, 2002.

Carver, J. "CEOs! Guiding Your Board Toward Better Governance." *Board Leadership*, 1997e, no. 29. Reprinted in J. Carver, *John Carver on Board Leadership*. San Francisco: Jossey-Bass, 2002.

Carver, J. "A City Council Creates Ends Policies." *Board Leadership*, 1997f, no. 33. Reprinted in J. Carver, *John Carver on Board Leadership*. San Francisco: Jossey-Bass, 2002.

Carver, J. "Corporate Governance Model from an Unexpected Source—Nonprofits." *The Corporate Board*, Mar.–Apr. 1997g, pp. 18–22. Reprinted in J. Carver, *John Carver on Board Leadership*. San Francisco: Jossey-Bass, 2002.

Carver, J. "Giving Measurement Its Due in Policy Governance." *Board Leadership*, 1997h, no. 30. Reprinted in J. Carver, *John Carver on Board Leadership*. San Francisco: Jossey-Bass, 2002.

Carver, J. "A Hospital Board Creates Ends Policies." *Board Leadership*, 1997i, no. 34. Reprinted in J. Carver, *John Carver on Board Leadership*. San Francisco: Jossey-Bass, 2002.

Carver, J. "If You Want It Done Right, Delegate It!" *Board Leadership*, 1997j, no. 29. Reprinted in J. Carver, *John Carver on Board Leadership*. San Francisco: Jossey-Bass, 2002.

Carver, J. "Is Policy Governance an All-or-Nothing Choice?" *Board Leadership*, 1997k, no. 34.

Carver, J. "A Public School Board Establishes Ends Policies." *Board Leadership*, 1997m, no. 32. Reprinted in J. Carver, *John Carver on Board Leadership*. San Francisco: Jossey-Bass, 2002.

Carver, J. "Reinventing the Governance in City Government: The Next Frontier for City Councils." *Nation's Cities Weekly*, Jan. 27, 1997n, p. 10.

Carver, J. "What If the Committee Chair Just Wants to Know?" *Board Leadership*, 1997o, no. 29. Reprinted in J. Carver, *John Carver on Board Leadership*. San Francisco: Jossey-Bass, 2002.

Carver, J. "What to Do When All Your Policies Are in Place." *Board Leadership*, 1997p, no. 32. Reprinted in J. Carver, *John Carver on Board Leadership*. San Francisco: Jossey-Bass, 2002.

Carver, J. "What to Do When Staff Take Complaints Directly to Board Members." *Board Leadership*, 1997q, no. 31. Reprinted in J. Carver, *John Carver on Board Leadership*. San Francisco: Jossey-Bass, 2002.

Carver, J. "What to Do with Your Board's Philosophy, Values, and Beliefs." *Board Leadership*, 1997r, no. 34. Reprinted in J. Carver, *John Carver on Board Leadership*. San Francisco: Jossey-Bass, 2002.

Carver, J. "When the Founding Parent Stays on the Board." *Board Leadership*, 1997s, no. 31. Reprinted in J. Carver, *John Carver on Board Leadership*. San Francisco: Jossey-Bass, 2002.

Carver, J. "Your Board's Market Surrogate Obligation." *Board Leadership*, 1997t, no. 30. Reprinted in J. Carver, *John Carver on Board Leadership*. San Francisco: Jossey-Bass, 2002.

Carver, J. "Beware the Quality Fetish." *Board Leadership*, 1998a, no. 37. Reprinted in J. Carver, *John Carver on Board Leadership*. San Francisco: Jossey-Bass, 2002.

Carver, J. "Board Committees: Essential and Non-Essential." *Contributions*, July–Aug. 1998b, *12*(4), 20, 35.

Carver, J. "A Board Learns That Proper Policy Categories Aren't Just a Nicety." *Board Leadership*, 1998c, no. 36.

Carver, J. "Bullies on the Board." *Board Leadership*, 1998d, no. 36.

Carver, J. "The Consent Agenda and Responsible Rubber Stamping." *Board Leadership*, 1998e, no. 38. Reprinted in J. Carver, *John Carver on Board Leadership*. San Francisco: Jossey-Bass, 2002.

Carver, J. "Does Your Board Drive Away Its Most Promising Members?" *Board Leadership*, 1998f, no. 35. Reprinted in J. Carver, *John Carver on Board Leadership*. San Francisco: Jossey-Bass, 2002.

Carver, J. "Give, Get, or Get Off?" *Contributions*, Sept.–Oct. 1998g, *12*(5), 8–12.

Carver, J. "Group Responsibility—Requisite for Good Governance." *Board Leadership*, 1998h, no. 38.

Carver, J. "If Your Board Isn't Worth the Cost of Competence, It Isn't Worth Much." *Board Leadership*, 1998i, no. 35.

Carver, J. "Is Policy Governance the One Best Way?" *Board Leadership*, 1998j, no. 37. Reprinted in J. Carver, *John Carver on Board Leadership*. San Francisco: Jossey-Bass, 2002.

Carver, J. "Leading, Following, and the Wisdom to Know the Difference." *Board Leadership*, 1998k, no. 36. Reprinted in J. Carver, *John Carver on Board Leadership*. San Francisco: Jossey-Bass, 2002.

Carver, J. "The Mechanics of Direct Inspection Monitoring." *Board Leadership*, 1998m, no. 39. Reprinted in J. Carver, *John Carver on Board Leadership*. San Francisco: Jossey-Bass, 2002.

Carver, J. "Policy Governance Won't Work Because . . . " *Board Leadership*, 1998n, no. 36. Reprinted in J. Carver, *John Carver on Board Leadership*. San Francisco: Jossey-Bass, 2002.

Carver, J. "Reining in a Runaway Chair." *Board Leadership*, 1998o, no. 38. Reprinted in J. Carver, *John Carver on Board Leadership*. San Francisco: Jossey-Bass, 2002.

Carver, J. "The Secret to Productive Board Meetings." *Contributions*, Mar.–Apr. 1998p, *12*(2), 20, 22.

Carver, J. "Watch Out for Misleading Interpretations of Governance Research." *Board Leadership*, 1998q, no. 40. Reprinted in J. Carver, *John Carver on Board Leadership*. San Francisco: Jossey-Bass, 2002.

Carver, J. "Why Is Conceptual Wholeness So Difficult for Boards?" *Board Leadership*, 1998r, no. 39. Reprinted in J. Carver, *John Carver on Board Leadership*. San Francisco: Jossey-Bass, 2002.

Carver, J. "Why Not Set Your Quorum Requirement at 100 Percent?" *Board Leadership*, 1998s, no. 37. Reprinted in J. Carver, *John Carver on Board Leadership*. San Francisco: Jossey-Bass, 2002.

Carver, J. "Are Boards Searching for the Holy Grail?" *Association*, Dec. 1998–Jan. 1999, *16*(1), 27–29. Reprinted in J. Carver, *John Carver on Board Leadership*. San Francisco: Jossey-Bass, 2002.

Carver, J. "Can a Board Establish Ends Policies Without Identifying Its Owners First?" *Board Leadership*, 1999a, no. 41.

Carver, J. "Governing the Community Organisation." *Community Management* (Australia), Mar. 1999b, *1*(1), 22–23.

Carver, J. "Living Up to Your Own Expectations." *Board Leadership*, 1999c, no. 42.

Carver, J. "Nine Steps to Implementing Policy Governance." *Board Leadership*, 1999d, no. 41. Reprinted in J. Carver, *John Carver on Board Leadership*. San Francisco: Jossey-Bass, 2002.

Carver, J. "Performance Reviews for Board Members." *Contributions*, Jan.–Feb. 1999e, *13*(1), 16, 19.

Carver, J. "Reinventing Corporate Governance—An Opportunity." *Boardroom*, July 1999f, *7*(4), 1, 7.

Carver, J. "Reinventing Governance." *Association Management*, Aug. 1999g, *51*(8), 70–77. Reprinted in J. Carver, *John Carver on Board Leadership*. San Francisco: Jossey-Bass, 2002.

Carver, J. *The Unique Double Servant-Leadership Role of the Board Chairperson*. Voices of Servant-Leadership Series, no. 2. Indianapolis, Ind.: Greenleaf Center for Servant-Leadership, Feb. 1999h.

Carver, J. "What Can Boards Do to Ensure That They Are Providing Full Representation of an Organization's Ownership?" *Board Leadership*, 1999i, no. 43.

Carver, J. "Who Sets the Board Agenda?" *Board Leadership*, 1999j, no. 41.

Carver, J. "Why Only the CEO Can Interpret the Board's Ends and Executive Limitations Policies." *Board Leadership*, 1999k, no. 46. Reprinted in J. Carver, *John Carver on Board Leadership*. San Francisco: Jossey-Bass, 2002.

Carver, J. "Does Your Board Need Its Own Dedicated Support Staff?" *Nonprofit World*, Mar.–Apr. 2000a, *18*(2), 6–7.

Carver, J. "Good Governance Is Not About Control—It's About Remote Control." *Board Leadership*, 2000b, no. 49.

Carver, J. "It's Not the Board's Role to Act as Management Consultant to the CEO." *Board Leadership*, 2000c, no. 49.

Carver, J. "Leadership du conseil: 'The Policy Governance Model'" [Board leadership: The Policy Governance model]. *Gouvernance Revue Internationale* (Canada), Spring 2000d, *1*(1), 100–108. Reprinted under the title "A Theory of Corporate Governance: Finding a New Balance for Boards and Their CEOs" in J. Carver, *John Carver on Board Leadership*. San Francisco: Jossey-Bass, 2002.

Carver, J. "The Opportunity for Re-Inventing Corporate Governance in Joint Venture Companies." *Corporate Governance—An International Review* (Great Britain), Jan. 2000e, 8(1), 75–80.

Carver, J. "Policy Governance as a Social Contract." *Board Leadership*, 2000f, no. 50.

Carver, J. "Remaking Governance: The Creator of 'Policy Governance' Challenges School Boards to Change." *American School Board Journal*, Mar. 2000g, *187*(3), 26–30. Reprinted in J. Carver, *John Carver on Board Leadership*. San Francisco: Jossey-Bass, 2002.

Carver, J. "Rethinking the Executive Committee." *Board Leadership*, 2000h, no. 52.

Carver, J. "Toward Coherent Governance." *The School Administrator*, Mar. 2000i, 57(3), 6–10. Reprinted in J. Carver, *John Carver on Board Leadership*. San Francisco: Jossey-Bass, 2002.

Carver, J. "When Bad Laws Require Bad Governance." *Board Leadership*, 2000j, no. 50.

Carver, J. "When Owners and Customers Are the Same People." *Board Leadership*, 2000k, no. 47.

Carver, J. "Board Members as Amateur CEOs." *Board Leadership*, 2001a, no. 53. Reprinted in J. Carver, *John Carver on Board Leadership*. San Francisco: Jossey-Bass, 2002.

Carver, J. "Can Things Go Horribly Wrong for Boards That Use Policy Governance?" *Board Leadership*, 2001b, no. 56. Reprinted in J. Carver, *John Carver on Board Leadership*. San Francisco: Jossey-Bass, 2002.

Carver, J. "The Case for a 'CGO.'" *Board Leadership*, 2001c, no. 56.

Carver, J. "Clarifying the Distinction Between Owners and Customers." *Board Leadership*, 2001d, no. 55.

Carver, J. "Does Policy Governance Give Too Much Authority to the CEO?" *Board Leadership*, 2001e, no. 55. Reprinted in J. Carver, *John Carver on Board Leadership*. San Francisco: Jossey-Bass, 2002.

Carver, J. "Does the Balanced Scorecard Have Governance Value?" *Board Leadership*, 2001f, no. 58.

Carver, J. "How Can Staff Know That Board Advice Is Not Actually Veiled Instruction?" *Board Leadership*, 2001g, no. 59.

Carver, J. "How Executive Limitations Policies Can Go Awry." *Board Leadership*, 2001h, no. 57.

Carver, J. "A New Game Plan for Co-op Boards." *Cooperative Business Journal*, Apr. 2001i, *15*(3), 4.

Carver, J. "A New Job Design for Board Leadership." *Cooperative Business Journal*, May 2001j, *15*(4), 5, 9.

Carver, J. "Rethinking Governance Research: Do Good Boards Produce Effective Organizations?" Unpublished paper for the University of Georgia Institute for Nonprofit Organizations, Apr. 10, 2001k. Reprinted in J. Carver, *John Carver on Board Leadership*. San Francisco: Jossey-Bass, 2002.

Carver, J. *Una Teoria de Gobierno Corporativo* [A theory of corporate governance]. Mexico City: Oficina de la Presidencia para la Innovación Gubernamental, 2001m.

Carver, J. "A Theory of Governing the Public's Business." *Public Management* (Great Britain), Mar. 2001n, *3*(1), 53–71. Reprinted in J. Carver, *John Carver on Board Leadership*. San Francisco: Jossey-Bass, 2002.

Carver, J. "The Unique Double Servant-Leadership Role of the Board Chair." In L. C. Spears and M. Lawrence (eds.), *Focus on Leadership: Servant-Leadership for the Twenty-First Century*. New York: Wiley, 2001o.

Carver, J. "What Use Is Business Experience on a Nonprofit or Governmental Board?" *Board Leadership*, 2001p, no. 58. Reprinted in J. Carver, *John Carver on Board Leadership*. San Francisco: Jossey-Bass, 2002.

Carver, J. "FAQ: Does Policy Governance Prohibit Staff from Talking with Board Members?" *Board Leadership*, 2002a, no. 63.

Carver, J. "FAQ: Isn't the Hierarchical Nature of Policy Governance Out of Step with Modern Participative Organizational Styles?" *Board Leadership*, 2002b, no. 60.

Carver, J. "Filling Board Vacancies." *Board Leadership*, 2002c, no. 63.

Carver, J. "The Governance Obsession Syndrome." *Board Leadership*, 2002d, no. 60.

Carver, J. "How Can an Organization's Statements of Vision, Beliefs, Values, and Philosophy Be Integrated into Policy Governance Policy?" *Board Leadership*, 2002e, no. 64.

Carver, J. "Is There a Fundamental Difference Between Governance and Management?" *Board Leadership*, 2002f, no. 60.

Carver, J. *John Carver on Board Leadership: Selected Writings from the Creator of the World's Most Provocative and Systematic Governance Model*. San Francisco: Jossey-Bass, 2002g.

Carver, J. "Organizational Ends Are Always Meant to Create Shareholder Value." *Board Leadership*, 2002h, no. 63.

Carver, J. "Rules Versus Principles: Comments on the Canadian Debate." *Institute of Corporate Directors Newsletter*, Nov. 2002i, no. 105, pp. 14–15.

Carver, J. "Teoriya Corporativnogo Upravleniya: Poisk Novogo Balansa Mezhdu Sovetom Directorov i Generalnym Directorom" [Corporate governance theory: New balance between the board of directors and the chief executive officer]. A summary. In E. Sapir (ed.), *Russian Enterprises in the Transitive Economy: Materials of the International Conference*. Vol. 1. Yaroslavl, Russia: Yaroslavl State University, 2002j.

Carver, J. "Title Versus Function: The Policy Governance Definition of a CEO." *Board Leadership*, 2002k, no. 59.

Carver, J. "What Should Government Funders Require of Nonprofit Governance?" *Board Leadership*, 2002m, no. 59.

Carver, J. "Why Should the Board Use Negative Wording About the Staff's Means?" *Board Leadership*, 2002n, no. 61.

Carver, J. "Board Access to the Internal Auditor." *Board Leadership*, 2003a, no. 68.

Carver, J. "Boards Should Add Value: But Which Value and to Whom?" *Institute of Corporate Directors Newsletter*, Jan. 2003b, no. 106, pp. 1, 2, 14.

Carver, J. "Committee Mania Among City Councils." *Board Leadership*, 2003c, no. 68.

Carver, J. "Compliance Versus Excellence." *Board Leadership*, 2003d, no. 67.

Carver, J. "Controlling Without Meddling—The Role of Boards." *Business Strategies*, Oct. 2003e, pp. 10–11.

Carver, J. "Dealing with the Board's First-Order and Second-Order Worries: Borrowing Trouble Effectively." *Board Leadership*, 2003f, no. 66.

Carver, J. "FAQ: Doesn't Policy Governance Require Too Much Confidence in the CEO?" *Board Leadership*, 2003g, no. 68.

Carver, J. "Is Governance a Fad?" *Board Leadership*, 2003h, no. 70.

Carver, J. "Is There a Fundamental Difference Between Governance and Management?" *Boardroom*, Mar.–Apr. 2003i, *11*(2), 1, 7.

Carver, J. "Model corporativnogo upravleniya: novyi balance mezhdu sovetom directorov i managementom companii" [The model of corporate governance: New balance between the board of directors and company's management]. *Economicheski Vestnic* (Yaroslavl, Russia: Yaroslavl State University), 2003j, no. 9, pp. 101–110.

Carver, J. "A New Basis for Governance Effectiveness Research." *Board Leadership*, 2003k, no. 67.

Carver, J. "The New Chairman: A Chief Governance Officer (CGO) for Tomorrow's Board." *Institute of Corporate Directors Newsletter*, Aug. 2003m, no. 109, pp. 1–2.

Carver, J. "'One Size Fits All': The Lingering Uninformed Complaint." *Board Leadership*, 2003n, no. 65.

Carver, J. "The Orphan Topic: Making Sense of the Governors' Dilemma." *FEnow* (Association of Colleges, London), Spring 2003o, pp. 26–27.

Carver, J. "Separating Chair and CEO Roles with Smoke and Mirrors." *Board Leadership*, 2003p, no. 68.

Carver, J. "Shareholder Value Is *Not* the Problem: Corporate Misdeeds Cannot Be Blamed on Putting Shareholders First." *Institute of Corporate Directors Newsletter*, Mar. 2003q, no. 107, pp. 1–2.

Carver, J. "Thoughts on Owners and Other Stakeholders." *Board Leadership*, 2003r, no. 68.

Carver, J. "The Trap in Greater Board Activism: Investors Need More Governing, Not More Micromanaging." *Institute of Corporate Directors Newsletter*, May 2003s, no. 108, pp. 14–15.

Carver, J. "The Trap of Answering Your CEO's Request for More Guidance." *Board Leadership*, 2003t, no. 66.

Carver, J. "What Do the New Federal Governance Requirements for Corporate Audit Committees Mean for the Policy Governance Board?" *Board Leadership*, 2003u, no. 67.

Carver, J. "What If Board Members 'Just Want to Know' About Some Aspect of Operations?" *Board Leadership*, 2003v, no. 65.

Carver, J. "Why in Policy Governance Are Customary Management Words Like *Goal, Objective, Procedure,* and *Strategy* Discouraged?" *Board Leadership,* 2003w, no. 68.

Carver, J. "FAQ: Why Shouldn't a Board Set Ends Policies One Program at a Time?" *Board Leadership,* 2004a, no. 76.

Carver, J. "FAQ: You Claim That Policy Governance Is a Universal Model for Governance. Why Is a Universal Model Even Needed?" *Board Leadership,* 2004b, no. 73.

Carver, J. "Hands On or Off?" *Contributions,* May–June 2004c, *18*(3), 22.

Carver, J. "If Corporate Governance Is a Fad, We Need More Fads." *Board Leadership,* 2004d, no. 71.

Carver, J. "The Invisible Republic." *Board Leadership,* 2004e, no. 74.

Carver, J. "Now Let's *Really* Reform Governance." *Directors Monthly* (National Association of Corporate Directors), Nov. 2004f, pp. 16–17.

Carver, J. "The Servant-Leadership Imperative in the Invisible Republic." Keynote address, Greenleaf Center for Servant-Leadership 14th Annual International Conference, Indianapolis, Ind., June 11, 2004g.

Carver, J. "So How About Half a Loaf?" *Board Leadership,* 2004h, no. 73.

Carver, J. "The Unique Double Servant-Leadership Role of the Board Chairperson." In L. C. Spears and M. Lawrence (eds.), *Practicing Servant Leadership: Succeeding Through Trust, Bravery, and Forgiveness.* San Francisco: Jossey-Bass, 2004i.

Carver, J. "Won't a Larger Board Mean There Is Greater Diversity in Governance?" *Board Leadership,* 2004j, no. 73.

Carver, J. "The Contrast Between Accountability and Liability." *Board Leadership,* 2005a, no. 78.

Carver, J. "Our Second Legal Issue." *Board Leadership,* 2005b, no. 79.

Carver, J. "Policy Governance and the Law." *Board Leadership,* 2005c, no. 78.

Carver, J. "Foreword." In P. Wallace and J. Zinkin, *Corporate Governance: Mastering Business in Asia.* Singapore: Wiley, 2005d.

Carver, J. "Un modelo de Gobierno Corporativo para el Mexico moderno" [A corporate governance model for a modern Mexico]. *Ejecutivos de Finanzas* (Instituto Mexicano de Ejecutivos de Finanzas), in press.

Carver, J., and Carver, M. "Governing (Not Managing) the Library." *Indiana Libraries,* 1998, *17*(1), 8–10.

Carver, J., and Carver, M. "A Board Member's Approach to the Job." *Board Leadership,* 1999a, no. 46.

Carver, J., and Carver, M. "A Finely Tuned Instrument." *Credit Union Management,* July 1999b, *22*(7), 54, 56.

Carver, J., and Carver, M. "Good to Go." *Credit Union Management*, June 1999c, *22*(6), 47–49.

Carver, J., and Carver, M. "Meeting the Challenge: Credit Union Survival Calls for Strong Governance and Strong Management." *Credit Union Management*, Apr. 1999d, *22*(4), 20–23.

Carver, J., and Carver, M. "The CEO's Role in Policy Governance." *Board Leadership*, 2000, no. 48.

Carver, J., and Carver, M. "Le modèle Policy Governance et les organismes sans but lucrative" [The Policy Governance model and nonprofit organizations]. *Gouvernance Revue Internationale* (Canada), Winter 2001, *2*(1), 30–48.

Carver, J., and Carver, M. "How to Tell Board Means from Staff Means." *Board Leadership*, 2004, no. 73.

Carver, J., and Carver, M. *Reinventing Your Board, Revised Edition*. San Francisco: Jossey-Bass, 2006.

Carver, J., and Carver, M. M. *Basic Principles of Policy Governance*. The Carver-Guide Series on Effective Board Governance, no. 1. San Francisco: Jossey-Bass, 1996a.

Carver, J., and Carver, M. M. *Your Roles and Responsibilities as a Board Member*. The CarverGuide Series on Effective Board Governance, no. 2. San Francisco: Jossey-Bass, 1996b.

Carver, J., and Carver, M. M. *The CEO Role Under Policy Governance*. The CarverGuide Series on Effective Board Governance, no. 12. San Francisco: Jossey-Bass, 1997a.

Carver, J., and Carver, M. M. *Making Diversity Meaningful in the Boardroom*. The CarverGuide Series on Effective Board Governance, no. 9. San Francisco: Jossey-Bass, 1997b.

Carver, J., and Carver, M. M. *Reinventing Your Board: A Step-by-Step Guide to Implementing Policy Governance*. San Francisco: Jossey-Bass, 1997c.

Carver, J., and Clemow, T. "Redeeming the Church Board." Unpublished paper, 1990.

Carver, J., and Mayhew, M. *A New Vision of Board Leadership: Governing the Community College*. Washington, D.C.: Association of Community College Trustees, 1994.

Carver, J., and Oliver, C. *Conselhos de Administração que Geram Valor: Dirigindo o Desempenho da Empresa a Partir do Conselho* [Boards that create value: Governing company performance from the boardroom]. (P. Salles, trans.). São Paulo: Editora Cultrix, 2002a.

Carver, J., and Oliver, C. "The Case for a CGO" (Appendix B). *Corporate Boards That Create Value*. San Francisco: Jossey-Bass, 2002b.

Carver, J., and Oliver, C. *Corporate Boards That Create Value: Governing Company Performance from the Boardroom.* San Francisco: Jossey-Bass, 2002c.

Carver, J., and Oliver, C. "Crafting a Theory of Governance." *Corporate Governance Review,* Oct.–Nov. 2002d, *14*(6), 10–13.

Carver, J., and Oliver, C. "Financial Oversight Reform—The Missing Link." *Chartered Financial Analyst* (Institute of Chartered Financial Analysts of India), Dec. 2002e, 8(12), 31–33.

Carver, M. "Governance Isn't Ceremonial; It's a Real Job Requiring Real Skills." *Board Leadership,* 1997, no. 31.

Carver, M. "The Board's Very Own Peter Principle." *Nonprofit World,* Jan.–Feb. 1998a, *16*(1), 20–21.

Carver, M. "Governing the Child and Family-Serving Agency: Putting the Board in Charge." *Georgia Academy Journal,* Spring 1998b, *5*(4), 8–11.

Carver, M. "What Is a CEO?" *Association,* June–July 1998c, *15*(4), 18–20.

Carver, M. "Enabling Boards to Be Accountable for the Agency." In "Best Practices/Promising Practices" special section. *Georgia Academy Journal,* 6(2), 1998d, 10.

Carver, M. "Speaking with One Voice: Words to Use and Not to Use." *Nonprofit World,* July–Aug. 2000, *18*(4), 14–18.

Carver, M. "Governance Rehearsal: A New Tool." *Board Leadership,* 2003a, no. 68.

Carver, M. "Transforming the Governance of Local Government." *IGNewsletter,* Nov. 2003b, *12,* 4–5.

Carver, M. "FAQ: In Policy Governance, the Board Is Supposed to Speak with One Voice to the CEO. Yet Our Board Relies to Some Extent on CEO Advice When We Make Our Decisions. Is This OK?" *Board Leadership,* 2004a, no. 75.

Carver, M. "FAQ: It Worries Me That in the Policy Governance System, the Board Gives a Huge Amount of Authority to the CEO. What Makes This OK?" *Board Leadership,* 2004b, no. 73.

Carver, M. "FAQ: When a Policy Governance Board Hires a New CEO, What Are Some Important Dos and Don'ts to Remember During the Hiring Process and the New CEO's Early Weeks?" *Board Leadership,* 2004c, no. 74.

Carver, M. "Of Potted Plants and Governance." *Board Leadership,* 2004d, no. 76.

Carver, M. "Independent? From Whom?" *Board Leadership,* 2005, no. 79.

Carver, M., and Charney, B. *The Board Member's Playbook: Using Policy Governance to Solve Problems, Make Decisions, and Build a Stronger Board.* San Francisco: Jossey-Bass, 2004.

Chait, R. P., Holland, T. P., and Taylor, B. E. *Improving the Performance of Governing Boards.* Phoenix, Ariz.: Oryx Press, 1996.

Chait, R. P., and Taylor, B. E. "Charting the Territory of Nonprofit Boards." *Harvard Business Review*, 1989, *129*, 44–54.

Charney, B. "'Messy Democracies': Should They Be Protected or Cleaned Up?" *Board Leadership*, 2003, no. 65.

Charney, B., and Hyatt, J. "When Legal Counsel Is Uninformed." *Board Leadership*, 2005, no. 79.

Chrislip, D., and Larson, C. *Collaborative Leadership: How Citizens and Civic Leaders Can Make a Difference*. San Francisco: Jossey-Bass, 1994.

Columbia Electronic Encyclopedia. (6th ed.) New York: Columbia University Press, 2003.

Conduff, M. "Sustaining Policy Governance." *Board Leadership*, 2000, no. 51.

Conduff, M., and Paszkiewicz, D. "A 'Reasonable Interpretation of Ends': What Exactly Does It Mean?" *Board Leadership*, 2001, no. 54.

Crosby, P. B. *Quality Is Free*. New York: McGraw-Hill, 1979.

Crosby, P. B. *Quality Without Tears*. New York: McGraw-Hill, 1984.

Dalton, A. "What Happens When a Federation Board Adopts Policy Governance?" *Board Leadership*, 2000, no. 47.

Davis, G. "Policy Governance Demands That We Choose Our Words Carefully." *Board Leadership*, 2000, no. 49.

Dayton, K. N. *Governance Is Governance*. Washington, D.C.: Independent Sector, 1987.

Deming, W. E. *Out of Crisis*. Cambridge: Center for Advanced Engineering Study, Massachusetts Institute of Technology, 1986.

Dodds, E. R. "Progress in Classical Antiquity." In P. P. Wiener (ed.), *Dictionary of the History of Ideas*. New York: Scribner, 1973.

Drucker, P. F. *Management: Tasks, Responsibilities, Practices*. New York: Harper-Collins, 1974.

Ewell, C. M. "How Hospital Governing Boards Differ from Their Corporate Counterparts." *Trustee*, Dec. 1986, pp. 24–25.

Felton, E. "The Politics of Influence Peddling." *Insight*, Sept. 18, 1989, pp. 22–23.

Ferguson, M. Untitled paper presented at the World Future Society, Toronto, July 1980.

Financial Post (Canada), May 23, 2003.

Fram, E. H. "Nonprofit Boards: They're Going Corporate." *Nonprofit World*, 1986, *4*(6), 20–36.

Fram, E. H. *Policy vs. Paper Clips: Selling the Corporate Model to Your Nonprofit Board*. Milwaukee, Wis.: Family Service America, 1988.

Geneen, H. S. "Why Directors Can't Protect the Shareholders." *Fortune*, 1984, *110*, 28–29.

Gillies, J. *Boardroom Renaissance*. Toronto: McGraw-Hill Ryerson and National Centre for Management Research and Development, 1992.

Globe and Mail (Toronto), Nov. 22, 2003.

Greenleaf, R. K. *Servant Leadership: A Journey into the Nature of Legitimate Power and Greatness*. New York: Paulist Press, 1977.

Greenleaf, R. K. *The Power of Servant Leadership*. (L. C. Spears, ed.). San Francisco: Berrett-Koehler, 1998a.

Greenleaf, R. K. "Servant: Retrospect and Prospect." In R. K. Greenleaf, *The Power of Servant Leadership*. (L. C. Spears, ed.). San Francisco: Berrett-Koehler, 1998b.

Gregory, T. W. "How to Implement Policy Governance." *Trustee Quarterly*, 1996a, no. 1, pp. 5–6.

Gregory, T. W. "What Is Policy Governance?" *Trustee Quarterly*, 1996b, no. 1, pp. 3–4.

Gregory, T. "Board Erosion Prevention." *Governing Excellence* (International Policy Governance Association), Winter 2003.

Guy, J. "Good Investment Decisions Are Policy Driven." *Board Leadership*, 1992, no. 4, p. 8.

Guy, J. "Making Decisions: The Role of Governance." *Journal of Financial Planning*, 1995, 8(1), 34–38.

Haskins, C. P. "A Foundation Board Looks at Itself." *Foundation News*, Mar.–Apr. 1972, 13(2).

Hough, A. *The Policy Governance Model: A Critical Examination*. Working paper no. CPNS6. Brisbane, Australia: Centre of Philanthropy and Nonprofit Studies, Queensland University of Technology, July 2002.

Hough, A., McGregor-Lowndes, M., and Ryan, C. "Policy Governance: 'Yes, But Does It Work?'" *Corporate Governance Quarterly*, Summer 2005, pp. 25–29.

Hume, D. *Philosophical Essays on Morals, Literature, and Politics*. Washington, D.C.: Duffy, 1817.

Hyatt, J., and Charney, B. "The Legal and Fiduciary Duties of Directors." *Board Leadership*, 2005a, no. 78.

Hyatt, J., and Charney, B. "Legal Concerns with Policy Governance." *Board Leadership*, 2005b, no. 78.

Hyatt, J., and Charney, B. "Sarbanes-Oxley: Reconciling Legal Compliance with Good Governance." *Board Leadership*, 2005c, no. 79.

Imai, M. *Kaizen*. New York: Random House, 1986.

Juran, J. M., and Louden, J. K. *The Corporate Director*. New York: American Management Association, 1966.

Kelly, H. M. "Carver Policy Governance in Canada: A Lawyer's Defense." *Miller-Thompson Charities and Not-for-Profit Newsletter*, July 2003, pp. 7–8. Reprinted in *Board Leadership*, 2004, no. 71.

Kiernan, M. "Your Guy in Washington: Members of Congress May Be More Useful Than You Think." *U.S. News & World Report*, 1989, *107*(6), 54–56.

Kirk, W. A. *Nonprofit Organization Governance: A Challenge in Turbulent Times*. New York: Carlton Press, 1986.

Koontz, H. *The Board of Directors and Effective Management*. New York: McGraw-Hill, 1967.

Kradel, E. "Just How Should Boards Communicate with Owners?" *Board Leadership*, 1999, no. 45.

Kuhn, T. S. *The Structure of Scientific Revolutions*. (3rd ed.) Chicago: University of Chicago Press, 1996.

Leblanc, R., and Gillies, J. *Inside the Boardroom: How Boards Really Work and the Coming Revolution in Corporate Governance*. Mississauga, Ontario, Canada: Wiley, 2005.

Leighton, D.S.R., and Thain, D. H. *Making Boards Work: What Directors Must Do to Make Canadian Boards Effective*. Whitby, Canada: McGraw-Hill Ryerson, 1997.

Lemieux, R. "Making the Commitment to Policy Governance." *Board Leadership*, 1999, no. 41.

Levitt, A. Remarks at Tulane University conference "Corporate Governance: Integrity in the Information Age," New Orleans, Mar. 12, 1998.

Lorsch, J. W., and MacIver, E. *Pawns or Potentates: The Reality of America's Corporate Boards*. Boston: Harvard Business School, 1989.

Loucks, R. "Surviving the Transition: Igniting the Passion." *Board Leadership*, 2002, no. 59.

Louden, J. K. *The Effective Director in Action*. New York: AMACOM, 1975.

Maas, J.C.A.M. "Besturen-op-afstand in de praktijk, Het Policy Governance Model van John Carver" [To bring "non-meddling governance" to life, the Policy Governance model of John Carver]. *VBSchrift*, 1997, *7*, 7–10.

Maas, J.C.A.M. "Besturen-op-afstand in praktijk brengen" [To bring "non-meddling governance" to life]. *Gids voor Onderwijsmanagement, Samsom H. D. Tjeenk Willink bv*, Oct. 1998.

Maas, J.C.A.M. "Besturen en schoolleiders doen elkaar te kort" [Boards and principals fail in their duties toward each other]. *Tijdschrift voor het Speciaal Onderwijs*, Nov. 1998, *71*(8), 291–293.

Maas, J.C.A.M. "De kwaliteit van besturen, Policy Governance Model geeft antwoord op basisvragen" [The quality of governance: Policy Governance answers fundamental questions]. *Kader Primair,* Jan. 2002, *7*(5), 26–29.

Maas, J.C.A.M. "Policy Governance: naar het fundament van goed bestuur" [Policy Governance: To the foundation of good governance]. *TH&MA, Tijdschrift voor Hoger onderwijs & Management,* 2004, *11*(3).

Massinger, P. Quote from *The Bondman,* I.iii (originally published 1624) in *Oxford Dictionary of Quotations.* (3rd ed.) New York: Oxford University Press, 1979.

Mill, J. S. *Considerations on Representative Government.* New York: Harper, 1867.

Mogensen, S. "What Are the Other Models?" *Board Leadership,* 2002, no. 64.

Mogensen, S. "The Big Picture: Policy Governance and Democracy." *Board Leadership,* 2003, no. 70.

Mogensen, S. "Sticking to the Process Without Getting Stuck." *Board Leadership,* 2004, no. 74.

Monks, R.A.G. "Shareholder Activism: A Reality Check." *The Corporate Board,* 2001, *22*(129), 23–26.

Monks, R.A.G., and Minow, N. *Corporate Governance.* (3rd ed.) Oxford, U.K.: Blackwell, 2004.

Moore, J. "Linking with Owners: The Dos and Don'ts." *Board Leadership,* 1999, no. 46.

Moore, J. "Meaningful Monitoring." *Board Leadership,* 2001a, no. 53.

Moore, J. "Meaningful Monitoring: The Board's View." *Board Leadership,* 2001b, no. 54.

Moore, J. "A Governance Information System." *Board Leadership,* 2002a, no. 60.

Moore, J. "Policy Governance as a Value Investment: Succession Planning." *Board Leadership,* 2002b, no. 60.

Moore, J. *Governance for Health System Trustees.* Ottawa, Canada: CHA Press, 2003.

Mueller, R. K. *The Incompleat Board: The Unfolding of Corporate Governance.* Lexington, Mass.: Heath, 1981.

Murray, V. "Is Carver's Model Really the One Best Way?" *Front and Centre,* Sept. 1994, p. 11.

Murray, V., and Brudney, J. L. "Improving Nonprofit Boards: What Works and What Doesn't?" *Nonprofit World,* 1997, *15*(3), 11–16.

Murray, V., and Brudney, J. L. "Do Intentional Efforts to Improve Boards Really Work?" *Nonprofit Management and Leadership,* 1998a, 8(4), 333–348.

Murray, V., and Brudney, J. L. "Letters to the Editor." *Nonprofit World,* 1998b, 16(1), 4–5.

Nason, J. W. *Foundation Trusteeship: Service in the Public Interest.* New York: Foundation Center, 1989.

National School Boards Association. Untitled advertising flyer. Alexandria, Va.: National School Boards Association, n.d.

Nobbie, P. D. "Testing the Implementation, Board Performance, and Organizational Effectiveness of the Policy Governance Model in Nonprofit Boards of Directors." Unpublished doctoral dissertation, Department of Public Administration, University of Georgia, 2001.

Nobbie, P. D., and Brudney, J. L. "Testing the Implementation, Board Performance, and Organizational Effectiveness of the Policy Governance Model in Nonprofit Boards of Directors." *Nonprofit and Voluntary Sector Quarterly*, 2003, *32*(4), 571–595.

Odiorne, G. S. *Management and the Activity Trap.* New York: HarperCollins, 1974.

Oliver, C. "Policy Governance in the Regulatory Environment." Information sheet. Toronto: Canadian Society of Association Executives, 1998.

Oliver, C. "Understanding and Linking with the Moral Ownership of Your Organization." *Board Leadership*, 1999, no. 44.

Oliver, C. "Boards Behaving Badly." *Board Leadership*, 2000a, no. 51.

Oliver, C. "Creating Your Policy Governance Tool Kit." *Board Leadership*, 2000b, no. 50.

Oliver, C. "Cultivating Good Board Manners." *Board Leadership*, 2000c, no. 52.

Oliver, C. "Getting Personal." *Board Leadership*, 2001a, no. 55.

Oliver, C. "He Who Pays the Piper Calls the Tune." *Board Leadership*, 2001b, no. 57.

Oliver, C. "Uncovering the Value of the Right Word." *Board Leadership*, 2001c, no. 59.

Oliver, C. "The Board and Risk." *The Bottom Line, the Independent Voice for Canada's Accounting and Financial Professionals*, Oct. 2002a.

Oliver, C. "The Cult of Efficiency." *Board Leadership*, 2002b, no. 61.

Oliver, C. "Getting Off Lightly." *The Bottom Line, the Independent Voice of Canada's Accounting and Financial Professionals*, May 2002c, *18*(6), 11.

Oliver, C. "Keeping Tabs on the CEO." *Association Magazine*, Oct.–Nov. 2002d, *19*(6), 9–11.

Oliver, C. "Policy Governance and Other Governance Models Compared." *Board Leadership*, 2002e, no. 64.

Oliver, C. "Questions and Answers About Good Governance." *Board Leadership*, 2002f, no. 63.

Oliver, C. "Best Practice Governance in Charities." *LawNow* (University of Alberta), Apr.–May 2003a, *27*(5), 33–34.

Oliver, C. "Developing Group Discipline." *Board Leadership*, 2003b, no. 68.

Oliver, C. "Do unto Others: Cultivating Good Board Manners." *Association and Meeting Management Directory.* Winnipeg, Canada: August Communications, 2003c.

Oliver, C. "In the Minority." *Board Leadership*, 2003d, no. 65.

Oliver, C. "The Strange World of Audit Committees." *Ivey Business Journal* (University of Western Ontario), Mar.–Apr. 2003e, 67(4), 1–4. (Also available as reprint no. 9B03TB09 at www.iveybusinessjournal.com.)

Oliver, C. "What's Really Missing?" *Boardroom*, 2003f, *11*(1), 4, 7.

Oliver, C. "When Owners Don't Agree." *Board Leadership*, 2003g, no. 70.

Oliver, C. "Why Size Matters." *Board Leadership*, 2003h, no. 67.

Oliver, C. "The Mighty Meeting." *Board Leadership*, 2004, no. 75.

Oliver, C. "Board Accountability in Highly Constrained Environments." *Board Leadership*, 2005a, no. 80.

Oliver, C. "A Debatable Alliance." *Board Leadership*, 2005b, no. 77.

Oliver, C. (gen. ed.), with Conduff, M., Edsall, S., Gabanna, C., Loucks, R., Paszkiewicz, D., Raso, C., and Stier, L. *The Policy Governance Fieldbook: Practical Lessons, Tips, and Tools from the Experiences of Real-World Boards.* San Francisco: Jossey-Bass, 1999.

Peters, T. J. *Thriving on Chaos: Handbook for a Management Revolution.* New York: Knopf, 1988.

Peters, T. J., and Waterman, R. H. *In Search of Excellence: Lessons from America's Best-Run Companies.* New York: HarperCollins, 1982.

Price, W. S. *Manual on Governance and Policy Planning for Board Members.* Silver Spring, Md.: Wolfgang S. Price Associates, 1977.

Raso, C. "Two People in the CEO Role: Can It Work?" *Board Leadership*, 2000, no. 48.

Reddin, W. J. *Effective Management by Objectives: The 3-D Method of MBO.* New York: McGraw-Hill, 1971.

Rehfeld, J. "Nose In, Hands In, Too: Optimizing the Board's Talent." *Directors Monthly*, 2005, 29(5), p. 1.

RE-THINK Group. *Benefits Indicators: Measuring Progress Towards Effective Delivery of the Benefits of Parks and Recreation.* Calgary, Canada: RE-THINK Group, 1997.

Rogers, S. "Policy Governance Top Ten." *Board Leadership*, 2005, no. 77.

Rousseau, J. J. "Discourse on Political Economy." In J. J. Rousseau, *Jean-Jacques Rousseau: The Social Contract* (C. Betts, trans.). Oxford, U.K.: Oxford University Press, 1999. (Originally published 1758.)

Rousseau, J. J. *Jean-Jacques Rousseau: The Social Contract* (C. Betts, trans.). Oxford, U.K.: Oxford University Press, 1999. (Originally published 1762.)

Royer, G. "Proactive About What?" *American School Board Journal*, 1996a, *183*(6), 34–39.

Royer, G. *School Board Leadership 2000: The Things Staff Didn't Tell You at Orientation.* Houston: Brockton, 1996b.

Skinner, W. "The Productivity Paradox." *Harvard Business Review*, 1986, 64, 55–59.

Smith, C. J. "Eight Colleges Implement Policy Governance." *Trustee Quarterly*, 1996, no. 1, pp. 8–10.

Smith, D. K. "Making Change Stick." *Leader to Leader*, 1996, no. 2, pp. 24–29.

Smith, E. E. "Management's Least-Used Asset: The Board of Directors." In *The Dynamics of Management*. AMA Management Report, no. 14. New York: American Management Association, 1958. Cited in H. Koontz, *The Board of Directors and Effective Management*. New York: McGraw-Hill, 1967.

Spears, L. C. (ed.). *Reflections on Leadership: How Robert K. Greenleaf's Theory of Servant Leadership Influenced Today's Top Management Thinkers*. New York: Wiley, 1995.

Spears, L. C., and Lawrence, M. (eds.). *Practicing Servant Leadership: Succeeding Through Trust, Bravery, and Forgiveness*. San Francisco: Jossey-Bass, 2004.

Stein, J. G. *The Cult of Efficiency*. Toronto: Anansi, 2001.

Sternberg, E. *Just Business: Business Ethics in Action*. New York: Little, Brown, 1994.

Swanson, A. "Who's in Charge Here? Board of Directors and Staff—The Division of Responsibility." *Nonprofit World*, 1986, 4(4), 14–18.

Tooley, R. "Using Information Technology to Sustain Policy Governance." *Board Leadership*, 2004, no. 76.

Tremaine, L. "Finding Unity and Strength Through Board Diversity." *Board Leadership*, 1999, no. 43.

Waterman, R. H., Jr. *The Renewal Factor: How the Best Get and Keep the Competitive Edge*. New York: Bantam Books, 1988.

Wolfe, J. *An Introduction to Political Philosophy*. Oxford, U.K.: Oxford University Press, 1996.

Index

A

Able, E., 295
Absence, excused, 367
Abstracting up to broader issues, 243, 244, 261
Accountability: accepted principles of governance, 329; approval syndrome effect on, 69–70; of the board as a whole, 158, 185–209, 239–243; to constituents, 31; as cumulative responsibility, 158–161, 172, 174; definition of, 371–372; financial, 218–219; leaky, 19; traditional and legal, 265–267, 304–305; a vision of group, 5–33
Accountability chain, 27, 160–161, 226, 325–326, 331
Accounting activities, 117
Accreditation, 304
Achard, F. K., 323
Acheson, B., 221
Ackoff, R., 9, 35
Activities, commendable organizational, 85–86; are means not ends, 90, 99; board "doing" jobs, 229–330; board hands-on, 203–208; board hands-on versus hands-off, 174, 175; policy control of outputs and, 147, 148. See also Staff operations
Adams 12 Five Star Schools, 59, 307–308

Adams, J. H., 110, 160, 296
Administrative Parameters. See Executive Limitations policies
Advisory bodies or boards, 23, 226–227, 354–355, 372
Agenda: annual, 198; consent (automatic approval), 198, 266, 304, 373–374; discussion readiness of, 263–264; long term or perpetual, 268–269; starting the Policy Governance, 273–276. See also Meetings, board
Agenda planning, board, 197, 198, 267–276
Aging persons, board policies toward, 247–249
Albee, E., 193
American Institutes of Research, 221–222
Anderson, G. L., 39
Andrews, J., 124
Applications, Policy Governance, 345–358. See also names of organizations
"Approval syndrome" policymaking flaws, 68–72, 157; and budgets, 135–140
Approvals, board hands-on versus hands-off, 174, 175
Architecture, policy, 67–68, 239; "terraced" format of, 253–254
Argenti, J., 114

Armstrong, R., 324, 341, 343

Assessment: of executive means, 118–119; of executive performance, 47, 159–160

Asset protection, Executive Limitations policy, 142, 144

Association organization boards, 19, 95, 304, 352–353

Attendance: quorum and board, 366–367; required, 282, 367

Audit, external, 167–168, 169

Australian Department of Defense, 241

Authority: "any reasonable interpretation" rule of, 307, 333, 372; of the board Chair, 222; board hands-on versus hands-off, 174, 175; of board over staff, 327, 331; diffusion of, 20, 267; of government boards, 348–349; group, 332; top-down hierarchy of, 325–326

Automatic approval agenda, 198, 266, 304, 334, 373–374

B

Baker, G. C., 119

Baker, H. H., Jr., 357–358

Barth, N., 124, 145

Beliefs, definition of, 378

Beneficiaries: definition of, 374; Ends policy, 94, 96, 99–100, 332; and ownership, 186; results for, 97, 99, 332

Benefits, staff, 141

Biery, R. M., 340, 362

Bissell Centre, 231, 232

Black, C., 29

Board (advisory), 23, 226–227, 354–355; definitions of, 9, 372

Board committees. *See* Committees, board

Board means, 332, 372

Board Policymaking circles. *See* Policy Circle

Board products: core, 199; job description, 197–201, 202, 203,
220; market test of, 14–15, 101; minutes, 223–224, 281; visual enhancement of, 294. *See also* Products of governance

Board varieties: by economic organization, 10–13; by organizational position, 9–10. *See also* Applications, Policy Governance

Board-Executive relationship, 153–180; and monitoring executive performance, 161–172, 310; role distinction in, 172–178, 217–219, 225, 242, 267. *See also* Executive Limitations policies

Board-Management Delegation policies, 74, 132, 153, 242, 244, 333; board means, 332, 372; definitions of, 52, 372; development of, 253; examples, 156, 202, 203. *See also* CEO (Chief Executive Officer)

Boards (governing): CEO recommendations to, 173–174; consensus of, 279; definitions of, 9, 372; governance flaws of, 18–20, 32–33, 37–38, 218–219, 225–226; ground rules of, 243–245; holistic, 220–224, 227–231; intraboard conflict within, 327–328; neglected study of, 16–17, 312, 319–320, 328–329, 339; overloads of, 20; self-discipline of, 31, 188–190, 332, 360; self-evaluation of, 306–308; size of, 366; the standards and policies of, 128–129, 304–305; as trustees, 26; typical shortcomings of, 18–20; as unique decision makers, 26–27; varieties of, 8–13

Bowers, R., 72

Branca, F., 178

Brandau, M., 260

British Petroleum, 241

Brudney, J. L., 342, 342, 343

Budget policy, 44–45, 241; Executive Limitations, 135–140; government, 357

Business corporations, 8, 10, 11, 16, 28–29, 90, 355–356

Bylaws, 274, 347; guidelines concerning characteristics of, 365–368

C

Cadbury, A., 6–7, 28, 182
California Park & Recreation Society, 93, 97, 110–111, 160, 295–296
Capital, Preservation of (policies), 250–252
Carver, J., 1–2, 3, 8, 34, 35, 36, 53, 54, 68, 76, 77, 114, 150, 151, 157, 181, 182, 183, 184, 209, 210, 211, 212, 213, 236, 237, 254, 263, 283, 284, 285, 313, 314, 315, 316, 317, 329, 355–356, 358, 359, 360, 361, 362, 363, 364, 368, 369, 371
Carver, M., 1–2, 3, 8, 35, 68, 181, 184, 212, 301–302, 310, 314, 315, 317, 360, 361, 371
Carver, M. M., 3, 181, 213, 263, 284
Castlereagh College, 92–93
CEO (Chief Executive Officer), the: accountability of as leaky, 19; accountability to the board, 159–161; backup policy, 131; board messages to, 132; as board treasurer or secretary, 368; CGO distinguished from, 216–217, 218, 220–221, 242; confounding domains of board and, 71–72, 120, 157; defining, 154–161; definition of the term, 373; and Ends Policies, 74, 272; expertise or competence of, 327–328; financial questions, 138, 198; freedom within limitations, 123–124, 145, 146–147, 327–328; independently elected, 346–347; job contributions list, 161; leadership, 177–178, 325; monitoring the performance of, 161–172, 310; protecting the role of, 217–219, 225–227, 267; recommendations to the board from, 173–174, 277; reports, 167, 169; self-development, 171–172; as sole employee of the board, 159, 333. *See also* Executive Limitations policies

CEO-Board relationship. *See* Board-Executive relationship
CGO (Chief Governance Officer), the, 175, 242, 277, 307, 333; board chair as, 74, 220–223; bylaw about, 367–368; CEO distinguished from, 216–217, 218, 220–221; definition of, 373
Chair of the board, 65; and board process, 196–197; CEO role separation from the, 157–158; job description, 222
Chait, R. P., 18, 19, 33, 145, 301
Change: creative or reactive, 309–310; enabling proactive, 31, 123–124
Charities, boards of, 247–249, 350
Charney, B., 2, 283, 301–302, 310, 315, 317, 340
Chavez, D., 287
Cheerleader function, 22
Church boards, 96, 351
City council boards, 346–347
Civic club boards, 354
Clean-the-desk syndrome, 258
Clemow, T., 361
Code of Conduct, board members', 193, 194–195
Codes, corporate governance, 28–29, 356
Colleges and universities, boards of, 92–93, 155, 156, 221, 349
Collegiality or hierarchy, 160
Colorado Springs Christian School, 92
Combs, L., 204
Committee, staff, 373
Committees, board, 195–196, 224–232, 368; advice from, 226–227; CEO role protection by, 225–227; comments on traditional, 233–235; decision making, 228–231; definition of, 373; finance, 219; legitimate, 231–232; minimalism of, 224–225; principles for, 232. *See also* Delegation

Communications activities, 117, 176, 294; and support to the board, 142, 143

Communicator, board as, 23

Community organizations, boards of, 99, 141, 204, 207, 350

Compensation: CEO, 198; staff, 117, 141, 261–262

Conditions, commendable, 86

Conduff, M., 182, 317

Conflict of interest: board chair-CEO, 157; intraboard, 327–328

Confrontation and board diversity, 190, 192–193, 195–197

Congresses and parliaments, 356–358

Consent agenda: automatic approval, 198, 266, 304, 334, 373–374; definition of, 373

Constituents, 31, 374

Constraints: budgeting, 139; freedom through, 17, 116, 122–125, 145, 176; legal, 140; personnel policy, 140–141; proactive, 121–125, 126; reasonable, 129; unnecessary, 128. *See also* Executive Limitations policies

Consultants, use of, 305–306

Consumers, 374; judgments by, 14–15; record keeping, 117

Contact, personal, 205

Control: of budgeting, 136–140; effectiveness or short-term, 88; of ends targets and barriers, 145–147; of large and small issues, 62, 64; of means, legitimate, 120–121; by personalities, 196–197; through proactive constraint, 121–125; tight versus loose, 32

Cooperatives, boards of, 111, 350

Corporate boards, for-profit, 11, 28–29, 90, 355–356

Costs: Ends concept of, 100–103; reduction seduction, 290; return on CEO, 176; return on education, 300; sliding fee, 44, 100; unit, 85. *See also* Budget policy

"Cradle" vision, 30

Credit unions, boards of, 139, 350

Criteria: preestablished monitoring, 161–163, 171–172; superfluous or extraneous evaluative, 171

Criticisms of the Policy Governance model, 320–329; as a one-size-fits-all approach, 321–322; rules of too rigid, 322

Crosby, P. B., 290, 313

Currency of policy categories, 58

Customers, 374; owners as, 350, 352–353

D

Davis, G., 314

Dayton, K. N., 182

Decision making: "approval syndrome," 68–72; below the board, 18–19, 65; board committees, 228–231; board hands-on, 203–208, 297; board hands-on versus hands-off, 174, 175; board-CEO-staff chain of, 27, 160–161, 226, 325–326; the board's unique, 26–27, 64; broad to narrow, 64–65, 241–243, 326; and executive recommendations, 173–174; fragmentation of, 71; information, 162, 244; lack of clarity in, 70; levels matrix, 66–67; low-level, 18–19; Policy Circle and board, 242; reaching consensus on, 278–279; staff-level, 174–176, 179–180; top-down hierarchy of, 325–326; and valuing, 40, 296–297

Delegation: balanced, 217; to board sub-groups, 206–207, 231–232, 354; board-management, 50–51, 143, 264–265; CEO-staff, 87; decreasingly enveloping layers of, 240–243; and empowerment, 292, 297; with Ends and Executive Limitations, 146–148; an irony of, 122; monitoring of board-management, 169; on the Policy Circle, 179–180, 209, 242; to the President, 155,

156; and proactive constraint,
121–125; of smaller issues, 52–53,
64–65; unitary, 217–218, 330, 333.
See also Committees, board
Deming, W. E., 290, 313
Dialogue, board-to-board, 207, 272,
290. *See also* Language
Disapproval of means, 120
Discipline, board: a common basis for,
31, 188–190, 360; Policy Governance rules and, 322, 326–327
Discrimination among employees,
140, 141
Discussion: informal, 281; with other
boards, 272, 290; readiness for,
263–264; within policy categories,
260–263
Diversity: and board unity, 31,
276–279; and interpersonal dynamics, 190, 192–193, 195–197; and
ownership, 205–207
Documents: approval of, 125; board
policy, 67, 203, 223, 247–253, 294;
establishment, 365; the hierarchy
of, 365; Internet management of,
300–301; maintaining the integrity
of board, 293–294; operational, 67;
policies or pronouncement, 292–
294, 365; Policy Governance versus
old policy, 274–275; separate-page
policy, 248. *See also* Bylaws
Drucker, P. F., 16
Durham Regional Police Services
Board, 92
Dutch Primary Education, 241
Dynamics, interpersonal, 190,
192–193, 195–197
Dysfunctional board members,
192–193

E

E pluribus unum, 276–279
Education: of board members,
298–302; boards of, 260, 287, 349
Effectiveness research, model, 16–17,
312, 328–329, 337–338; impedi-

ments to, 319–320. *See also* Policy
Governance model
Effects for people, 287–291
Elected boards, 346–347
Ends and means: confusing, 82–90;
the difference between, 82; evaluation of, 106–110; reasons to separate, 48–50, 326
Ends, organizational (results, outcomes), 48, 52–53; as a transaction
with the environment, 81–82;
attack and don't ponder, 287–288;
board product of satisfactory, 103,
199, 202, 271; the difficult concept
of, 110–112; effectiveness of,
118–119; effects for people as,
287–291; evaluation of, 105–110;
focusing on, 79–113, 287–290; mission versus, 83–84; mistaken for
means, 88–90; subresults are not,
89–90; subtopics of, 96
Ends policies, 74; and advisory boards,
354–355; board updates of, 270–
273; CEO evaluation and, 171–172,
333; definitions of, 52, 332, 374;
development and growth, 247–250;
examples of, 92–93, 94–99, 247–
249; expressing, 90–93; and long-
range planning, 103–105, 268–270;
on the Policy Circle, 112, 113, 242;
as policy product, 103
Ends test for Ends policies,
111–112
Ends-means distinction, the Policy
Governance, 82
Environment, transaction with the,
81–82, 88
Equality: of board members and the
CEO, 160; of owners and stakeholders, 336
Equity boards. *See* Profit boards
(equity or business boards)
Equivalence, ownership-board, 188
Ethics and prudence, 115–149; board
standards of, 128–129; legitimate
control of means and, 120–121;

and proactive constraint, 121–125; of staff operations, 50, 115–116

Evaluation: board's self, 306–308; of the CEO, 168–170, 330, 333, 334; crude or precise, 110; of ends not means, 110; misplaced concern about, 107–108; of organizational results, 105–110; placing concern about, 109–110; well-placed concern about, 106–107

Ewell, C. M., 204

Excellence: board pursuit of, 308–312; Policy Governance and board leadership, 339–340

Exchange, the organization-world, 81–82, 107

Executive committees, board, 233–234

Executive Limitations policies, 332; and board "worry areas," 130–131, 137, 244; and CEO authority, 64–65, 74, 101, 123–124; and CEO evaluation, 171–172; definitions of, 52, 374–375; development and growth, 250–253, 306; examples of, 135, 139, 141, 143, 250–252; governing staff action, 125–131; number of, 145, 149; on the Policy Circle, 148–149, 242; and proactive constraint, 121–125, 126; range of, 142–145; the reason for, 126; reasonable interpretation of, 129, 156, 165–167, 167–168, 169, 333, 334; typical topics of, 131–145

Executive means as staff issues, 117–118

Executive reports, 167, 169

Expectations, board-CEO, 176–178

Expertise, CEO. See CEO (Chief Executive Officer)

Explicitness of policy categories, 58

External forces: and consent agendas, 198, 266, 304, 334, 373–374; demanding board time, 259; focus on, 30, 80; influence and conventional wisdom of, 302–306; the larger context of, 80–81; legal and traditional, 140, 265–267, 304–305, 334

F

Facilities issues, 117

Failures of governance, 190, 357

Federations of organizations, 352–353

Felton, E., 357

Ferguson, M., 308

Fetterly, R., 167

Field, P., 62

Finance committees, board, 234–235

Financial condition policies, Executive Limitations, 132–135, 306, 334; examples of, 134, 135, 250–252

Fitzpatrick, J., 177, 287

Food bank organization, 111

Forward thinking: pursuit of excellence, 309–310; strategic, 31, 104, 130–131, 160–161, 232

Foundation boards, 351

Fram, E. H., 123, 157

Freedom through limits, 17, 116, 122–125, 145, 176

Fundraising, 47; board roles in, 23, 200–201, 323–324

G

Gale, R., 33

Gallon, J., 50

Garden City Community College, 155, 156

Geneen, H. S., 16, 157

Generic principles. See Policy Governance model

Georgia State Board of Education, 349

Gerards, J., 177

Gillies, J., 17, 192, 212

Glendale Elementary School, 193, 194–195

Global Ends, 84

Global Ends policy statements, 90–93; attributes of, 91–92; broad to narrow, 93–94, 102, 245, 278–279; examples of, 92–93; expanding on the, 93–103; reasonable interpretation of, 129
Global Executive Limitations policy, 250
Goals: and ends, 82; and objectives as problematic, 375
Goals, organization. *See* Ends, organizational (results, outcomes)
Gómez, A. P., 6
Governance: as a means, 311; as a social construct, 335, 337; confusion over purpose of, 319–320; definition of, 375; as empowerment, 292; information needed for, 31, 143; management difference from, 27, 241, 324–325, 338; not a dependent variable, 338; principles of accountable, 329, 331–333; the process of, 51; pursuing excellence in, 308–312, 339–340; reforms of corporate, 28–29, 356; research on effectiveness of, 335–339; responsibility for integrity of, 188–190; shaped by personalities, 196–197; toward a new, 29–33; as unique management, 24–27
Governance framework: designing a new model of, 29–32; the foundational technology of, 7; need for a, 32–33. *See also* Policy Governance model
Governance Process: board means, 332, 372; compliance with, 143
Governance Process policies, 74, 204, 333; and agenda planning, 197, 198, 258–267; board decision making on, 227–231, 242, 244; continual use of, 310; definitions of, 52, 375; development of, 253; examples of, 191, 194–195, 197, 198, 222, 232, 299, 307
Governing boards, 372; a vision of, 5–8

Governments: national, 88, 356–358; state and provincial, 11, 12, 348–349
Grantors and owners, 187
Greenleaf, R. K., 2, 3, 217, 291, 313, 339, 344, 377
Gregory, T., 298, 317
Gregory, T. W., 360
Grievance procedures, 140, 141
Guy, J., 135

H

Haskins, C. P., 233
Health care organization boards, 141, 197, 198, 351–352
Heifer Project International, 206
History of values, 94, 262, 309
Hoff-Israël, M. van der, 241
Holding company and subsidiary boards, 353–354
Holism, board, 220–224, 227–231
Holland, T. P., 18, 19, 33, 301
Homeowners' association boards, 354
Horen, I. R., 32, 301–302
Hospital boards, 197, 198, 351–352
Hough, A., 340, 343
Houser, R. V., 347
Human rights organizations, 99
Hume, D., 211, 287
Hyatt, J., 283, 315

I

Imai, M., 309
Incidental information, 162–163
Inclusivity, board, 206–207
Information: carefully managed knowledge and, 300–301; needed to govern, 31, 143, 157, 298–301; three types of, 162–163, 244
Inspection, direct, 168, 169, 170
Insurance and liability, 144
Intellectual property, 144
International organizations, 99, 202, 203, 206, 223, 338
International Policy Governance Association, 202, 203, 223, 338

Internet, using the, 300–301
Investments and endowments, organization, 134–135, 142, 144, 250–252
Involvement, board: Policy Governance requires, 326–327; prescribing more or less, 21

J

Jackson, J., 281
Jenkins, P. T., 33
Jeopardy, fiscal, 134, 135
Job products. *See* Products of governance
Juran, J. M., 17

K

Kelly, H. M., 315, 340
Kerr, J., 196
Kiernan, M., 357
Kirk, W. A., 83
Koontz, H., 279
Kradel, E., 213
Kuhn, T. S., 28

L

Lancaster County Bible Church, 96
Language: "any reasonable interpretation" rule, 61, 156, 165–167, 307, 333, 334, 372; of board ground rules, 243–245; board meetings managing, 258–267; board respect for policy document, 292–294; board values and policy, 165, 293–294; board-room dialogue and, 75; brevity of, 59; broad proscriptive policy control, 125–128, 332; generality or fuzziness of policy, 145; literal policy category, 58; meticulous precision of, 245; negative limitations versus positive ends, 122–124, 146; results not activity, 208; shaping policy, 246–253
Law, protections and constraints of, 140, 347
Law Society of Manitoba, 95

Lawrence, M., 3, 314, 344
Leadership, board: and the board-CEO-staff relationship, 160–161, 176–178; excellence of, 311–312, 339–340; of leaders, 291–292; linkage with other boards, 207, 289–290; member qualifications, 296–297; preparedness for, 298–302; reasons for policy-focused, 41–42; religious, 351; strategic or tactical decisions, 160–161; a useful framework of, 30–32; a vision of, 5–8, 282
Leblanc, R., 192, 212
LeFevre, R. J., 105
Legal membership, 186–187, 349
Legal review of the bylaws, 368
Legislatures, conduct of, 356–358
Leighton, D.S.R., 17, 182
Lemieux, R., 284
Levels. *See* Policy levels
Levitt, A., 17
Library boards, 350–351
LifeStream Services Ends policies, 247–249
Line board, 9
Linkage: Board-CEO, 53, 143, 155, 157–158; with the external environment, 47, 272; organization-ownership, 199, 202, 204–207, 253, 271. *See also* Board-Management Delegation policies
Logical containment principle, 60–63, 131, 240–241
Lorsch, J. W., 155, 182
Loucks, R., 284
Louden, J. K., 17, 33
Luck, J., 123
Lyon, G. Taft, Jr., 124

M

MacIver, E., 155, 182
Macroeffectiveness of governance, 337
Management by boards, 22–23; governance not a dependent variable of,

338; hands-on and hands-off, 174, 175, 203–208; ownership-centered versus traditional, 325, 338; and proactive constraint, 121–125

Management Limitations. *See* Executive Limitations policies

Management (or staff) means, 375; methods, 117; policy separation from, 326

Management sequence, 179

Manuals, board policy versus staff, 67

Market: compensation, 262; focus on needs and, 30; serving a muted, 13–15

Market test of result or product worth, 14–15, 101

Massinger, P., 188–189

Mayhew, M. M., 360

McGillicuddy, S., 227

Means, board, 332, 372

Means decisions: definition of, 375; the management sequence of, 179

Means, organizational, 48–50, 115–116; approvability of, 119–120; are never ends, 82; effectiveness of, 118–119, 337; executive, 117–118, 147, 159–160, 179; legitimate control of, 120–121; mistaken for ends, 84–88

Measurement: denigration of, 323; and evaluation, 109–110; of productivity, 85; unit cost, 85

Meetings, board, 257–282; the character of, 282; choosing the issues for, 259–260; Ends justify, 270–273; form before content of, 260–263; frequency of, 233–234; participation in, 21, 297, 326–327; structured practice during, 301–302. *See also* Agenda

Megaproduct, the board's, 197

Members, board: collegiality or hierarchy of, 160; definition of, 374; diversity of, 276–277, 289; elected, 346, 347–348; intraboard conflict between, 327–328; involvement of,

21, 326–327; legally required, 186–187, 349; as owners and customers, 350, 352–353; preparation and job training of, 298–302, 337; pursuit of excellence by, 308–312, 339–340; qualifications of, 296–297; quotes from, 123–124; selection of, 276–277, 294–297; turnover of, 280

Membership: the board as the only, 366; termination of, 367

Memory, institutional, 280–282

Mennonite Mutual Aid, 141

Microeffectiveness of governance, 337–338

Micromanaging, 115

Mill, J. S., 187, 210

Minutes, board, 223–224, 281

Miracle Hill Ministries, 142, 143

Mission: avoiding the term, 84; board responsibility for, 79–80; outcome-driven, 30; versus ends, 83–84

Mission (or mission statement), 53, 83; definition of, 375; ends terminology of vision or, 105. *See also* Ends, organizational (results, outcomes)

Mission Resource Network, 168, 169–170

Mitstifer, D. I., 292

Model (governance), 329–335; definition of, 376. *See also* Policy Governance model

Mogensen, S., 212, 342, 364

Monitoring: adherence to Governance Process Policies, 307; data, 143, 162–163, 179; executive performance, 161–172, 310, 333; information, 162; and measurement, 323; methods of board, 167–168, 169; ongoing or periodic, 170, 308; performance, 106, 109–110, 199, 232, 333, 338; preestablished criteria for, 161–163, 171–172, 235; two components of, 166–167

Monks, R.A.G., 356, 364

Moore, J., 182, 213, 314, 315, 362
Moral ownership, 26, 185–188, 336
Morale, high staff, 86
Mueller, R. K., 27
Murray, V., 341, 342

N

Nader, R., 357
Nason, J. W., 366
National School Boards Association, 19
Nested set of policies, 61–62, 67–68
NGOs (nongovernmental organizations), 11
Nobbie, P. D., 338, 343
Nominating committees, board, 205, 235
Nonprofit boards, 10–11, 204, 350–353
Number: of board officers, 215–216; of Executive Limitations policies, 145, 149; policy system component, 246

O

Objectives and ends, 82, 375
Observers, including, 302–303
O'Connell, B., 279
Officers, 215–224; describing board, 367–368; minimalism in establishing, 215–216
Oliver, C., 3, 7, 8, 35, 114, 150, 151, 157, 181, 210, 211, 212, 236, 237, 314, 316, 317, 329, 340, 341, 342, 343, 344, 355–356, 358, 359, 360, 361, 362, 363, 369, 371
Oparah, D., 218
Optional job products, 200–201, 323–324
Orchard County Day School, 140
Ordinances, 347
Orientation, board member, 298–299
Osborne, G. S., 86, 114
Outcome-driven mission, 30
Oversight, congressional, 357–358
Owner-accountable organizational performance, 338

Owners (ownership): and the "approval syndrome," 68–70; board as subset of, 188, 205; board volunteers as, 25, 350; board-CEO relationship and, 178; bridge between producers and, 197, 199; commitment to, 296, 303, 331; as customers, 14–15, 117, 350, 352–353, 374; definition of, 376; diversity of board and, 205–207, 276–277, 289; of elected boards, 346–347; of meeting issues, 261; moral, 26, 185–188, 336; organization obligation to its, 324–325, 331; other representatives of, 272, 289–290; shareholders as, 11, 90, 355–356; a subset of stakeholders, 336, 377–378; three intentions of, 15–16; and trusteeship, 291
Oxfam Community Aid Abroad, 99

P

Paperwork reduction (board), 125
Parent-subsidiary boards, 353–354
Parks and recreation agencies, 93, 97, 295–296; about, 349
Paskewicz, M. F., 59
Pass-fail Ends policies, 103
Paszkiewicz, D., 182
Peckham, R. J., 18, 287
Pension Fund, Unnamed, 250–252
Perpetual agenda, board, 269
Personnel: committees, 233; policies, 45, 117, 264, 306; return on, 176
Perspective, definition of, 39
Peters, T. J., 41, 105, 309
Philosophy, Policy Governance as a, 335–336, 338–339
Physicians and hospital boards, 351–352
Planning: board agenda, 197, 198, 258–267, 267–276; board approval of staff, 123; by boards, 23; definition of, 376; Ends policies and long-range, 103–105, 268–270; financial, 135–140. *See also* Strategy

Police services organization, 92

Policies: explicit, 202; leadership through, 41–42; logical containment of, 60–63, 131, 240–241; a nested set of, 61–62; transforming worries into, 130–131, 137; as values and perspectives, 38–41

Policy (board), 333; the four categories of, 47, 51–53, 203, 244, 376; good development of, 72–75; principles and formats guiding, 57–59; reinventing the meaning of, 42–46; staff policy versus, 63–67, 326

Policy categories: central availability of, 58–59; classification of, 57; comprehensiveness of, 59, 202; creation within, 244; defined, 376; discussing issues within, 260–263; the four, 37, 46–53, 199, 203, 244, 333, 376

Policy Circle, 73, 74, 254; board decision making issues on the, 242; board-management delegation policies on the, 179–180, 209, 242; Ends quadrant, 112, 113, 242; Executive Limitations on the, 148–149, 242; Governance Process Policies on the, 208, 209

Policy Governance: as a philosophy, 335–336, 338–339; as a system, 329–335; as a tool or means, 311; actual use of, 319; for board committees, 227; board members' commitment to, 273–274, 296, 339–340; concept of ends, 110–112; the conceptual model of, 1–3, 328, 331–333, 376–377; criticisms of, 320–329; entire use of, 324; the freedom of, 124–125; implementation, 8; managing the transition to, 275–276; "monitoring" criteria, 161–163, 171–172; and policy development, 72–75; practice and rehearsals, 301–302, 310; sequence of writing, 274–275; ten minimum requirements of, 331–333; theory

utility of, 328; training in, 298–302; using only parts of, 330

Policy Governance Association, International, 202, 203, 223, 338

Policy Governance model, 1–3, 328, 376–377; as generic, 321–322, 345–346; ten minimum requirements of the, 331–333

Policy levels, 239–255; board committees and, 225–226; board versus staff, 63–67, 102–103, 148–149; board-management, 179–180, 326; definition of, 377; and delegation, 209; form and function of, 243–246; format of, 245–246; lists differ from, 239–243; screening issues by, 261–262; top-down, 245, 278–279, 325–326; and worry areas, 130–131

Policy sizes, the nature of, 59–68

Power: board uses of, 32, 33; of legislators, 357

Practice, structured, 301–302

Prescriptions for boards: about activity and involvement, 21, 326–327; about board work and skills, 22–23; about board-staff relations, 22; problem-based, 23–24, 309–310; reforms and codes as, 28–29

Principles: of accountable governance, 329, 331–333; for board committees, 232; guiding board policy, 57–59; sample violations of, 334; universality of, 321–322, 333. See also Policy Governance model

Proactivity, enabling, 31, 123–124

Procedures, definition of, 377

Process evaluation, 106–108

Productivity measures, 85

Products of governance, 294, 331; basic board job description, 201–203; board job description, 197–199, 220, 222, 269; board optional, 200–201, 323–324; undelegatable, 199. See also Board products

Professional society organizations, 95, 98, 348, 353

Profit boards (equity or business boards), 8, 10, 11, 16, 28–29, 90, 355–356
Programs: as ends, 234; as means, 85–86
Project Management Institute, 98
Prudence. *See* Ethics and prudence
Public and private boards, 10–11, 12–13, 291; the muted market of, 13–15, 106–107; results evaluation by, 105–110
Purchasing decisions, 19
Putnam, G., 19, 309
PVOs (private voluntary organizations), 11, 350

Q

Quality, perpetual redefinition of, 308–312
Questions: board debate and exposure of ends, 277, 288–290; board screening, 260–263; macroeffectiveness or microeffectiveness, 337–338; value alternative, 306; "why" issues, 49
Quorum, board, 366–367

R

Raso, C., 181
Reactive stance of boards, 19
Reactivity, board, 68–69
"Reasonable interpretation" rule, 61, 156, 165–167, 333, 334, 372
Recipients, definition of, 374
Reddin, W. J., 199
Reforms, corporate governance, 28–29, 356
Regulations, external, 140, 304, 347
Rehfeld, J., 29, 36
Relief agencies, 351
Remuneration: CEO, 198; staff, 117, 141, 261–262
Reporting activities, 117, 275
Reports: monitoring, 166–167; types and methods of CEO, 167–168
Research on governance effectiveness, 335–339; and all Policy Gover-

nance components, 331–335; macroeffectiveness or microeffectiveness, 337–338; needed, 16–17, 312, 328–329, 339; three impediments to, 319–320. *See also* Policy Governance model
Responsibility: accountability as cumulative, 158–161, 172, 174; of board for board performance, 188–190; definition of, 371; optional, 207–208
Results: board core, 199; board optional, 200–201; cost and, 100–103; ends statement, 90, 96, 97, 99; evaluation of organizational, 105–110; expanding on global, 94, 96; means assessment based on, 118–119; planning, 103–105
Return on investment in education, 300
Rhode Island Board of Regents, 289
Risk management issues, 117
Rituals, expected, 303
Rockhill, L., 111, 124, 145
Rogers, S., 342
Roles articulating board, 31
Romanko, B., 20
Rousseau, J. J., 187, 210, 339, 344
Royer, G., 259, 359
Rubberstamping, 115, 190, 228, 230; responsibly, 264–265

S

Salaries, 141, 198
Sarbanes-Oxley legislation, 28
Saunier, A., 124
Scandals, congressional, 357
Schedules, monitoring, 170, 308
School boards, 19, 55–56, 59, 92, 140, 193, 194–195, 204, 264, 287, 304, 307–308; four peculiar conditions facing, 347–348
Schukken, F., 50
Screening form before content, 260–263
Second Harvest Food Bank of East Central Indiana, 111, 124, 134, 135

Secretary, board, 220, 223–224; CEO as, 368

Selection, board. *See* Members, board

Servant-leadership, 2, 217, 291, 331, 339; definition of, 377

Services and programs as means, 85–86

Shareholders, equity corporation, 11, 90, 355–356

Shea, G., 124, 145

Short-term bias, 19

Sicile, M., 220

Size: board, 366; of board minutes, 224; of issues, 18–19, 29–30, 33, 66; of material for approval, 69, 326; policy encompasses, 59–63

"Size of issue" matrix, 66

Skills: CEO work, 159–160; training or occupational, 89

Skinner, W., 290

Sliding fee schedule (sliding scale), 44, 100

Slogans, 92

Smith, C. J., 343, 360

Smith, D. K., 312

Smith, E. E., 16–17

Social construct of governance, 335, 337

Social contract, the, 186–187

Social service agency boards, 99, 141, 206, 247–249, 350

Southeast Booksellers Association, 95

Speaking with one voice, 27, 31, 155, 156, 178, 191, 217–218, 327, 330; definition of, 377

Spears, L. C., 3, 313, 314, 344

Staff: advice from, 305–306, 327; approval syndrome effects on, 69–71, 122–125, 259; board policies about, 49–50, 125–131, 140–141, 243, 332; boards without, 354; compensation, 117, 141, 198; credentials or morale, 86; as leaders or bureaucrats, 291–292; means issues, 117–118; medical, 352; no bylaws about, 368; and policymaking, 102–103, 104, 277, 305–306, 327; talking with, 327

Staff Means Proscriptions. *See* Executive Limitations policies

Staff operations: board intrusions in, 174–176, 225–226; the board's stake in, 118–121; the enticing complexity of, 116–118; policies to limit, 125–131; prudence and ethics of, 50, 115–116, 120–121, 125

Staff policy versus board policy, 63–67, 194–195

Staff work: board work versus, 225–226; effectiveness of, 118–119, 327–328; reviewing, 19, 69–71, 118, 267–268

Stakeholders, 377–378; moral ownership by, 26, 185–188, 336

State Employees Credit Union, 139

Stein, J. G., 112

Sternberg, E., 312

Stewardship, responsible, 188–190

Strategy, 378; forward thinking, 31, 104, 130–131, 160–161, 232; leadership, 160–161, 345–346

Structure, commendable means, 87

Subsidies, differential, 44

Supply activities, 117

Swanson, A., 184

Swap with the world, an organization's, 81, 107

Systems thinking, 246–253, 296, 324; and improvement, 310, 330; Policy Governance model as, 329–336, 338–339

T

Tax status of nonprofit organizations, 11, 135

Taylor, B. E., 18, 19, 33, 145, 301

Teamwork, board-CEO, 176–177

Technology, commendable techniques and, 87–88

Tennessee Managed Care, 141

Termination of membership, 367

Terminology. *See* Language; Titles

Thain, D. H., 17, 182

Theory, Policy Governance as just, 328

Thinking. *See* Forward thinking; Systems thinking

Three Rivers Area Hospital, 197, 198

Time: efficient use of, 32, 164, 258; spent on low-level decisions, 18–19, 69

Time horizon: for board decisions, 19; of policy development, 263–264; short-term, 70

Titles: CEO, 155; of Executive Limitation policies, 131–132, 142; of global Ends policies, 247; of governing boards, 9, 12; of policy categories, 52–53

Tooley, R., 315

Topics, board committee, 226

Training: of board members, 298–302, 337; skills, 89

Treasurer, board, 218–219, 368

Tremaine, L., 213

Trust, board-CEO, 310

Trustees, boards as, 26, 188

Trusteeship, 186–187, 291

Two-tier Ends policies, 103

U

Unanimous votes, 279

Unit cost measurement, 85

United Kingdom, 28

U.S. Environmental Protection Agency, 88

V

Value map, 94, 262

Values: board linkage, 204–205; the board's own policies and, 128–129; codifying group, 165; collecting

board wisdom and, 280–282; definitions of, 39, 378; ends, 48, 52–53, 100–102, 105; focus on, 30, 296–297, 306; history of, 94, 262, 309; integrated board, 228–229; means, 48–50, 52–53; and priorities of intended results, 100–101; respect for expression of, 292–294; shareholder, 355–356

Vertical integration, 92, 93–94

Vision statement. *See* Mission (or mission statement)

Visual presentation of governance declarations, 294

Voice, speaking with one, 27, 31, 155, 156, 178, 191, 217–218, 327, 330

Voluntarism: CEO-led, 200–201, 350; the red herring of, 25

Volunteers, board members as, 25, 350

Voting, board, 243, 279

W

Watchdog function, 22

Waterman, R. H., 41

Weeks, J. P., 45

What's going on, learning, 162–163

"Why" issues, 49

Williams, N., 298

Wisdom: collecting board, 280–282; surmounting conventional, 302–306

Wolfe, J., 210, 211, 212

Words. *See* Language

Workgroup board, 10

"Worry areas" and policies, 130–131, 137, 281–282